W9-BWW-122

PYTHON® PROJECTS

Python® Projects

Python® Projects

Laura Cassell
Alan Gauld

wrox
A Wiley Brand

Python® Projects

Published by
John Wiley & Sons, Inc.
10475 Crosspoint Boulevard
Indianapolis, IN 46256
www.wiley.com

Copyright © 2015 by John Wiley & Sons, Inc., Indianapolis, Indiana

Published simultaneously in Canada

ISBN: 978-1-118-90866-2
ISBN: 978-1-118-90889-1 (ebk)
ISBN: 978-1-118-90919-5 (ebk)

Manufactured in the United States of America

10 9 8 7 6 5 4 3 2 1

No part of this publication may be reproduced, stored in a retrieval system or transmitted in any form or by any means, electronic, mechanical, photocopying, recording, scanning or otherwise, except as permitted under Sections 107 or 108 of the 1976 United States Copyright Act, without either the prior written permission of the Publisher, or authorization through payment of the appropriate per-copy fee to the Copyright Clearance Center, 222 Rosewood Drive, Danvers, MA 01923, (978) 750-8400, fax (978) 646-8600. Requests to the Publisher for permission should be addressed to the Permissions Department, John Wiley & Sons, Inc., 111 River Street, Hoboken, NJ 07030, (201) 748-6011, fax (201) 748-6008, or online at http://www.wiley.com/go/permissions.

Limit of Liability/Disclaimer of Warranty: The publisher and the author make no representations or warranties with respect to the accuracy or completeness of the contents of this work and specifically disclaim all warranties, including without limitation warranties of fitness for a particular purpose. No warranty may be created or extended by sales or promotional materials. The advice and strategies contained herein may not be suitable for every situation. This work is sold with the understanding that the publisher is not engaged in rendering legal, accounting, or other professional services. If professional assistance is required, the services of a competent professional person should be sought. Neither the publisher nor the author shall be liable for damages arising herefrom. The fact that an organization or Web site is referred to in this work as a citation and/or a potential source of further information does not mean that the author or the publisher endorses the information the organization or Web site may provide or recommendations it may make. Further, readers should be aware that Internet Web sites listed in this work may have changed or disappeared between when this work was written and when it is read.

For general information on our other products and services please contact our Customer Care Department within the United States at (877) 762-2974, outside the United States at (317) 572-3993 or fax (317) 572-4002.

Wiley publishes in a variety of print and electronic formats and by print-on-demand. Some material included with standard print versions of this book may not be included in e-books or in print-on-demand. If this book refers to media such as a CD or DVD that is not included in the version you purchased, you may download this material at http://booksupport.wiley.com. For more information about Wiley products, visit www.wiley.com.

Library of Congress Control Number: 2014946683

Trademarks: Wiley, Wrox, the Wrox logo, Programmer to Programmer, and related trade dress are trademarks or registered trademarks of John Wiley & Sons, Inc. and/or its affiliates, in the United States and other countries, and may not be used without written permission. Python is a registered trademark of Python Software Foundation Corporation. All other trademarks are the property of their respective owners. John Wiley & Sons, Inc., is not associated with any product or vendor mentioned in this book.

For my truly great boys—Nathan, Ben, and Matt:
We will do so many things now that I'm not writing.
Thank you for all the quiet time while I was writing;
you can come out of your rooms now.

—Laura Cassell

To my wife, Heather, for her continued support and
patience with my eccentric working hours.

—Alan Gauld

ABOUT THE AUTHORS

LAURA CASSELL has been poking at code on the web since 1997. She taught herself Perl in the early 2000s where she discovered that programming materials were in dire need of an overhaul and the barrier to entry to teach programming was incredibly high. Thus, her journey to learn programming so she can bring it to other people began.

Originally from Atlanta, GA, Laura founded PyLadies Atlanta, and got her start teaching Python and JavaScript for Big Nerd Ranch. She has since moved on to engineering management and currently resides in Portland, OR where she manages a team of Pythonistas doing software analytics for New Relic, Inc. She still volunteers for teaching and speaking gigs when time permits.

ALAN GAULD is an enterprise architect with more than 40 years of experience in IT, working mainly in the telecommunications and customer service areas. He has programmed in more than 20 languages, producing everything from mainframe billing systems through embedded micro-controllers. For the last 15 years, his preference has been for Python. He is the author of a beginner's book on Python and is co-moderator of the python-tutor mailing list.

When not programming, he likes climbing, backpacking, and skiing. He is also a keen photographer, artist, and acoustic music enthusiast. He lives in Scotland with his wife, Heather.

ABOUT THE TECHNICAL EDITORS

ALEX BRADBURY is a compiler hacker, Linux geek, and Free Software enthusiast. He has been a long time contributor to the Raspberry Pi project and also co-authored *Learning Python with Raspberry Pi*. He is currently a researcher at the University of Cambridge Computer Laboratory and is a co-founder of lowRISC, a non-profit project to produce a complete open-source System-on-Chip (SoC).

TODD SHANDELMAN fondly remembers coding assembly language programs on punch cards for IBM System/370 mainframes. After occupying various other ecological niches in software technology over the years (C, C++, and Perl, to name but a few), Todd's best days are now spent coding pure Python 2.x and 3.x from the Linux command line. In his spare time he is a professional translator of Russian and Hebrew, specializes in foreign-language typography, and can find his way in the dark around Unicode and UTF-8. Todd earned a Bachelor of Science degree in Business Administration from the University of the State of New York. He lives in Houston, Texas, with his wife and son.

CREDITS

Acquisitions Editor
Jim Minatel

Project Editor
Jennifer Lynn

Technical Editors
Alex Bradbury
Todd Shandelman

Production Editor
Christine Mugnolo

Copy Editor
Kimberly A. Cofer

Production Manager
Kathleen Wisor

Manager of Content Development and Assembly
Mary Beth Wakefield

Marketing Director
David Mayhew

Marketing Manager
Carrie Sherrill

Professional Technology & Strategy Director
Barry Pruett

Business Manager
Amy Knies

Associate Publisher
Jim Minatel

Project Coordinator, Cover
Patrick Redmond

Proofreader
Sarah Kaikini, Word One New York

Indexer
Johnna Dinse

Cover Designer
Wiley

Cover Image
© iStock.com/skodonnell

ACKNOWLEDGMENTS

I'D LIKE TO GIVE a big thank you to Alan Gauld, who helped put so much of this book together, and to Mary James and Jennifer Lynn for making sure this idea came to fruition. It's a better book because of all of you.

Thank you also to the Python community, you are all the most welcoming community that I've ever found. You have created a place where people feel welcome and able to approach everyone, experts to novices alike. Keep up the good work and thank you for allowing me to be a part of this wonderful community.

—LAURA CASSELL

I'D LIKE TO GIVE a shout out to Laura Cassell for kick-starting this project, Jennifer Lynn for steering us through it, and the Python community for their support over the last 15 years.

—ALAN GAULD

CONTENTS

INTRODUCTION

AFTER A CONFERENCE ONE YEAR, an e-mail went around the PyLadies organizers mailing list asking, "Is anyone interested in writing a Python book?" I had kicked around the idea of a programming book for a while. After teaching for a couple years and mentoring at PyLadies and other coding meetups, I realized there was a need for a new, specific sort of programming book. I didn't jump to replying to the e-mail, however. I knew that writing a book would be a big process (boy is it!) and that it would take a lot of time and effort on my part, in the way of working on the weekends and holidays (yep, check!). I also knew that I had a full-time job teaching programming, I was the lead organizer for my local PyLadies chapter in Atlanta, Georgia, and I had children that would soon start asking, "Are you writing this weekend?"

All of the above was true (a little more than I originally thought, actually), but I knew that the book was important. There were so many of my students asking me at the end of class, "Now that I know the basics of Python, what do I do?" My answer was always something along the lines of, "You can get involved in open-source projects!" or "Take the advanced Python class!" But none of those answers satisfied them or me. The answer is, "You have to really start looking for something to work on—a problem to solve, a need that must be met." Because, the only way to really know and understand programming and a programming language is to solve problems with said language.

But then the problem of "But I don't have a problem that really needs to be solved" cropped up. So while I could send my students off to look at open-source projects that do, in fact, need the help, if they didn't understand the technology, they'd be lost and give up. Then the community loses yet another programmer who may have brought interesting things to the table. So, that's when, after lots of talking to friends and family, I realized that this book needed to be written.

WHY WE WROTE THIS BOOK

For all those people who came up to us and asked, over the years, "What can I do now that I understand Python basics? What things can I learn? Where do I go?" That's why we wrote this book.

The most chronic problem in programming books that we've experienced and that others have also felt they experienced is that it goes from "These are the basics of a language" into very deep concepts that only people who hold Computer Science (CS) degrees would understand. And that's not cool. Programming should be open to anyone who is interested. We should all be working toward making the bar into programming a little lower. We feel that Python accomplishes this, but we need to take it a step further and begin to understand how people learn abstract ideas and concepts, to help us help them learn.

Think of programming like learning how to build a house, but only understanding that wood is needed and how the wood works to build a house. You still need to understand structural engineering, electrical, plumbing, ventilation, HVAC, etc. The same concept is true for programming. Languages just explain the wood being used in a house. There is plenty more that is happening in harmony with the wood, and we want to help you uncover those concepts.

WHO THIS BOOK FOR

This book is not for beginners who want to learn Python. Rather, as a reader of this book, you need to already have some Python programming under your belt. That means you've done some tutorials. You also understand that whitespace matters in Python and that lists are denoted with hard braces ([ ]) while dicts (dictionaries) are denoted with curly braces ({ }). This book is for those people who are still beginners, but who have completed a tutorial or two—folks who understand the basics of Python, but are interested to learn what all they can do with Python.

"Need is the mother of invention" goes the saying, and when you're learning to program, this is very true. If you need a piece of software that can perform a specific function or task, it's easy to learn a language around that need. You have a need, the language will help you, you learn the language, you solve the problem, you've learned a thing, and you've put it to use immediately. This is awesome and fantastic! However, what if you think programming is interesting, but you're missing the need? What if you don't know what to make? That's where this book comes in.

This book will help you to learn the parts of Python that most people don't think to tell new programmers about. Most of the things covered in this book are tools and technologies that one may only discover when they are faced with working with them. However, for new programmers who don't have a specific problem to solve, learning these tools can be difficult. Most of the time no one thinks to introduce these topics to programmers because they are used so regularly. We hope to take you on a journey through the power of Python and all of its splendor.

You will learn how to make a web app, how to talk to a database using Python libraries, and which system tools can help speed up your workflow, if you're a systems administrator. We will briefly touch on topics such as security and best practices. You'll get an overview of creating graphical user interfaces (GUIs) using Python libraries. We will cover consuming and producing application programming interfaces (APIs) and many other topics that are beneficial to Python programmers.

WHAT YOU WILL LEARN

We hope to take you on a small tour of the basics that are available in the Python ecosystem. We'll introduce you to many concepts that are usually discovered only while working on a problem to solve. While we can't put everything into the context of problems that you may need to solve in the future, we hope that we can illustrate the powerful features of the Python language and the available packages and technology that are available to you, the new Python programmer.

We will start out with a brief "crash course" in Python, in case you've forgotten anything. We'll go over the basics, and then you can decide if you want to read that chapter in its entirety or not. Next, we go over Python as a scripting language. You'll get to get your hands dirty, as it were, by writing small scripts to access parts of your system, using Python. This should illustrate the very basic power you have with the language. Third, we'll start talking about data, which is what programming is all about—manipulating data. You'll get to dive in and work through some examples using some of the standard libraries that come out of the box with Python. We'll even discuss databases so that you can get a quick intro into those. We want you to see and touch every part of a system that you may come in contact with.

After the first three chapters, you'll dive into desktop applications. While these aren't incredibly popular in Python, it is a feature of the language, and it could be useful down the line in your tenure as a Python programmer. Next, we will step out of the desktop and onto the Internet with Python as a data communicator. You'll learn all about HTTP and the Web and how websites work under the hood. You'll even be able to play with producing and consuming APIs. APIs confuse many new programmers; we hope to have removed much of the mystery with this chapter.

In the final chapters, we'll show more advanced topics in Python, such as how to work with Python in bigger projects, debugging your code, creating testing-harnesses, handling errors, and even creating your own exceptions and exception handlers! Finally, there are appendices for reference while you are going through the book and after, when you're spreading your Python wings and programming.

It is a lot of information, and it's like a huge sandbox of tools and ideas to get you started on your journey with the language. We hope that you try things out and research more on your own time with certain concepts and ideas that interest you. We've included plenty of hands-on exercises to help you try out the concepts as they are presented, as well as some challenge questions in most chapters to help you exercise your newfound knowledge.

WHAT YOU NEED TO USE THIS BOOK

In order to get the most out of this book, we recommend you have a modern computer running Python 3.3 or later, a good text editor that you are comfortable using, an Internet connection (for some parts of the book), and a healthy dose of patience and wonderment. We also recommend that you utilize Internet searching for any problems that may arise. Professional programmers don't actually know it all; they usually only know those problems that they deal with day in and day out. A lot of the time of a professional programmer is spent researching and tracking down why a behavior is occurring. No one should ever feel bad for relying on a Google search to solve a problem. Sometimes, your Googling abilities are just as important as your programming ones.

To work through the examples and projects in this book, you will also need the source code. The source code for the samples is available for download from the Wrox website at:

www.wrox.com/go/pythonprojects

CONVENTIONS

To help you get the most from the text and keep track of what's happening, we've used a number of conventions throughout the book.

TRY IT OUT

The *Try It Out* is an exercise you should work through, following the text in the book.

1. They usually consist of a set of steps.

2. Each step has a number.

3. Follow the steps through with your copy of the database.

How It Works

After each *Try It Out*, the code you've typed will be explained in detail.

> **WARNING** *Warnings hold important, not-to-be-forgotten information that is directly relevant to the surrounding text.*

> **NOTE** *Notes indicate notes, tips, hints, tricks, or asides to the current discussion.*

As for styles in the text:

➤ We highlight new terms and important words when we introduce them.

➤ We show keyboard strokes like this: Ctrl+A.

➤ We show filenames, URLs, and code within the text like so: `persistence.properties`.

➤ We present code in two different ways:

```
We use a monofont type with no highlighting for most code examples.
```

```
We use bold to emphasize code that is particularly important in the present
context or to show changes from a previous code snippet.
```

SOURCE CODE

As you work through the examples in this book, you may choose either to type in all the code manually, or to use the source code files that accompany the book. All the source code used in this book is available for download at www.wrox.com. Specifically for this book, the code download is on the Download Code tab at:

www.wrox.com/go/pythonprojects

You can also search for the book at www.wrox.com by ISBN (the ISBN for this book is 978-1-118-90866-2 to find the code. And a complete list of code downloads for all current Wrox books is available at www.wrox.com/dynamic/books/download.aspx.

Most of the code on www.wrox.com is compressed in a .ZIP, .RAR archive, or similar archive format appropriate to the platform. Once you download the code, just decompress it with an appropriate compression tool.

ERRATA

We make every effort to ensure that there are no errors in the text or in the code. However, no one is perfect, and mistakes do occur. If you find an error in one of our books, like a spelling mistake or faulty piece of code, we would be very grateful for your feedback. By sending in errata, you may save another reader hours of frustration, and at the same time, you will be helping us provide even higher quality information.

To find the errata page for this book, go to:

www.wrox.com/go/pythonprojects

And click the Errata link. On this page you can view all errata that has been submitted for this book and posted by Wrox editors.

If you don't spot "your" error on the Book Errata page, go to www.wrox.com/contact/ techsupport.shtml and complete the form there to send us the error you have found. We'll check the information and, if appropriate, post a message to the book's errata page and fix the problem in subsequent editions of the book.

P2P.WROX.COM

For author and peer discussion, join the P2P forums at http://p2p.wrox.com. The forums are a Web-based system for you to post messages relating to Wrox books and related technologies and interact with other readers and technology users. The forums offer a subscription feature to e-mail you topics of interest of your choosing when new posts are made to the forums. Wrox authors, editors, other industry experts, and your fellow readers are present on these forums.

At http://p2p.wrox.com, you will find a number of different forums that will help you, not only as you read this book, but also as you develop your own applications. To join the forums, just follow these steps:

1. Go to http://p2p.wrox.com and click the Register link.
2. Read the terms of use and click Agree.
3. Complete the required information to join, as well as any optional information you wish to provide, and click Submit.
4. You will receive an e-mail with information describing how to verify your account and complete the joining process.

> **NOTE** You can read messages in the forums without joining P2P, but in order to post your own messages, you must join.

Once you join, you can post new messages and respond to messages other users post. You can read messages at any time on the Web. If you would like to have new messages from a particular forum e-mailed to you, click the Subscribe to this Forum icon by the forum name in the forum listing.

For more information about how to use the Wrox P2P, be sure to read the P2P FAQs for answers to questions about how the forum software works, as well as many common questions specific to P2P and Wrox books. To read the FAQs, click the FAQ link on any P2P page.

1

Reviewing Core Python

WHAT YOU WILL LEARN IN THIS CHAPTER:

> ➤ The basic features of the Python language
>
> ➤ How to use the Python module mechanism
>
> ➤ How to create a new module
>
> ➤ How to create a new package

WROX.COM CODE DOWNLOADS FOR THIS CHAPTER

You can find the wrox.com downloads for this chapter at www.wrox.com/go/pythonprojects on the Download Code tab. The code is in the Chapter 1 download and individually named according to the names throughout the chapter.

This chapter starts with a brief review of Python—in case you have forgotten some of the basics—and provides a foundation upon which the rest of the book is built. If you are confident in your ability with basic Python coding, feel free to skip ahead until you see content that might be of interest to you. After all, you can always come back to this chapter later if you find you need a refresher.

In this chapter you start off by looking at the Python ecosystem, the data types, and the major control structures and then move on to defining functions and classes. Next, you look at the Python module and package system. And, finally, you create a basic new package of modules.

By the end of this chapter, you should be ready to take the next step and start working with the standard Python modules on real project tasks.

EXPLORING THE PYTHON LANGUAGE AND THE INTERPRETER

Python is a dynamic but strictly typed programming language. It is both interpreted and compiled in that the original source code is compiled into byte code and then interpreted, but this happens transparently to the user; you do not have to explicitly ask Python to compile your code.

The Python language has several implementations, but the most common is the version written in C, often referred to as *CPython*. Other implementations include Jython, written in Java, and IronPython, written for the Microsoft .NET platform. CPython is the implementation used in this book.

> **NOTE** *At the time of writing, there are two version streams of Python: versions 2.x and 3.x. This book focuses on version 3, and the code has been tested on several releases within that stream—up to release 3.4. Where major compatibility issues arise with 2.x, reference will be made to version 2.7.*

Python programs are written in text files that customarily have the extension .py. The Python interpreter, called *python* (in lowercase) does not actually care about the extension; it is only for the user's benefit (and in some operating systems to allow the file and interpreter to be linked).

You can also input Python code directly to the interpreter. This method makes for a highly interactive development style where ideas are prototyped or tested in the interpreter and then transferred into a code editor. The Python interpreter is a powerful learning tool when you are starting to use a new concept or code module.

When working in this mode, you start the interpreter by typing **python** at an operating system command prompt. The system will respond with a message telling you the Python version and some build details, followed by the interactive prompt at which you type code. It looks like this:

```
ActivePython 3.3.2.0 (ActiveState Software Inc.) based on
Python 3.3.2 (default, Sep 16 2013, 23:10:06) [MSC v.1600 32 bit (Intel)] on win
32
Type "help", "copyright", "credits" or "license" for more information.
>>>
```

This message says that this interpreter is for version 3.3.2.0 of Python, it is the ActiveState distribution (as opposed to the `python.org` distribution), and it was built for 32-bit Windows. Your message may differ slightly, but should contain the same types of information.

If instead of running the Python interpreter interactively you want to execute a program stored in a file, then at the operating system prompt you simply append the name of the file after the `python` command:

```
$ python myscript.py
```

> **NOTE** Usually you can also double-click the file in your file explorer tool, and the operating system makes the connection to python and runs the program automatically. However, this often results in the program opening in a window, completing, and the window closing again before you can see the results, so you may prefer to type the python `filename` command in full at a command-line prompt.

Python comes with two helpful functions that assist you in exploring the language: `dir(name)` and `help(name)`. `dir(name)` tells you all of the names available in the object identified by `name`. `help(name)` displays information about the object called `name`. When you first import a new module, you will often not know what functions or classes are included. By looking at the `dir()` listing of the module, you can see what is available. You can then use `help()` on any of the features listed. Be sure to experiment with these functions; they are an invaluable source of information.

REVIEWING THE PYTHON DATA TYPES

Python supports many powerful data types. Superficially, these look like their counterparts in other programming languages, but in Python they often come with super powers. Everything in Python is an object and, therefore, has methods. This means that you can perform a host of operations on any variable. The built-in `dir()` and `help()` functions will reveal all. In this section you look at the standard data types and their most important operations.

> **TIP** The Python Reference Manual (`http://docs.python.org/3.3/reference/`) provides the full detail should you need it.

You need to be aware of some underlying concepts in Python. First, Python variables are just names. You create variable names by assigning them to objects that are instances of types. Variables do not, of themselves, have a type; it is the object to which they are bound that has a type. The name is just a label and, as such, it can be reassigned to a completely different object. Assignment is performed using =, so assigning a value to a variable looks like this:

```
aVariable = aValue
```

This code binds the value `aValue` to the variable name `aVariable` and, if the name does not already exist, the interpreter adds the name to the appropriate namespace.

The distinction between a variable and its underlying value (an object) is thus crucial in Python. You can test variables for equality using a double equal sign (`==`) and object identity (that is, if two names refer to the same object) is compared using the `is` operator, as shown:

```
>>> aString = 'I love spam'
>>> anotherString = 'I love spam'
```

```
>>> anInt = 6
>>> intAlias = anInt
>>> aString == anotherString      # test equality of value
True
>>> aString is anotherString      # test object identity
False
>>> anInt == intAlias             # same value
True
>>> anInt is intAlias             # also same object identity
True
```

Python groups types according to how you can use them. For example, all types are either categorized as *mutable* or *immutable*. If a type is immutable, it means you can't change an object of that type once it's created. You can create a new data item and assign it to the same variable, but you cannot change the original immutable value.

Python also supports several collection types, sometimes referred to as *sequences*. (Strictly speaking collections are a subset of sequences, the distinction will be made clearer later in the chapter.) Sequences share a common set of operations, although not all sequences support all of the operations.

Some Python data types are *callable*. That means you can use the type name like a function to produce a new instance of the type. If no value is given, a default value is returned. You will see examples of this behavior in the following descriptions of the individual data types.

Now that you understand the basics of working with Python data types, it's time to take a look at the different data types, including the numeric, boolean, and None types, as well as the various collection types.

Numeric Types: Integer and Float

Python supports several numeric types including the most basic forms: integer and floating point.

Python integers are unusual in that they are theoretically of infinite size. In practice, integers are limited by the size of your computer's memory. Integers support all the usual numeric operations, such as addition, subtraction, multiplication and so on. You perform arithmetic operations using traditional infix notation. For example, to add two integers,

```
>>> 5 + 4
9
```

or:

```
>>> result = 12 + 8
>>> print (result)
20
```

Literal integer values are, by default, expressed in decimal. You can use other bases by prefixing the number with a zero and the base's initial. Thus, binary is represented as 0bnnn, octal as 0onnn, and hexadecimal as 0xnnn.

The type of an integer is `int`, and you can use it to create integers from floating-point numbers or numeric string representations such as `'123'`, like this:

```
>>> int(5.0)
5
>>> int('123')
123
```

`int` can also convert from nondecimal bases (covering any base up to 36, not just the usual binary, octal, and hexadecimal) using a second, optional, parameter. To convert a hexadecimal (base 16) string representation to an integer, you can use:

```
>>> intValue = int('AB34',16)
43828
```

Python floating-point numbers are of type `float`. Like `int` you can use `float()` to convert string representations, like `'12.34'` to float, and you can also use it to convert an integer number to a float value. Unlike integers, `float()` cannot handle strings for different bases.

The `float` type also supports the normal arithmetic operations, as well as several rounding options. Python floats are based on the Institute of Electrical & Electronic Engineering (IEEE) standards and have the same ranges as the underlying computer architecture. They also suffer the same levels of imprecision that make comparing float values a risky option. Python provides modules for handling fixed precision decimal numbers (`decimal`) and rational fractions (`fractions`) to help alleviate this issue. Python also natively supports a complex, or imaginary, number type called `complex`. These are all typically used for fairly special purposes, so they are not covered here.

The Boolean Type

Python supports a Boolean type, `bool`, with literal values `True` and `False`. The default value of a `bool` is `False`; that is, `bool()` yields `False`.

Python also supports the concept of *truth-like* values for other types. For example, integers are considered `False` if their value is zero. Anything else is considered `True`. The same applies to float values where `0.0` is `False` and anything else is `True`.

You can convert Boolean values to integers using `int()`, in which case `False` is represented as `0` and `True` as `1`.

The Boolean type has most of the Boolean algebra operations you'd expect, including `and`, `or`, and `not`, but—surprisingly—not `xor`.

> **NOTE** Booleans are implemented as a subclass of integer and so also support a bunch of operations that you might not expect, such as exponentiation. You can type things like `True**False` and get a result of 1. You should basically just pretend these "features" don't exist and treat them as an implementation detail; otherwise, your code will become very confusing.

In addition to the Boolean type, Python also supports bitwise Boolean operations on integers. That is to say that Python treats each corresponding pair of bits within two integers as Boolean values in their own right and applies the corresponding operation to each pair of bits. These operations include bitwise and (&), or (|), not (^) and, this time, xor (~), as well as bit shift operators for moving bit patterns left (<<) or right (>>). You look more closely at these bitwise operations later in the chapter.

The None Type

The None type represents a null object. There is only one None object in the Python environment, and all references to None use that same single instance. This means that equality tests with None are usually replaced by an identity test, like so,

```
aVariable is None
```

rather than:

```
aVariable == None
```

None is the default return value of a Python function. It is also often used as a place marker or flag for default parameters in functions. None is not callable and so cannot be used as a conversion function to convert other types to None. None is considered to have a Boolean value of False.

Collection Types

As already mentioned Python has several types representing different kinds of collections or sequences. These are: strings, bytes, tuples, lists, dictionaries and sets. You will see the similarities and differences in each as they are discussed in the following sections. A standard library module called collections provides several other more specialized collection types. You will see occasional references to these in the sections that follow.

> **NOTE** In many of the following discussions, you will see references to operations accepting a collection type. Usually this includes what Python calls iterables, which are objects that conform to Python's iteration protocol. In simple terms iterables are objects that you can use in loop constructs. In most cases you will not need to worry about them, but they are described in the Python documentation if you are interested in reading the technical details. A good place to start is: https://wiki.python.org/moin/Iterator.

Several common features apply to all collections, and rather than bore you by repeating them for each type, they are covered here.

You can get the length of any collection in Python by using the built-in len() function. It takes a collection object argument and returns the number of elements.

You can access the individual elements of a collection using indexing. You do this by providing an index number (or a valid key value for dictionaries) inside square brackets. Collection indices start at zero. You can also index backward from the end by using negative indices so that the last item in the collection will have an index of –1.

Whereas indexing is used to access just one particular element of a collection, you can use *slicing* to access multiple items in the collection. Slicing consists of a start index, an end index, and a step size, and the numbers are separated by colons. Slicing is not valid for dictionaries or sets. The step size argument enables you to, for example, select every other element. All values are optional, and the defaults are the start of the collection, the last item in the collection, and a step size of one. The slice returned consists of all (selected) elements from start to end-1.

Here are a few examples of slicing applied to a string, entered at the Python interactive prompt:

```
>>> '0123456789'[:]
'0123456789'
>>> '0123456789'[3:]
'3456789'
>>> '0123456789'[:3]
'012'
>>> '0123456789'[3:7]
'3456'
>>> '0123456789'[3:7:2]
'35'
>>> '0123456789'[::3]
'0369'
```

You can sort most collections by using the sorted() function. The return value is a sorted list containing the original collection elements. Optional arguments to sorted() provide flexibility in how the elements are sorted and in what order.

In general, empty collections are treated as False in Boolean expressions and True otherwise. Two functions, any() and all(), refine the concept to allow more precise tests. The any() function takes a collection as an argument and returns True if any member of the collection is true. The all() function takes a collection as an argument and returns True if—and only if—all the members are true.

Strings

Python strings are essentially collections of Unicode characters. (The implications of using Unicode are discussed in Chapter 4.) The default encoding is UTF8. If you are working in English, most things will work as you expect. Once you start to use non-English characters, things get more interesting! For now you will be working in English and sticking with UTF8.

Python requires that literal strings be enclosed within quotation marks. Python is extremely flexible in this regard and accepts single quotes ('Joe'), double quotes ("Joe"), triple single quotes ('''Joe'''), and triple double quotes ("""Joe""") to delimit a string. Obviously, the start and end quotes must be of the same type, but any other quote can be contained inside the string. This is most useful for apostrophes and similar grammatical cases ('He said, "Hi!"' or "My brother's hat"). Triple quotes of either type can span multiple lines. Here are a few examples:

```
>>> 'using single quotes'
'using single quotes'
>>> "using double quotes"
```

```
'using double quotes'
>>> print('''triple single quotes spanning
... multiple lines ''')
triple single quotes spanning
multiple lines
```

A literal string at the start of a module, class, or function that is not assigned to a variable is treated as documentation and displayed as part of the built-in help() output for that object.

Special characters such as tabs (\t) or newlines (\n) must be prefixed, or quoted, with a backslash character, and literal backslashes must be quoted so they look like double backslashes. You can avoid this by preceding the entire string with the letter r (for *raw*) to indicate that special character processing should not be done. Nonprintable characters can be included in a string using a backslash followed by their hex code. For example, the escape character is \x1A. (Note that there is no leading zero as is used for hexadecimal integer literals.)

Strings are immutable in that you cannot directly modify or add to a string once it is formed. You can, however, create a new string based on an existing one, and that is how many of the Python string operations work. Python supports a wide range of operations on strings, and these are mostly implemented as methods of the string class. Some of the most common operations are listed in Table 1-1.

Several other string operations are available, but those listed in Table 1-1 are the ones you will use most often.

Empty strings are treated as False in Boolean expressions. All other strings are treated as True.

Bytes and ByteArrays

Python supports two byte-oriented data types. A byte is an 8-bit value, equivalent to an integer from 0–255, and represents the raw bit patterns stored by the computer or transmitted over a network. They are very similar to strings in use and support many of the same methods. The type names are spelled as byte and bytearray respectively.

Literal byte strings are represented in quotes preceded by the letter b. Byte strings are immutable. Byte arrays are similar, but they are mutable.

In practice you will rarely use byte strings or byte arrays unless handling binary data from a file or network. One issue that can catch you by surprise is that if you access an individual element using indexing, the returned value is an integer. This means that comparing a single character byte string with an indexed string value results in a False response, which is different from what would happen using strings in the same way. Here is an example:

```
>>> s = b'Alphabet soup'
>>> c = b'A'
>>> s[0] == c
False
>>> s[0] == c[0]
True
```

As you can see, the key is to use indexing on both sides of the comparison.

TABLE 1-1: String Operations

OPERATION	DESCRIPTION
`+`	Concatenation. This is a somewhat inefficient operation, and you can usually avoid it by using `join()` instead.
`*`	Multiplication. This produces multiple copies of the string concatenated together.
`upper, lower, capitalize`	These change the case of a string.
`center, ljust, rjust`	These justify the string as needed within a given character width, padding as needed with the specified fill character (defaulting to a space).
`startswith, endswith`	These test a substring matching the start or end of a line. Optional parameters control the actual subsection of the string that is tested so the names are slightly misleading. They can also test multiple substrings at once if they are passed as a tuple.
`find, index, rfind`	These return the lowest index where the given substring is found. `find` returns `-1` on failure whereas `index` raises a `ValueError` exception. `rfind` starts at the right-hand side and, therefore, returns the highest index where the substring is found.
`isalpha, isdigit, isalnum, and so on.`	These test the string content. Several test types exist, the most commonly used being those listed; for alphabetic, numeric, and alphanumeric characters respectively.
`join`	This joins a list of strings using the active string as the separator. It is common to build a string using either a single space or no space as the separator. This is faster and more memory efficient than using string concatenation.
`split, splitlines, partition`	These split a string into a list of substrings based on a given separator (the default is whitespace). Note that the separators are removed in the process. `splitlines()` returns a list of lines, effectively splitting using the newline character. `partition()` splits a string based on the given separator, but only up to the first occurrence; it then returns the first string, the separator, and the remaining string.
`strip, lstrip, rstrip`	These strip whitespace (the default) or the specified characters from the ends of the string. `lstrip` strips only the left side; `rstrip` strips only the right. None of them remove whitespace from the middle of a string; they only remove outer characters. To globally remove characters, use the `replace` operation.
`replace`	This performs string replacement. By specifying an empty string as the replacement, it can be used to effectively delete characters.
`format`	This replaces the older C printf-style string formatting used in Python version 2. Printf style is still available in version 3, but is deprecated in favor of `format()`. String formatting is explained in detail in the Python documentation. The basic concept is that pairs of braces embedded in the string form placeholders for data passed as arguments to `format()`. The braces can contain optional style information, such as padding characters. (You can find examples throughout this book.)

You can use the `struct` module to convert binary data from the bytes representation to normal Python types. Of course, to use this you will still have to know what types the byte patterns represent in the first place.

Empty byte strings are treated as `False` in Boolean expressions. All other byte strings are treated as `True`.

Tuples

Tuples are collections of arbitrary objects. The fact that they are collected together suggests that there is probably a logical connection between them, but the language puts no restriction on the objects contained. Tuples are often described as being the Python equivalent to records, or structs, in other languages.

Literal tuples consist of a series of values (or variables) separated by commas. Often, to prevent syntax ambiguity, the tuple as a whole will be contained in parentheses, but this is not a requirement of the tuple itself.

Tuples are immutable, so you cannot modify or extend the tuple once it is created. You can create a new tuple based on an existing one in the same way you did for strings, and you can create a new empty tuple using the `tuple()` type function. You can use a tuple as a key in a dictionary because they are immutable.

One feature of Python tuples that is very useful is known as *unpacking*. This enables you to extract the values of a tuple into discrete variables. You most often see this when a function returns a tuple of values and you want to store the individual values in separate variables. An example is shown here using the `divmod()` function, which returns the quotient and remainder of an integer division as a tuple:

```
>>> print(divmod(12,7))
(1, 5)
>>> q,r = divmod(12,7)
>>> print (q)
1
>>> print (r)
5
```

Notice how q and r can be treated as new, single-valued variables.

A `namedtuple` class in the `collections` module allows elements to be indexed by name rather than position. This combines some of the advantages of a dictionary with the compactness and immutability of a tuple.

Empty tuples are treated as `False` in Boolean expressions. All other tuples are treated as `True`.

Lists

Lists in Python are highly flexible and powerful data structures. They can be used to mimic the behavior of many classic data structures and to form the basis of others in the form of custom classes. They are dynamic and, like tuples, can hold any kind of object but, unlike tuples, they are mutable, so you can modify their contents. You can also use tuple-style unpacking to assign list items to discrete variables.

A literal list is expressed as a comma-separated sequence of objects enclosed in square brackets. You can create an empty list either by specifying a pair of empty square brackets or by using the default value of the `list()` type function. Lists come with several methods for adding and removing members, and they also support some arithmetic-style operations for concatenating and copying lists in a similar fashion to strings.

You can initialize a list directly by using lists of values, or you can build them programmatically using list comprehensions. The latter looks like a single-line `for` loop inside list brackets. Here is an example that builds a list of the even squares from 1 to 10:

```
>>> [n*n for n in range(1,11) if not n*n % 2]
[4, 16, 36, 64, 100]
```

Table 1-2 lists some of the most common list operations.

Empty lists are treated as `False` in Boolean expressions. All other lists are treated as `True`.

TABLE 1-2: List operations

OPERATION	DESCRIPTION
+	This concatenates two lists.
*	This creates a list of multiple copies of the first list. Note that the copies all refer to the same object, which often results in surprising side effects when an object is modified. Often, list slicing or list comprehension is a better option.
append	This adds an element to the end of an existing list. The new element could itself be a list. The operation is effective in-place, and `None` is returned.
extend	This adds the contents of a list to the end of another list, effectively joining the two lists. The original list is modified in place. `None` is returned.
pop	This removes an item from the end of a list or at the specified index if one is provided. Returns the item.
index	This returns the index of the first occurrence of an item in a list. Raise a `ValueError` if not found. (The string operation of the same name has similar behavior.)
count	This returns a count of the specified item in the list.
insert	This inserts an element before the specified index. If the index is too large, it is appended to the end of the list.
remove	This removes the first occurrence of the specified item. It raises a `ValueError` if the item does not exist.
reverse	This reverses the elements of the list in-place.
sort	This sorts the elements of the list in-place. Optional parameters provide flexibility in how the sort is performed. To get a sorted copy of the list without modifying the original, use the `sorted()` function.

Dictionaries

Dictionaries are super powerful data structures that beginners frequently overlook. They offer solutions to lots of common programming problems. A dictionary is used like a list, but its elements are accessed by using a key-value mechanism rather than a numeric index. The elements of a Python dictionary are thus a (non-ordered) sequence of key-value pairs.

The key can be any immutable value, including a tuple. Keys must be unique. The value can be any kind of Python object, including another dictionary, a list, or anything else that Python recognizes as an object.

Dictionaries are highly optimized, so lookup times are very fast. In fact Python makes extensive use of dictionaries internally, to implement namespaces and classes, among other things. Dictionaries also provide a solution anywhere that dynamically named values need to be stored and accessed. Dictionaries are also efficient where the keys are not sequential because Python uses a hashing algorithm to map the keys into a sparse array structure. (If you didn't understand that last sentence, don't worry, you are not alone, and you don't really need to know. What it means for you is that Python dictionaries are fast, and they use memory efficiently.)

Dictionary literals are composed of comma-separated key-value pairs. The keys and their values are separated by colons, and the whole is contained in a pair of curly braces, or {}. It looks like this:

```
>>> {'aKey':'avalue', 2:7, 'booleans':{False:0,True:1}}
{'aKey': 'avalue', 2: 7, 'booleans': {False: 0, True: 1}}
```

You access the stored values by "indexing" the dictionary using the key rather than a numeric index. If the preceding example were stored in a variable called D, you could access the aKey and the True values like this:

```
>>> D['aKey']
'avalue'
>>> D['booleans'][True]
1
```

You can create an empty dictionary by using an empty pair of braces or by using the default value of the dict() type function.

Dictionaries come with some extra operations for extracting lists of keys and values and handling default values. Some of these are described in Table 1-3.

Dictionaries are, by the nature of their implementation, unsorted. Indeed the order may change when new data is inserted. The collections module contains an OrderedDict class that maintains the order of insertion should that be required. The sorted() function returns a sorted list of keys if the keys are comparable. If the keys are incompatible (as in the preceding example), sorted() raises a TypeError.

The collections module also provides a defaultdict class that enables you to specify a default value that is returned any time a nonexistent key is used. In addition to returning the default value, it also creates a new element for the given key with the default value. This is similar to the setdefault method described earlier. This can be a mixed blessing because it can result in bogus entries for badly spelled keys!

TABLE 1-3: Dictionary Operations

OPERATION	DESCRIPTION
keys, values, items	These methods return list-like objects (called *dictionary views*) containing the keys, values, and key-value tuples respectively. These views are dynamic, so any changes to the dictionary (deletions and so on) after they are created are reflected in the view.
get, pop	These methods take a key and an optional default value. get returns the value for a key from the dictionary if the key exists or a specified default if the key does not exist. pop works the same way, but also removes the item from the dictionary if it exists. get has a default value of None, but pop raises a KeyError if no default is given.
setdefault	This operation acts like get, but also creates a new key-value pair in the dictionary using the given key and the default value if the key does not exist.
fromkeys	This operation initializes a dictionary using a sequence to provide the keys and a given default value (or None if no value is given). Usually called directly as dict.fromkeys() rather than on an existing dictionary.

Empty dictionaries are treated as False in Boolean expressions. All other dictionaries are treated as True.

Sets

Sets embody a mathematical concept that is frequently used in programming where a unique group of elements is required. In Python, sets are a lot like dictionaries with keys but no corresponding values.

Sets have the Python type set. The same basic rules apply as for dictionary keys in that set values must be immutable and unique (indeed that's what makes it a set!). The default value from set() is the empty set, and this is the only way to express an empty set because {} is already used for an empty dictionary. The set() function accepts any kind of collection as its argument and converts it to a set (dictionary values will be lost).

There is another type of set in Python, called frozenset, that is immutable and is basically a read-only set. Its constructor works like set(), but it supports only a subset of the operations. You can use a frozenset as an element of a regular set because frozenset is immutable.

Set literals are expressed with curly braces surrounding elements separated by commas:

```
myset = {1,2,3,4,5}
```

Sets do not support indexing or slicing and, like dictionaries, they do not have any inherent order. The sorted() function returns an ordered list of values. Sets have a bunch of math-style set operations that are distinct from other collections. Table 1-4 shows those operations that are common to both the set and frozenset types.

TABLE 1-4: Set Operations

OPERATION	DESCRIPTION
`in`	This tests whether a single element exists in the set. Note: If the tested item is itself a set, S1, the result will be true only if S1, as a set, is an element of the target set. This is different from the `subset()` test.
`issubset, <=, <`	These test whether one set is a subset of the target—that is, whether all members of the tested set are also members of the target. If the sets are identical, the test will return `True` in the first two cases, but `False` for the `<` operator.
`issuperset, >=, >`	These test whether one set is a superset of the other—that is, whether all the members of the target set are members of the source. If they are equal, the first two operations return `True`; the last operation will return `False`.
`union, |`	These return the union of two (or more) sets. The union method takes a comma-separated list of sets as arguments while the pipe operator is used infixed between the sets.
`intersection, &`	These return the intersection set of two (or more) sets. Usage is similar to `union()`.
`difference, -`	These return the members of the source set that are not members of the target set.
`symmetric_difference, ^`	Returns the elements of both sets that are not in the intersection. The method works only for two sets, but the `^` operator can be applied to multiple sets in infix style.

Note that the method variations in Table 1-4 will accept any collection type as an argument whereas the infix operations will work only with sets.

Table 1-5 looks at the modifier operations that are applicable only to sets. These cannot be used on a `frozenset`, although a `frozenset` can be used as an argument for several of them. Note that these operations adjust the source set itself; they do not return a set—they return the Python default value of `None`. The infix operations work only on two sets (unlike those in Table 1-4) and work only on actual sets, not other collection types. You can use the methods on multiple sets, and other collection types are converted to a set where needed.

Empty sets are treated as `False` in Boolean expressions. All other sets are treated as `True`.

In the next section, you will use the data types in code as you explore the different control structures that Python offers.

TABLE 1-5: Set Modifier Operations

OPERATION	DESCRIPTION
`update, |=`	These add the elements of the target set (or sets) to the source set.
`intersection_update, &=`	These remove all elements except those in the intersection of source and target sets. If more than two sets are involved, the result is the intersection of all sets involved.
`difference_update, -=`	These remove all elements found in the intersection of the sets. If multiple sets are provided, the items removed are in the intersection of the source with any of the other sets.
`symmetric_difference_update, ^=`	These return the set of values in both sets involved excepting those in the intersection. Note that this operation works only on two sets at a time.
`add`	This adds the given element to the set.
`remove`	This removes the specified element from the set. If the element is not found it raises a `KeyError`.
`discard`	This removes the given element from the set if it is present. No `KeyError` is raised in this case if the element is not found.
`pop`	This removes and returns an arbitrary member from the set. Raises `KeyError` if the set is empty.
`clear`	This removes all elements from a set.

USING PYTHON CONTROL STRUCTURES

In this section you first look at the overall structure of a Python program and then consider each of the basic structures: sequence, selection, and iteration. Finally, you look at how Python handles errors, review context managers, and investigate how to exchange data with the outside world.

Structuring Your Program

Python programs do not have any required, predefined entry point (for example a `main()` function) and are simply expressed as source code in a text file that is read and executed in order starting at the top of the file. (Definitions, such as functions, are executed in the sense that the function is created and assigned to a name, but the internal code is not executed until the function is called.)

Python does not have any special syntax to indicate whether a source file is a program or a module and, as you will see, a given file can be used in either role. A typical executable program file consists of a set of import statements to bring in any code modules needed, some function and class definitions, and some directly executable code.

In practice, for a nontrivial program, most function and class definitions will exist in module files and be included in the imports. This leaves a short section of driver code to start the application. Often this code will be placed in a function, and the function will often be called `main()`, but that is purely a nod to programming convention, not a requirement of Python.

Finally this "main" function needs to be called. This is often done within a special `if` statement at the end of the main script. It looks like this:

```
if __name__ == "__main__":
    main()
```

When Python detects that a program file is being executed by the interpreter rather than imported as a module, it sets the special variable `__name__` (note the double underscores on either side) to `"__main__"`. This means that any code inside this `if` block is executed only when the script is run as a main program and not when the file is imported by another program. If the file is only ever expected to be used as a module, the `main()` function may be replaced by a `test()` function that executes a set of unit tests. Again, the actual name used is of no significance to Python.

Using Sequences, Blocks and Comments

The most fundamental programming structure is a sequence of statements. Normally Python statements occur on a line by themselves, so a sequence is simply a series of lines.

```
x = 2
y = 7
z = 9
```

In this case the statements are all assignments. Other valid statements include function calls, module imports or definitions. Definitions include functions and classes. The various control structures described in the following sections are also valid statements.

> **NOTE** *Python does enable you to include multiple statements on a single line by separating them with a semicolon. Thus the following line of code consists of three statements:*
>
> ```
> x = 2; y = 7; z = 9
> ```
>
> *This style is not recommended by the Python community; using separate lines is preferred.*

Python is a block-structured language, and blocks of code are indicated by indentation level. The amount of indentation is quite flexible; although most Python programmers stick to using three or four spaces to optimize readability, Python doesn't care. Different Integrated Development Environments (IDEs) and text editors have their own ideas about how indentation is done. If you use multiple programming tools, you may find you get indentation errors reported because the tools have used different combinations of tabs and spaces. If possible, set up your editor to use spaces instead of tabs.

The exception to the indentation rule is comments. A Python comment starts with a # symbol and continues to the end of the line. Python accepts comments that start anywhere on the line regardless of current indentation level, but by convention, programmers tend to retain indentation level, even for comments.

Selecting an Execution Path

Python supports a limited set of selection options. The most basic structure is the if/elif/else construct. The elif and else parts are optional. It looks like this:

```
if pages < 9:
    print("It's too short")
elif pages > 99:
    print("It's too long")
else: print("Perfect")
```

Notice the colon at the end of each test expression. That is Python's indicator that a new block of code is coming up. It has no start and end block markers (such as {}); the colon is the only indication, and the block must either occur on the same line as the colon, if it's only a single line block, or as an indented block of code. Many Python programmers prefer the indented block style even for single line blocks.

Also note that there can be an arbitrary number of elif tests, but only a single else clause—or none at all.

The other selection structure you will find in Python is the conditional expression selector. This produces one of several values depending on the given test conditions. It looks like this:

```
<a value> if <an expression> else <another value>
```

An example might be where a screen coordinate is being incremented until a certain limit (perhaps the screen's maximum resolution) and then reset to 0. That could be written as:

```
coord = coord + increment if coord < limit else 0
```

This is equivalent to the more traditional structure shown here:

```
if coord < limit
    coord += increment
else:
    coord = 0
```

You should use caution when using conditional expressions because it is very easy to create obscure code. If in doubt you should use the expanded if/else form.

One final comment on Python's comparison expressions is worth making here. In many programming languages, if you want to test whether a value lies between two limits, you need two separate tests, like this:

```
if aValue < upperLimit and aValue > lowerLimit:
    # do something here
```

Python will be quite happy to process code like that, but it offers a useful shortcut in that you can combine the comparisons as shown here:

```
if lowerLimit < avalue < upperLimit:
    # do something here
```

Iteration

Python offers several alternatives for iteration. The most fundamental and general is the `while` loop. It looks like this:

```
while BooleanExpression:
    aBlockOfCode
else:
    anotherBlock
```

Notice the colon (:) at the end of the `while` statement, which signifies that a block of code follows. Also notice the indentation of the block. The block will, in principle, be executed for as long as `BooleanExpression` remains true. However, there are two ways you can exit out of a `while` loop regardless of the `BooleanExpression` value. These are the `break` statement, which exits the loop immediately, and a `return` statement if the loop is inside a function definition. A `return` statement exits the function immediately and so will also exit any loop within the function.

The `else` clause is optional and is rarely used in practice. It is executed any time the `BooleanExpression` is `False`, including when the loop exits normally. It will not be executed if the loop is exited by a `break` or `return` statement.

One very common `while` loop idiom is to use `True` as the test condition to create an infinite loop and then have a `break` test within the body of the loop. Here is an example where the loop reads user commands and processes them. If the command contains the letter q, it exits.

```
while True:
    command = input('Enter a command[rwq]: ')
    if 'q' in command.lower(): break
    if command.lower() == 'r':
        # process 'r'
    elif command.lower() == 'w':
        # process 'w'
    else:
        print('Invalid command, try again')
```

There is a companion statement to `break`, namely `continue`. Whereas `break` exits both the block and the loop, `continue` exits the block for the current loop iteration only. Control then returns to the `while` statement and, if appropriate, a new iteration of the block will commence.

The next significant looping construct in Python is the `for` loop, which looks like this:

```
for item in <iterable>:
    code block
else:
    another code block
```

The `for` loop takes each item in the iterable and executes the code block once per item. You can terminate the loop early using `break` or `return` as described for the `while` loop. You can terminate a single iteration of the loop using `continue` as described earlier.

The `else` block is executed when all the iterations are completed. It will not be executed if the loop exits via a `break` or `return`.

The iterable is anything that complies with Python's iterator protocol. In practice this is usually a collection such as a list, tuple, or a function that returns a collection of values such as `range()`. The `open()` function returns a file iterator that enables you to loop over a file without first reading it into memory. It's possible to define your own custom iterable classes, too.

One common function that is particularly used with `for` loops is `enumerate()`. This function returns tuples containing both the iterable item and a sequence number that, by default, is equivalent to a list index. This means that the `for` block can more easily update the iterable directly. `enumerate()` takes a second optional argument that specifies the sequence starting number, which you could use, for example, to indicate the line number in a file, starting with 1 rather than the 0 default.

Here is an example that illustrates some of these points printing a file with associated line numbers:

```
for number, line in enumerate(open('myfile.txt')):
    print(number, '\t', line)
```

Finally, Python has a couple of inline loop structures. You saw one of these, the list comprehension, in the discussion of lists earlier in the chapter.

A list comprehension is a specific application of a more general loop form known as a *generator expression* that you can use where you might otherwise have a sequence of literal values. If you recall the list comprehension example earlier in the chapter, you used it to populate a list with the even squares from 1 to 10, like this:

```
>>> [n*n for n in range(1,11) if not n*n % 2]
[4, 16, 36, 64, 100]
```

The part inside the square brackets is a generator expression and the general form is as follows:

```
<result expression> for <loop variable> in <iterable> if <filter expression>
```

Comparing that with the list comprehension example you see that the result expression was n*n, the loop variable was n, and the iterable was `range(1,11)`. The filter expression was `if not n*n % 2`.

You can rewrite that as a conventional `for` loop, like this:

```
result = []
for n in range(1,11):
    if n*n % 2:
        result.append(n)
```

One important point to appreciate about generator expressions is that they do not generate the whole data set at once. Rather they generate (hence the name) the data items on demand, which can lead to a significant saving in memory resources when dealing with large data sets. You find out more about this later in the chapter when you look at a special type of function called a *generator function*.

Handling Exceptions

There are two approaches to detecting errors. The first involves explicitly checking each action as it's performed; the other attempts the operations and relies on the system generating an error condition, or *exception*, if something goes wrong. Although the first approach is appropriate in some situations, in Python, it's far more common to use the second. Python supports this technique with the `try/except/else/finally` construct. In its general form, it looks like this:

```
try:
      A block of application code
except <an error type> as <anExceptionObject>:
    A block of error handling code
else:
    Another block of application code
finally:
    A block of clean-up code
```

The `except`, `else`, and `finally` are all optional, although at least one of `except` or `finally` must exist if a `try` statement is used. There can be multiple `except` clauses, but only one `else` or `finally`. You can omit the as… part of an `except` statement line if the exception details are not required.

The `try` block is executed and, if an error is encountered, the exception class is tested. If an `except` statement exists for that type of error, the corresponding block is executed. (If multiple exception blocks specify the same exception type, only the first matching clause is executed.) If no matching `except` statement is found, the exception is propagated upwards until the top-level interpreter is reached and Python generates its usual traceback error report. Note that an empty `except` statement will catch any error type; however, this is usually a bad idea because it hides the occurrence of any unexpected errors.

The `else` block is executed if the `try` block succeeds without any errors. In practice the `else` is rarely used. Regardless of whether an error is caught or propagated, or whether the `else` clause is executed, the `finally` clause will always be executed, thus providing an opportunity to release any computing resources in a locked state. This is true even when the `try/except` clause is left via a `break` or `return` statement.

You can use a single `except` statement to process multiple exception types. You do this by listing the exception classes in a tuple (parentheses are required). The optional exception object contains details of where the exception occurred and provides a string conversion method so that a meaningful error message may be provided by printing the object.

It is possible to raise exceptions from your own code. It is also possible to use any of the existing exception types or to define your own by subclassing from the `Exception` class. You can also pass arguments to exceptions you raise, and you can access these in the exception object in the `except` clause using the `args` attribute of the error object.

Here is an example of raising a standard `ValueError` with a custom argument and then catching that error and printing the given argument.

```
>>> try:
...     raise ValueError('wrong value')
... except ValueError as error:
...     print (error.args)
...
('wrong value',)
```

Note that you didn't get a full traceback, only the print output from the `except` block. You can also re-raise the original exception after processing by simply calling `raise` with no arguments.

Managing Context

Python has the concept of a runtime *context*. This typically includes a temporary resource of some kind that your program wants to interact with. A typical example might be an open file or a concurrent thread of execution. To handle this Python uses the keyword `with` and a *context manager* protocol. This protocol enables you to define your own context manager classes, but you will mostly use the managers provided by Python.

You use a context manager by invoking the `with` statement:

```
with open(filename, mode) as contextName:
        process file here
```

The context manager ensures the file is closed after use. This is fairly typical of a context manager's role—to ensure that valuable resources are freed after use or that proper sharing precautions are taken on first use. Context managers often remove the need for a `try/finally` construct. The `contextlib` module provides support for building your own context managers.

You have now seen the different types of data that Python can process as well as the control structures you can use to do that processing. It is now time to find out how to get data into and out of your Python programs and that is the subject of the next section.

GETTING DATA IN AND OUT OF PYTHON

Basic input and output of data is a major requirement of any programming language. You need to consider how your programs will interact with users and with data stored in files.

Interacting with Users

To send data to users via `stdout`, you use the `print()` function, which you've seen several times already. You learn how to control the output more precisely in this section. To read data from users, you use the `input()` function, which prompts the user for input and then returns a string of raw characters from `stdin`.

The `print()` function is more complex than it first appears in that it has several optional parameters. At its simplest level, you simply pass a string and `print()` displays it on `stdout` followed by an end-of-line (eol) character. The next level of complexity involves passing non-string data that print() then converts to a string (using the str() type function) before displaying the result. Stepping up a gear, you can pass multiple items at once to print(), and it will convert and display them in turn separated by a space.

The previous paragraph identified three fixed elements in print()'s behavior:

➤   It displays output on stdout.

➤   It terminates with an eol character.

➤   It separates items with a space.

In fact, none of these are really fixed, and print() enables you to modify any or all of them using optional parameters. You can change the output by specifying a file argument; the separator is defined by the sep argument, and the terminating character is defined by the end argument. The following line prints the infamous "hello world" message, specified as two strings, to a file using a hyphen separator and the string "END" as an end marker:

```
with open("tmp.txt", "w") as tmp:
    print("Hello", "World", end="END", sep="-", file=tmp)
```

The content of the file should be: "Hello-WorldEND".

The string format() method really comes into its own when combined with print(). This combination is capable of presenting your data neatly and clearly separated. In addition using format() can often be more efficient that trying to print a long list of objects and string fragments. There are many examples of how to use format() in the Python documentation.

You can also communicate with the user using the input() function that reads values typed by the user in response to a given on-screen prompt. It is your responsibility to convert the returned characters to whatever data type is represented and handle any errors resulting from that conversion.

> **NOTE** In Python version 2, the raw _ input() function was used instead of input(). The version 2 input() function behaved rather differently. It evaluated whatever the user typed. This created a security issue because malicious code could be input. The version 2 input() function was removed in version 3 and raw _ input() was renamed to input().

Here is an example that asks the user to enter a number. If the number is too high or too low it prints a warning. (This could form the core of a guessing game if you cared to experiment with it.)

```
target = 66

while True :
    value = input("Enter an integer between 1 and 100")
    try:
```

```
            value = int(value)
            break
        except ValueError:
            print("I said enter an integer!")

    if value > target:
        print (value, "is too high")
    elif int(value) < target:
        print("too low")
    else:
        print("Pefect")
```

Here the user is provided with a prompt to enter an integer in the appropriate range. The value read is then converted to an integer using `int()`. If the conversion fails, a `ValueError` exception is raised, and the error message is then displayed. If the conversion succeeds, you can break out of the `while` loop and proceed to test it against the target, confident that you have a valid integer.

Using Text Files

Text files are the workhorses of programming when it comes to saving data, and Python supports several functions for dealing with text files.

> **NOTE** The file interface in Python is really a specialization of a higher-level abstract interface starting with a class called `io.IOBase`. You can mostly ignore these; they simply create a standardized set of operations that applies to text files and other "file like" objects.

You saw the `open()` function used in previous sections and it takes a filename and a mode as arguments. The mode can be any of `r`, `w`, `rw`, and `a` for read, write, read-write, and append respectively. (Some other modes are less often used. There are also a few optional parameters that control how the data is interpreted, see the documentation for details.) The `r` mode requires the file to exist; the `w` and `rw` modes create a new empty file (or overwrite any existing file of the same name). The `a` mode opens an existing file or creates a new empty file if a file of the specified filename does not already exist. The file object returned is also a context manager and can be used in a `with` block as you saw in the context manager section. If a `with` block is not used, you should explicitly close the file using the `close()` method when you are finished with it, thus ensuring that any data sitting in memory buffers is sent to the physical file on disk. The `with` construct calls `close()` automatically, which is one of the advantages of using the context manager approach.

Once you have an open file object, you can use `read()`, `readlines()`, or `readline()` as required. `read()` reads the entire file contents as a single string complete with embedded newline characters. `readlines()` reads line by line into a list, and the newline characters are retained. `readline()` reads the next line in the file, again retaining the newline. The file object is an iterable, so you can use it directly in a `for` loop without the need for any of the read methods. The recommended pattern for reading the lines in a file is therefore:

```
with open(filename, mode) as fileobject:
    for line in fileobject:
        # process line
```

You can write to a writable file object using the `write()` or `writelines()` methods, which are the equivalents to the similarly named read methods. Note that there is no `writeline()` method for writing a single line.

If you are using the `rw` mode, you might want to move to a specific position in the file to overwrite the existing data. You can find your current position in the file using the `tell()` method. You can go to a specific position (possibly one you recorded with `tell()` earlier) using the `seek()` method. `seek()` has several modes of calculating position; the default is simply the offset from the start of the file.

You now have all of the basic skills to write working Python programs. However, to tackle larger projects, which are the focus of this book, you will want to extend Python's capabilities. The next section starts to explore how you can do just that.

EXTENDING PYTHON

The simplest way of extending Python is by writing your own functions. You can define these in the same file as the code that uses them, or you can create a new module and import the functions from there. You look at modules in the next section; for now you will create the functions and use them in the same file. In fact, you will mostly be using the interactive prompt for the examples in this section.

The next step in creating new functionality in Python is to define your own classes and create objects from them. Again, it is common to create classes in modules, and you see how to do so in the next section. The examples here are simple enough that you can just use the Python prompt.

Python programmers frequently use documentation strings in their programs. Documentation strings are string literals that are not assigned to a variable and respect the indentation level at which they are defined. You use documentation strings to describe functions, classes, or modules. The `help()` function reads and presents documentation strings.

Defining and Using Functions

Several types of functions are available in Python. This section looks at the standard variety first, followed by a generator function, and concludes with the slightly enigmatic lambda function.

You define functions in Python using the `def` keyword. The form looks like this:

```
def functionName(parameter1, param2,...):
    function block
```

Python functions always return a value. You can specify an explicit return value using the `return` keyword; otherwise, Python returns `None` by default. (If you find unexpected `None` values appearing in your output, check that the function concerned has an explicit `return` statement in its body.) You can give default values to parameters by following the name with an equals sign and the value. You see an example in the `odds()` generator function in the next section.

You can most easily understand how a function definition is created and used by trying it out.

TRY IT OUT Creating and Using a Function

In this Try It Out, you create a new function that takes several input parameters and returns a value. This function uses the mathematical equation of a straight line to return the corresponding y-coordinate for a given gradient, x-coordinate, and constant. You then use the function to generate a set of coordinates for a line.

1. Start the Python interpreter.

2. Type the following code to define the function:

```
>>> def straight_line(gradient, x, constant):
...         ''' returns y coordinate of a straight line
        -> gradient * x + constant'''
...         return gradient*x + constant
...
>>>
```

3. Now that you have defined the function, test it using some simple values that you can calculate in your head. Try calling the function with a `gradient` of 2, an x value of 4, and a `constant` of `-3`:

```
>>> # test with a single value first
>>> straight_line(2,4,-3)
5
```

4. Let's now try a more complex test of the function, using the following code:

```
>>> for x in range(10):
...     print(x,straight_line(2,x,-3))
...
0 -3
1 -1
2 1
3 3
4 5
5 7
6 9
7 11
8 13
9 15
```

5. Finally, check that the `help()` function correctly recognizes the function:

```
>>> help(straight_line)
Help on function straight_line in module __main__:

straight_line(gradient, x, constant)
    returns y coordinate of a straight line
    -> gradient * x + constant
(END)
```

How It Works

In the first line in step 2, you created the function definition. You named it `straight_line` and said it had three required parameters: `gradient`, `x`, and `constant`. These parameters correspond to the values used in the mathematical equation $y = mx+c$, where m is the gradient and c is a constant.

The second line is a documentation string that describes what the function is for and how it should be used.

The third line is the function code block. It could be arbitrarily complex and several lines long, but in this case it's a one-liner and you are returning the result so you prefixed it with the keyword `return`. Note that the code line has to start at the same indentation level as the start of the documentation string; otherwise, you will get an indentation error.

You then tested the function with some simple values. Some mental arithmetic confirms that the return value of 5 does indeed equal (2*4-3). The function seems to work, at least for a simple case.

You then used the function to generate a set of x-,y-coordinate pairs using a `for` loop with a fixed value for the `gradient` (2) and `constant` (-3) but supplying the loop variable as x. If you have some paper handy, you can try plotting the coordinates listed to confirm that they form a straight line.

Finally, you used the `help()` function to confirm that the documentation string was correctly detected and displayed.

Generator Functions

The next form of function you look at is the generator function. Generator functions look exactly like standard functions except that instead of using `return` to pass back a value, they use the keyword `yield`. (In theory they can use return in addition to `yield`, but only the `yield` expressions produce the generator behavior.)

The bit of Pythonic magic that makes generator functions special is that they act like a freeze-frame camera. When a standard function reaches a `return` statement, it returns the value and the function then throws away all of its internal data. The next time the function is called, everything starts off from scratch.

The `yield` statement does something different. It returns a value, just like `return` does, but it doesn't cause the function to throw away its data; instead, everything is preserved. The next call of the function picks up from the `yield` statement, even if that's in the middle of a block or part of a loop. There can even be multiple `yield` statements in a single function. Because the `yield` statement can be inside a loop, it is possible to create a function that effectively returns an infinite series of results. Here is an example that returns an incrementing series of odd numbers:

```
def odds(start=1):
    ''' return all odd numbers from start upwards'''
    if int(start) % 2 == 0: start = int(start) + 1
    while True:
        yield start
        start += 2
```

In this function you first check that the `start` argument passed is an odd integer (an even integer divided by 2 has a zero remainder), and if not, you force it to be the next highest odd integer by adding 1. You then create an infinite `while` loop. Normally this would be a very bad idea because your program would just block forever. However, because this is a generator function, you are using `yield` to return the value of `start` so the function exits at this point, returning the value of `start` at this moment in time. The next time the function is called, execution starts right where you left off. So `start` is incremented by 2, and the loop goes round again, yielding the next odd number and exiting the function until the next time.

Python ensures that generator functions become iterators so that you can use them in `for` loops, like so:

```
for n in odds():
        if n > 7: break
        else: print(n)
```

You use `odds()` just like a collection. Every time the loop goes around, it calls the generator function and receives the next odd value.

You avoid an infinite loop by inserting the `break` test so you never call `odds()` beyond 7.

> **NOTE** If you use `odds()` *a second time in the same program, it creates a brand-new instance of the iterator and the sequence starts over.*

Now that you understand how generator functions work, you may have realized that the generator expressions introduced earlier in this chapter are effectively just anonymous generator functions. Generator expressions are effectively a disguised form of a generator function without a name.

This provides a perfect segue to the final function type we will be learning about here—the lambda function.

Lambda Functions

The term *lambda* comes from a form of mathematical calculus invented by Alonzo Church. The good news is that you don't need to know anything about the math to use lambda functions! The idea behind a lambda function is that it is an anonymous function block, usually very small, that you can insert into code that then calls the lambda function just like a normal function. Lambda functions are not things you will use often, but they are very handy when you would otherwise have to create a lot of small functions that are used only once. They are often used in GUI or network programming contexts, where the programming toolkit requires a function to call back with a result.

A lambda function is defined like this:

```
lambda <param1, param2, ...,paramN> : <expression>
```

That's the literal word `lambda`, followed by an optional, comma-separated list of parameter names, a colon, and an arbitrary Python expression that, usually, uses the input parameters. Note that the expression does not have the word `return` in front of it.

Some languages allow lambda functions to be arbitrarily complex; however, Python limits you to a single expression. The expression can become quite complex, but in practice it's better to create a standard function if that is the case because it will be easier to read and debug if things go wrong.

You can assign lambda functions to variables, in which case those variables look exactly like standard Python function names. For example, here is the `straight _ line` example function re-implemented as a lambda function:

```
>>> straight_line = lambda m,x,c: m*x+c
>>> straight_line(2,4,-3)
5
```

You see lambda functions popping up later in the book. Just remember that they are simply a concise way to express a short, single expression, function.

Defining and Using Classes and Objects

Python supports object-oriented programming using a traditional class-based approach. Python classes support multiple inheritance and operator overloading (but not method overloading), as well as the usual mechanisms of encapsulation and message passing. Python classes do not directly implement data hiding, although some naming conventions are used to provide a thin layer of privacy for attributes and to suggest when attributes should not be used directly by clients. Class methods and data are supported as well as the concepts of *properties* and *slots*. Classes have both a constructor (__new__ ()) and an initializer (__init__ ()), as well as a destructor mechanism (__del__ ()), although the latter is not always guaranteed to be called. Classes act as namespaces for the methods and data defined therein.

Objects are instances of classes. Instances can have their own attributes added after instantiation, although this is not normal practice.

A class is defined using the `class` keyword followed by the class name and a parenthesized list of super-classes. The class definition contains a set of class data and method definitions. A method definition has as its first parameter a reference to the calling instance, traditionally called `self`. A simple class definition looks like this:

```
class MyClass(object):
    instance_count = 0
    def __init__(self, value):
        self.__value = value
        MyClass.instance_count += 1
        print("instance No {} created".format(MyClass.instance_count))
    def aMethod(self, aValue):
        self.__value *= aValue
    def __str__(self):
        return "A MyClass instance with value: " + str(self.__value)
    def __del__(self):
        MyClass.instance_count -= 1
```

The class name traditionally starts with an uppercase letter. In Python 3 the super class is always `object` unless specifically stated otherwise, so the use of `object` as the super class in the preceding example is actually redundant. The `instance _ count` data item is a class attribute because it does not appear inside any of the class' methods. The __ init __ () function is the initializer (constructors are rarely used in Python unless inheriting from a built-in class). It sets the instance variable self.__ value, increments the previously defined class variable instance _ count, and then prints a message. The double underscores before value indicate that it is effectively private data and should not be used directly. The __ init __ () method is called automatically by Python immediately after the object is constructed. The instance method aMethod() modifies the instance attribute created in the __ init __ () method. The __ str __ () method is a special method used to return a formatted string so that instances passed to the print function, for example, will be printed in a meaningful way. The destructor __ del __ () decrements the class variable instance _ count when the object is destroyed.

You can create an instance of the class like this:

```
myInstance = MyClass(42)
```

This creates an instance in memory and then calls MyClass.__ init __ () with the new instance as self and 42 as value.

You can call the aMethod() method using dot notation like this:

```
myInstance.aMethod(66)
```

This is translated to the more explicit invocation,

```
MyClass.aMethod(myInstance, 66)
```

and results in the desired behavior whereby the value of the __ value attribute is adjusted.

You can see the __ str __ () method in action if you print the instance, like this:

```
print(myInstance)
```

This should print the message:

```
A MyClass instance with value: 2772
```

You could also print the instance _ count value before and after creating/destroying an instance:

```
print(MyClass.instance_count)
inst = MyClass(44)
print(MyClass.instance_count)
del(inst)
print(MyClass.instance_count)
```

This should show the count being incremented and then later decremented again. (There may be a slight delay before the destructor is called during garbage collection, but it should only be a few moments.)

The __ init __ (), __ del __ (), and __ str __ () methods are not the only special methods. Several of these exist, all signified by the use of double underscores (they are sometimes called *dunder* methods). Operator overloading is supported via a set of these special methods including: __ add __ (), __ sub __ (), __ mul __ (), __ div __ (), and so on. Other methods provide for the implementation of Python protocols such as iteration or context management. You can override these methods in your own classes. You should never define your own dunder methods; otherwise, future enhancements to Python could break your code.

You can override methods in subclasses, and the new definitions can invoke the inherited version of the method by using the `super()` function, like this:

```
class SubClass(Parent):
    def __init__(self, aValue):
        super().__init__(aValue)
```

The call to `super().__init__()` translates to a call to the `__init__()` method of `Parent`. Using `super()` avoids problems, particularly with multiple inheritance, where a class could be inherited multiple times and you usually don't want it to be initialized more than once.

> **NOTE** The use of `super()` in Python 3 has been greatly simplified compared to its Python 2 form. The `super()` line in Python 2 would look like `super(SubClass, self).__init__(aValue)`, which is much less intuitive to use.

Slots are a memory-saving device, and you invoke them by using the `__slots__` special attribute and providing a list of the object attribute names. Often `__slots__` are a premature optimization, and you should use them only if you have a specific, known need.

Properties are another feature available for data attributes. They enable you to make an attribute read only (or even write only) by forcing access to be via a set of methods even though the usual method syntax is not used. This is best seen by an example where you create a `Circle` class with a `radius` attribute and `area()` method. You want the `radius` value to always be positive, so you don't want clients changing it directly in case they pass a negative value. You also want `area` to look like a read-only data attribute even though it is implemented as a method. You achieve both objectives by making `radius` and `area` properties.

TRY IT OUT   Creating a Property within a Class (testCircle.py)

In this Try It Out, you start by creating a simple `Circle1` class that has only one attribute and two callable methods: `setRadius()` and `area()`. You then create a second class, `Circle2`, which makes `radius` and `area` properties. Finally, you see how the use of properties simplifies the use of the class in client code.

1. Start your favorite programming editor or IDE and create a new file called `testCircle.py` (or load the file from the book download site).

2. Enter the following code:

```
class Circle1:
    def __init__(self, radius):
        self.__radius = radius
    def setRadius(self,newValue):
        if newValue >= 0:
```

```
            self.__radius = newValue
        else: raise ValueError("Value must be positive")
    def area(self):
        return 3.14159 * (self.__radius ** 2)

class Circle2:
    def __init__(self, radius):
        self.__radius = radius

    def __setRadius(self, newValue):
        if newValue >= 0:
            self.__radius = newValue
        else: raise ValueError("Value must be positive")
    radius = property(None, __setRadius)

    @property
    def area(self):
        return 3.14159 * (self.__radius ** 2)
```

3. Save the code.

4. Start the Python interpreter and type the following code to use `Circle1`:

```
>>> import testCircle as tc
>>> c1 = tc.Circle1(42)
>>> c1.area()
5541.76476
>>> print(c1.__radius)
Traceback (most recent call last):
  File "<interactive input>", line 1, in <module>
AttributeError: 'Circle1' object has no attribute '__radius'
>>> c1.setRadius(66)
>>> c1.area()
13684.766039999999
>>> c1.setRadius(-4)
Traceback (most recent call last):
  File "<interactive input>", line 1, in <module>
  File "D:\PythonCode\Chapter1\testCircle.py", line 7, in setRadius
    else: raise ValueError("Value must be positive")
ValueError: Value must be positive
```

5. Play with `Circle 2` using the following code:

```
>>> c2 = Circle2(42)
>>> c2.area
5541.76476
>>> print(c2.radius)
Traceback (most recent call last):
  File "<interactive input>", line 1, in <module>
AttributeError: unreadable attribute
>>> c2.radius = 12
>>> c2.area
452.38896
>>> c2.radius = -4
Traceback (most recent call last):
```

```
  File "<interactive input>", line 1, in <module>
  File "D:\PythonCode\Chapter1\testCircle.py", line 18, in __setRadius
    else: raise ValueError("Value must be positive")
ValueError: Value must be positive
>>>
```

How It Works

In `testCircle.py` you created two classes. The first, `Circle1`, achieved what you wanted to do by forcing the user to change the radius value via the `setRadius()` method. You did this by prefixing the attribute `self.__radius` with two underscores, which is how Python makes things appear private. You then created the `setRadius()` method that validated the supplied value before applying it and raised an error if a negative value was found. You also provided an `area()` method so that the user could evaluate the area using the usual method calling technique.

The second class, `Circle2`, went about things rather differently. It used Python's property definition feature to create an attribute called `radius` that was write only. It also created the `area` method as a read-only attribute. This made the user code for `Circle2` much more intuitive, as you saw when you exercised the classes in the interpreter. The key lies in the `property()` type function that you called like this:

```
radius = property(None, __setRadius)
```

This code takes as arguments a set of functions for read, write, and delete (as well as a documentation string). The default value of each is `None`. In this case you created the `radius` property with a `None` read function but with the (now private) `__setRadius()` method as a write function. The other values were left at their default of `None`. The result was that `radius` could be accessed by the user as if it were a public data attribute when assigning a value but, under the covers, Python called the `__setRadius()` method. Any attempt to read (or delete) the attribute would be ignored because the action gets routed to `None`.

The `area` property is slightly different and uses a Python property decorator (`@property`), which is just a shortcut for creating a read-only property. This is a very common use of properties.

Looking at the interactive session, you created a `Circle1` instance and printed the area using the `area()` method. You then tried to print the radius directly by accessing `__radius`, but Python pretended that it had no such attribute (because of the double underscore private setting) and raised an `AttributeError`. When you used the `setRadius()` method, all was well, and printing the area a second time showed that the modification worked. Finally, you tried to set a negative radius and, as expected, the method raised a `ValueError` exception with a custom error message: "Value must be positive."

In the session using `Circle2`, you can see how much simpler the code is. You simply evaluate the `area` property name to get the area and you assign a value to the `radius` property name. When you try to assign a negative value, the method again raises a `ValueError`. Printing the radius directly again generates an `AttributeError`, although this time it has a slightly different message.

Properties require a small amount of extra effort on the programmer's part, but can greatly simplify the usage of the class.

Having seen how to extend Pythons capabilities using functions and classes, the next section shows you how to enclose these extensions in modules and packages for reusability.

CREATING AND USING MODULES AND PACKAGES

Modules are fundamental to most programming environments intended for nontrivial programming tasks. They allow programs to be broken up into manageable chunks and provide a mechanism for code reuse across projects. In Python, modules are simply source files, ending in .py and located somewhere that Python can find them. In practice, that means the file must be located in the current working directory or a folder listed in the sys.path variable. You can add your own folders to this path by specifying them in the PYTHONPATH environment variable for your system or dynamically at run time.

Although modules provide a useful way of packaging up small amounts of source code for reuse, they are not entirely satisfactory for larger projects such as GUI frameworks or mathematical function libraries. For these Python provides the concept of a *package*. A package is essentially a folder full of modules. The only requirement is that the folder should contain a file called __init__.py, which may be empty. To the user a package looks a lot like a module, and the submodules within the package look like module attributes.

Using and Creating Modules

You access modules using the import keyword, which has many variations in Python. The most common forms are shown here:

```
import aModule
import aModule as anAlias
import firstModule, secondModule, thirdModule...
from aModule import anObject
from aModule import anObject as anAlias
from aModule import firstObject,secondObject, thirdObject...
from aModule import *
```

The last form imports all the visible names from aModule into the current namespace. (You learn how to control visibility shortly.) This carries a significant risk of creating naming conflicts with built-in names or names you have defined, or will define, locally. It is therefore recommended that you use only the last import form for testing modules at the Python prompt. The small amount of extra typing involved in using the other forms is a small price to pay compared to the confusion that can result from a name clash. The other from... forms are much safer because you only import specified names and, if necessary, rename them with an alias. This makes clashes with other local names much less likely.

Once you import a module using any of the first three forms, you can access its contents by prefixing the required name with the module name (or alias) using dot notation. You have already seen examples of that in the previous sections; for example, sys.path is an attribute of the sys module.

Having said that modules are simply source files, in practice, you should observe some do's and don'ts when creating modules. You should avoid top-level code that will be run when the module is imported, except, possibly, for some initialization of variables that may depend on the local environment. This means that the code you want to reuse should be packaged as a function or a class. It's also common to provide a test function that exercises all the functions and classes in the module. Module names are also traditionally lowercase only.

> **NOTE** *There is a Python style guide known as PEP8 that provides guidance on naming conventions and code layout rules. Its use is not mandatory, but you are strongly recommended to follow it, especially if submitting code for inclusion in the standard library. PEP8 can be found here:* `http://legacy .python.org/dev/peps/pep-0008/`*.*

You can control visibility of the objects within your module in one of two ways. The first is similar to the privacy mechanism used in classes in that you can prefix a name with an underscore. Such names will not be exported when a `from x import *` style statement is used. The other way to control visibility is to list only the names that you want exported in a top-level variable called __ all __ . This ensures that only the names you specifically want to be exported will be and is recommended over the underscore method if visibility is important to you.

> **NOTE** *One very important gotcha with modules is that the* `sys.path` *list is searched in order. This usually means that any modules you create will be found before the built-in or standard library modules. It is very important that you do not use a standard module name for your own module files; otherwise, strange things may happen and, even if you realize that it's your module, that's being accessed, other readers are likely to be fooled.*

You put most of this into practice in the next Try It Out, but first, you need to look at packages and how they differ from modules.

Using and Creating Packages

You discovered at the start of this section that a Python package is just a folder with a file called __ init __ .py. All other Python files within that folder are the modules of the package. Python considers packages as just another type of module, which means that Python packages can contain other packages within them to an arbitrary depth—provided each subpackage also has its own __ init __ .py file, it is a valid package.

> **NOTE** *Having just said that a package was defined by having an* __ init __ *.py, this is not strictly true. The real defining feature of a package is that it has a* __ path __ *attribute. However, in practice, you don't need to provide that because Python does it for you. So, if you create an* __ init __ *.py, all will be well.*

The __ init __ .py file itself is not particularly special; it is just another Python file, and it will be loaded when you import the package. This means that the file can be empty, in which case importing the package simply gives access to the included modules, or it can have Python code within it like any other module. In particular it can define an __ all __ list, as described earlier, to control visibility, effectively enabling a package to have private implementation files that are not exported when a client imports the package.

A common requirement when you create a package is to have a set of functions or data shared between all the included modules. You can achieve this by putting the shared code into a module file called, say, common.py at the top level of the package and having all of the other modules import common. It will be visible to them as part of the package, but if it is not explicitly included in the __ all __ list, external consumers of the packages will not see it.

When it comes to using a package, you treat it much like any other module. You have all the usual styles of import available, but the naming scheme is extended by using dot notation to specify which submodules you need from the package hierarchy. When you import a submodule using the dot notation, you effectively define two new names: the package and the module. Consider, for example, this statement:

```
import os.path
```

This code imports the path submodule of the os package. But it also makes the whole of the os module visible as well. You can proceed to access os functions without having a separate import statement for os itself. One implication of this is that Python automatically executes all of the __ init __ .py files that it finds in the imported hierarchy. So in the case of os.path, it executes os. __ init __ .py and then path. __ init __ .py.

On the other hand, if you use an alias after the import, like this,

```
import os.path as pth
```

only the os.path module is exposed. If you want to use the os module functions, you will need an explicit import. Although only path is exposed, as the name pth, both os and path __ init __ .py files will still be run.

The Python standard library contains several packages including the os package just mentioned. Others of note include the UI frameworks tkinter and curses, the email package, and the web-focused urllib, http, and html packages. You use several of these later in the book.

NAMESPACE PACKAGES

Python 3.3 introduced a new type of package called a *namespace package*. A namespace package contains a number of *portions*. A portion is a reference to an object that may, or may not, have a physical representation and may be located on the network or in a different part of the local file system. Namespace packages do not use the __ init __ .py file technique; rather, they depend on being part of the sys.path definition used to find modules during imports.

Namespace packages are so new that, at the time of writing, it is not clear how extensively they will be used. In the short term, you will probably not meet many of them in practice, and the intention is that, to a user, they should not appear significantly different from the traditional-style packages.

You have now covered all of the theory about modules and packages. In the next section, you put this information to work by creating some modules and a package.

CREATING AN EXAMPLE PACKAGE

You've read the theory; now it's time to put it into practice. In this section you create a couple of modules and bundle them as a package. You utilize the bitwise logical operators mentioned in "The Boolean Type" section. The intention is to provide a functional interface to those operators and extend their scope to include testing of individual bit values. In doing this you also see several of the Python core language features that were discussed previously. The modules you develop are not optimized for performance, but are designed to illustrate the concepts. However, it would not be difficult to refine them into genuinely useful tools.

> **TRY IT OUT** Creating a Module (bits.py)

In this Try It Out, you start out by creating a simple, conventional module based on integer inputs. You then create another module that defines a class that can be used to represent a piece of binary data and expose the bitwise functions as methods. Finally, you create a package containing both modules.

1. Create a new folder called `bitwise`. This eventually becomes your package.

2. In that folder create a Python script called `bits.py` containing the following code (or load it from the book's downloadable filenamed `bits.py`):

```
#! /bin/env python3
''' Functional wrapper around the bitwise operators.
Designed to make their use more intuitive to users not
familiar with the underlying C operators.
Extends the functionality with bitmask read/set operations.

The inputs are integer values and
return types are 16 bit integers or boolean.
bit indexes are zero based

Functions implemented are:
    NOT(int)              -> int
    AND(int, int)         -> int
    OR(int,int)           -> int
    XOR(int, int)         -> int
    shiftleft(int, num)   -> int
    shiftright(int, num)  -> int
    bit(int,index)        -> bool
    setbit(int, index)    -> int
    zerobit(int,index)    -> int
    listbits(int,num)     -> [int,int...,int]
'''

def NOT(value):
    return ~value
```

```
def AND(val1,val2):
    return val1 & val2

def OR(val1, val2):
    return val1 | val2

def XOR(val1,val2):
    return val1^val2

def shiftleft(val, num):
    return val << num

def shiftright(val, num):
    return val >> num

def bit(val,idx):
    mask = 1 << idx     # all 0 except idx
    return bool(val & 1)

def setbit(val,idx):
    mask = 1 << idx     # all 0 except idx
    return val | mask

def zerobit(val, idx):
    mask = ~(1 << idx)    # all 1 except idx
    return val & mask

def listbits(val):
    num = len(bin(val)) - 2
    result = []
    for n in range(num):
        result.append( 1 if bit(val,n) else 0 )
    return list( reversed(result) )
```

3. Save the file and, while still in your `bitwise` folder, start the Python interpreter.

4. Type the following code to test your new module:

```
>>> import bits
>>> bits.NOT(0b0101)
-6
>>> bin(bits.NOT(0b0101))
'-0b110'
>>> bin(bits.NOT(0b0101) & 0xF)
'0b1010'
>>> bin(bits.AND(0b0101, 0b0011) & 0xF)
'0b1'
>>> bin(bits.AND(0b0101, 0b0100) & 0xF)
'0b100'
>>> bin(bits.OR(0b0101, 0b0100) & 0xF)
'0b101'
>>> bin(bits.OR(0b0101, 0b0011) & 0xF)
'0b111'
>>> bin(bits.XOR(0b0101, 0b11) & 0xF)
```

```
'0b110'
>>> bin(bits.XOR(0b0101, 0b0101) & 0xF)
'0b0'
>>> bin(bits.shiftleft(0b10,1))
'0b100'
>>> bin(bits.shiftleft(0b10,4))
'0b100000'
>>> bin(bits.shiftright(0b1000,2))
'0b10'
>>> bin(bits.shiftright(0b1000,6))
'0b0'
>>> bits.bit(0b0101,0)
True
>>> bits.bit(0b0101,1)
False
>>> bin(bits.setbit(0b1000,1))
'0b1010'
>>> bin(bits.zerobit(0b1000,1))
'0b1000'
>>> bits.listbits(0b10111)
[1, 0, 1, 1, 1]
```

How It Works

The module is a fairly straightforward list of functions that wrap the built-in bitwise operators for not (~), and (&), or (|), xor (^), shift left (<<), and shift right (>). These operations work on binary data—that is, simply a sequence of 1s and 0s stored as a unit within the computer. All data in the computer is, ultimately, stored in binary form.

These wrapper operations are complemented by a set of functions that test whether a bit has a value of 1 (this is known as being "set"), set a bit (to 1), or zero a bit (also known as "resetting" the bit). The bit number counts from the right, starting at zero. The tests are done using a bit pattern (also known as a *bitmask*) that, in all cases except zerobit(), consists of all zeros except for the bit you want to test or set. You created the mask by shifting 1 left by the required number of bits. zerobit() uses the bitwise complement of the usual mask to create one that consists of all 1s apart from a 0 where you want to reset the bit.

Finally, you have a function that lists the individual bits of the given value. This last function is slightly more complex and demonstrates some of Python's coding features. You first determine the length of the number by converting to a binary string with bin() and subtracting 2 (to account for the leading 0b characters). You then create an empty result list and loop over the bits. For each bit you append either a 1 or 0, depending on whether or not the bit is set, using Python's conditional expression construct.

The testing of the module throws up some interesting issues. You start off by importing your new module. Because you are in the folder where the file lives, Python can see it without modifying the sys.path value. You start testing with the NOT() function (prefixed, of course, with the module name, bits), and straightaway you can see an anomaly in that the Python interpreter prints the decimal representation as the result. To get around that, you can use the bin() function to convert the number to a binary string representation. However, there is still a problem because the number is negative. This is because Python integers are signed, that is, they can represent positive or negative numbers. Python does this internally by having the leftmost bit represent the sign. By inverting all of the bits, you also invert the sign! You can avoid the confusion by using a bitmask of 0xF (or decimal 15 if you prefer) to retrieve only the rightmost 4 bits. By converting this with bin(), you now see the inverted bit pattern you expected. Obviously, if the value you were inverting was bigger than 16, you would need to use a longer bitmask. Just remember that each hex digit is 4 bits, so all you need to do is add an extra F to your mask.

The next set of tests—covering the functions AND() through to shiftleft()—should be straightforward, and you can check the results by visually inspecting the input bit patterns and the results. The shiftright() examples do show one interesting outcome in that shifting the bits too far to the right produces a zero result. In other words, Python fills the "empty" space left by the shift operations with zeros.

Moving on to the new functionality, you used bit(), setbit(), and zerobit() to test and modify individual bits within the given value. Again, you can visually inspect the input and result patterns to see that the correct results are produced. Remember that the index parameter counts from zero starting from the right.

Finally, you tested the listbits() function. Once more, you can easily compare the binary input pattern with the resultant list of numbers.

So you see that you now have a working module that you can import and use just like any other module in Python. You could enhance the module further by providing a test function and wrapping that in an if __ name __ clause if you wanted, but for now you can proceed to look at how to move from a single module to a package.

TRY IT OUT Creating a Package (bitmask.py)

In this Try It Out, you build a class that replicates the functions in bits.py as a set of methods. You then bundle both modules into a package.

1. Navigate into your bitwise folder.

2. Create a new file called bitmask.py with the following code (or load it from the book's downloadable filename bitmask.py):

```
#! /bin/env python3
''' Class that represents a bit mask.
It has methods representing all
the bitwise operations plus some
additional features. The methods
return a new BitMask object or
a boolean result. See the bits
module for more on the operations
provided.
'''

class BitMask(int):
    def AND(self,bm):
        return BitMask(self & bm)
    def OR(self,bm):
```

```
        return BitMask(self | bm)
    def XOR(self,bm):
        return BitMask(self ^ bm)
    def NOT(self):
        return BitMask(~self)
    def shiftleft(self, num):
        return BitMask(self << num)
    def shiftright(self, num):
        return BitMask(self > num)
    def bit(self, num):
        mask = 1 << num
        return bool(self & mask)
    def setbit(self, num):
        mask = 1 << num
        return BitMask(self | mask)
    def zerobit(self, num):
        mask = ~(1 << num)
        return BitMask(self & mask)
    def listbits(self, start=0,end=-1):
        end = end if end < 0 else end+2
        return [int(c) for c in bin(self)[start+2:end]]
```

3. Now save it so that you can test it in the Python interpreter.

4. Staying in the `bitwise` folder, start Python and type the following code:

```
>>> import bitmask
>>> bm1 = bitmask.BitMask()
>>> bm1
0
>>> bin(bm1.NOT() & 0xf)
'0b1111'
>>> bm2 = bitmask.BitMask(0b10101100)
>>> bin(bm2 & 0xFF)
'0b10101100'
>>> bin(bm2 & 0xF)
'0b1100'
>>> bm1.AND(bm2)
0
>>> bin(bm1.OR(bm2))
'0b10101100'
>>> bm1 = bm1.OR(0b110)
>>> bin(bm1)
'0b110'
>>> bin(bm2)
'0b10101100'
>>> bin(bm1.XOR(bm2))
'0b10101010'
>>> bm3 = bm1.shiftleft(3)
>>> bin(bm3)
'0b110000'
>>> bm1 == bm3.shiftright(3)
True
>>> bm4 = bitmask.BitMask(0b11110000)
>>> bm4.listbits()
```

```
[1, 1, 1, 1, 0, 0, 0]
>>> bm4.listbits(2,5)
[1, 1, 0]
>>> bm4.listbits(2,-2)
[1, 1, 0, 0]
```

5. Quit the interpreter.

   Now that you have proved the new module works, you can go ahead and convert the bitwise directory into a Python package.

6. Create a new empty __init.py__ file.

7. To test that the package works, you need to change your working directory to the directory above bitwise. Do that now.

   You now need to test that you can import the package and its contents and access the functionality.

8. Start the Python interpreter and type the following test code:

```
>>> import bitwise.bits as bits
>>> from bitwise import bitmask
>>> bits
<module 'bitwise.bits' from 'bitwise/bits.py'>
>>> bitmask
<module 'bitwise.bitmask' from 'bitwise/bitmask.py'>
>>> bin(bits.AND(0b1010,0b1100))
'0b1000'
>>> bin(bits.OR(0b1010,0b1100))
'0b1110'
>>> bin(bits.NOT(0b1010))
'-0b1011'
>>> bin(bits.NOT(0b1010) & 0xFF)
'0b11110101'
>>> bin(bits.NOT(0b1010) & 0xF)
'0b101'
>>> bm = bitmask.BitMask(0b1100)
>>> bin(bm)
'0b1100'
>>> bin(bm.AND(0b1110))
'0b1100'
>>> bin(bm.OR(0b1110))
'0b1110'
>>> bm.listbits()
[1, 1, 0]
```

How It Works

You created a class based on the built-in integer type, int. Because you are only providing new methods for the class and not storing any additional data attributes, you don't need to provide a __ new __ () constructor or __ init __ () initializer. The methods are all very similar to the functions written in bits.py except that you created a BitMask instance as the return type. The listbits() method also shows an alternative approach to deriving the list using the bin() string representation, and creating the list using a list comprehension based on a character-to-integer conversion using int(). listbits() has also been extended to provide a pair of start and end parameters that default to the full length of the binary number, but could be used to extract a subset of bits. There is a small piece of work involved in adjusting the end value depending on whether it is a positive or negative index. Negative indices do not need the addition of two characters because they automatically apply from the right-hand end, so a Python conditional assignment ensures the correct end value is set.

Having created the class, you then tested it as a standard module by importing it from the local directory. You then repeated a similar set of tests to the ones you did for bits.py. A few points to note include the fact that you can mix and match the traditional bitwise operators with the new functional versions. You can also compare BitMask objects just like any other integer, as you saw in the shiftright() example. Finally, you proved that your new listbits() algorithm worked and the new additional arguments function as expected for both positive and negative values.

At this stage you had created two standard modules in a folder. You then created a blank __ init __ .py file that turned the folder into a Python package. To test that it worked, you moved up a directory level so that the package was visible to the interpreter. You then confirmed that you could import the package and modules within it and access some of the functionality. Congratulations, you now have a package with two contained modules.

Knowing how to create—and use—the standard modules and packages, as well as ones you create yourself, is a great starting point. However, there are many more modules and packages available on the internet, just waiting to be downloaded. The next section explains how you can do that.

USING THIRD-PARTY PACKAGES

Many third-party packages are available for Python. Binary distributions of many of these packages, complete with installer programs, are available for most common operating systems. If a binary installer is available, either on the package website or, for Linux users, in your package management tool, you should use it because it will be the simplest way of getting things up and running. If a binary package is not available, you need to download and install the base package.

You can find many of these third-party packages in the Python Package Index (PyPI) at https://pypi.python.org/pypi. They are distributed in a special format that itself requires the installation of a third-party package! This chicken-and-egg situation often confuses beginners, so this section describes how to set up your environment such that you can access these third-party packages.

PyPI packages come in the form of something called an *egg*. A Python egg is capable of delivering either a standard Python package or a binary package written in C, or a mix of Python and C code.

> ### THE FUTURE OF PYTHON PACKAGING
>
> The egg format has some issues and is itself being replaced by something called a *wheel*. This is all part of a wider strategy to rationalize the multiple methods of distributing Python packages and applications. The Python Package Authority is leading this project. Eventually, all the tools needed to both build and install Python

packages should be available in a standard Python installation. The roadmap starts to take effect in Python 3.4 with the inclusion of `pip` in the standard distribution.

You should refer to the latest guidance on the Python Package Authority website (`https://python-packaging-user-guide.readthedocs.org/en/latest/`) if you want to create your own distributable packages.

Installing an egg requires a tool called *pip*. Fortunately, installing pip does not require pip. As of version 3.4 of Python, pip is included in the standard library, which simplifies the process somewhat. If pip is not included in your version of Python, you can install pip by going to `https://pip.pypa.io/en/latest/reference/pip_install.html` and following the instructions.

Download the `get-pip.py` file using the link on the page into any convenient folder on your computer. Change into that folder, make sure you are connected to the Internet, and run the following:

```
python get-pip.py
```

This will take a few moments and downloads some stuff from the Internet. You will see a few messages like this:

```
$ python3 get-pip.py
Downloading/unpacking pip
  Downloading pip-1.5.2-py2.py3-none-any.whl (1.2MB): 1.2MB downloaded
Installing collected packages: pip
Successfully installed pip
Cleaning up...
```

Once pip is installed, you can use it to install a PyPI package using:

```
pip install SomePackageName
```

This installs the latest version of the specified package. You can uninstall a package just as easily using:

```
pip uninstall SomePackageName
```

Many other options are available to use, and they are described on the pip documentation page at: `https://pip.pypa.io/en/latest/reference/index.html`.

Not all packages use pip, and other install options and tools exist. The package documentation should explain what you need to do. The current state of confusion should resolve itself in the near future as explained in the earlier sidebar box: "The Future of Python Packaging."

SUMMARY

In this chapter you reviewed the core language features of Python. You looked at the interpreter environment, the core data types, and the language control structures and syntax. You also considered how Python can be extended by writing functions, classes, modules, and packages.

The core data types are Boolean (`bool`), integer (`int`), and floating point (`float`) numbers, as well as the special `None` type. Python also supports several collection types including strings, bytes, lists, tuples, dictionaries, and sets.

The control structures cover all of the structured programming concepts including sequences, selection, and iteration. Selection is done using `if`/`elif`/`else` and a conditional expression form. Iteration is supported via two loop constructs: `for`, which iterates over a collection or iterable object, and `while`, which is a more general, and potentially infinite, loop. Python also supports exception management via a `try`/`except`/`finally` construct.

In addition to a large number of built-in functions and a standard library of modules, Python enables you to extend its capabilities by writing your own functions using the `def` or `lambda` keywords. You can also extend the standard data types by creating your own data types using the `class` keyword and then creating instances of those classes. Functions and classes can be stored in separate files, which constitute Python modules that can be imported into other code, thus facilitating cross program reuse. Modules can in turn be grouped into packages, which are simply folders containing an __ init __ .py file.

EXERCISES

1. How do you convert between the different Python data types? What data quality issues arise when converting data types?

2. Which of the Python collection types can be used as the key in a dictionary? Which of the Python data types can be used as a value in a dictionary?

3. Write an example program using an `if`/`elif` chain involving at least four different selection expressions.

4. Write a Python `for` loop to repeat a message seven times.

5. How can an infinite loop be created using a Python `while` loop? What potential problem might this cause? How could that issue be resolved?

6. Write a function that calculates the area of a triangle given the base and height measurements.

7. Write a class that implements a rotating counter from 0 to 9. That is, the counter starts at 0, increments to 9, resets to 0 again, and repeats that cycle indefinitely. It should have `increment()` and `reset()` methods, the latter of which returns the current count then sets the count back to 0.

Answers to exercises can be found in Appendix A.

▶ WHAT YOU LEARNED IN THIS CHAPTER

TOPIC	KEY CONCEPTS
Python infrastructure	The Python interpreter can be called without arguments to get an interactive shell. If a filename is given as an argument, the interpreter will execute it and exit.
Simple data types	Python supports integers, floating-point Boolean, and `None` data types. The type names can be used as conversion functions. Python types are objects and support a rich set of operations.
Collection data types	Python supports Unicode and byte strings plus lists, tuples, dictionaries, and sets. Strings and tuples are immutable (cannot be changed), and dictionaries and sets require immutable types as keys. Most collections are iterables and can be used in `for` loops.
Basic control structures	Python supports sequences, selection, and repetition. Sequences are simple lines of code; there are no block markers or statement terminators required. Selection is via the `if/elif/else` structure. Two loops are provided: `for` and `while`.
	Code blocks are indicated by a terminating colon on the previous line, and the block will be indented under that line. Restoring the indentation level ends the block.
Error handling	Python supports exception handling through the `try/except/.else/finally` structure.
	Users can define their own exceptions or parameterize the built-in errors.
Input/output	User input can be read, as a string, using the `input()` function.
	User output can be displayed via the `print()` function.
	Text files can be opened, read from, and written to. File navigation is possible using `tell()` and `seek()`.
Defining functions	New functions can be defined using the `def` or `lambda` keywords. Functions can receive input via parameters and provide results via the `return` keyword.
Defining classes	Classes are defined using the `class` keyword. Classes support single and multiple inheritance, polymorphism, operator overloading, and method overriding. Class attributes can be treated as properties and/or slots. Attributes are accessed via dot notation. Classes are objects, too.
Modules and packages	Modules are just files containing Python code that exist in any of the folders listed in `sys.path`. Packages are folders containing modules and a (possibly empty) file called `__init__.py`. Packages are modules, too. Names within a module are accessed via dot notation.

2

Scripting with Python

WHAT YOU WILL LEARN IN THIS CHAPTER:

➤ Accessing and managing computer resources via the operating system

➤ Handling common file formats such as CSV and XML

➤ Working with dates and times

➤ Automating applications and accessing their APIs

➤ Using third-party modules to extend automation beyond the standard library capabilities

WROX.COM DOWNLOADS FOR THIS CHAPTER

For this chapter the wrox.com code downloads are found at www.wrox.com/go/
pythonprojects on the Download Code tab. The code is in the Chapter 2 download, called
Chapter2.zip, and individually named according to the names throughout the chapter.

Often, you may find yourself undertaking tasks that involve many repetitive operations.
To combat this repetition of work, it may be possible to write a macro to automate those
operations within a single application but, if the operations span several applications,
macros are rarely effective. For example, if you back up and archive a large multimedia web
application, you may have to deal with content produced by one or more media tools, code
from an IDE, and probably some database files, too. Instead of macros, you need an external
programming tool to drive each application, or utility, to perform its part of the whole.
Python is well suited to this kind of orchestration role.

WHAT IS SCRIPTING?

Scripting is a term that means different things to different people so it's important to clarify up front what it means when you see it in this chapter. It means coordinating the actions of other programs or applications to perform a task such as bulk file printing or an automated workflow, such as adding a new user. You could be using operating system utilities or large general purpose packages like an office productivity suite. Think of the way that a script in a play tells the actors what to say, where to stand and when to enter or exit the stage. That's what Python "scripting" does; it coordinates the behavior of other programs.

In this chapter you learn how to use Python modules to check user settings as well as directory and file access levels; set up the correct environment for an operation; and launch and control external programs from your script. You also discover how Python modules help you access data in common file formats, how to handle dates and times and, finally, how to directly access the low-level programming interfaces of external applications using the very powerful `ctypes` module and, for Windows, the `pywin32` package.

SYSTEM-SPECIFIC ISSUES

By the nature of the discussion, much of this chapter's content is operating system specific. Some modules try to be portable across operating systems whereas others support only a subset of operations on some systems. Others come with dedicated modules that work only on that platform. If you find an example that doesn't seem to work for you, make sure it is not for a different operating system. Whenever possible, we try to point out which modules are specific to a particular system.

Also, in the Try It Out sections the output is often quite specific to the user and operating system, so don't expect to get exactly the same results as shown. For example, when checking user details, you should see your own username, not the one shown.

ACCESSING THE OPERATING SYSTEM

Most of the tasks that a typical programmer needs to undertake using the operating system—for example, collecting user information or navigating the file system—can be done in a generic way using Python's standard library of modules. (Recall that modules are reusable pieces of code that can be shared across multiple programs.) The key modules have been written in such a way that the peculiarities of individual operating system behaviors have been hidden behind a higher level set of objects and operations. The modules that you consider in this section are: *os/path*, *pwd*, *glob*, *shutil*, and *subprocess*. The material here focuses on how to use these modules in common scenarios; it does not try to cover every possible permutation or available option.

The *os* module, as the name suggests, provides access to many operating system features. It is, in fact, a package with a submodule, *os.path,* that deals with managing file paths, names, and types. The *os* module is supported by a number of other modules that you meet as you work through the various topics in this chapter. These myriad modules are collectively referred to as the *OS* modules (uppercase) and the actual *os* module as *os* (lowercase). If you are familiar with systems programming on a UNIX system, or even with using a UNIX shell such as Bash, many of these operations will be familiar to you.

The OS is primarily there to manage access to the computer's hardware in the form of CPU, memory, storage, and networking. It regulates access to these resources and manages the creation, scheduling, and removal of processes. The OS module functions provide insight and control over these OS activities. In the next few sections, you look at these common tasks:

➤ Collecting user and system information

➤ Managing processes

➤ Determining file information

➤ Manipulating files

➤ Navigating folders

> **NOTE** *One of the biggest changes in Python version 3 is its increased focus on internationalization and recognition and use of Unicode. The os module is no exception and the functions accept Unicode strings. However, the underlying OS functions and filenames are not necessarily Unicode aware and Python will, in those cases, do a conversion to bytes using the system encoding found in* `sys.getfilesystemencoding()`. *This is not guaranteed to work in every case so, very occasionally, a* `UnicodeError` *may be raised. In those cases, you either have to convert the string into a more OS-friendly form before calling the function or look for an alternative approach to solving your problem.*

Obtaining Information About Users and Their Computer

One of the first things you can do when exploring the OS modules is to find out what they can tell you about users. Specifically, you can find out the user's ID, login name, and some of his default settings.

Like most new things in Python, the best way to get familiar is via the interactive prompt, so fire up the Python interpreter and try it out.

TRY IT OUT Identifying the User

In this Try It Out, you find out some information about the current user. To do so, follow these steps:

1. Start the Python interpreter.

2. Type the following code into the interpreter:

```
>>> import os
>>> os.getlogin()
'agauld'
>>> os.getuid()                   # Not Windows
1001
>>> import pwd                    # Not Windows
>>> pwd.getpwuid(os.getuid())     # Not Windows
pwd.struct_passwd(pw_name='agauld', pw_passwd='unused', pw_uid=1001,
pw_gid=513, pw_gecos='Alan Gauld,U-DOCUMENTATION\\agauld,
S-1-5-21-2472883112-933775427-2136723719-1001',
pw_dir='/home/agauld', pw_shell='/bin/bash')
>>> for id in pwd.getpwall():
...     print(id[0])
...
SYSTEM
LocalService
NetworkService
Administrators
TrustedInstaller
Administrator
agauld
Guest
HomeGroupUser$
????????
>>>
```

How It Works

After importing the os module in the first line, you got the login name as a string. That is generally most useful for creating personalized prompts or screen messages. Unfortunately, for Windows users, that's it; the rest of the Try It Out code is suitable for UNIX-based systems only. However, all is not lost because you can also find some of this information from environment variables which you look at a little later in the section "Obtaining Information About the Current Process."

If you have a UNIX-based system, you use os.getuid() to get the user ID as the OS sees it, namely a numeric value, which you can then use with various other functions. The next lines import and use functions from the password module, pwd, to translate the OS user ID into a more complete set of information that includes the real name, default shell and home directory. This is obviously much more informative, but it requires the UID from os.getuid() as a starting point. An alternative function, os.getpwnam(), takes the login name instead and returns the same information. Finally, you used pwd.getpwall() and a for loop to extract all of the user names for this system.

Next you find out what kind of permissions the users have on files they create. This is significant because it affects any files your code produces. It may be that you need to temporarily alter the permissions—for example, if you need to create a file that you execute later in the program, it needs to have execute privileges. In UNIX, these settings are stored in something known as a *umask* or user mask. It is a bitmask, like the ones you used at the end of Chapter 1, where each bit represents a user-access data point, as described next.

Python lets you look at the umask value, even on Windows, using the os.umask() function. The os.umask() function has a slight quirk in its usage, however. It expects you to pass a new value to the function; it then sets that value and returns the old value. But if you only want to find out the current value, you can't do it. Instead you need to set the umask to a temporary new value, read the old one, and then reset the value to the original. The format of the mask is very compact, consisting of 3 groups of 3 bits, 1 group for each of Owner, Group, and World permissions, respectively.

> **NOTE** *3 bits can be concisely shown as an octal digit, and for that reason you will often find UNIX documentation that expresses these values in octal. Python can use octal values, too, by representing the numbers with 0o in front, so that 0o777 represents 9 bits, all set to 1.*

Within a group the 3 bits each represent one type of access—read, write, or execute. These are most conveniently written using explicit binary notation. Table 2-1 shows how each 3-bit binary value maps onto permissions.

TABLE 2-1: Umask Binary Mappings

UMASK BINARY VALUE	READ, WRITE, EXECUTE VALUES		
000	Read = True,	Write = True,	Execute = True
001	Read = True,	Write = True,	Execute = False
010	Read = True,	Write = False,	Execute = True
011	Read = True,	Write = False,	Execute = False
100	Read = False,	Write = True,	Execute = True
101	Read = False,	Write = True,	Execute = False
110	Read = False,	Write = False,	Execute = True
111	Read = False,	Write = False,	Execute =False

Now that you understand what you are trying to do, it's time to try it out.

TRY IT OUT Reading and Modifying umask Values

In this Try It Out, you read, modify, and restore the current user's umask value. To do so, follow these steps:

1. Start the Python interpreter.

2. Type the following code into the interpreter:

```
>>> import os
>>> os.umask(0b111111111)   # binary for all false - 111 x 3
18
>>> bin(18)
'0b10010'
>>> os.umask(18)
511
```

How It Works

You started out by calling os.umask() with a binary value of 111111111. That sets all permissions to false, which you did as a security feature in the event that something went wrong. It's better to have the mask too restrictive than leave the user vulnerable to security exploits.

Python then printed the decimal value 18. By calling the bin() function, you see that 18 has the binary mask value of 10010. If you pad that with zeros to get the full 9-bit mask and split it into 3-bit groups, you see that it is 000-010-010. Referring back to Table 2-1, you find that this value represents full access to the Owner, but only read and execute access to Group and World users.

Finally, you restored the user's original setting by calling os.umask() again with an argument of 18 (the original value returned by umask) and the previous mask value (111111111) that you had set was printed, in decimal, as 511.

Sometimes you want to know what kind of computer system the user is running, in particular the details of the OS itself. Python has several ways of doing this, but the one you look at first is the os.name property. At the time of writing, this property returns one of the following values: posix, nt, mac, os2, ce, or java.

> **NOTE** The java value is included, although not strictly an OS. For Java versions of Python (as opposed to the default C version), it is useful to know that you are running under a Java virtual machine (JVM).

Another place to look for the system the user is running is in the sys module and, in particular, the sys.platform attribute. This attribute often returns slightly different information than that found using os.name. For example, Windows is reported as win32 rather than nt or ce. On UNIX another function in os called os.uname() provides slightly more detail. If you have several different OSes available to you, it can be interesting to compare the results from these different techniques. It is recommended that you use the os.name option simply because it is universally available and returns a well-defined set of results.

One other snippet of information that is often useful to collect is the size of the user's terminal in terms of its lines and columns. You can use this information to modify the display of messages from your scripts. The shutil module provides a function for this called shutil.get _ terminal _ size(), and it is used like this:

```
>>> import shutil
>>> cols, lines = shutil.get_terminal_size()
>>> cols
80
>>> lines
49
```

> **NOTE** *On older versions of Python, the underlying* `os.get_terminal_size()` *must be used, but in version 3, the* `shutil` *version is recommended instead.*

If the terminal size cannot be ascertained, the default return value is 80 × 24. A different default can be specified as an optional argument, but 80 × 24 is usually a sensible option because it's the traditional size for terminal emulators.

Obtaining Information About the Current Process

It can be useful for a program to know something about its current status and runtime environment. For example, you might want to know the process identity or if the process has a preferred folder in which to write its data files or read configuration data. The OS modules provide functions for determining these values.

One such source of process information is the process environment, as defined by environment variables. The `os` module provides a dictionary called `os.environ` that holds all the environment variables for the current process.

> **NOTE** *The number of variables on any given system depends on all sorts of local considerations, including the number and nature of the applications installed, because many applications create their own environment values during installation.*

The disadvantage of environment variables is that they are highly volatile. Users can create them and remove them. Applications can do likewise, so it is dangerous to rely on the existence of an environment variable; you should always have a default value that you can fall back on. Fortunately, some values are fairly reliable and usually present. Three of these are particularly useful for Windows users because the `pwd.getpwuid()` and `os.uname()` functions discussed earlier are not available. These are HOME, OS, and PROCESSOR_ARCHITECTURE.

If you do try to access a variable that is not defined, you get the usual Python dictionary `KeyError`. On most, but not all, operating systems, a program can set, or modify, environment variables. If this feature is supported for your OS, then Python reflects any changes to the `os.environ` dictionary back into the OS environment. In addition to using environment variables as a source of user information, it is quite common to use them to define user-specific configuration details about a program—for example, the location of a database. This practice is slightly frowned upon nowadays, and it's considered better to use a configuration file for such details. But if you are working with older applications, you may need to refer to the environment for such things.

TRY IT OUT   Investigating the Process Environment

In this Try It Out, you investigate the process environment on your computer. Complete the following steps:

1. Start the Python interpreter.

2. Type the following code into the interpreter:

```
>>> import os
>>> os.getpid()
16432
>>> os.getppid()
3165
>>> os.getcwd()
/home/agauld
>>> len(os.environ)
48
>>> os.environ['HOME']
'/home/agauld'
>>> os.environ['testing123']
Traceback (most recent call last):
  File "<stdin>", line 1, in <module>
  File "/usr/lib/python2.7/UserDict.py", line 23, in __getitem__
    raise KeyError(key)
KeyError: 'testing123'
>>> os.environ['testing123'] = 42
Traceback (most recent call last):
  File "<stdin>", line 1, in <module>
  File "/usr/lib/python2.7/os.py", line 471, in __setitem__
    putenv(key, item)
TypeError: str expected, not int
>>> os.environ['testing123'] = '42'
>>> os.environ['testing123']
'42'
>>> del(os.environ['testing123'])
>>> os.environ['testing123']
Traceback (most recent call last):
  File "<stdin>", line 1, in <module>
  File "/usr/lib/python2.7/UserDict.py", line 23, in __getitem__
    raise KeyError(key)
KeyError: 'testing123'
```

How It Works

After importing os in the first line, the first thing you did was determine the current process ID. You are in the Python interpreter, so it is the interpreter process itself that you are identifying. The next line reads the parent process ID; in this case, that is the OS shell program. You can use these IDs when interacting with other operating system tools, as described in the next section.

You then used the os.getcwd() function (which stands for get current working directory) to determine which directory is currently the default. This is usually the directory from which the interpreter was invoked but, as you will see, it is possible to change directory within your program. os.getcwd() is a useful way of checking exactly where your code is working at any given time.

Next you found out how big your environment was by displaying the length of the os.environ dictionary. You then pulled out the value of the HOME environment variable that shows the user's home directory. You then tried to access a variable called testing123, but because it did not exist, you got a KeyError. You attempted to create a testing123 variable by assigning the number 42, but that yielded a TypeError because environment variables must be strings. You then assigned the string value '42' to the testing123 variable and succeeded in creating a new environment variable for this process. (Remember that the environment is local to this process and any subprocesses that it spawns. This is not visible in other external processes.) You next read the value again and this time got a value with no error messages, confirming that you had succeeded. Finally, you deleted the variable and proved that it was gone by once more attempting to read it—resulting in, as expected, an error.

Managing Other Programs

It is often useful to be able to run other programs from within a script, and the subprocess module is the preferred tool for this. The subprocess module contains a class called Popen that provides a very powerful and flexible interface to external programs. The module also has several convenience functions that you can use when a simpler approach is preferred. The documentation describes how to use all of these features; in this section you use only the simplest function, subprocess.call(), and the Popen class.

> **NOTE** Historically, Python has had several ways to run subprocesses. This has led to considerable confusion and a proliferation of options. Most of these mechanisms are still available so as not to break old code, but you are strongly advised to use the subprocess module discussed here for any new code you write.

The most basic use of the subprocess module is to call an external OS command and simply allow it to run its course. The output is usually displayed on screen or stored in a data file somewhere. After the program completes, you can ask the user to make some kind of selection based on what was displayed or you can access the data file directly from your code. You can force many OS tools, especially on UNIX-based systems, into producing a data file as output by providing suitable command-line options or by using OS file redirection. This technique is a very powerful way to harness the power of OS utilities in a way that Python can use for further processing.

This basic mechanism for calling a program is wrapped up in the subprocess.call() function. This function has a list of strings as its first parameter, followed by several optional keyword parameters that are used to control the input and output locations and a few other things.

The easiest way to see how it works is to try it out.

TRY IT OUT Starting External Programs

In this Try It Out, you call various programs from within Python. Complete the following steps to see how it works:

1. Create a test directory, called `root`, and populate it with a few text files. (Either create them from scratch or copy them from somewhere else.) It doesn't matter what they contain; you are only interested in their being there at this stage. To get the same results as shown here, the structure should look like this:

   ```
   root
   fileA.txt
   fileB.txt
   ```

2. Change into your `root` folder and start the Python interpreter.

3. Type the following code at the >>> prompt (be sure to use the right commands for your OS):

   ```
   >>> import subprocess as sub
   >>> sub.call(['ls'])     # Not Windows
   fileA.txt   fileB.txt
   0
   >>> sub.call(['ls'], stdout=open('ls.txt', 'w'))  # Not windows
   0
   >>> sub.call(['cmd', '/c', 'dir', '/b'])       # Windows only
   fileA.txt
   fileB.txt
   0
   >>> sub.call(['cmd', '/c', 'dir', '/b'], stdout=open('ls.txt','w'))    # Windows only
   0
   >>> sub.call(['more','ls.txt'])     # Not Windows
   fileA.txt
   fileB.txt
   ls.txt
   0
   >>> sub.call(['cmd','/c','type','ls.txt'])    # Windows only
   fileA.txt
   fileB.txt
   ls.txt
   0
   >>> for line in open('ls.txt'): print(line)
   ...
   fileA.txt

   fileB.txt

   ls.txt
   ```

How It Works

After importing `subprocess` with the alias `sub` in the first line (it just saves some typing later!), you called `sub.call()` for the first time, with an argument of `['ls']` or `['cmd', '/c', 'dir', '/b']` depending on your OS. (Notice that `dir` is actually a subcommand of the `cmd.exe` shell process. The Windows help system explains what the /c and /b flags do.) The output is displayed on `stdout` (your terminal), but the filenames are not accessible from within Python. The only thing returned by `call()` is the operating system return code, which tells you if the program completed successfully or not, but it does not help you interact with the data in any way. You then used `sub.call()` a second time, but this time you redirected `stdout` to a new file: `ls.txt`. Next you used the operating system tool `more` (or `type` on Windows) to display the file. The fact that `ls.txt` is a regular text file also means you can access the data by opening the file and processing it in the usual way using Python commands. In this case you simply looped over the lines and printed them, but you could have stored and used the data for some other purpose just as easily. It is worth noting that exposing a list of files in a text file like this is a potential security issue, and you should delete the file as soon as possible after processing it.

> **TIP** Note that it is possible to get the terminal session confused, especially when running processes in the background. The result is usually that the keyboard seems to stop responding or it produces strange characters. If this happens, the simplest way to restore order is to kill off any errant processes using the OS tools. This is one of the hazards of running subprocesses from inside Python. The `subprocess` module does its best to protect you from these scenarios, but you may inadvertently get things messed up from time to time.

One problem that can occur when running external programs is that the OS cannot find the command. You generally get an error message when this happens, and you need to explicitly provide the full path to the program file, assuming it does actually exist.

Finally, consider how to stop a running process. For interactive programs, the simplest way is for the user to close the external program in the normal way or issuing an interrupt signal using Ctrl+C or Ctrl+Z, or whatever is the norm on the user's OS. But for non-interactive programs, you may need to intervene from the OS, usually by examining the list of running processes and explicitly terminating the errant process.

> **NOTE** On Windows, another useful tool is `os.startfile()`. Instead of passing a command to the function, you pass a filename and Windows uses its file association database to start the appropriate command. As an example, if you pass it a text file, it may start the Notepad editor. A second optional parameter called `operation` specifies what the called program should do with the file, the most common options being `open`, which is the default, or `print`. The specified operation must be one that is recognized by Windows for the file type. You can see these by right-clicking the file in Windows Explorer; however, only a subset of that list is associated with an external program. An invalid operation results in an `OSError` exception being raised. If in doubt, use the Python interpreter to experiment with the options and find out which ones work.

You have just seen how easy it is to use `subprocess.call()` to start an external process. You now learn how the `subprocess` module gives you much more control over processes and, in particular, how it enables your program to interact with them while they are running, especially how to read the process output directly from your script.

Managing Subprocesses More Effectively

You can use the `Popen` class to create an instance of a process, or command. Unfortunately, the documentation can appear rather daunting because the `Popen` constructor has quite a few parameters. The good news is that nearly all of those parameters have useful default values and can be ignored in the simplest cases. Thus, to simply run an OS command from within a script, you only need to do this (Windows users should substitute the `dir` command from the previous example):

```
>>> import subprocess as sub
>>> sub.Popen(['ls', '*.*'], shell=True)
<subprocess.Popen object at 0x7fd3edec>
>>> book   tmp
```

Notice the `shell=True` argument. This is necessary to get the command interpreted by the OS command processor, or *shell*. Doing so ensures that the wildcard characters (`'*.*'`) as well as any string quotes and the like are all interpreted the way you expect. If you do not use the `shell` parameter, this happens:

```
>>> sub.Popen(['ls', '*.*'])
<subprocess.Popen object at 0x7fcd328c>
>>> ls: cannot access *.*: No such file or directory
```

Without specifying `shell=True`, the operating system tries to find a file with the literal name `'*.*'`, which doesn't exist.

The problem with using `shell=True` is that it also creates security issues in the form of a potential injection attack, so never use this if the commands are formulated from dynamically created strings, such as those read from a file or from a user.

> **NOTE** An injection attack is where a malicious (or very slapdash) user types an input string that is read and interpreted by your program but, rather than containing harmless data, it contains potentially harmful commands, possibly resulting in deletion of files or worse. The `shlex` module contains a `quote()` function that can mitigate the risks, but care should still be exercised when running dynamically generated strings.

To access the output of the command being run, you can add a couple of extra features to the call, like so:

```
>>> lsout = sub.Popen(['ls', '*.*'], shell=True, stdout=sub.PIPE).stdout
>>> for line in lsout:
...     print (line)
```

Here you specify that `stdout` should be a `sub.PIPE` and then assign the `stdout` attribute of the `Popen` instance to `lsout`. (A *pipe* is just a data connection to another process, in this case between your program and the command that you are executing.) Having done so, you can then treat the lsout variable just like a normal Python file and read from it—and so on.

You can send data into the process in much the same way by specifying that stdin is a pipe to which you can then write. The valid values that you can assign to the various streams include open files, file descriptors, or other streams (so that stderr can be made to appear on stdout, for example). Note that it's possible to chain external commands together by setting, for example, the input of the second program to be the output of the first. That produces a similar effect to using the OS pipe character (|) on a command line.

TRY IT OUT   Using subprocess.Popen to Access stdin/stdout

To see how to use subprocess.Popen to interact with processes, complete the following steps:

1.   Start the Python interpreter in your root folder.

2.   Type this code:

```
>>> import subprocess as sub
>>> sub.Popen(['ls'])      # Windows use: ("cmd /c dir /b")
<subprocess.Popen object at 0x7fd3eecc>
fileA.txt   fileB.txt   ls.txt
>>> # Windows use: ("cmd /c dir /b", stdout=sub.PIPE)
>>> ls = sub.Popen(['ls'], stdout=sub.PIPE)
>>> for f in ls.stdout: print(f)
...
b'fileA.txt\n'
b'fileB.txt\n'
b'ls.txt\n'
>>> ex = sub.Popen(['ex', 'test.txt'], stdin=sub.PIPE)   # Not Windows
>>> ex.stdin.write(b'i\nthis is a test\n.\n')             # Not Windows
19
>>> ex.stdin.write(b'wq\n')                               # Not Windows
3
>>>
1+  Stopped                 python3
>>> sub.Popen(['NonExistentFile'])
Traceback (most recent call last):
  File "<stdin>", line 1, in <module>
  File "/usr/lib/python3.2/subprocess.py", line 745, in __init__
    restore_signals, start_new_session)
  File "/usr/lib/python3.2/subprocess.py", line 1361, in _execute_child
    raise child_exception_type(errno_num, err_msg)
OSError: [Errno 2] No such file or directory: 'NonExistentFile'
```

How It Works

To start, you imported subprocess with the alias sub. The first couple of commands just duplicated what you did with subprocess.call() in that you initially produced a file listing on stdout, but again could not use that data. The second case is more interesting because you redirected stdout to a sub .PIPE that allowed you to read it via the stdout attribute. (Notice the difference between the stdout parameter, which you set to sub.PIPE within the Popen constructor call and the stdout attribute that you use for reading data from the Popen instance and is accessed via dot notation.) To use this, you also assigned the result of the `Popen` call to a variable called `ls`. `Popen` is actually a class and the result of the call is a new `Popen` object instance. The end result is very similar to the `subprocess.call()` case where you fed the output to a file, `ls.txt`, and then read the file, but in this case you don't wind up creating any files. Rather, you read directly from the process. This means you don't end up cluttering your file system with little temporary files that have to be tidied up afterwards.

The next example used the UNIX line editor `ex`, but this time you redirected `stdin` to `sub.PIPE` and then fed some commands into the editor to create a short text file. You also passed in a filename as an argument by providing a second string in the first argument to `Popen`. Note that the input to `stdin` must be a byte string (`b'xxxx'`) rather than a normal text string.

The penultimate example shows what happens if you try to open a non-existent file (or don't provide the correct path information). You get an `OSError` exception that you could, of course, catch using Python's `try/except` structure.

In the Try It Out examples, you accessed `stdin` and `stdout` directly; however, this can sometimes cause problems, especially when running processes concurrently or within threads, leading to pipes filling and blocking the process. To avoid these issues, it's recommended that you use the `Popen` `.communicate()` method and index the appropriate stream. This is slightly more complex to use, but avoids the problems just mentioned. `Popen.communicate()` takes an input string (equivalent to `stdin`) and returns a tuple with the first element being the content of `stdout` and the second the content of `stderr`. So, repeating the file listing example using `Popen.communicate()` looks like this:

```
>>> ls = sub.Popen(['ls'], stdout=sub.PIPE)
>>> lsout = ls.communicate()[0]
>>> print (lsout)
b'fileA.txt\nfileB.txt\nls.txt\n'
>>>
```

To conclude this section, it is worth pointing out that, for simplicity, you have been using fairly basic commands, such as `ls`, in the examples. Many of these commands can be performed equivalently from within Python itself (as you see shortly). The real value in mechanisms like `subprocess.call()` and `Popen()` is in running much more complex programs such as file conversion utilities and image-processing batch tools. Writing the equivalent functionality of these tools in Python would be a major project, so calling the external program is a more sensible alternative. You use Python where it is strongest, in orchestrating and validating the inputs and outputs, but leave the "heavy lifting" to the more specialized applications.

Obtaining Information About Files (and Devices)

The os module is heavily biased to the UNIX way of doing things. As such it treats devices and files similarly. So finding out about devices such as the current terminal session looks a lot like finding out about files. In this section you now look at how you can determine file status and permissions and even how to change some of their properties from within your programs. Consider the following code:

```
>>> import os
>>> os.listdir('.')
```

```
['fileA.txt', 'fileB.txt', 'ls.txt', 'test.txt']
>>> os.stat('fileA.txt')
posix.stat_result(st_mode=33204, st_ino=1125899907117103,
st_dev=1491519654, st_nlink=1, st_uid=1001, st_gid=513,
st_size=257, st_atime=1388676837, st_mtime=1388677418,
st_ctime=1388677418)
```

Here you checked the current directory ('.') listing with os.listdir(). (Now that you've seen os.listdir(), you hopefully realize that your use of ls or dir in subprocess was rather artificial because os.listdir() does the same job directly from Python, and does it more efficiently.) You then used the os.stat() function to get some information about one of the files. This function returns a named tuple object that contains 10 items of interest. Perhaps the most useful of these are st _ uid, st _ size, and st _ mtime. These values represent the file owner's user ID, the size, and the last modification date/time. The times are integers that must be decoded using the time module, like so:

```
>>> import time
>>> time.localtime(1388677418)
time.struct_time(tm_year=2014, tm_mon=1, tm_mday=2, tm_hour=15,
tm_min=43, tm_sec=38, tm_wday=3, tm_yday=2, tm_isdst=0)
>>> time.strftime("%Y-%m-%d", time.localtime(1388677418))
'2014-01-02'
```

Here you used the time module's localtime() function to convert the integer st _ mtime value into a time tuple showing the local time values and from there into a readable date string using the time.strftime() function with a suitable format string. (You look more closely at the time module in the "Using the Time Module" section later in this chapter.)

The simple 10-value tuple returned from os.stat() is generally convenient, but more details are available via os.stat() than the tuple provides directly. Some of these additional values are OS dependent, such as the st _ obtype attribute found on RiscOS systems. You need to do a little bit more work to dig these out. You can access the details by using object attribute dot notation.

Perhaps the most interesting field that you can access from os.stat() is the st _ mode value, which tells you about the access permissions of the file. You use it like this:

```
>>> import os
>>> stats = os.stat('fileA.txt')
>>> stats.st_mode
33204
```

But that's not too helpful; it's just an apparently random number! The secret lies in the individual bits making up the number; it's another bitmask. You may recall the umask bitmask that you looked at earlier in the chapter. The st _ mode is conceptually similar to the umask, but with the bit meanings reversed. You can see how the access details are encoded by looking at the last 9 bits, like this:

```
>>> bin(stats.st_mode)[-9:]
'111111101'
```

By using the bin() function in combination with a slice, you have extracted the binary representation of the last 9 bits. Looking at those as 3 groups of 3, you can see the read/write/execute values for Owner, Group, and World respectively. Thus, in this example, Owner and Group have all three bits set to one (True), but World only has the read and execute bits set to 1

(True), and the write access is 0 (False). (Note that these are the direct inverse of the meanings of the umask bits; do not confuse the two!)

The higher order bits also have meanings, and the stat module contains a set of bitmasks that can be used to extract the details on a bit-by-bit basis. For most purposes the preceding access bits are sufficient, and helper functions exist in the os.path module that enable you to access that information. You'll revisit this theme when you look at os.path later in the chapter.

You have several other ways to determine access rights to a file in Python. In particular the os module provides a convenience function—os.access()—that takes a filename and flag variable (one of os.F_OK, os.R_OK, os.W_OK, or os.X_OK) that returns a boolean result depending on whether the file exists, or is readable, writable, or executable, respectively. These functions are all easier to use than the underlying os.stat() and bitmask approach but it's useful to know where the functions are getting their data.

Finally, the os documentation points out a potential issue when checking for access before opening a file. There is a very short period between the two operations when the file could change either its access level or its content. So, as is usual in Python, it's better to use try/except to open the file and deal with failure if it happens. You can then use the access checks to determine the cause of failure if necessary. The recommended pattern looks like this:

```
try:
    myfile = open('myfile.txt')
except PermissionError:
    # test/modify the permissions here
else:
    # process the file here
finally:
    # close the file here
```

Having seen how to explore the properties of individual files, you now look at the mechanisms available for traversing the file system, reading folders, copying, moving, and deleting files, and so on.

Navigating and Manipulating the File system

Python provides built-in functions for opening, reading, and writing individual files. The os module adds functions to manipulate files as complete entities—for example, renaming, deleting, and creating links are all catered for. However, the os module itself provides only half of the story when it comes to working with files. You look at the other half when you explore the shutil module and other utility modules that work alongside os.

> **NOTE** In Python 3.4 a new module was introduced called pathlib, which aims to provide an object-oriented view of the file system. This potentially replaces much of that functionality discussed in this section. However, pathlib is marked as provisional, which means that the interfaces could change significantly in future releases or the module could even be removed from the library. Because of this uncertainty, pathlib is not used here.

You start with reading and navigating the file system. You've already seen how you can use os.listdir() to get a directory listing and os.getcwd() to tell you the name of the current working directory. You can use os.mkdir() to create a new directory and os.chdir() to navigate into a different directory.

TRY IT OUT   Accessing Directories in Python

In this Try It Out, you create and access directories using Python. Complete the following steps:

1. Change into the root directory you used previously.

2. Start the Python interpreter and type the following Python commands:

```
>>> import os
>>> cwd = os.getcwd()
>>> print (cwd)
/home/agauld/book/root
>>> os.listdir(cwd)
['fileA.txt', 'fileB.txt', 'ls.txt']
>>> os.mkdir('subdir')
>>> os.listdir(cwd)
['fileA.txt', 'fileB.txt', 'ls.txt', 'subdir']
>>> os.chdir('subdir')
>>> os.getcwd()
'/home/agauld/book/root/subdir'
>>> os.chdir('..')
>>> os.getcwd()
'/home/agauld/book/root'
```

How It Works

After importing os in the first line, you stored the current directory in cwd and then printed it to confirm that you were where you thought you were. You then listed its contents. Next, you created a folder called subdir and changed into that folder. You verified the move succeeded by calling os.getcwd() again from the new folder and found that the folder had indeed changed. Finally, you changed back up to the previous directory using the '..' shortcut and once again verified that it worked with os.getcwd().

One problem with the os.mkdir() function used here is that it can only create a directory in an existing directory. If you try creating a directory in a place that doesn't exist, it fails. Python provides an alternative function called os.makedirs()—note the difference in spelling—that creates all the intermediate folders in a path if they do not already exist.

You can see how that works with the following commands:

```
>>> os.mkdir('test2/newtestdir')
Traceback (most recent call last):
  File "<stdin>", line 1, in <module>
OSError: [Errno 2] No such file or directory: 'test2/newtestdir'
>>> os.makedirs('test2/newtestdir')
>>> os.chdir('test2/newtestdir')
>>> print( os.getcwd() )
/home/agauld/book/root/test2/newtestdir
```

Here the original os.mkdir() call produced an error because the intermediate folder test2 did not exist. The call to os.makedirs() succeeded, however, creating both the test2 and newtestdir folders, and you were able to change into newtestdir to prove the point. Note that os.makedirs() raises an error if the target folder already exists. You can use a couple of additional parameters to further tune the behavior, but the default values are usually what you need.

Another module, shutil, provides a set of higher level file manipulation commands. These include the ability to copy individual files, copy whole directory trees, delete directory trees, and move files or whole directory trees. One anomaly is the ability to delete a single file or group of files. That is actually found in the os module in the form of the os.remove() function for files (and os.rmdir() for empty directories, although shutil.rmtree() is more powerful and usually what you want).

Another useful module is glob. This module provides filename wildcard handling. You are probably familiar with the ? and * wildcards used to specify groups of files in the OS commands. For example, *.exe specifies all files ending in .exe. glob.glob() does the same thing in your code by returning a list of the matching filenames for a given pattern.

TRY IT OUT   Using Wildcards, Copying, Deleting, and Moving Files

In this Try It Out, you use the functions from os, glob, and shutil to manipulate whole files. Follow these steps:

1. Change into the root directory created earlier.

2. Create a new file called test.py; it doesn't really matter what is in it, you are only interested in the name!

3. Start the Python interpreter and type in the following code:

```
>>> import os,glob,shutil as sh
>>> os.listdir('.')    # everything in the folder
['fileA.txt', 'fileB.txt', 'ls.txt', 'subdir', 'test.py', 'test2']
>>> glob.glob('*')    # everything in the folder
['fileA.txt', 'fileB.txt', 'ls.txt', 'subdir', 'test.py', 'test2']
>>> glob.glob('*.*')  # files with an extension
['fileA.txt', 'fileB.txt', 'ls.txt', 'test.py']
>>> glob.glob('*.txt') # text files only
['fileA.txt', 'fileB.txt', 'ls.txt']
>>> glob.glob('file?.txt')  # text files starting with 'file'
['fileA.txt', 'fileB.txt']
>>> glob.glob('*.??')  # any file with a 2 letter extension
['test.py']
```

4. Look closely at the different result sets to see the effect of the different function/argument combinations.

5. Type the following code:

```
>>> sh.copy('fileA.txt','fileX.txt')
>>> sh.copy('fileB.txt','subdir/fileY.txt')
>>> os.listdir('.')
['fileA.txt', 'fileB.txt', 'fileX.txt', 'ls.txt', 'subdir', 'test.py', 'test2']
>>> os.listdir('subdir')
['fileY.txt']
```

```
>>> sh.copytree('subdir', 'test3')
>>> os.listdir('.')
['fileA.txt', 'fileB.txt', 'fileX.txt', 'ls.txt', 'subdir', 'test.py',
'test2', 'test3']
>>> os.listdir('test3')
['fileY.txt']
>>> sh.rmtree('test2')
>>> os.listdir('.')
['fileA.txt', 'fileB.txt', 'fileX.txt', 'ls.txt', 'subdir', 'test.py', 'test3']
```

6. Review the output from the commands you just typed and consider their impact before typing the following code:

```
>>> os.mkdir('test4')
>>> sh.move('subdir/fileY.txt', 'test4')
>>> os.listdir('test4')
['fileY.txt']
>>> os.listdir('subdir')
[]
>>> os.remove('test4/fileY.txt')
>>> os.listdir('test4')
[]
>>> os.remove('test4')
Traceback (most recent call last):
  File "<stdin>", line 1, in <module>
OSError: [Errno 1] Operation not permitted: 'test4'
>>> sh.rmtree('test4')
>>> sh.rmtree('test3')
>>> os.remove('fileX.txt')
>>> os.listdir('.')
['fileA.txt', 'fileB.txt', 'ls.txt', 'subdir', 'test.py']
```

How It Works

In the first set of commands, you compared the effect of os.listdir() with various patterns in the glob.glob() function. The first pattern ('*') replicated what os.listdir() did by listing the full contents of the folder. The second pattern ('*.*') listed all files with an extension. (Strictly speaking glob() does not know anything about files or folders; it works strictly with names, so it actually listed all names that had a period included regardless of what kind of object it was.) Next you used the '*.txt' pattern to find all the text files followed by 'file?.txt' to find any "txt" file whose name starts with file followed by a single character. Finally, you used a combination of wildcards to find any file whose name ends in two characters ('*.??').

The second set of commands looked at the shutil file manipulation commands.

You started by using shutil.copy() to copy single files: fileA.txt to a new file in the same folder called fileX.txt and fileB.txt to the subdirectory subdir with a new name fileY.txt. You then used os.listdir() twice to see the results in each folder.

You next looked at directory level operations with the shutil.copytree() function that copied the subdir directory and its contents to a new folder, test3, creating it in the process. Again, you used os.listdir() twice to confirm the results. You used shutil.rmtree() to delete the test2 folder and its contents. Once again os.listdir() proves the point.

You started the next sequence by creating another new folder, test4, using os.mkdir(). Into this new folder, you moved the file fileY.txt using sh.move(). Again, using os.listdir() on both folders proves that the operation succeeded and the file no longer exists in subdir but does exist in test4.

Finally, you looked at removing files with os.remove(). The first example removed the file from test4 and verified that it had been deleted. The next line attempted to remove test4 itself, but produced an error because os.remove()works only on files. If you need to remove a directory, you need to use shutil.rmtree() again (or you could have used the os.rmdir() function to the same end). You finished by using os.listdir() once more to confirm that the folder had gone.

If you look at the shutil documentation, you'll see several variations on the copy functions with subtly different behaviors. In most cases the standard shutil.copy() function does what you want. Other features of shutil include the ability to create archived or compressed files in either zip or tar formats. Also, you can extend the functionality of several of the functions using optional arguments. One of the most interesting is the shutil.copytree() function, which has an ignore parameter. You can set this to a function that takes two arguments: a root folder and a list of files. (The function must accept two parameters even if they are not actually used by it.) The function then returns another list of filenames that shutil.copytree() ignores. This function is then called by shutil.copytree() for each folder of the tree being copied, with the arguments being the current folder within the tree and the list of files produced by os.listdir() acting on that folder. This is useful for ignoring temporary or archive files, or files that can be re-created later. Here is a short example that copies a project directory tree but ignores any compiled Python files (i.e., those with an extension of .pyc).

```
>>> def ignore_pyc(root, names):
...     return [name for name in names if name.endswith('pyc')]
...
>>> # now test that it works
>>> ignore_pyc('fred',['1.py','2.py','2.pyc','4.py','5.pyc'])
['2.pyc', '5.pyc']
>>> sh.copytree('projdir', 'projbak', ignore=ignore_pyc)
```

In this case you used a list comprehension to build the ignore list, but you could equally just return a hard-coded filename (for example RCS to avoid copying version control files across) or you could have a much more complex piece of logic involving database lookups or other complex processing. The scenario of testing for a standard pattern ('*.pyc' in your case) is so common that shutil has a helper function called shutil.ignore _ patterns(), which takes a list of glob-style patterns and returns a function that can be used in shutil.copytree(). Here is the previous example again, but this time using shutil.ignore _ patterns():

```
>>> sh.copytree('projdir', 'projbak', ignore=sh.ignore_patterns('*.pyc') )
```

Remember that the ignore function is called for every folder being copied, so if it is very complex, the copytree() operation could become quite resource-intensive and slow.

Finally, consider a submodule of os called os.path. The os.path module contains several helpful tests and utility functions that can help you when using the higher-level functions already discussed. The most useful functions are for creating paths, deconstructing paths, expanding user details, testing for path existence, and obtaining some information about file properties.

You start your exploration of os.path by looking at some helpful test functions. You saw earlier how you can use os.stat() to extract information about a file. os.path provides some helper functions that get the more common features more easily. You can, for instance, determine the size of a file using os.path.getsize(), the modification time using os.path.getmtime(), and the creation time with os.path.getctime(). You can also tell whether a name, returned by os.listdir() for example, is a file or a directory using os.path.isfile() or os.path.isdir(). (You can even test for mount points and links if that is important to you.) All of these functions take a name as an argument and return True or False. That's a bit easier than calling os.stat() and then using a combination of indexing and bitmasking to extract the details.

The next thing that os.path helps with is processing paths. You can find the full path to your file using os.path.abspath() and, if it's a link, the path to the real file with os.path.realpath(). Having obtained that path, you can break it into its constituent parts. Python considers a full file path to look like this:

```
[<drive>]<path to folder><filename><extension>
```

Using os.path.splitdrive(), you can read the drive letter (if you are on Windows, otherwise it is empty). os.path.dirname() finds the folder, and os.path.basename() gets the filename (including the extension). You can even get the folder path and filename in one go with os.path.split(). Usually that's sufficient but, if necessary, you can further split the filename into its extension and core name with os.path.splitext(), in which case the extension includes the period, for example, myfile.exe returns myfile and .exe.

Often, after having inspected and worked with the various path components, you want to reassemble the path or even create one from scratch. os.path provides another convenience function for this called os.path.join(), which takes the various elements and combines them into a single string using the current OS path separator, as defined in the constant os.sep. This is very important because path format is one area that varies considerably across operating systems. Since MacOS X appeared, based on a UNIX kernel, things have been a little easier because Windows usually accepts the UNIX-style / separator in addition to its native \ style. But it is still safer to use os.path.join() to create file paths if you plan on running your script on multiple computer types.

You can see this operation in action on your test files and folders.

TRY IT OUT Working with Paths

In this Try It Out, you use the os.path functions to determine the status of various files. To see them in action, complete the following steps:

1. Change into the root directory you created earlier. Stay in the OS for the moment.

2. Using the OS, copy fileA.txt into the subdirectory subdir as fileC.txt.

3. Now create a symbolic link to fileB.txt in subdir and call it fileD.txt. (If you are on Windows, you probably don't create symbolic links, so you need to miss out on the steps associated with fileD.txt). The UNIX command for this is:

```
$ ln -s fileB.txt subdir/fileD.txt
```

4. Fire up Python and type the following code:

```
>>> import os
>>> from os import path
>>> os.listdir('.')
['fileA.txt', 'fileB.txt', 'ls.txt', 'subdir', 'test.py']
>>> path.getsize('fileA.txt')
257
>>> path.getctime('fileA.txt')
1389109373.1044922
>>> path.getsize('subdir/fileC.txt')
257
>>> path.getctime('subdir/fileC.txt')
1389274706.736207
>>> path.abspath('fileB.txt')
'/home/agauld/book/root/fileB.txt'
>>> path.abspath('subdir/fileD.txt')    # Not Windows
'/home/agauld/book/root/subdir/fileD.txt'
>>> path.islink('fileB.txt')            # Not windows
False
>>> path.islink('subdir/fileD.txt')     # Not windows
True
>>> path.realpath('subdir/fileD.txt')   # Not windows
'/home/agauld/book/root/subdir/fileB.txt'
>>> folder, filename = path.split(path.abspath('subdir/fileB.txt'))
>>> print (folder, filename)
/home/agauld/book/root/subdir fileB.txt
>>> path.join(folder,filename)
'/home/agauld/book/root/subdir/fileB.txt'
>>> path.splitext(filename)
('fileB', '.txt')
```

How It Works

You started off by importing the modules you need and checking the contents of the current folder, just to check that you are where you expect to be. You then compared the size and creation time of fileA.txt and subdir/fileC.txt (which was a copy of fileA.txt if you recall). You see that the sizes are identical but the creation times different, as you'd expect.

You next looked at fileB.txt and its linked relation fileD.txt. This time you looked first at the absolute path to each file. Both show up as you'd expect in their respective places. You then tested both files to see if they were links. Of course, fileB.txt is not, but fileD.txt yields a positive result. You next asked for the real path to fileD.txt, and it revealed that the original was, in fact, fileB.txt.

Finally, you looked at some path manipulation. You used os.path.split() to break the fileB.txt path into the folder and file parts. You joined them back together with os.path.join() and then you split up the filename to get the core name and the extension. Notice the period is preserved at the front of the extension.

Plumbing the Directory Tree Depths

One common automation operation is to start at a given location and apply a particular action to every file (or type of file) in the file system below that location. This is often called "walking the directory tree," and the os module contains a powerful and flexible function called os.walk() that helps you do just that. It is not the most straightforward function to use, so you spend this section looking at its key features.

You consider an example of os.walk() being used to find a specific file located somewhere within a given directory tree or subtree. You then create a new module with a findfile() function that you can use in your programs. That foundation can go on to form the basis for a whole group of functions that you can use to process directory trees.

First you need to create a test environment consisting of a hierarchy of folders under a root directory. (You can generate this structure by extracting the file TreeRoot.zip from the Chapter2.zip master file on the download site and then extracting the files within TreeRoot.zip, or you can use the OS tools to generate it manually.) Each folder contains some files, and one of the folders contains the file you want to find, namely target.txt. You can see this structure here:

```
TreeRoot
        FA.txt
        FB.txt
        D1
            FC.txt
            D1-1
                FF.txt
        D2
            FD.txt
        D3
            FE.txt
            D3-1
                target.txt
```

The os.walk() function takes a starting point as an argument and returns a generator yielding tuples with 3 members (sometimes called a *3-tuple* or *triplet*): the root, a list of directories in the current root, and a list of the current files in that root. If you look at the hierarchy you have created, you would expect the top-level tuple to look like this:

```
( 'TreeRoot', ['D1','D2','D3'], ['FA.txt','FB.txt'])
```

You can check that easily by writing a for loop at the interactive prompt:

```
>>> import os
>>> for t in os.walk('TreeRoot'):
...     print (t)
...
('TreeRoot', ['D1', 'D2', 'D3'], ['FA.txt', 'FB.txt'])
('TreeRoot/D1', ['D1-1'], ['FC.txt'])
('TreeRoot/D1/D1-1', [], ['FF.txt'])
('TreeRoot/D2', [], ['FD.txt'])
('TreeRoot/D3', ['D3-1'], ['FE.txt'])
('TreeRoot/D3/D3-1', [], ['target.txt'])
```

This clearly shows the path taken by os.walk(), starting with the first directory at the top level and drilling down before moving onto the next directory and so on. It also shows how you can take a file from the files list and construct its full path by combining the name with the root value of the containing tuple.

By writing your function to use regular expressions, and to return a list, you can create a function that is much more powerful (but also slower!) than the simple glob.glob() that you saw earlier.

TRY IT OUT   Building a File Finder (file_tree.py)

In this Try It Out, you build and test a module containing a file-finding function using the os.walk() function as a foundation. To build the module, complete the following steps:

1. If you haven't done so already, create a test directory structure like the one just described (or load it from the zip file).

2. Go to your project directory where you keep your Python modules.

3. Open your favorite text editor and type in the following code (or load it from the zip file):

```
# file_tree.py module containing functions to assist
# in working with directory hierarchies.
# Based on the os.walk() function.

import os, re
import os.path as path

def find_files(pattern, base='.'):
    """Finds files under base based on pattern

    Walks the file system starting at base and
    returns a list of filenames matching pattern"""

    regex = re.compile(pattern)
    matches = []
    for root, dirs, files in os.walk(base):
        for f in files:
            if regex.match(f):
                matches.append( path.join(root,f) )
    return matches
```

4. Save the file as file_tree.py.

5. Go to your root folder (that is, the one above TreeRoot).

6. Start the Python interpreter and type the following to test the new function:

```
>>> import file_tree
>>> help(file_tree)
Help on module file_tree:

NAME
    file_tree
```

DESCRIPTION
```
    # file_tree.py module containing functions to assist in
    # working with directory hierarchies.
    # Based on the os.walk() function.
```

FUNCTIONS
```
    find_files(pattern, base='.')
        Finds files under base based on pattern

        Walks the file system starting at base and
        returns a list of filenames matching pattern
```

FILE
```
    /cygdrive/d/PythonCode/Chapter2/file_tree.py
```

7. Type q to exit the help screen:

```
>>> file_tree.find_files('target.txt','TreeRoot')
['TreeRoot/D3/D3-1/target.txt']
>>> file_tree.find_files('F.*','TreeRoot')
['TreeRoot/FA.txt', 'TreeRoot/FB.txt', 'TreeRoot/D1/FC.txt',
'TreeRoot/D1/D1-1/FF.txt', 'TreeRoot/D2/FD.txt', 'TreeRoot/D3/FE.txt']
>>> file_tree.find_files('.*\.txt','TreeRoot')
['TreeRoot/FA.txt', 'TreeRoot/FB.txt', 'TreeRoot/D1/FC.txt',
'TreeRoot/D1/D1-1/FF.txt', 'TreeRoot/D2/FD.txt', 'TreeRoot/D3/FE.txt',
'TreeRoot/D3/D3-1/target.txt']
>>> file_tree.find_files('D.*','TreeRoot')
[]
```

How It Works

The function takes a regular expression as the parameter `pattern` and compiles it for efficiency. It then calls `os.walk()` in the usual way using the base parameter value and at each level of the tree tests each file found against the input pattern. If it finds a match, it generates the full path and adds it to the result list. Once all the files in the directory tree have been tested, it returns the list of found files.

You tested the code by importing the module and running the `help()` function on it. You saw the comments and doc string describing how to use the function.

After exiting help, you tested `find _ files()` by searching for the literal name of your file `target.txt` and found the result `TreeRoot/D3/D3-1/target.txt`. You then experimented with some regular expressions (note the differences between the `glob()` wildcard syntax and the regular expression form). `F.*` indicates any file starting with `F` followed by zero or more characters. `.*\.txt` indicates any sequence of characters followed by a literal period and the 3 characters `txt`.

Finally, you tried using a pattern that matched directory names and got back an empty list, which is to be expected because the function only checks the filenames; it doesn't look at the names in the `dirs` tuple element.

You've seen how Python helps you work with the OS. In the next section, you see how Python enables you to work with dates and times.

WORKING WITH DATES AND TIMES

One of the most common features of scripting tasks is the use of dates and times. This could be to identify files older than a certain date or between a certain range or it might be to set a process to run at a certain time or interval. You might need to compare dates and times in data to select an appropriate subset of a file's content. Reading dates and times and comparing their values is necessary in many scenarios.

Unfortunately, dates and times are not clearly defined values like integers or floats. They tend to be stored in strings with a multitude of formats. For example 2016-02-07, 02/07/2016, and 07/02/2016 are all possible representations for the 7th day in February, 2016. The situation is further complicated by the possibility of rendering months and days using name abbreviations such as Jan, Feb, or Mon, Tue, and so on. Add the fact that years may be abbreviated to two digits and the separators can be any of a number of characters, and you start to see the complexity. How can you reliably read a date value from a given string? Time values are almost as complex, especially if you have to consider time zones and daylight saving rules. Fortunately, Python offers several modules to help you do just that. The most basic is the `time` module, augmented by the `datetime` module and, for some tasks, the `calendar` module.

Using the time Module

The `time` module stores times (including dates) in two different formats. The first is the number of seconds since the *epoch*, which is simply a fixed date in history. For UNIX-based systems that's 1st January 1970. (Did you notice that's yet another date representation?) The other representation is as a tuple of fields representing the various parts of a date/time: year, month, day, hour, minute, second, and so on. The details are all found in the `time` module documentation, but you need to remember which underlying format you are using. The time modules contain various conversion functions to switch between them.

Two very important functions for reading and writing times as strings take into account most of the issues just discussed. These functions are called `strptime()` (the "p" stands for parse) and `strftime()` (the "f" stands for format). The secret to using these functions lies in a format string. This string tells the function how to map string values to/from time values. The format string uses `%` markers to indicate a field and a set of character codes to indicate what the field should contain. For example, `%Y` indicates a four-digit year whereas `%y` indicates a two-digit year. `%m` indicates a two-digit month, and `%B` indicates the full month name (taking into account the local language settings). A table in the `time` module documentation for `strftime()` provides the definitive list.

> **NOTE** One quirk of the time string functions of which you should be aware is that the `strftime()` function takes the format string as its first argument and the tuple to convert as its second. The `strptime()` function takes the input string as its first argument and the format string as its second.

The easiest way to come to grips with these functions is to play with them at the Python prompt. You can try it out now.

TRY IT OUT Formatting Dates and Time Strings

In this Try It Out, you see how to use the strptime() and strftime() functions. To do so complete the following steps, but also feel free to experiment with other variations to consolidate your understanding.

1. Start the Python interpreter and type the following code:

```
>>> import time as t
>>> now = t.time()        # Note: current time will be a different value each time
>>> now
1394536692.958137
>>> gmt = t.gmtime(now)
>>> gmt
time.struct_time(tm_year=2014, tm_mon=3, tm_mday=11, tm_hour=11,
tm_min=18, tm_sec=12, tm_wday=1, tm_yday=70, tm_isdst=0)
>>>
```

2. Look at the two formats for now: seconds since the epoch and gmt (a time tuple representing GMT, or UTC, time). Next, you use the tuple version to play with strftime().

3. Type the following code:

```
>>> t.strftime("The date is: %Y-%m-%d", gmt)
'The date is: 2014-03-11'
>>> t.strftime("The date is: %b %d, %Y", gmt)
'The date is: Mar 11, 2014'.s
>>> t trftime("The time is: %H:%M:%S", gmt)
'The time is: 11:18:12'
>>> t.strftime("It is now %I %M%p",gmt)
'It is now 11 18AM'
>>> t.strftime("The local time format is: %X", gmt)
'The local time format is: 11:18:12'
>>> t.strftime("The local date format is: %x", gmt)
'The local date format is: 03/11/14'
>>>
```

4. Look at the reverse operation using strptime() by typing the following code:

```
>>> dt = t.strptime("Saturday, March 8, 2014", "%A, %B %d, %Y")
>>> dt
time.struct_time(tm_year=2014, tm_mon=3, tm_mday=8, tm_hour=0,
tm_min=0, tm_sec=0, tm_wday=5, tm_yday=67, tm_isdst=-1)
>>> dt = t.strptime("Saturday, March 8th, 2014", "%A, %B %d, %Y")
Traceback (most recent call last):
  File "<stdin>", line 1, in <module>
  File "/usr/lib/python3.2/_strptime.py", line 482, in _strptime_time
    tt = _strptime(data_string, format)[0]
  File "/usr/lib/python3.2/_strptime.py", line 337, in _strptime
    (data_string, format))
ValueError: time data 'Saturday, March 8th, 2014' does not match
format '%A, %B %d, %Y'
>>> dt = t.strptime("Saturday, March 8th, 2014", "%A, %B %dth, %Y")
>>>
```

5. Notice that the format string must match the input string exactly. The use of a th postfix on the day completely confused the strptime() function.

6.   Try a few more examples:

```
>>> t.strptime("2014-01-01", "%Y-%m-%d")
time.struct_time(tm_year=2014, tm_mon=1, tm_mday=1, tm_hour=0,
tm_min=0, tm_sec=0, tm_wday=2, tm_yday=1, tm_isdst=-1)
>>> t.strptime("2014-01-01T15:05:45", "%Y-%m-%dT%H:%M:%S")
time.struct_time(tm_year=2014, tm_mon=1, tm_mday=1, tm_hour=15,
tm_min=5, tm_sec=45, tm_wday=2, tm_yday=1, tm_isdst=-1)
>>> t.asctime(gmt)
'Tue Mar 11 11:18:12 2014'
>>> t.mktime(dt)
1394236800.0
>>>
```

How It Works

You started by importing the time module and, to save typing, you assigned it an alias: t. You then used the time.time() function to get the current time. This should reflect the current time on your computer, so the values will be different from those shown. In fact, the values should be different every time you call the function! The now variable contains the time expressed as seconds from the epoch; note that it is a decimal value. The part after the decimal point is dependent on your operating system and computer clock for its accuracy, so may not be as precise as it appears. The seconds representation is useful for doing simple time calculations, such as timing the duration between two events in your code. (Consider using the datetime module discussed in the next section for more complex calculations.)

You next converted the time in seconds to a time tuple, which is the format you need for the string formatting functions to work. The tuple representation enabled you to confirm that the now value really is storing the current date and time.

You then used strftime() to print out the stored time in various formats. Note that the format string can have any string text within it, not just the special formatting characters.

For the next set of instructions, you used the strptime() function to convert a string into a date tuple. The first example used a well-formatted string to store the value in a variable called dt. The next example used a less well-formatted string in that it had a th postfix after the day value. The strptime() parser is not able to handle this format so you need to add the postfix to your string value. This becomes awkward when reading strings in this format, and you may need to use a try/except structure with a combination of postfixes (st, nd, rd, th) to get it right. You then tried a few other formats, including some times.

Finally, you saw two new functions. time.asctime() is a convenience function that prints a time tuple using a standard format regardless of local settings. time.mktime() converts a time tuple into a seconds representation.

The time module includes several other functions for managing time zones and for getting information about the system clocks. You can also tell if daylight savings time is in effect on the computer.

Finally, and far from least, the time module contains a sleep() function that pauses your program for the specified number of seconds. This is often useful in scripting when you are using background processes to perform a task that may require some time. It is also useful when polling a resource such as a network connection while waiting for data to arrive. You can use fractions of a second, but you should realize that the timing is only approximate because of OS process scheduling overheads and the like.

Introducing the datetime Module

The datetime module includes several objects and methods that represent both absolute dates and times as well as relative dates and times. Relative values are used for computing differences between times and avoid you having to do messy calculations on second-based values, dividing by 60 and 24, and so on. Some overlap exists between the time functions and the datetime objects. In general, if you are doing comparisons or time-based calculations, you should use the datetime module rather than time. If you are using both in the same code, use the most basic import style to ensure no name collisions occur.

The main classes exposed by the datetime module are date, time, and datetime, whose names are indicative of their scope. datetime and time objects can have a timezone attribute set to a timezone object to take account of time zone effects. If you have complex time processing to do, you may need to subclass the timezone class to provide any non-trivial algorithms required. In this book you only use the basic objects from the module. The other, and perhaps most useful, object type exposed is the timedelta class, which handles time durations such as the result of a time computation or a relative period such as a year or a month. The datetime module supports many time-based calculations using timedelta objects, including addition, subtraction, multiplication of a delta by a number, and even various forms of division.

You can initialize the date object by passing year, month, and day values, all of which are mandatory. You can initialize the time object passing hour, minute, and second values, all of which are optional and default to zero. The datetime object, you will not be surprised to learn, uses the full gamut of year, month, day, hour, minute, and second. Some helpful class methods return instances based on object arguments. An example is the date.today() method that returns today's date or the date.fromtimestamp() method that takes a time value in seconds as its argument. Various attributes and methods exist for extracting data about the date after it has been created. The date class includes a strftime() method similar to the one in the time module (but has no corresponding strptime(); for that, you must look to the datetime object).

The time object is conceptually similar but, as mentioned earlier, includes the capability to take account of time zone data including daylight savings information. time objects, like date objects, support a strftime() method only.

datetime objects are a combination of both date and time objects and support a combination of both objects' methods. datetime also adds a few extra methods of its own, including a now() class method for initialization to the current date and time, and combine() class method that takes date and time objects as arguments and returns a combined datetime object with the same values. You can do basic arithmetic using a combination of datetime and timedelta objects, the latter being either an argument or result as appropriate. datetime objects also support both strftime() and strptime() methods, which work in the same way as those in the time module described earlier.

You use the datetime objects as part of a larger example in the Try It Out "Parsing XML with ElementTree" later in the chapter.

Introducing the calendar Module

The `calendar` module is the simplest of the time-based modules in Python's standard library. Essentially, it generates a calendar for a given year. The calendar is a `calendar.Calendar` class instance that has several support methods that allow you to, for example, iterate over the days in a given month or produce various formatted text strings that can be useful in presenting user messages in a script. Calendars can be formatted as plaintext or in HTML.

`calendar` is probably the least used of the three modules discussed, but it has some useful features that are not available elsewhere and would be time consuming to reproduce. Among these are some utility functions such as `isleap()`, which reports whether or not the specified year is a leap year, and `timegm()`, which converts a `time.gmtime()` tuple into seconds (why it is located in the `calendar` module instead of `time` is something of a mystery).

Finally, a couple of printing functions, `prcal()` and `prmonth()`, take a year and a year/month combination, respectively, as arguments and display their output on `stdout`. These can be useful when you want to prompt your user to choose a date.

There are some third-party modules available that try to simplify date and time handling in Python by combining all the functions from all of the standard modules into a single more user-friendly module. Some examples include `arrow` and `delorean`, but an Internet search will reveal several others.

In the next section, you see how Python assists in reading and writing several common data file formats.

HANDLING COMMON FILE FORMATS

When writing scripts to control several applications or utilities, it's common to use files as the data transfer mechanism between applications. Unfortunately the output format of one application may not be in exactly the right format for the next application to read. At this point the script itself must convert the output file into the appropriate form for the next application to read. Most applications produce and consume variants of a few standard formats such as CSV (comma-separated values), HTML (HyperText Markup Language), XML (eXtended Markup Language), Windows INI (named after the file extension) and, more recently, JSON (JavaScript Object Notation). You now look at how Python's standard library supports these various formats. (JSON is covered in Chapter 5, "Python on the Web," because it is most commonly associated with web applications.) These modules make it easier to read and write data than if you tried to do it using the standard Python text-processing tools such as string methods or regular expressions.

Using Comma-Separated Values

The comma-separated value (CSV) format has been around for many years. Its name is something of a misnomer because, though commas are the most common separator, the term CSV is often applied to files using tabs or pipes (|) or, indeed, just about any other kind of character, as a separator. At first glance it might seem easy to parse data from such a file using the built-in string `split()` method. The problem is that the format is not absolutely standardized, and different files have different ways of representing fields that contain the separator within them. Also, lines of data can sometimes be split over multiple physical lines in the file. To make dealing with this diversity easier, Python includes the csv module in its standard library.

The csv module provides two mechanisms for reading CSV files. The simplest just reads each line into a tuple, and the programmer has to keep track of what each position in the tuple represents. The second method reads the data into a dictionary, often using the first line of the file as the keys of the dictionary. This is a particularly flexible mechanism because it accommodates changes in the file format (such as adding new keys) without breaking existing code.

> **NOTE** *One big issue with the standard* csv *module is that it does not handle Unicode input. If you need to process files containing Unicode characters, you should investigate third-party modules such as* unicodecsv.

The module defaults to the CSV format used by Microsoft Excel, but you can define your own formats too; it just takes a bit of extra work. In this chapter you are dealing with the Excel format only.

The examples that follow are based on a simple spreadsheet, toolhire.xlsx, as shown in Figure 2-1. (All of the data files discussed are included in the ToolhireData folder of the Chapter2 .zip download file in case you don't have access to Excel.) The spreadsheet describes a small tool hire facility set up by some friends to keep track of who is borrowing what from whom.

	A	B	C	D	E	F	G
	ItemID	Name	Description	Owner	Borrower	DateLent	DateReturned
2	1	LawnMower	Small Hover mower	Fred	Joe	4/1/2012	4/26/2012
3	2	LawnMower	Ride-on mower	Mike	Anne	9/5/2012	1/5/2013
4	3	Bike	BMX bike	Joe	Rob	7/3/2013	7/22/2013
5	4	Drill	Heavy duty hammer	Rob	Fred	11/19/2013	11/29/2013
6	5	Scarifier	Quality, stainless steel	Anne	Mike	12/5/2013	
7	6	Sprinkler	Cheap but effective	Fred			
8							

FIGURE 2-1: The toolhire spreadsheet

The data was saved to CSV format in the file toolhire.csv. The raw data in that file looks like this:

```
ItemID,Name,Description,Owner,Borrower,DateLent,DateReturned
1,LawnMower,Small Hover mower,Fred,Joe,4/1/2012,4/26/2012
2,LawnMower,Ride-on mower,Mike,Anne,9/5/2012,1/5/2013
3,Bike,BMX bike,Joe,Rob,7/3/2013,7/22/2013
4,Drill,Heavy duty hammer,Rob,Fred,11/19/2013,11/29/2013
5,Scarifier,"Quality, stainless steel",Anne,Mike,12/5/2013,
6,Sprinkler,Cheap but effective,Fred,,,
```

This is a fairly simple file, but does include one of the complexities described earlier. Notice that Anne's scarifier description is surrounded by double quotes because it contains a comma.

After importing the module, you can read the file into a list of tuples like so:

```
>>> import csv
>>> with open('toolhire.csv') as th:
...         toolreader = csv.reader(th)
...         print(list(toolreader))
...
[['ItemID', 'Name', 'Description', 'Owner', 'Borrower',
'DateLent', 'DateReturned'],
['1', 'LawnMower', 'Small Hover mower', 'Fred', 'Joe', '4/1/2012', '4/26/2012'],
['2', 'LawnMower', 'Ride-on mower', 'Mike', 'Anne', '9/5/2012', '1/5/2013'],
['3', 'Bike', 'BMX bike', 'Joe', 'Rob', '7/3/2013', '7/22/2013'], ['4', 'Drill',
'Heavy duty hammer', 'Rob', 'Fred', '11/19/2013', '11/29/2013'], ['5',
'Scarifier', 'Quality, stainless steel', 'Anne', 'Mike', '12/5/2013', ''],
['6', 'Sprinkler', 'Cheap but effective', 'Fred', '', '', '']]
>>>
```

Notice that Anne's scarifier description no longer has double quotes, but does still contain the original comma. Figuring out how to do that is the value that the `csv` module adds to your programs. You can apply lots of options both to the file in the call to `open()` and in the creation of the `csv.reader` object. The example shows the minimal set.

> **NOTE** *The reader object is not limited to files. It can also take a list of strings as its input instead. This can be a powerful tool if you are using* `subprocess` *to generate CSV format data on* `stdout`.

Writing to a CSV file is just as easy. In this example, you create a new page of data for the `toolhire.xlsx` spreadsheet that lists the various tools available, along with some details about when they were made available, their condition, and original price. You save the data as a CSV file called `tooldesc.csv` that you can load into Excel as a new worksheet.

Here is the code:

```
>>> import csv
>>> items = [
...         ['1','Lawnmower', 'Small Hover mower', 'Fred','$150','Excellent',
'2012-01-05'],
...         ['2','Lawnmower','Ride-on mower','Mike','$370','Fair','2012-04-01'],
...         ['3','Bike','BMX bike','Joe','$200','Good','2013-03-22'],
...         ['4','Drill','Heavy duty hammer','Rob','$100','Good','2013-10-28'],
...         ['5','Scarifier','Quality, stainless steel','Anne','$200','2013-09-14'],
...         ['6','Sprinkler','Cheap but effective','Fred','$80','2014-01-06']
...         ]
>>> with open('tooldesc.csv','w', newline='') as tooldata:
...         toolwriter = csv.writer(tooldata)
...         for item in items:
...             toolwriter.writerow(item)
...
```

```
44
39
33
34
34
33
>>>
```

As you can see, the `writer.writerow()` method returns the number of characters written to the file. Mostly you just ignore that! The output file looks like this:

```
1,Lawnmower,Small Hover mower,Fred,$150,Excellent,2012-01-05
2,Lawnmower,Ride-on mower,Mike,$370,Fair,2012-04-01
3,Bike,BMX bike,Joe,$200,Good,2013-03-22
4,Drill,Heavy duty hammer,Rob,$100,Good,2013-10-28
5,Scarifier,"Quality, stainless steel",Anne,$200,2013-09-14
6,Sprinkler,Cheap but effective,Fred,$80,2014-01-06
```

Notice that the scarifier description once again has quotes around it, and the date fields are written exactly as is. If you want to get the dates in the same format as Excel produced in the original CSV file, you need to do that manipulation before you write the data. This is very typical of the kinds of inconsistencies you find when using CSV files as a transport between different applications. You can use the `datetime` module to convert the date formats. `datetime` contains the `datetime.strptime()` function, which can parse an input string to a `datetime` object and the `datetime.strftime()` function to write that `datetime` object out in the format you want. Try that out now.

TRY IT OUT   Reformatting Data and Writing to a CSV File (change_date.py)

In this Try It Out, you read a list of tools from the `tooldesc.csv` file, then extract each date field from the list, convert the format of the date and, finally, write the entire data structure back to the CSV file. To do this, complete the following steps:

1. Change to the folder where you saved the CSV files, or create a new folder and copy the CSV files from the zip file.

2. Open your favorite IDE or editor. Type the following code and save it as `change_date.py` (or load it from the `ToolHire` folder of the `Chapter2.zip` download file):

```python
import csv
from datetime import datetime

def convertDate(item):
    theDate = item[-1]
    dateObj = datetime.strptime(theDate, '%Y-%m-%d')
    dateStr = datetime.strftime(dateObj, '%m/%d/%Y')
    item[-1] = dateStr
    return item

with open('tooldesc.csv') as td:
    rdr = csv.reader(td)
    items = list(rdr)

items = [convertDate(item) for item in items]
```

```
with open('tooldesc2.csv', 'w', newline='') as td:
    wrt = csv.writer(td)
    for item in items:
        wrt.writerow(item)
```

3. Run the script. Check that a new `tooldesc2.csv` file has been created.

4. Open the new file, `tooldesc2.csv`, in a text editor such as Notepad.

5. Confirm that it has the new date format, like this:

```
1,Lawnmower,Small Hover mower,Fred,$150,Excellent,01/05/2012
2,Lawnmower,Ride-on mower,Mike,$370,Fair,04/01/2012
3,Bike,BMX bike,Joe,$200,Good,03/22/2013
4,Drill,Heavy duty hammer,Rob,$100,Good,10/28/2013
5,Scarifier,"Quality, stainless steel",Anne,$200,09/14/2013
6,Sprinkler,Cheap but effective,Fred,$80,01/06/2014
```

How It Works

You started off with the imports that you need: `csv` and the `datetime` class from the `datetime` module. You then created a function to convert the dates. This starts by extracting the date field from the record and then uses the `datetime.strptime()` function to parse the date field. The format string (`"%Y-%m-%d"`) tells it to select a four-digit year (`%Y`) followed by a hyphen, followed by a two-digit month (`%m`), another hyphen, and a two-digit day (`%d`). That produces a date object. You then used the `datetime.strftime()` function to format that date object in the required format by rearranging the fields and using slash (/) as a separator.

(Note that the `datetime` versions of `strptime()` and `strftime()` do not have the parameter order anomalies of the `time` module versions.)

Finally, you replaced the original date field with the new string and returned the modified record.

The main code of the script opens the original CSV file, reads the records, and stores them as a list called `items`. You then replaced `items` using a list comprehension that called your `convertDate()` function on each record in `items`.

Finally, you wrote the modified `items` list out to a new CSV file called `tooldesc2.csv`.

So far you have been using the basic reader and writer components of the `csv` module that work with lists of data items. You may recall from earlier that `csv` also supports a dictionary-based approach. You now use that to access the original `toolhire.csv` file. If you look again at the content of the CSV file, you notice that the first line is a list of headings that describe the columns. The `csv` module can exploit that by using the headings as keys in a dictionary. This makes accessing individual fields much more reliable because you no longer need to rely on the numeric position of the field in the file.

The way it works is very similar to the previous code, but instead of using a `csv.reader` object, you use a `csv.DictReader`. It looks like this:

```
>>> with open('toolhire.csv') as th:
...     rdr = csv.DictReader(th)
```

```
...       for item in rdr:
...           print(item)
...
{'DateReturned': '4/26/2012', 'Description': 'Small Hover mower',
'Owner': 'Fred', 'ItemID': '1', 'DateLent': '4/1/2012',
'Name': 'LawnMower', 'Borrower': 'Joe'}
{'DateReturned': '1/5/2013', 'Description': 'Ride-on mower',
'Owner': 'Mike', 'ItemID': '2', 'DateLent': '9/5/2012',
'Name': 'LawnMower', 'Borrower': 'Anne'}
{'DateReturned': '7/22/2013', 'Description': 'BMX bike',
'Owner': 'Joe', 'ItemID': '3', 'DateLent': '7/3/2013',
'Name': 'Bike', 'Borrower': 'Rob'}
{'DateReturned': '11/29/2013', 'Description': 'Heavy duty hammer',
'Owner': 'Rob', 'ItemID': '4', 'DateLent': '11/19/2013',
'Name': 'Drill', 'Borrower': 'Fred'}
{'DateReturned': '', 'Description': 'Quality, stainless steel',
'Owner': 'Anne', 'ItemID': '5', 'DateLent': '12/5/2013',
'Name': 'Scarifier', 'Borrower': 'Mike'}
{'DateReturned': '', 'Description': 'Cheap but effective',
'Owner': 'Fred', 'ItemID': '6', 'DateLent': '',
'Name': 'Sprinkler', 'Borrower': ''}
>>>
```

Notice that, as is normal with a dictionary, the fields are not in the original order, and they are keyed using the labels from the first line. You can see that, as before, the scarifier description has lost the quotes but retained its comma.

If, instead of printing the items, you store them in a variable, you can do some interesting analysis of the data using list comprehensions. For example, to see all of the items owned by Fred, you can do this:

```
>>> with open('toolhire.csv') as th:
...     rdr = csv.DictReader(th)
...     items = [item for item in rdr]
...
>>> [item['Name'] for item in items if item['Owner'] == 'Fred']
['LawnMower', 'Sprinkler']
>>>
```

You could do the same thing using the basic reader and its lists, but you'd need to use numeric indices, which are much less readable. For example, the list comprehension using the earlier list would look like this:

```
>>> [item[1] for item in toolList if item[3] == 'Fred']
['LawnMower', 'Sprinkler']
```

It isn't nearly so obvious what you are returning or what the selection criteria are. Also, if the file format ever changed, you would need to change the indices everywhere in your code.

There is a matching `DictWriter` object that can write a dictionary out to a CSV file. You use it in the next Try It Out exercise.

You can use the `DictReader` even if your CSV file contains no labels. For example, the `tooldesc2.csv` file that you created in the previous Try It Out had no label line. You can remedy that by reading it into a `DictReader` and then writing it out with a `DictWriter`. The trick is to provide the labels as an argument to the `DictReader` constructor. Try it out now.

TRY IT OUT Adding a Label Line to a CSV File (add_labels.py)

In this Try it Out, you define a set of labels for the `tooldesc2.csv` file and then open the file and read it into a `DictReader` object. You then write the data out to a new file using a `DictWriter` that automatically inserts a label heading row. To do this, complete the following steps:

1. Change to your project folder and open your IDE or editor.

2. Type the following code and save it as `add_labels.py` (or load it from the zip file):

    ```python
    import csv

    fields = ['ItemID', 'Name', 'Description', 'Owner',
              'Price', 'Condition', 'DateRegistered']

    with open('tooldesc2.csv') as td_in:
        rdr = csv.DictReader(td_in, fieldnames = fields)
        items = [item for item in rdr]

    with open('tooldesc3.csv', 'w', newline='') as td_out:
        wrt = csv.DictWriter(td_out, fieldnames=fields)
        wrt.writeheader()
        wrt.writerows(items)
    ```

3. Run the code and confirm that a new file, `tooldesc3.csv`, has been created.

4. Check that `tooldesc3.csv` has indeed acquired a header row by opening it in your text editor. It should look like this:

    ```
    ItemID,Name,Description,Owner,Price,Condition,DateRegistered
    1,Lawnmower,Small Hover mower,Fred,$150,Excellent,01/05/2012
    2,Lawnmower,Ride-on mower,Mike,$370,Fair,04/01/2012
    3,Bike,BMX bike,Joe,$200,Good,03/22/2013
    4,Drill,Heavy duty hammer,Rob,$100,Good,10/28/2013
    5,Scarifier,"Quality, stainless steel",Anne,$200,09/14/2013,
    6,Sprinkler,Cheap but effective,Fred,$80,01/06/2014,
    ```

How It Works

After importing `csv` in the first line, you defined the field names as a list of strings.

You then opened the original file, `tooldesc2.csv`, and read it into a list, `items`, using a `DictReader` that had been initialized with your `fields` list as its `fieldnames` parameter.

The next step was to write this out to a new file with a header line. To do that you opened the new file, `tooldesc3.csv`, and created a `DictWriter` object specifying the desired order of the fields via the `fieldname` parameter (remember that a dictionary stores the fields in an arbitrary order). You simply passed the same `fields` list that you used to read the file, thus maintaining the same order. You then called the `writeheader()` method of the writer object and followed that by using the `writerows()` method that writes out the entire `items` list in one go.

You've seen how to use the `csv` reader and writer objects to convert between the CSV file format and Python lists as well as the `DictReader` and `DictWriter` objects to do the same with dictionaries. You've also seen two examples of modifying a CSV file format to make it more suitable for subsequent processing. The `csv` module contains a few other features for dealing with non-Excel based CSV files, but you can read about those in the documentation if you need them.

Working with Config Files

Config files or, as they are often called, Windows "INI" files, have a very readable format that is also easy to work with programmatically. They have fallen out of favor in recent years because Microsoft now advocates the Windows Registry and non-Microsoft applications are moving to XML-based storage. However, there are plenty of legacy applications around that use this format. (A search for `*.ini` on a relatively clean installation of Windows 8.1 found several hundred files, so it is far from dead!)

The format is very good at storing multiple instances of similar data, such as per-node settings on a network, or for multiple categories of options, such as various screen sizes, or online versus offline operational parameters. The disadvantage of the Config format is that it can sometimes be too simple with the result that complex data is harder to fit into the format. Python provides the `configparser` module for reading and writing Config format data.

> **NOTE** The `configparser` module is one that has had a name change for Python version 3. In Python 2 it was known as `ConfigParser` (capitalized), but in Python 3, it is now all lowercase: `configparser`. If you are working across Python versions, be aware of the name change. The functionality remains the same.

The basic structure of a Config file is as shown here:

```
[DEFAULT]
Option1=value1

[SECTION1]
Option2=value2
Option3=value3

[SECTION2]
Option4=value4
etc.
```

The DEFAULT section is noteworthy because options defined there apply to all following sections. The format has a lot of flexibility, with spaces and indentation optional, embedded sections, and various other variants, including the ability to interpolate a value from one option into another option. The `configparser` module can handle all of these and much more. It converts the data into, or from, a dictionary format similar to the kind used for the CSV files described in the previous section.

Basic usage is shown very clearly in the documentation with examples of creating a file and reading from it. Because there is little point in repeating that here, you can browse it at your leisure and then try it out in the following example.

TRY IT OUT Creating and Reading a Config File

In this Try It Out, you create a Config file such as might be used for the tool lending application discussed earlier. This Config file describes the standard settings and any user-specific overrides to those values. The settings are limited to the lending period (expressed in days) and the maximum value of items that can be borrowed (zero implies no limit and is the default value).

To create the file, complete the following steps:

1. Create a project directory and change into it.

2. Start the Python interpreter and type the following code:

```
>>> import configparser as cp
>>> conf = cp.ConfigParser()
>>> conf['DEFAULT'] = {'lending_period' : 0, 'max_value' : 0}
>>> conf['Fred'] = {'max_value' : 200}  # Fred's a bit rough with things!
>>> conf['Anne'] = {'lending_period' : 30}  # She is a bit forgetful sometimes
>>> with open('toolhire.ini', 'w') as toolhire:
...     conf.write(toolhire)
...
>>>
```

3. Check that a new file `toolhire.ini` has been created in your folder.

4. Open this new file in your text editor (but keep your Python session running) and confirm that it looks like this:

```
[DEFAULT]
lending_period = 0
max_value = 0

[Fred]
max_value = 200

[Anne]
lending_period = 30
```

Having created the file, you can now read back some values.

5. Go back to your Python interpreter session and type the following:

```
>>> del(conf)   # get rid of the old one
>>> conf = cp.ConfigParser()  # create a new one
>>> conf.read('toolhire.ini')
['toolhire.ini']
>>> conf.sections()
['Fred', 'Anne']
```

```
>>> conf['DEFAULT']['max_value']
'0'
>>> conf['Anne']['max_value']
'0'
>>> conf['Anne']['lending_period']
>>> conf['Fred']['max_value']
'200'
```

6. Finally, to investigate a bit of irregular behavior type the following:

```
>>> conf['Joe']
Traceback (most recent call last):
  File "<interactive input>", line 1, in <module>
  File "C:\Python33\lib\configparser.py", line 954, in __getitem__
    raise KeyError(key)
KeyError: 'Joe'
>>> conf.options('Anne')
['lending_period', 'max_value']
>>> conf.options('DEFAULT')
Traceback (most recent call last):
  File "<interactive input>", line 1, in <module>
  File "C:\Python33\lib\configparser.py", line 667, in options
    raise NoSectionError(section)
configparser.NoSectionError: No section: 'DEFAULT'
>>> conf.defaults()
OrderedDict([('lending_period', '0'), ('max_value', '0')])
>>>
```

How It Works

After importing the module in the first line, you created a ConfigParser object and then assigned a dictionary of name/value pairs to the DEFAULT section. You then stipulated a limit on the value of what Fred could borrow (he has a track record of breaking things!) as well as a limit on Anne's lending _ period (because she tends to "forget" to return things, so she needs a reminder). You then opened the file "toolhire.ini" in write mode and used the ConfigParser object to write the data to the file.

Having checked that the file existed and contained the correct data, you then set about reading the data back from the file.

In preparation for doing that, you deleted the original parser object and created a new one, reusing the name conf.

You used conf to read the toolhire.ini file. You checked that the expected sections were available and saw that the DEFAULT section was not included in the list. You then read some option values from the parser and saw that you could read the DEFAULT values even though it was not listed as a section. Furthermore, the DEFAULT values are used when a particular option is not explicitly declared for a user. (For example, the default max _ value is returned for Anne even though she only had lending _ period specified.)

You then tried pushing the boundaries a bit to see how the parser handles error conditions. The first attempt was to access a user for which no values had been provided. This gave a typical dictionary KeyError. You then read the available options for Anne and discovered that the parser returned the default values as well as those explicitly defined. You also discovered that options() does not work for the DEFAULT section, and you needed to use the explicit defaults() method to fetch those options. The nonstandard behavior for DEFAULTS is one of the few annoyances you will experience in using configparser.

Working with XML and HTML files

You are probably familiar with HTML as the language of web pages. XML is also widely used, as a so-called self-describing data format. XML and HTML are closely related formats. XML is a much more rigidly defined format, and that makes it easier to process using a computer. HTML is very forgiving of malformed content and, although that makes it easy to create by hand, as well as with specialized editors, HTML is much more hit or miss to process accurately. HTML also has many variations because of web browser proprietary extensions. All of this means that HTML parsers have a trickier job and often yield less than perfect results when faced with badly formatted files. Because XML is easier to handle programmatically, you look at parsing it first and then extend the technique to cover HTML.

> **NOTE** A form of HTML, known as XHTML, is also valid XML. XHTML is starting to appear on websites as increasing numbers of web publishing tools support it. This means that you can use XML parsers to parse XHTML as well as other forms of XML. However, HTML5 has, in effect, deprecated XHTML, so its use in the future is likely to diminish rather than increase.

Parsing XML Files

Many different parsers are available for parsing XML. The Python standard library contains no less than five (dom, minidom, expat, ElementTree, and sax). These all fall into two categories: those that read the entire file into a tree-like data structure called a document object model (DOM) or those that read the file looking for items of interest (an "event") and triggering a response as the items are found. The former are more flexible for complex, or multiple, queries on the same set of data. The latter tend to be faster and slightly simpler to use. In this book you only look at two of the parsers, each representing one of these two approaches.

The first parser you consider is sax, which is an example of an event-based parser. To understand how event-based parsers work, consider the following example that parses some plaintext:

```
>>> text = """mary had a little lamb
... its fleece was white as snow
... and everywhere that mary went
... the lamb was sure to go"""

>>> def has_mary(aLine):
...     print( "We found: ", aLine)
...
```

```
>>> def parse_text(theText, aPattern, function):
...     for line in theText.split('\n'):
...         if aPattern in line:
...             function(line)
...
>>> parse_text(text,'mary',has_mary)
We found:  mary had a little lamb
We found:  and everywhere that mary went
>>>
```

Here you create some text that you want to parse. You then define a function, has_mary(), that you want to be called every time mary is found in the text.

Next you create your event-driven parsing function, parse_text(). This function iterates over the input text line by line. If the search string, in this case mary, is found, then it calls the function that has been passed in.

When you execute parse_text() with your text string and the has_mary() function as arguments, it prints out the two lines containing mary.

The sax module works in a similar way to your parse_text() function; however, it uses events, such as detecting the start of an XML element, rather than plaintext patterns. It takes in an XML source text and a collection of events and associated event-handler functions. It then processes the XML text section by section, and if it finds a match to a given event, it calls the associated handler to deal with it. The parser does not store the XML data, it simply iterates over it. If you need to go back to access earlier data, you need to re-parse the entire file.

To investigate the sax parser, you need an XML file. You can find one, called toolhire.xml, in the ToolhireData folder of the Chapter2.zip file. This is simply an XML export of the toolhire.xlsx spreadsheet that you used earlier. A fragment of that file, including the parts you will be extracting, slightly edited for readability, is shown here:

```
<?xml version="1.0"?>
<?mso-application progid="FileName_Excel.Sheet"?>
<Workbook xmlns="urn:schemas-microsoft-com:office:spreadsheet"
...
<Worksheet ss:Name="Sheet1">
  <Table ss:ExpandedColumnCount="1025" ss:ExpandedRowCount="7" x:FullColumns="1"
   x:FullRows="1" ss:DefaultRowHeight="15">
  <Column ss:AutoFitWidth="0" ss:Width="36"/>
...
  <Row ss:StyleID="s36">
   <Cell><Data ss:Type="String">ItemID</Data></Cell>
   <Cell><Data ss:Type="String">Name</Data></Cell>
   <Cell><Data ss:Type="String">Description</Data></Cell>
   <Cell><Data ss:Type="String">Owner</Data></Cell>
   <Cell><Data ss:Type="String">Borrower</Data></Cell>
   <Cell><Data ss:Type="String">DateLent</Data></Cell>
   <Cell><Data ss:Type="String">DateReturned</Data></Cell>
  </Row>
  <Row>
   <Cell><Data ss:Type="Number">1</Data></Cell>
```

```
    <Cell><Data ss:Type="String">LawnMower</Data></Cell>
    <Cell><Data ss:Type="String">Small Hover mower</Data></Cell>
    <Cell><Data ss:Type="String">Fred</Data></Cell>
    <Cell><Data ss:Type="String">Joe</Data></Cell>
    <Cell ss:StyleID="s37"><Data ss:Type="DateTime">
2012-04-01T00:00:00.000</Data></Cell>
    <Cell ss:StyleID="s37"><Data ss:Type="DateTime">
2012-04-26T00:00:00.000</Data></Cell>
    </Row>
...
</Worksheet>
</Workbook>
```

Assume you want to find the average length of loan. You use sax to extract just the DateLent and DateReturned fields for each item and store them as a tuple in a dates list. You can then later process those dates to find the duration for each lent item.

To initialize the parser, you need to create your handler and specify the events that you are interested in. sax actually uses a handler object, an instance of the xml.sax.handler .ContentHandler class, or more specifically, a subclass of it, to combine the event and function. Several predefined handler subclasses exist, including one for dealing with errors. The advantage of this approach is that many default methods are already defined and others can be easily overridden, such as startDocument() called at the very beginning of parsing and useful for setting up state variables and the like. For simple XML parsing tasks, you normally create a custom subclass of ContentHandler and then write your own versions of the startElement(), endElement(), and possibly, the character() methods.

By inspecting the XML file, you can see that the data you want is contained in a <Data> element and is identified by the ss:Type attribute being set to DateTime. The actual data is character data that sits between the start and end <Data> tags, so the expected event sequence is startElement(), followed by character(), followed by endElement().

The code for your ToolHireHandler class looks like this (and is in the ToolHire folder of Chapter2.zip as toolhiresax.py):

```
import xml.sax
import xml.sax.handler

class ToolHireHandler(xml.sax.handler.ContentHandler):
    def __init__(self):
        super().__init__()
        self.dates = []
        self.dateLent = ''
        self.dateCounter = 0
        self.isDate = False

    def startElement(self, name, attributes):
        if name == "Data":
            data = attributes.get('ss:Type', None)
            if data == 'DateTime':
                self.isDate = True
                self.dateCounter += 1
```

```
            else:
                self.dateCounter = 0
    def endElement(self, name):
        self.isDate = False

    def characters(self, data):
        if self.isDate:
            if self.dateCounter == 1:
                self.dateLent = data
            else:
                self.dates.append((self.dateLent, data))

if __name__ == '__main__':
    handler = ToolHireHandler()
    parser = xml.sax.make_parser()
    parser.setContentHandler(handler)
    parser.parse('toolhire.xml')
    print(handler.dates)
```

The initializer calls the superclass initializer and then sets up various data attributes that you use in the parsing and need to use across methods. It also creates an empty dates list to hold the results.

The main parsing method is the startElement() method that looks out for Data elements and, when one is found, refines the search by selecting only those with a ss:Type attribute of DateTime. (You have to identify these values by inspecting the XML file manually.) Because you can have up to two dates in a single row, you use the self.dateCounter to keep track of which date within the row you are handling. You use the self.isDate value to indicate to the character() method that it is inside a date element. If the data is not a DateTime type, then you reset the self.dateCounter to 0.

The endElement() method ensures the self.isDate flag is reset to False ready for the next startElement() event to come along.

The character() method is called whenever content outside a tag element is encountered. You are only interested in the date information so, if the self.isDate flag is not set, you simply ignore the character data. If the data is a date, then you check if it's the first date, in which case you store it in the self.dateLent attribute; if it's the second date, you store both dates in the self.dates list. If only one date is found, the character handler is not called a second time, and the date is not added to the dates list, thus ensuring you store only pairs of dates, which is what you need for the duration calculations.

Finally, the driver code at the bottom creates the handler and parser instances. It then sets the handler within the parser to your ToolHireHandler instance and executes the parse() operation on your XML file. After parsing is complete, it prints out the collected dates from the handler.

You repeat this exercise using the ElementTree DOM-based parser in the Try It Out at the end of this section. There you can compare and contrast the two techniques. First, though, you look at parsing HTML because the standard library HTML parser is very similar in style to the sax XML parser.

Parsing HTML Files

The standard library provides the html.parser module for parsing HTML. It works in a similar way to the sax parser, in that it is event driven. It is slightly simpler to use because it only has a single class with the handler methods defined within it. To show how it works, you once again extract the dates from the `toolhire.xlsx` spreadsheet, but this time from the HTML export. You can find this file in the zip file under the `ToolhireData/toolhire_files` folder as `sheet001.htm`.

The file looks, in part, like this:

```
<html xmlns:v="urn:schemas-microsoft-com:vml"
xmlns:o="urn:schemas-microsoft-com:office:office"
xmlns:x="urn:schemas-microsoft-com:office:excel"
xmlns="http://www.w3.org/TR/REC-html40">

<head>
<meta http-equiv=Content-Type content="text/html; charset=windows-1252">
<meta name=ProgId content=Excel.Sheet>
...
<body link=blue vlink=purple>

<table border=0 cellpadding=0 cellspacing=0 width=752 style='border-collapse:
 collapse;table-layout:fixed;width:564pt'>
 <col width=64 style='width:48pt'>
 <col width=115 style='mso-width-source:userset;mso-width-alt:4205;width:86pt'>
 ...
 <tr class=xl66 height=21 style='height:15.75pt'>
  <td height=21 class=xl66 width=64 style='height:15.75pt;width:48pt'>ItemID</td>
  <td class=xl66 width=115 style='width:86pt'>Name</td>
  <td class=xl66 width=153 style='width:115pt'>Description</td>
  <td class=xl66 width=80 style='width:60pt'>Owner</td>
  <td class=xl66 width=120 style='width:90pt'>Borrower</td>
  <td class=xl66 width=99 style='width:74pt'>DateLent</td>
  <td class=xl66 width=121 style='width:91pt'>DateReturned</td>
 </tr>
 <tr height=20 style='height:15.0pt'>
  <td height=20 align=right style='height:15.0pt'>1</td>
  <td>LawnMower</td>
  <td>Small Hover mower</td>
  <td>Fred</td>
  <td>Joe</td>
  <td class=xl65 align=right>4/1/2012</td>
  <td class=xl65 align=right>4/26/2012</td>
 </tr>
 ...
</tabular>
</body>
</html>
```

You can see that the dates have a unique class, namely `xl65`. This means you can look for `<td>` tags with that class attribute value in a similar way that you did with the earlier XML example.

The `HTMLParser` class works very like the `saxContentHandler` class in that it has methods corresponding to HTML document elements. In the example you override the `handle_starttag()`, `handle_endtag()`, and `handle_data()` methods that are directly analogous to the `startElement`, `endElement`, and `character` methods for XML.

You can find the code for this example in the zip file `ToolHire` folder as `toolhirehtml.py`. It looks like this:

```python
import html.parser

class ToolHireParser(html.parser.HTMLParser):
    def __init__(self):
        super().__init__()
        self.dates = []
        self.dateLent = ''
        self.isDate = False
        self.dateCounter = 0

    def handle_starttag(self, name, attributes):
        if name == 'td':
            for key, value in attributes:
                if  key == 'class' and value == 'xl65':
                    self.isDate = True
                    self.dateCounter += 1
                    break
        else:
            self.dateCounter = 0

    def handle_endtag(self, name):
        self.isDate = False

    def handle_data(self, data):
        if self.isDate:
            if self.dateCounter == 1:
                self.dateLent = data
            else:
                self.dates.append((self.dateLent, data))

if __name__ == '__main__':
    htm = open('sheet001.htm').read()
    parser = ToolHireParser()
    parser.feed(htm)
    print(parser.dates)
```

If you compare that with the `sax` example, you see that the code inside the methods is nearly identical. The `HTMLParser` presents its attributes as a list of tuples. You iterate over that list looking for a class attribute of value `xl65` to identify a date field. (Note that's an x-ELL not x-ONE; remember that this is an export from Microsoft Excel, hence the class name.) The parser conveniently takes care of mixed-case HTML tags or by converting tag names to lowercase, so you don't need to worry about that. It also does its best to make sense of badly formed HTML although it's not perfect and really bad code can trip it up.

You conclude this section on reading data files with a look at another of Python's XML parsers. This time it's `ElementTree`, and you investigate it in the following Try It Out.

TRY IT OUT **Parsing XML with ElementTree (toolhireET1.py and toolhireET.py)**

In this Try It Out, you use the `ElementTree` XML parser to extract the same set of dates that you did in the earlier examples. You also use the data to calculate the average loan period for the items in the spreadsheet. To get the answer, complete the following steps:

1. Create a new project folder and copy the `toolhire.xml` file, which you used earlier, into it.

2. Open your IDE or text editor and type in and save the following code as `toolhireET.py` (or grab `toolhireET1.py` from the zip file):

```python
import xml.etree.ElementTree as ET
import datetime as dt

def parseDates(filename):
    dates = []
    rows = []
    dom = ET.parse(filename)
    root = dom.getroot()
    for node in dom.iter('*'):
        if 'Row' in node.tag:
            rows.append(node)
    for row in rows:
        row_dates = []
        for node in row.iter('*'):
            for key,value in node.attrib.items():
                if 'Type' in key and 'DateTime' in value:
                    row_dates.append(node.text)
        if len(row_dates) == 2:
            dates += row_dates
    return dates

def main():
    print(parseDates('toolhire.xml'))

if __name__ == '__main__':
    main()
```

3. Open an OS console window and navigate to your project folder.

4. Run the file from your console using `python3 toolhireET.py` (or `toolhireET1.py` if using the zip file).

5. Check that the output looks like this:

```
['2012-04-01T00:00:00.000', '2012-04-26T00:00:00.000', '2012-09-05T00:00:00.000',
'2013-01-05T00:00:00.000', '2013-07-03T00:00:00.000', '2013-07-22T00:00:00.000',
'2013-11-19T00:00:00.000', '2013-11-29T00:00:00.000', '2013-12-05T00:00:00.000']
```

6. Go back into your IDE or editor and add a `calculateAverage()` function and modify `main()` as shown (or load `toolhireET.py` from the zip file):

```python
def calculateAverage(dates):
    loan_periods = []
    while dates:
        lent = dates.pop(0).split('T')[0]
        ret = dates.pop(0).split('T')[0]
        lent_date = dt.datetime.strptime(lent,'%Y-%m-%d')
        ret_date = dt.datetime.strptime(ret,'%Y-%m-%d')
        loan_periods.append( (ret_date - lent_date).days )
    average = sum(loan_periods)/len(loan_periods)
    return average
```

```
def main():
    dates = parseDates('toolhire.xml')
    avg = calculateAverage(dates)
    print('Average loan period is: {} days'.format(avg))
```

7. Save the file and run the code. You should see a message telling you that the average loan period is 44 days.

How It Works

You started by importing the `ElementTree` parser and assigning it an alias, `ET`. You then imported the `datetime` module as `dt` in anticipation of the date calculations to follow.

You created the `parseDates()` function that starts off by parsing the XML file into a DOM. Notice that the `parse()` function takes a filename as an argument, not a file object. You then obtained the root node from that DOM using the `getroot()` method. You used the `iter()` method to find all nodes, as signified by the `'*'` argument. You then inspected the node, and if it had `Row` in its tag, you added the node to the `rows` list.

Having built a list of rows, you then drilled into each row and examined the cells. You checked their attributes looking for a `key` of `Type` with a `value` of `DateTime`. Once found, you inserted the date nodes into the `row_dates` list. At the end of each row, if the `row_dates` list contained two dates, you added it to the `dates` list; otherwise, you just ignored it. You returned the final `dates` list at the end of the function.

You then tested the function and checked that the output was the expected list of dates.

You next added the new function `calculateAverage()` and modified the `main()` function accordingly.

In the `calculateAverage()` function, you initialized a list to hold the length of each loan. You then iterated over the dates list extracting them in pairs. You knew the pairs matched because you only added pairs of dates in the `parseDates()` function. The extraction process involved splitting the date strings on the letter `T` and only keeping the first part of the string. (You had to split the strings because the `datetime.strptime()` method cannot handle the decimal seconds value.) The next step was to convert the date strings into `datetime` objects using the `strptime()` method. You then used the `datetime` object's arithmetic capabilities to compute a `timedelta` representing the loan period and stored the `days` value in the `loan_period` list. Finally, you calculated the average of the stored periods and returned the result.

Some applications do not lend themselves to generating data files. In these cases, you may need to interact with the program via an application programmer's interface (API). The next section shows you how.

ACCESSING NATIVE APIS WITH ctypes AND pywin32

Some applications or OS functions are not easily accessed from regular Python code because no Python API exists or no user-friendly operations are exposed that you can call from Python. The `ctypes` module can provide an alternative means of access by exposing to Python the C code libraries from which the application is built. In Windows these libraries are typically a set of DLL files or, in UNIX, a set of shared object libraries. `ctypes` enables you to load those libraries into your application and call their functions directly from Python. This only works, of course, if you know what functions are in the library, what arguments are required, and the return values. This may not be published, and you then have to resort to trial and error, or reverse engineering, which may, in turn, be prohibited by the manufacturer or vendor. However, if the library has a published interface, `ctypes` provides an effective, although non-trivial, method of access.

SOME WORDS OF CAUTION
_____

Using `ctypes` requires a basic knowledge of C programming. If you don't have that skill, you may want to skip this section because it may not make much sense. On the other hand, skimming it lets you see what the potential is, should you need it.

When you use `ctypes`, you leave the safety net of the Python interpreter behind. Remember that you are working with the raw OS libraries and sometimes directly accessing memory locations. The libraries also work with the raw file system and input/output streams, and so they may not show the results you expect in an IDE like IDLE or Pythonwin.

If you make a mistake, you can easily cause the Python interpreter to crash. In extreme cases, you could even cause the OS to crash! This is why you should treat `ctypes` and its friends as a last resort, only to be used when all else fails.

Another package, installed by default in the ActiveState distribution of Python for Windows, or available for download on other distributions, is `pywin32`. This package provides access to the Windows native libraries and, in particular, to any Microsoft component object model (COM) interfaces. Being Windows specific, it is usually easier to use than `ctypes` which works generically on any operating system. The same caveats apply when using `pywin32` as apply to `ctypes`.

Accessing the Operating System Libraries

One area that is usually well documented is the OS application programming interface (API) that is exposed in standard system libraries. In this section you use the OS libraries to perform some fairly simple tasks that are nonetheless not available via Python's `os` module. This method is particularly useful for Windows users because many of the UNIX-like features in the `os` module do not work, or only work partially, under Windows. Accessing the Win32 API directly via `ctypes` (or `pywin32`) is often the only option.

> **NOTE** `ctypes` *does not work with static libraries nor does it work with C++ libraries, unless the functions have been explicitly exported as C functions from the C++ code.*

The following sections show `ctypes` being used on Windows and Linux systems, but the principles are identical, apart from getting the initial reference to the C library.

Using ctypes with Windows

On Windows systems the basic C library is found in the msvcrt library. Some functions in msvcrt
.dll, mainly concerned with console input/output operations, are exposed in the Python msvcrt
module, but many more are not available by that route. You can easily access the native msvcrt
library from ctypes using the following code:

```
>>> import ctypes as ct
>>> libc = ct.cdll.msvcrt     # Windows only
```

Once you have a reference to the standard library, you can call the familiar C functions. The only
complication is that you need to ensure the arguments are type-compatible with C. In general,
integer arguments work just fine, but strings usually need to be explicitly marked as byte strings,
and floats need a special ctypes type conversion. Many type conversion functions are included in
ctypes; you can find a full list in the module documentation. Here are two examples:

```
>>> libc.printf(b"%d %s %s hanging on a wall\n", 6, b"green", b"bottles")
6 green bottles hanging on a wall
34
>>> libc.printf(b"Pi is: %f\n", ct.c_double(3.14159))
Pi is: 3.141590
16
```

Notice the use of b to indicate a byte string and, in the second example, the use of the ctypes.c_
double() conversion function. Also, note that the return value of printf(), which is the number of
characters printed, is displayed after the message is printed.

Many C functions require pointers to data (effectively memory addresses) as arguments.
ctypes enables you to do this using the byref() function. You can create an object of a given
type and then pass that object using byref() into the ctypes function call you want to perform.
Here is an example of using sscanf() that reads an integer value from a string into a Python
variable:

```
>>> d = ct.c_int()
>>> print(d.value)
0
>>> libc.sscanf(b"6", b"%d", ct.byref(d))
1
>>> print(d.value)
6
```

Next you look at a slightly more practical function in the Windows library: msvcrt._
getdrives(). This returns a list of available drives on a Windows system, something not easily done
using Python's standard os module. The only complication is that the returned list is a bitmask, so
you need to write a loop to test each bit to find out which bits are set and map the bit position into a
drive letter. Here is the code:

```
>>> drives = "ABCDEFGHIJKLMNOPQRSTUVWXYZ"
>>> drivelist = libc._getdrives()
```

```
>>> for n in range(26):
...     mask = 1 << n   # use left bit shifting to build a mask
...     if drivelist & mask: print (drives[n], 'is available')
...
C is available
D is available
E is available
P is available
```

The Microsoft Developers Network (`msdn.microsoft.com`) has full documentation for the standard Windows library functions.

Using ctypes on Linux

You can use `ctypes` on non-Windows systems, too. Here is an example using `printf()` on a Linux system accessed via the standard C library `libc.so.6`. (You can also use other UNIX-like OSes if you can find out the name of the library that implements the standard C library functions.)

```
>>> import ctypes as ct
>>> libc = ct.CDLL('libc.so.6')
>>> libc.printf(b"My name is %s\n", b"Fred")
My name is Fred
16
```

The `printf()` and `sscanf()` examples in the previous section should also work using the Linux `libc`, as will the `byref()` function and the various type conversion functions.

Accessing a Windows Application Using COM

Accessing an application library is almost as easy as accessing an OS system library, provided you can get documentation for the contents of the library. However, that is not always readily available. Another option on Windows is to use the OS functions to access the COM objects and then manipulate the COM objects from Python. Unfortunately, COM is a complex technology and has been extended over time to include features such as distribution over a network as well as various data access mechanisms. Compounding the difficulty is the fact that documentation for COM objects is often sparse and hard to find. Nonetheless, COM is often the most effective option for automating Windows applications.

The easiest way to use COM objects in Python is to use the `pywin32` package, written by Mark Hammond and available for download from the SourceForge website or included as standard in the ActiveState distribution of Python. The following Try It Out demonstrates the use of `pywin32` to open Excel preloaded with the `toolhire.xlsx` file you used in the earlier sections of this chapter.

TRY IT OUT Using COM to Present a File-Open Dialog (toolhireCOM.py)

This Try It Out demonstrates how to use the Excel COM interface to open the application and let the user select a file—all from within Python. If you are using Windows, follow along with these steps (this example works under Windows only):

1. If you do not have the ActiveState version of Python installed, download and install the `pywin32` extension package from the SourceForge website: `http://sourceforge.net/projects/pywin32/`.

2. Open your Python IDE and create a new file called `toolhireCOM.py` (or load it from the zip file). Enter the following code (making sure to set the filepath to your own file location):

```python
import win32com.client as com
# set the file path as required on your PC
filepath = r"D:\PythonCode\Chapter2\CSVexamples\toolhire.xlsx"
fileopen = 1   # found by trial and error!
app = com.Dispatch("Excel.Application")
app.Visible = True
fd = app.FileDialog(fileopen)
fd.InitialFileName = filepath
fd.Title = "Open the toolhire spreadsheet"
if fd.Show() == -1:
    fd.Execute()
```

3. Save and run the file.

4. Click OK in the dialog box that opens.

5. Confirm that the spreadsheet contains the data from the spreadsheet you used earlier.

How It Works

After importing the `win32com.client` module and aliasing it as `com`, you set the file path to a variable so it's easy to change if needed. (Note: You should use the path to your own folder, not the one that is used here.) The next line sets a `filemode` variable to 1. This determines what kind of file dialog is opened, in this case a File-Open dialog. (The value was found by trial and error, valid values lie between 1 and 4.)

You then created the `Application` COM object using the `Dispatch()` function and made the window visible by setting its `Visible` property to `True`. At this point the window appeared on screen but without the usual grid of cells. This is because Excel actually stores the grid in another COM object called a `Workbook`. You could have created a `Workbook` (or more accurately a set of `Workbooks`, or tabs) and opened the file directly instead of using a dialog box if you knew which file you were interested in. `Workbook` objects contain `Cells`, and it is these you would use if you wanted to create or modify data within a spreadsheet.

The next step was to create the dialog object using the `FileDialog()` method of the `Application`. This took your `filemode` value as an argument. You then set a couple of attributes of the object to ensure it opened in the right place and with an instructive title.

Finally, you called the `Show()` method of the dialog that displays the dialog box on screen, with all the usual functionality available to the user. If the user selects the OK button, the return value is `-1`. In this case you can call the `Execute()` method of the dialog object that proceeds to open (or save, if necessary) the selected file. At this point the spreadsheet gets populated with the `Workbooks` and appears as you would normally see the application.

You have now seen many techniques for integrating different applications in a scripting program. The next section gives you some advice on how to bring these techniques together to complete a scripting project.

AUTOMATING TASKS INVOLVING MULTIPLE APPLICATIONS

Scripting was defined at the start of this chapter as "coordinating the actions of other programs or applications to perform a task." So far, you have seen several enabling modules that can help you to interface with these external programs, but the bigger picture of how to automate a full workflow has not been discussed.

Normally, when you approach a workflow automation project, you look at what the human process is. You identify the systems used and the actions taken. You look at the input and output data. You then try to replicate that using whatever automation options are available for each system and process. You should take one other step before jumping in too quickly and that is to eliminate any steps that are done purely for the human user's convenience—for example, formatting data into a more readable layout when the data is only an intermediate result. If the computer can read the data without that formatting, it's an unnecessary step. Once you have identified the necessary steps, along with the systems and tools to be used, you can look at the automation options.

This section considers some guidelines that should minimize the pain in developing such multi-application scripts. As a general rule, use the following techniques in the order discussed.

Using Python First

Python comes with many support modules that enable you to replicate the OS functions and commands directly from your code. Other modules provide access to different file formats and network protocols. For example, Python has modules for directly manipulating the Windows registry and the UNIX password file that avoid calling external programs. Using Python directly provides an efficient and flexible solution that will be easier to maintain in the future. This should always be the first choice if possible.

Using Operating System Utilities

The OS provides many tools and commands for performing system administration. Many of these tools have command line interfaces (CLIs) that make them easy to call from Python code using the `subprocess` module. Tools that operate without interaction are the easiest to work with, even if this means using data files as an intermediate step because the files can be used as a recovery point should the process fail: You simply restart with the last successful step.

Using Data Files

Many tools and OS commands use configuration files to control how they function. By creating or modifying these configuration files prior to running the command, you can often control the behavior without the complexity of interacting with the processes in real time. In addition, you can usually drive such tools by using input files and generating output files rather than interactively providing data at prompts. You can build such files (or read them) using Python code, and you have seen how Python modules can assist in parsing many common data formats.

Using a Third-Party Module

Many popular applications have third-party modules that facilitate interacting with the application or direct manipulation of their data files. Microsoft Excel is a good example, with several modules available to assist in manipulating spreadsheets. You can manipulate many other proprietary file formats using third-party modules. Use your favorite search engine to find such modules. Include keywords like the application name, "python", and "module", and you should find what you are looking for fairly quickly.

The main caveat with this approach is that third-party modules often work only with older Python versions and may not be updated to the latest build. Most such modules are open source, with generous license conditions, so you usually have the option of updating the code yourself or, if that is too big a project, perhaps copying just the code that you need for your project. Due credit to the original authors should, of course, be given.

Interacting with Subprocesses via a CLI

If a tool has a CLI but cannot be driven using a data file, you can still use the `subprocess` module and interact with the process using `stdin` and `stdout` as was demonstrated with the `ex` editor earlier in the "Managing Subprocesses" section of this chapter. This is a potentially complex strategy because you have to anticipate every possible response or input request that the application may make. Similarly, error handling can be difficult to control and often, if an application deviates from the expected interaction, you may have no choice but to abort your script and try to recover manually. This is why using data files is preferable if at all possible.

> **NOTE** On Mac OS X there is an alternative technology, which is not covered in detail in this book, but can be useful for scripting Mac applications. It is based on AppleScript technology and its command-line interface: `osascript`. By writing small AppleScript programs and calling them from Python via `osascript`, you can often get Apple programs to "join in the dance" so to speak. Third-party modules are available for interacting with `osascript`, but you can run it directly, using the `subprocess` module, too.

There is a third-party module called *pexpect* that makes interacting with an external console-based program easier. It works by looking for expected (hence the name) prompt strings from the target application and then responding by allowing the programmer to send responses. This works well for login dialogs and similar interactions.

Using Web Services for Server-Based Applications

Some applications provide web services as an interface option. This is often an attractive alternative to using a third-party module, although the trade-off is often slower performance and the added complexity of parsing the XML or JSON data format used by such services. Web services are discussed in more detail in Chapter 5.

Using a Native Code API

If the application you need to control offers a C library as an API, you can use `ctypes` to access it from Python. The biggest problem you are likely to face with this approach is finding good documentation for the API. If documentation exists, this can be a very effective technique, but if not, it can involve a lot of painful trial and error. The Python interactive prompt is an invaluable tool in these scenarios.

For Windows applications you can often find a COM interface and access that via the win32 package. As with using `ctypes`, the lack of documentation is often the biggest obstacle.

Using GUI Robotics

The final option for GUI applications with no API is to interact with the GUI itself by sending user event messages into the application. Such events could include key-presses, mouse-clicks, and so forth. This technique is known as *robotics* because you are simulating a human user from your Python program. It is really an extension of the native code access described in the previous section, but operating at a much lower level.

This is a frustrating technique that is very error prone and also very vulnerable to changes in the application being controlled—for example, if an upgrade changes the screen layout, your code will likely break. Because of the difficulty of writing the code, as well as the fragility of the solution, you should avoid this unless every other possibility has failed.

SUMMARY

This chapter looked at how to automate tasks involving several different applications or OS utilities. You saw that Python's standard library contains several powerful modules to assist in this. The `os`, `os.path`, `shutil`, and `glob` modules, for example, can provide much information about computer resources and help you manage files directly from within Python.

The `subprocess` module provides a mechanism to launch and interact with command line programs from within your scripts.

The `time`, `datetime`, and `calendar` modules can assist with time-related tasks and calculations. The `time.sleep()` function can introduce a pause to your script's execution while waiting for other processes to complete.

You also saw that common data files that can be generated, or used as input by applications, can be created or read by Python using modules such as `csv`, `configparser`, `htmllib`, and `xml.etree`.

If no other form of access is available, it may be possible to use `ctypes` to access C functions exposed by dynamic libraries. On Windows similar functions exposed as a COM interface may be available, and the `pywin32` modules simplify access somewhat. These techniques are usually more complex than using data files or calling `subprocess` functions.

Finally, you reviewed the options available for scripting with their pros and cons, including the last resort option for GUIs of sending OS events to the application windows. This last option is fraught with difficulty and should only ever be used when all other means have been explored and exhausted.

EXERCISES

1. Explore the os module to see what else you can discover about your computer. Be sure to read the relevant parts of the Python documentation for the `os` and `stat` modules.

2. Try adding a new function to the `file_tree` module called `find_dirs()` that searches for directories matching a given regular expression. Combine both to create a third function, `find_all()`, that searches both files and directories.

3. Create another function, `apply_to_files()`, that applies a function parameter to all files matching the input pattern. You could, for example, use this function to remove all files matching a pattern, such as `*.tmp`, like this:

```
findfiles.apply_to_files('.*\.tmp', os.remove, 'TreeRoot')
```

4. Write a program that loops over the first 128 characters and displays a message indicating whether or not the value is a control character (characters with ordinal values between 0x00 and 0x1F, plus 0x7F). Use `ctypes` to access the standard C library and call the `iscntrl()` function to determine if a given character is a control character. Note this is not one of the built-in test methods of the string type in Python.

▶ **WHAT YOU LEARNED IN THIS CHAPTER**

TOPIC	DESCRIPTION
Scripting	Automation of a task involving multiple tools or applications. Python is used as the glue that binds these tools together, converting data formats to compatible forms, synchronizing the activities, and if necessary driving the functionality as a pseudo user.
OS environment	When the OS runs a process, it creates an environment consisting of certain configuration details. These include things like the process priority, its home directory, file permissions, and formats. Scripts often need to customize the environment prior to launching a program to ensure that it performs in the correct way.
Process and subprocesses	Programs run by the OS are known as processes. A single application may consist of a process hierarchy with a top-level process spawning multiple child or subprocesses. Subprocesses, by default, inherit their parent's environment. Scripts frequently launch other programs as subprocesses.
Tree walking	The file system exists as a tree structure with a root node and subtrees attached to the root. It is possible to recursively descend through this structure to the leaf nodes, which are the individual files. Scripts frequently need to process multiple files within a given subtree of the file system.
Absolute dates and times	A fixed date and time in history. A date such as July 4th, 1776 is an absolute date.
Relative dates and times	A date or time relative to another date or time. Usually expressed as a period such as three hours or as a repeating date or time, such as the third hour of every day or first day of every month.
Parser	A function that breaks down structured data into its component parts. Parsers can be based on several different algorithms and the most common types are either event based or tree based. Python supports both styles for XML parsing.
Libraries	Programming languages make reusable code available in code libraries. These are conceptually like Python modules, but in compiled languages are generated with special tools and can be either static or dynamically linked into an application. `ctypes` can access dynamically linked C libraries.
COM	The Windows Common Object Model (COM) mechanism enables external applications (or frequently an internal macro language) to manipulate the functionality of a program. The pywin32 package simplifies Python access to COM objects.

3

Managing Data

WHAT YOU WILL LEARN IN THIS CHAPTER:

- ➤ What data persistence means
- ➤ How to store data in files
- ➤ How to store data in a database
- ➤ How databases search, sort, and access data
- ➤ Other options for data storage

WROX.COM DOWNLOADS FOR THIS CHAPTER

For this chapter the wrox.com code downloads are found at www.wrox.com/go/pythonprojects on the Download Code tab. The code is in the Chapter 3 download, called Chapter3.zip, and individually named according to the names throughout the chapter.

In many scenarios you need to store data between executions of your program. The data you want to store could be local status information, such as the current location in an e-book reader or the current working filename, or it could be administrative data such as usernames and passwords or server addresses. Often it will be large volumes of business-oriented data such as customer orders, inventory, or address information. Many business applications consist of little more than a mechanism to create, view, and edit stored data.

This capability to store data in such a way that it is available for use on subsequent invocations of your program is known as *data persistence* because the data persists beyond the lifetime of the process that created it. To implement data persistence you need to store the data somewhere, either in a file or in a database.

This chapter is a bit like a history of computing storage technologies. That's because the need to store data has grown—and continues to grow—ever more complex with the passage of time. You now have a broad range of technologies available covering every storage need, from a few simple configuration settings to sophisticated distributed data sources representing thousands of logical entities. In this chapter learn about the different options available for storing data and the advantages and disadvantages of each. Along the way, you see how Python modules assist in this fundamental programming task.

STORING DATA USING PYTHON

The simplest storage is a plaintext file. You have already seen in Chapter 2 how to use a text file to store data in various formats, such as CSV and XML, as well as how to store unformatted text. These formats are fine if you need to store the data only when the program closes and read it back when the program is started again. This situation makes these formats very suitable for configuration data or application status information. These flat-file formats are less useful when you need to handle large volumes of data non-sequentially or search for specific records or fields. For that, you need a database.

A database is just a data storage system that enables you to create, read, update, and delete individual records—this set of four fundamental data management functions is often referred to as a *CRUD* interface. Database records consist of one or more key fields that uniquely identify the record, plus any other fields needed to represent the attributes of the entity that the record represents.

A Python dictionary can be used as a type of non-persistent database in that you can use the dictionary key to create, read, update, or delete a value associated with a given dictionary key; that could be a tuple of fields, or a record. All that's missing is the ability to store the data between sessions. The concept of a dictionary as a database has been exploited over the years, and various forms of persistent dictionaries exist. The oldest are the database management (DBM) family of files.

Using DBM as a Persistent Dictionary

DBM files originated in UNIX but have been developed over the years for other platforms as well. Python supports several variations. These variations are hidden by the dbm module that automatically determines the best solution based on which libraries are supported by the OS installation at hand. If no native DBM library can be found, a basic, pure Python version is used.

The DBM system is a simplified version of a dictionary in that both the keys and values must be strings, which means that some data conversion and string formatting is necessary if you are using non-string data. The advantages of a DBM database are that it is simple to use, fast, and fairly compact.

You can see how DBM works by revisiting the tool-hire example from Chapter 2. When you last looked at it you were working from a spreadsheet as the master data source. Suppose you decided to migrate the solution to a pure Python application? You would need a storage mechanism for the various data elements.

Recall that the spreadsheet had two sheets, one representing the tools for hire and the other the actual loans by the members. The record formats are shown in Table 3-1.

TABLE 3-1: Tool-Hire Data Entities

TOOL	LOAN
ItemID	ItemID
Name	Name
Description	Description
Owner	Owner
Price	Borrower
Condition	Date Borrowed
Date Registered	Date Returned

That design is fine for a human working with a spreadsheet, but if you want to convert it into a full-blown data application you need to overcome a number of issues with it:

➤ First, there is a lot of duplication between the two entities. The `Name`, `Description`, and `Owner` fields are all duplicated, and therefore need to be changed in two places whenever they are edited.

➤ Both entities use the `ItemID` as a key, which suggests the `ItemID` represents both a `Tool` and a `Loan` which is confusing.

➤ Several fields store names of subscribers to the service, but it would be better to have a separate entity to describe those members and reference that member entity from the other entities.

➤ Finally, although this started out as a tool-hire application, there is no reason to limit it to tools. The members could just as well borrow books or DVDs or anything else. So rather than restrict it to tools, you can rename the `Tool` entity as `Item`. And in keeping with that, you can rename the application to reflect its more generic approach. Call it `LendyDB`.

> **NOTE** *The changes to the tool-hire data involving removal of duplication and splitting of data into single entities are typical of those performed during a data design process known as normalization. This is a highly formalized discipline, and whole books have been written on the subject. This book only touches on the principles, but it is an important component of good database design. If you need to design a high-performance, high-volume database, you should research normalization to become familiar with the technique.*

With very little effort, you can rearrange things to overcome the issues with the spreadsheet. Table 3-2 shows the resulting database design.

You now have three entities, so you need to store the data in three data files. You can use the DBM format for this because each entity now has a unique identifier field, which, in string format, works well as a DBM key. You need to populate these files with data, and that means reformatting the data from the spreadsheet. You could write a Python program to do that but, because the sample data set is small, it's easier to just cut and paste the data into the new format. (Or you can extract the files from the LendyDB folder of the Chapter3.zip file from the download site.) Once you have the data you can save it into DBM files quite easily, as shown in the following Try It Out.

TABLE 3-2: LendyDB Data Design

ITEM	MEMBER	LOAN
ItemID	MemberID	LoanID
Name	Name	ItemID
Description	Email	BorrowerID
OwnerID		Date Borrowed
Price		Date Returned
Condition		
Date Registered		

TRY IT OUT Creating a LendyDB DBM Database (create-lendyDB.py)

In this Try It Out you translate the data from the tool-hire spreadsheet into the LendyDB data format and save it as three sets of DBM files. You then prove that it worked by reading the files and printing their contents. To do so, follow these steps:

1. Create a project folder and name it LendyDB.

2. Start your favorite editor or IDE and type the following code (or load the file create-lendyDB.py from the book's website):

```
import dbm

# ID, Name, Description, OwnerID, Price, Condition, DateRegistered
items = [
['1','Lawnmower','Tool','1','$150','Excellent','2012-01-05'],
['2','Lawnmower','Tool','2','$370','Fair','2012-04-01'],
['3','Bike','Vehicle','3','$200','Good','2013-03-22'],
['4','Drill','Tool','4','$100','Good','2013-10-28'],
['5','Scarifier','Tool','5','$200','Average','2013-09-14'],
['6','Sprinkler','Tool','1','$80','Good','2014-01-06']
]

# ID, Name, Email
members = [
['1', 'Fred', 'fred@lendylib.org'],
['2', 'Mike', 'mike@gmail.com'],
['3', 'Joe', 'joe@joesmail.com'],
['4', 'Rob', 'rjb@somcorp.com'],
['5', 'Anne', 'annie@bigbiz.com'],
]
```

```
# ID, ItemID, BorrowerID, DateBorrowed, DateReturned
loans = [
['1','1','3','4/1/2012','4/26/2012'],
['2','2','5','9/5/2012','1/5/2013'],
['3','3','4','7/3/2013','7/22/2013'],
['4','4','1','11/19/2013','11/29/2013'],
['5','5','2','12/5/2013','None']
]

def createDB(data, dbName):
    try:
        db = dbm.open(dbName, 'c')
        for datum in data:
            db[datum[0]] = ','.join(datum)
    finally:
        db.close()
        print(dbName, 'created')

def readDB(dbName):
    try:
        db = dbm.open(dbName, 'r')
        print('Reading ', dbName)
        return [db[datum] for datum in db]
    finally:
        db.close()

def main():
    print('Creating data files...')
    createDB(items, 'itemdb')
    createDB(members, 'memberdb')
    createDB(loans, 'loandb')

    print('reading data files...')
    print(readDB('itemdb'))
    print(readDB('memberdb'))
    print(readDB('loandb'))

if __name__ == "__main__": main()
```

3. Save the file as create-lendyDB.py and run it. Verify that your output looks like this:

```
Creating data files...
itemdb created
memberdb created
loandb created
reading data files...
Reading  itemdb
[b'2,Lawnmower,Tool,2,$370,Fair,2012-04-01', b'3,Bike,Vehicle,3,$200,
Good,2013-03-22', b'1,Lawnmower,Tool,1,$150,Excellent,2012-01-05',
 b'6,Sprinkler,Tool,1,$80,Good,2014-01-06', b'4,Drill,Tool,4,$100,
Good,2013-10-28', b'5,Scarifier,Tool,5,$200,Average,2013-09-14']
Reading  memberdb
[b'2,Mike,mike@gmail.com', b'3,Joe,joe@joesmail.com', b'1,Fred,
fred@lendylib.org', b'4,Rob,rjb@somcorp.com', b'5,Anne,annie@bigbiz.com']
Reading  loandb
[b'2,2,5,9/5/2012,1/5/2013', b'3,3,4,7/3/2013,7/22/2013', b'1,1,3,4/1/2012,
4/26/2012', b'4,4,1,11/19/2013,11/29/2013', b'5,5,2,12/5/2013,None']
```

4.   Inspect the contents of your `LendyDB` folder. You should see three sets of three files: one set per entity, with extensions of `.bak`, `.dat`, and `.dir`.

How It Works

You started off by importing the `dbm` module. (The module internally analyzes your system to determine which DBM library is available and initializes it for use.) You then created the raw data items by extracting the values from the Excel spreadsheet data. Note that you changed the item `Description` field so that it now records what kind of item you have (tool, book, DVD, and so on). You could have created an extra field instead and that would have been equally valid, but for this exercise you chose to reuse the existing field name.

You then defined the `createDB()` function, which opens the DBM database file in c, for create mode. (The c mode creates a new file if one does not exist or opens the existing file if it has already been created.) You then used a `for` loop to read each data item and store it in the database using the first field as the key and joining all the fields as a comma-separated string for the value.

You used a `try/finally` construct to ensure all data was written to the file and it was closed properly.

The `readDB()` function is the converse operation to `createDB()`. It opens the file using r, for read mode, and then returns the contents as a list using a list comprehension. If you expected the database to be very large you could have made this function into a generator instead and yielded each line in turn. Because you don't expect the lending library to contain vast numbers of items or members, returning a list is fine.

Finally, the `main()` function calls the `createDB()` function once for each data entity. Note that you do not provide any file extension; `dbm` does that itself. `main()` then checks that the data has been created correctly by printing the output from `readDB()` for each database. The databases created by `dbm` consist of three files. One file contains the actual data; the other two files hold the index information that `dbm` uses to find the records in the data file. It is this indexing mechanism that makes `dbm` so much faster than simply searching sequentially through a plaintext file. You should not try to edit the `dbm` files directly because this could corrupt the database.

> **NOTE** The mode strings used for `dbm` file operations are slightly different from the normal file modes. The default r mode is for read-only access to an existing database. w is for read/write access to an existing database. c creates a new database or opens an existing one. n always creates a new, empty database.

Having created your database, you can now use it to read or edit the contents. This is best demonstrated from an interactive session at the Python prompt, so fire up the Python interpreter from the folder where you saved the data files and type the following:

```
>>> import dbm
>>> items = dbm.open('itemdb')
>>> members = dbm.open('memberdb')
>>> loans = dbm.open('loandb','w')
```

```
>>> loan2 = loans['2'].decode()
>>> loan2
'2,2,5,9/5/2012,1/5/2013'
>>> loan2 = loan2.split(',')
>>> loan2
['2', '2', '5', '9/5/2012', '1/5/2013']
>>> item2 = items[loan2[1]].decode().split(',')
>>> item2
['2', 'Lawnmower', 'Tool', '2', '$370', 'Fair', '2012-04-01']
>>> member2 = members[loan2[2]].decode().split(',')
>>> member2
['5', 'Anne', 'annie@bigbiz.com']
>>> print('{} borrowed a {} on {}'.format(
... member2[1],item2[1],loan2[3]))
Anne borrowed a Lawnmower on 9/5/2012
```

With the preceding commands, you opened the three databases, extracted loan number 2 (using `decode()` to convert from the `dbm` bytes format into a normal Python string), and split it into its separate fields. You then extracted the corresponding member and item records by using the loan record values as keys. Finally, you printed a message reporting the data in human-readable form.

Of course, you can create new records in the data set, too. Here is how you create a new loan record:

```
>>> max(loans.keys()).decode()
'5'
>>> key = int(max(loans.keys()).decode()) + 1
>>> newloan = [str(key),'2','1','4/5/2014']
>>> loans[str(key)] = ','.join(newloan)
>>> loans[str(key)]
b'6,2,1,4/5/2014'
```

With the preceding code, you used the built-in `max()` function to find the highest existing key value in the `loans` database. You then created a new key by converting that maximum value to an integer and adding one. Next, you used the string version of the new key value to create a new loan record. You then wrote that record out to the database using the new key field. Finally, you checked that the new record existed by using the new key value to read the record back.

You can see that DBM files can be used as a database, even with multiple entities. However, if the data is not naturally string-based, or has many fields, extracting the fields and converting to the appropriate format becomes tedious. You can write helper functions or methods to do that conversion for you, but there is an easier way. Python has a module that can store arbitrary Python objects to files and read them back without you having to do any data conversion. It's time to meet the `pickle` module.

Using Pickle to Store and Retrieve Objects

The `pickle` module is designed to convert Python objects into sequences of binary bytes. The object types converted include the basic data types, such as integers and boolean values, as well as system- and user-defined classes and even collections such as lists, tuples, and functions (except those defined using `lambda`). A few restrictions exist on objects that can be pickled; these are described in the module documentation.

pickle is not of itself a data management solution; it merely converts objects into binary sequences. These sequences can be stored in binary files and read back again so they can be used as a form of data persistence. But pickle does not provide any means to search the stored objects or retrieve a single object from among many stored items. You must read the entire stored inventory back into memory and access the objects that way. pickle is ideal when you just want to save the state of a program so that you can start it up and continue from the same position as before (for example, if you were playing a game).

> **NOTE** *Converting data to strings (or bytes) for storage or transmission over a network is a common operation in computing; as such, the process has a generic name: serialization (sometimes known as marshalling). Pickle is a Python-specific form of serialization. The JavaScript Object Notation (JSON) data format is another form of serialization that is widely used across languages, especially on the web. You find out more about JSON in Chapter 5. Pickle is more powerful than JSON but less general because it is restricted to Python applications.*

The pickle module provides several functions and classes, but you normally only use the dump() and load() functions. The dump() function dumps an object (or objects) to a file and the load() function reads an object from a file (usually an object previously written with dump).

To see how this works, you can use the interactive prompt and experiment with the Item data definition from LendyDB in the previous section. You start off by creating a single item and this time, instead of using a single string for all the values, you use a tuple, like this:

```
>>> import pickle
>>> anItem = ['1','Lawnmower','Tool','1','$150','Excellent','2012-01-05']
>>> with open('item.pickle','wb') as pf:
...     pickle.dump(anItem,pf)
...
>>> with open('item.pickle','rb') as pf:
...     itemCopy = pickle.load(pf)
...
>>> print(itemCopy)
['1', 'Lawnmower', 'Tool', '1', '$150', 'Excellent', '2012-01-05']
>>>
```

Notice that you have to use binary file modes for the pickle file. Most importantly, notice that you got a list back from the file, not just a string. Of course, these elements are all strings, so just for fun try pickling some different data types:

```
>>> funData = ('a string', True, 42, 3.14159, ['embedded', 'list'])
>>> with open('data.pickle','wb') as pf:
...     pickle.dump(funData, pf)
...
>>> with open('data.pickle','rb') as pf:
...     copyData = pickle.load(pf)
...
```

```
>>> print (copyData)
('a string', True, 42, 3.14159, ['embedded', 'list'])
>>>
```

That all worked as expected, and you got back the same data that you put in. The only other thing you need to know about `pickle` is that it is not secure. It potentially executes objects that get unpickled, so you should never use `pickle` to read data received from untrusted sources. But for local object persistence in a controlled environment, it does a great job very simply. If you are using `pickle` in your own projects you should be aware that you can get some `pickle`-specific exceptions raised so you might want to wrap your code inside a `try/except` construct.

For your `LendyDB` project, the big problem with `pickle` is that you can only access the data by reading the whole file into memory. Wouldn't it be great if you could have an indexed file of arbitrary Python objects by combining the features of `pickle` and `dbm`? It turns out that you can, and the work has been done for you in the `shelve` module.

Accessing Objects with shelve

The `shelve` module combines the `dbm` module's ability to provide random access to files with `pickle`'s ability to serialize Python objects. It is not a perfect solution in that the key field must still be a string and the security issue with `pickle` also applies to `shelve`, so you must ensure your data sources are safe. Also, like `dbm` files the module cannot tell if you modify data read into memory, so you must explicitly write any changes back to the file by reassigning to the same key. Finally, `dbm` files impose some limits around the size of objects they can store and are not designed for concurrent access from, for example, multiple threads or users. However, for many projects, `shelve` provides a simple, lightweight, and fairly fast solution for storing and accessing data.

So as far as you are concerned, `shelve` acts just like a dictionary. Almost everything you do with a dictionary you can also do with `shelve` instances. The only difference is that the data remains on the disk rather than being in memory. This has obvious speed implications, but on the other hand, it means you can work with very large dictionaries even when memory is limited.

Before you build `LendyDB` with `shelve`, you'll experiment with some dummy data that includes a bigger selection of data types, including a user-defined class. The first thing you do is create the `shelve` database file (or, as they are sometimes known, a *shelf*):

```
>>> shelf = shelve.open('fundata.shelve','c')
```

The `open` function takes the same arguments as the `dbm` version discussed earlier. Because you are creating a new shelf, you use mode c for create. Now you can start adding items to the shelf:

```
>>> shelf['tuple'] = (1,2,'a','b',True,False)
>>> shelf['lists'] = [[1,2,3],[True,False],[3.14159, -66]]
```

With these commands, you saved two items, each of which contains a mix of Python data types, and `shelve` happily stored them without any data conversion required by you. You can check that `shelve` saved the items by reading the values back:

```
>>> shelf['tuple']
(1, 2, 'a', 'b', True, False)
>>> shelf['lists']
[[1, 2, 3], [True, False], [3.14159, -66]]
```

To make the data changes permanent you need to call `close` (normally you would use a try/
finally construct or, unlike dbm, you can use a context manager style):

```
>>> shelf.close()
>>> shelf['tuple']
Traceback (most recent call last):
  File "C:\Python33\lib\shelve.py", line 111, in __getitem__
    value = self.cache[key]
KeyError: 'tuple'

During handling of the above exception, another exception occurred:

Traceback (most recent call last):
File "<stdin>", line 1, in <module>
File "C:\Python33\lib\shelve.py", line 113, in __getitem__
  f = BytesIO(self.dict[key.encode(self.keyencoding)])
File "C:\Python33\lib\shelve.py", line 70, in closed
  raise ValueError('invalid operation on closed shelf')
ValueError: invalid operation on closed shelf
>>>
```

You can see that after closing the shelf you can no longer access the data; you need to reopen the shelf.

Now you can try something slightly more complex. First, you define a class, create some instances,
and then store them to a shelf:

```
>>> class Test:
...     def __init__(self,x,y):
...         self.x = x
...         self.y = y
...     def show(self):
...         print(self.x, self.y)
...
>>> shelf = shelve.open('test.shelve','c')
>>> a = Test(1,2)
>>> a.show()
1 2
>>> b = Test('a','b')
>>> b.show()
a b
>>> shelf['12'] = a
>>> shelf['ab'] = b
```

So far, so good. You have saved two instances of the class. Getting them back is just as easy:

```
>>> shelf['12']
<__main__.Test object at 0x01BD1570>
>>> shelf['ab']
<__main__.Test object at 0x01BD1650>
>>> c = shelf['12']
>>> c.show()
1 2
>>> d = shelf['ab']
>>> d.show()
a b
>>> shelf.close()
```

Notice that the object returned was reported as a __main__.Test object. That raises one very important caveat about saving and restoring user-defined classes. You must make sure that the very same class definition used by shelf for the save is also available to the module that reads the class back from the shelf, and the class definitions must be the same. If the class definition changes between writing the data and reading it back, the result is unpredictable. The usual way to make the class visible is to put it into its own module. That module can then be imported, and used in the code that writes, as well as the code that reads, the shelf.

> **NOTE** *You can define two special methods in your class (__getstate__ and __setstate__) that tell* pickle *(and therefore shelve) exactly which attributes to save; this can avoid some issues with changes to class definitions provided these two methods themselves don't change. The documentation contains examples of this mechanism at work. In general, it's best to avoid changes to the class definitions if at all possible.*

It's time to revisit your lending library, LendyDB. This time you replicate what you did with the dbm database, but use the shelve module instead.

TRY IT OUT   Using shelve to Store LendyDB (shelve-lendyDB.py)

In this Try It Out, you replicate the functionality of the dbm example but use shelve instead. The code is simpler as a result. To do this, complete the following steps:

1.   Change into your LendyDB project folder.

2.   Open your favorite editor or IDE and type in the following code (or load shelve-lendyDB.py from the LendyDB folder of the downloaded files):

```
import shelve

# ID, Name, Description, OwnerID, Price, Condition, DateRegistered
items = [
['1','Lawnmower','Tool','1','$150','Excellent','2012-01-05'],
['2','Lawnmower','Tool','2','$370','Fair','2012-04-01'],
['3','Bike','Vehicle','3','$200','Good','2013-03-22'],
['4','Drill','Tool','4','$100','Good','2013-10-28'],
['5','Scarifier','Tool','5','$200','Average','2013-09-14'],
['6','Sprinkler','Tool','1','$80','Good','2014-01-06']
]

# ID, Name, Email
members = [
['1', 'Fred', 'fred@lendylib.org'],
['2', 'Mike', 'mike@gmail.com'],
['3', 'Joe', 'joe@joesmail.com'],
['4', 'Rob', 'rjb@somcorp.com'],
['5', 'Anne', 'annie@bigbiz.com'],
]
```

```
# ID, ItemID, BorrowerID, DateBorrowed, DateReturned
loans = [
['1','1','3','4/1/2012','4/26/2012'],
['2','2','5','9/5/2012','1/5/2013'],
['3','3','4','7/3/2013','7/22/2013'],
['4','4','1','11/19/2013','11/29/2013'],
['5','5','2','12/5/2013','None']
]

def createDB(data, shelfname):
    try:
        shelf = shelve.open(shelfname,'c')
        for datum in data:
            shelf[datum[0]] = datum
    finally:
        shelf.close()

def readDB(shelfname):
    try:
        shelf = shelve.open(shelfname,'r')
        return [shelf[key] for key in shelf]
    finally:
        shelf.close()
def main():
    print('Creating data files...')
    createDB(items, 'itemshelf')
    createDB(members, 'membershelf')
    createDB(loans, 'loanshelf')

    print('reading items...')
    print(readDB('itemshelf'))
    print('reading members...')
    print(readDB('membershelf'))
    print('reading loans...')
    print(readDB('loanshelf'))

if __name__ == "__main__": main()
```

3. Save the file as `shelve-lendyDB.py` and run it.

4. Check that your output matches the following output:

```
Creating data files...
reading items...
[['1', 'Lawnmower', 'Tool', '1', '$150', 'Excellent', '2012-01-05'], ['3', 'Bike
', 'Vehicle', '3', '$200', 'Good', '2013-03-22'], ['2', 'Lawnmower', 'Tool', '2'
, '$370', 'Fair', '2012-04-01'], ['5', 'Scarifier', 'Tool', '5', '$200', 'Averag
e', '2013-09-14'], ['4', 'Drill', 'Tool', '4', '$100', 'Good', '2013-10-28'], ['
6', 'Sprinkler', 'Tool', '1', '$80', 'Good', '2014-01-06']]
reading members...
[['1', 'Fred', 'fred@lendylib.org'], ['3', 'Joe', 'joe@joesmail.com'], ['2', 'Mi
ke', 'mike@gmail.com'], ['5', 'Anne', 'annie@bigbiz.com'], ['4', 'Rob', 'rjb@som
corp.com']]
reading loans...
[['1', '1', '3', '4/1/2012', '4/26/2012'], ['3', '3', '4', '7/3/2013', '7/22/201
3'], ['2', '2', '5', '9/5/2012', '1/5/2013'], ['5', '5', '2', '12/5/2013', 'None
'], ['4', '4', '1', '11/19/2013', '11/29/2013']]
```

5. Start the Python interpreter and experiment with the data by typing the following:

```
>>> import shelve
<module 'shelve' from 'C:\\Python33\\lib\\shelve.py'>
>>> items = shelve.open('itemshelf','w')
>>> members = shelve.open('membershelf','w')
>>> loans = shelve.open('loanshelf','w')
>>> loan2 = loans['2']
>>> loan2
['2', '2', '5', '9/5/2012', '1/5/2013']
>>> item2 = items[loan2[1]]
>>> item2
['2', 'Lawnmower', 'Tool', '2', '$370', 'Fair', '2012-04-01']
>>> member2 = members[loan2[2]]
>>> print('{} borrowed a {} on {}'.format(
... member2[1],item2[1],loan2[3]))
Anne borrowed a Lawnmower on 9/5/2012
>>>
```

6. Add a new loan record by typing the following:

```
>>> key = int(max(loans.keys())) + 1
>>> newloan = [str(key), '2','1','4/5/2014']
>>> loans[str(key)] = newloan
>>> loans[str(key)]
['6', '2', '1', '4/5/2014']
>>> loans.close()   # make the change permanent
```

How It Works

The file is very similar to the one using dbm. You start off by importing shelve instead of dbm. The three sets of data definitions that follow are identical to the earlier example. You then define the two functions: createDB() and readDB().

This is where the shelve version starts to simplify the code. For creation, the shelf is opened and the data is written to the shelf directly instead of having to use the string join() method. For reading, things are almost identical but you use a list comprehension to retrieve, store, and return the shelf content.

The main() function is also very similar to the dbm example except for a few tweaks to the printed messages.

At this stage the shelve solution doesn't seem to have been a huge advantage. However, when you start to access the database and modify it, the situation begins to improve. You open the three shelves and repeat the exercises from the dbm section. But this time you do not need to split() the values to get a list and you do not need to mess with decode() to get from bytes to normal strings. This makes the code shorter and easier to read. (If the records had contained mixed types, the savings would have been even more obvious.)

Finally, you create a new loan record. Again, this does not require any decoding or joining of strings. When you close the shelf, you ensure the data is written to disk.

You've now seen the various options Python offers for storing objects and retrieving them. The `shelve` module, in particular, offers a persistence mechanism that is compact, fairly fast, and simple to use. If you have a solution that uses Python dictionaries in memory, switching to a `shelve` solution is almost a trivial task. However, this is still a long way short of what is needed for complex data handling. Operations like finding a set of records based on non-key values or sorting the data essentially still require a complete read of the data into memory. The only way to avoid that is to move to a full-blown database solution. However, before you look at that you should consider some aids that Python provides to make data analysis of in-memory data sets easier.

ANALYZING DATA WITH PYTHON

Once you have a set of data, you usually want to ask questions about it. For example, in the lending library example, you might want to know the total cost of the items or even the average cost of an item. You might want to know who contributed the most items, which items are out on loan at any given time, and so on. You can do that using Python, and you could write functions using all the standard Python features that would answer those questions. However, Python has some powerful features that often get overlooked that are especially useful for analyzing data sets.

In this section you look at some of the built-in features you can use, especially the functional programming features of the language. Then you turn your attention to the `itertools` module, which offers more advanced features that often save time and computing resources when compared with the standard alternatives.

Analyzing Data Using Built-In Features of Python

When you analyze data, it is important to select the right data structure. For example, Python includes a `set` data type that automatically eliminates duplicates. If you care only about unique values, converting (or extracting) the data to a set can simplify the process considerably. Similarly, using Python dictionaries to provide keyword access rather than numeric indices often improves code readability, and thus reliability (you saw an example of that in Chapter 2 that compared the CSV dictionary-based reader with the standard tuple-based reader). If you are finding that your code is getting complicated, it's often worthwhile to stop and consider whether a different data structure would help.

In addition to the wide variety of data structures, Python also offers many built-in and standard library functions that you can use, such as `any`, `all`, `map`, `sorted`, and slicing. (Slicing isn't technically a function but an operation, however it does return a value in a similar way that a function would.) When you combine these functions with Python generator expressions and list comprehensions, you have a powerful toolkit for slicing and dicing your data.

You can apply these techniques to your `LendyDB` data to answer the questions raised in the opening paragraph of this "Analyzing Data with Python" section. You can try that now.

TRY IT OUT Analyzing LendyDB with Python (lendydata.py)

In this Try It Out, you use standard Python features to answer the questions about the `LendyDB` data raised earlier: 1) What is the total cost of all items? 2) What is the average cost of an item?

3) Who contributed the most items? 4) Which items are currently on loan? To do this, complete the following steps.

1. Create a module called `lendydata.py` containing the following code (or load it from the `Analysis` folder of the downloadable files):

```
items = [
['ID','Name', 'Description', 'OwnerID', 'Price', 'Condition', 'Registered'],
['1','Lawnmower','Tool','1','$150','Excellent','2012-01-05'],
['2','Lawnmower','Tool','2','$370','Fair','2012-04-01'],
['3','Bike','Vehicle','3','$200','Good','2013-03-22'],
['4','Drill','Tool','4','$100','Good','2013-10-28'],
['5','Scarifier','Tool','5','$200','Average','2013-09-14'],
['6','Sprinkler','Tool','1','$80','Good','2014-01-06']
]

members = [
['ID', 'Name', 'Email'],
['1', 'Fred', 'fred@lendylib.org'],
['2', 'Mike', 'mike@gmail.com'],
['3', 'Joe', 'joe@joesmail.com'],
['4', 'Rob', 'rjb@somcorp.com'],
['5', 'Anne', 'annie@bigbiz.com'],
]

loans = [
['ID','ItemID','BorrowerID','DateBorrowed','DateReturned'],
['1','1','3','4/1/2012','4/26/2012'],
['2','2','5','9/5/2012','1/5/2013'],
['3','3','4','7/3/2013','7/22/2013'],
['4','4','1','11/19/2013','11/29/2013'],
['5','5','2','12/5/2013','None']
]
```

2. Start the Python interpreter and import the data using the following command:

```
>>> from lendydata import *
```

3. To answer the question, "What is the total cost of all items?" type the following code:

```
>>> def cost(item):
...     return int(item[4][1:])
...
>>> cost(items[2])
370
>>> sum(cost(item) for item in items[1:])
1100
```

4. To answer the question, "What is the average cost of an item?" type this:

```
>>> sum(cost(item) for item in items[1:])/len(items)-1
183.33333333334
>>>
```

5. To answer the question, "Who contributed the most items?" type this:

```
>>> def owner(item): return item[3]
...
```

```
>>> for member in members[1:]:
...     count = 0
...     for item in items[1:]:
...         if owner(item) == member[0]:
...             count += 1
...     print(member[1],':',count)
...
Fred : 2
Mike : 1
Joe : 1
Rob : 1
Anne : 1
>>>
```

6. To answer the question, "Which items are currently on loan?" type this:

```
>>> def onLoan(loan): return loan[-1] == 'None'
...
>>> [items[int(loan[1])] for loan in loans if onLoan(loan)]
[['5', 'Scarifier', 'Tool', '5', '$200', 'Average', '2013-09-14']]
>>>
```

How It Works

You started by creating a Python module containing your sample data and importing that data into the interpreter. Note the handy trick of using the first entry (having index 0) in each data section to store a list of that section's field descriptions.

This has two useful effects:

1. Every ID value of any given data section (of the three sections) now matches the zero-relative index of that same row in its section. For example, the 'Mike' row of the members data section, having an ID of '3', can now be accessed as members[3].

2. You have access to the field names, both programmatically and as an *aide-de-memoir* in the interpreter, by accessing the first record.

The downside is that, in your processing code, you must remember to adjust by 1 the length, and indices, of the data sections, to account for the extra header-line record of each section.

You then used standard Python tools to answer several questions about the data using standard Python tools. For each question you defined a small helper function that typically just extracted a field from a data entry. For the first question it returned the cost as an integer value by extracting the string value and stripping the dollar sign from the front before converting to an integer. You then used Python's built-in sum() function applied to a generator expression to calculate the total cost of the items. And you computed the average item cost by dividing that total cost by the number of items.

To find out who contributed which items, you defined a function owner() that simply extracted the ownerID field from an item record. You then looped over all the members checking how many items each member owned.

Finally, you determined which items were out on loan by creating a helper function, called onLoan(), that returned a boolean result depending on whether or not the DateReturned field was None. You then used this in a list comprehension with a filter condition using the onLoan() function.

In the preceding Try It Out you saw that you can use the built-in functions and data structures combined with loops and generators to answer most questions about data. The problem is that for volumes of data this technique requires storing large lists in memory and may involve looping over those lists many times. This can become very slow and resource-intensive. The Python itertools module provides several functions that can reduce the load significantly.

Analyzing Data with itertools

The itertools module of the standard Python library provides a set of tools that utilize functional programming principles to consume iterable objects and produce other iterables as results. This means that the functions can be combined to build sophisticated data filters.

Before looking at how itertools can be used on the LendyDB data, you should look at some of the functions provided using simpler data sets. These functions are powerful, but operate in slightly different ways than most of the functions you have dealt with in the past. In particular, they are all geared around processing iterators. You should recall that all the standard Python collections, as well as objects such as files, are iterators. You can also create your own custom iterators by defining some methods that adhere to the Python iterator protocol. The simplest iterators are strings, so that's mainly what the documentation uses to demonstrate the itertools functions, but remember that these functions work with any kind of iterator, not just strings.

Utility Functions

The first group of functions you look at includes relatively simple functions that you typically use to provide input to the other functions in the module. The count() function works a lot like the built-in range() function, except where range() generates numbers up to a limit, count() generates an indefinite series of numbers from a start point, incrementing by a given, optional, stepsize. It looks like this:

```
>>> import itertools as it
>>> for n in it.count(15,2):
...     if n < 40: print(n, end=' ')
...     else: break
...
15 17 19 21 23 25 27 29 31 33 35 37 39
```

The repeat() function is even simpler; it just repeats its argument continuously, or for the number of repetitions specified, like this:

```
>>> for n in range(7):
...     print(next(it.repeat('yes ')), end='')
...
yes yes yes yes yes yes yes >>>
>>> list(it.repeat(6,3))
[6, 6, 6]
>>>
```

> **NOTE** *Several of the* `itertools` *functions produce a potentially infinite series of output data. This has the potential to lock your program into an infinite loop. You need to take extra care to ensure you provide an exit mechanism when using these functions.*

The `cycle()` function rotates over the input sequence over and over again. This is useful for building round-robin–style iterations for load balancing or resource allocation. Consider the case where you have a number of resources and want to allocate data to each resource in turn. You can build a list of resources, then cycle over that list until you run out of data. You can simulate this technique using lists as resources, like this:

```
>>> res1 = []
>>> res2 = []
>>> res3 = []
>>> resources = it.cycle([res1,res2,res3])
>>> for n in range(30):
...        res = next(resources)
...        res.append(n)
...
>>> res1
[0, 3, 6, 9, 12, 15, 18, 21, 24, 27]
>>> res2
[1, 4, 7, 10, 13, 16, 19, 22, 25, 28]
>>> res3
[2, 5, 8, 11, 14, 17, 20, 23, 26, 29]
>>>
```

The `chain()` function concatenates all the input arguments into a single collection and then returns each element. If the arguments were all of the same type, you could achieve the same result by adding the collections together with the plus operator, but `chain()` also works for types of collections that are not compatible with the plus operator. Here is an example using a list, a string, and a set:

```
>>> items = it.chain([1,2,3],'astring',{'a','set','of','strings'})
>>> for item in items:
...     print(item)
...
1
2
3
a
s
t
r
i
n
g
a
of
set
strings
```

Finally, there is the `islice()` function that works like the slice operator but, because it uses a generator, is more memory efficient. It does have one significant difference from the normal slice: You cannot use negative indices to count backward from the end, because iterators do not always have well-defined endpoints.

You could use `islice()`like this:

```
>>> data = list(range(20))
>>> data[3:12:2]
[3, 5, 7, 9, 11]
>>> for d in it.islice(data,3,12,2): print(d, end=' ')
...
3 5 7 9 11
```

`itertools` can do much more than just generate data. It can also help analyze data using a variety of data processing functions.

Data Processing Functions

`itertools` has many data processing functions that either take input data and transform the elements, or filter the contents in some way. By combining these functions you can build sophisticated data processing tools. One feature that many of these functions have in common is that they accept a function object as a parameter.

> **NOTE** Passing functions as arguments is a common feature of functional programming style and can seem a little strange at first. You just need to remember that, in Python, a function is an object, too. A function name is just like any other variable; it is simply a reference to a function object. As such, you can pass a function name, such as f, into another function, say, g, and function g can call the input function f internally. Functions that return a boolean result are often referred to as predicates.

The `compress()` function acts a little bit like a higher-order version of the bitmasks that you explored in Chapters 1 and 2. It takes a collection of data as its first argument and a collection of boolean values as its second. It returns those items of the first collection that correspond to the `True` values of the second collection. Here is a basic example:

```
>>> for item in it.compress([1,2,3,4,5],[False,True,False,0,1]):
...     print(item)
...
2
5
```

Note that the boolean values do not need to be pure boolean values; they can be anything that Python can convert to boolean, even expressions. (The `itertools.filterfalse()` function works in exactly the same way, but in reverse; it returns those elements whose corresponding boolean flags are `False` instead of `True`.)

Likewise, the `dropwhile()` and `takewhile()` functions have related, but opposite, effects. Both take an input function and a collection, or iterator, as arguments and then apply the function to the input data elements one at a time. `dropwhile()` ignores all of the input elements until the function argument evaluates to `False`, whereas `takewhile()` returns the elements until the result is `False`. You can see the difference in these examples that use the same input data and argument function:

```
>>> def singleDigit(n): return n < 10
...
>>> for n in it.dropwhile(singleDigit,range(20)): print(n,end=' ')
...
10 11 12 13 14 15 16 17 18 19
>>> for n in it.takewhile(singleDigit,range(20)): print(n,end=' ')
...
0 1 2 3 4 5 6 7 8 9
```

Note that both of these functions stop processing the data after the first time a trigger is detected. Consider this example:

```
>>> for n in it.dropwhile(singleDigit, [1,2,12,4,20,7,999]): print(n,end=' ')
...
12 4 20 7 999
```

Notice that the output includes the single-digit numbers following the first non–single-digit number, for the reason just indicated: Once `dropwhile` stops dropping, nothing else is dropped thereafter. (And `takewhile`'s taking behavior is analogous.)

The `accumulate()` function applies its input function to each element of the input data along with the result of the previous operation. (The default function is addition and the first result is always the first element.) Thus, for an input data set of [1,2,3,4] the initial value, `result1`, is 1, followed by the function applied to `result1` and 2 to produce `result2`, and to `result2` and 3 to create `result3`, and to `result3` and 4 to create `result4`. The output is `result1`, `result2`, `result3`, and `result4`. (The final result value is the same as applying the `reduce()` function from the `functools` module.) Here is an example using `accumulate()`'s default addition operator:

```
>>> for n in it.accumulate([1,2,3,4,]): print(n, end=' ')
...
1 3 6 10
```

Taming the Vagaries of groupby()

`groupby()` is one of the most useful and powerful of the `itertools` functions, but it has a number of little foibles that can catch you out. Its basic role is to collect the input data into groups based on a key derived by an input function and return those groups as iterators in their own right.

The first problem is that the function only groups for as long as it finds the same key, but it creates a new group if a new key is found. Then, if the original key is found later in the sequence, it creates a new group with the same key rather than adding the new element to the original group. To avoid this behavior, it is best if the input data is sorted using the same key function used by `groupby()`.

The second snag is that the groups generated by `groupby()` are not really independent iterators; they are effectively views into the original input collection. Thus, if the function moves on to the next group of data, the previous groups become invalid. The only way to retain the groups for later processing is to copy them into a separate container—a list, for example.

To reinforce these concepts, you look at an example that produces a set of data groups that can be processed independently. The example is built up to the final, correct solution starting from an initial, naïve, but broken solution.

First, you define several groups of data and use the built-in `all()` function as a key. The `all()` function returns `True` when all of its input data items are `True`.

```
>>> data = [[1,2,3,4,5],[6,7,8,9,0],[0,2,4,6,8],[1,3,5,7,9]]
>>> for d in data: print(all(d))
...
True
False
False
True
```

Next, you apply the `groupby()` function to your data:

```
>>> for ky,grp in it.groupby(data,key=all):
...     print(ky, grp)
...
True <itertools._grouper object at 0x7fd3ee2c>
False <itertools._grouper object at 0x7fd3ee8c>
True <itertools._grouper object at 0x7fd3ee2c>
```

You can see that `groupby()` returned two separate groups both keyed on `True`. To avoid that you must sort the data before processing it with `groupby()`, like this:

```
>>> for ky,grp in it.groupby(sorted(data,key=all), key=all):
...     print(ky, grp)
...
False <itertools._grouper object at 0x7fd3ef4c>
True <itertools._grouper object at 0x7fd3ee2c>
```

Now you want to try to access these groups, so you store each one in a variable:

```
>>> for ky,grp in it.groupby(sorted(data,key=all), key=all):
...     if ky: trueset = grp
...     else: falseset=grp
...
>>> for item in falseset: print(item)
...
>>>
```

As you can see, `falseset` is empty. That's because the `falseset` group was created first and then the underlying iterator (`grp`) moved on, thus invalidating the value just stored in `falseset`. To save the sets for later access, you need to store them as lists, like this:

```
>>> groups = {True:[], False:[]}
>>> for ky,grp in it.groupby(sorted(data,key=all), key=all):
...     groups[ky].append(list(grp))
...
```

```
>>> groups
{False: [[[6, 7, 8, 9, 0], [0, 2, 4, 6, 8]]],
 True: [[[1, 2, 3, 4, 5], [1, 3, 5, 7, 9]]]}
>>>
```

Notice that you created a dictionary whose keys are the expected ones (True and False), and whose values are lists. You then had to append the groups, converted to lists, as you found them. This may seem complex, but if you remember to sort the input data first and copy the groups into lists as groupby() generates them, you will find that groupby() is a powerful and useful tool.

Using itertools to Analyze LendyDB Data

You've seen what itertools has to offer, so now it's time to try using it with your LendyDB data. You want to repeat the analysis that you did using the standard tools, but see how the itertools functions can be brought to bear, too. Remember, the real point of the itertools module is not so much that it gives you new features, but rather that it lets you process large volumes of data more efficiently. Given the tiny amount of data you are using in this chapter, you won't actually see any efficiency improvements, but as you scale the data volumes up, it does make a difference.

TRY IT OUT   Analyzing the LendyDB Data Using itertools

In this Try It Out, you repeat the earlier analysis of the LendyDB data using some of the itertools functions. To achieve this, follow these steps:

1. Change into the folder where you stored the lendydata.py file.

2. Start the Python interpreter and import the data file using the following command:

   ```
   >>> from lendydata import *
   ```

3. Import the itertools module:

   ```
   >>> from itertools import *
   ```

4. To answer the question, "What is the total cost of all items?" type this:

   ```
   >>> def cost(item):
   ...     return int(item[4][1:])
   ...
   >>> for n in islice(accumulate(cost(item) for item in items[1:]),
   ...              len(items)-2,None):
   ...     print(n)
   ...
   1100
   ```

5. To answer the question, "What is the average cost of an item?" type this:

   ```
   >>> n/len(items)-1
   183.33333333334
   >>>
   ```

6. To answer the question, "Who contributed the most items?" type this:

   ```
   >>> def owner(item): return item[3]
   ...
   ```

```
>>> owners = {}
>>> for ky,grp in groupby(sorted(items[1:], key=owner), key=owner):
...       owners[ky] = len(list(grp))
...
>>> for member in members[1:]:
...     print(member[1],' : ', owners[member[0]])
...
Fred  :  2
Mike  :  1
Joe   :  1
Rob   :  1
Anne  :  1
```

7. To answer the question, "Which items are currently on loan?" type this:

```
>>> def returned(loan): return not (loan[-1] == 'None')
...
>>> [items[int(loan[1])] for loan in filterfalse(returned,loans)]
[['5', 'Scarifier', 'Tool', '5', '$200', 'Average', '2013-09-14']]
```

How It Works

As in the previous Try It Out you created small helper functions to improve the readability of the code. To answer the first question you used the accumulate() function to produce a running count of the costs, then used islice() to extract only the last item by specifying a start index of len(items)-2 and a stop index of None. (You had to subtract 2 to account for the headers line at the start of items.) Because the result, n, was still in scope, you could calculate the average by simply dividing n by the number of items.

The question of who contributed most is answered quite differently from the previous Try It Out because you used groupby() to gather the related items. In this case you are interested only in the size of the group, not the details, so you used len() to calculate the size of the group. You then iterated over the members, in conventional style, to print the names and counts.

You answered the final question by inverting the logic of the helper function, returned(), to return whether an item has been returned. By using that in the filterfalse() function, you could find those items that had not been returned and, therefore, were still out on loan.

In this section you have seen how a mix of the conventional Python data structures, functions, and operators, combined with the functional techniques of the itertools module, enable you to perform complex analysis of quite large data sets. However, there comes a point when the volume and complexity of the data call for another approach, and that means introducing a new technology: relational databases powered by the *Structured Query Language* (SQL).

MANAGING DATA USING SQL

In this section you are introduced to some of the concepts behind SQL and relational databases. You find out how to use SQL to create data tables and populate them with data, and how to manipulate the data contained within those tables. You go on to link tables to capture the relationships between data and finally apply all of these techniques to your lending library data.

Relational Database Concepts

The basic principle of a relational database is very simple. It's simply a set of two-dimensional *tables*. Columns are known as *fields* and rows as *records*. Field values can refer to other records, either in the same table, or in another table—that's the "relational" part.

A table holding data about employees might look like Table 3-3.

TABLE 3-3: Employee Data

EMPID	NAME	HIREDATE	GRADE	MANAGERID
1020304	John Brown	20030623	Foreman	1020311
1020305	Fred Smith	20040302	Laborer	1020304
1020307	Anne Jones	19991125	Laborer	1020304

Notice a couple of conventions demonstrated by this data:

➤ You have an identifier (ID) field to uniquely identify each row; this ID is known as the *primary key*. It is possible to have other keys too, but conventionally, there is nearly always an ID field to uniquely identify a record. This helps should an employee decide to change her name, for example.

➤ You can link one row to another by having a field that holds the primary key value for another row. Thus an employee's manager is identified by the ManagerID field, which is simply a reference to another EmpID entry in the same table. Looking at your data, you see that both Fred and Anne are managed by John who is, in turn, managed by someone else, whose details are not visible in this section of the table.

> ### RELATIONSHIP CARDINALITY
>
> Relationships within a database link two or more entities together. The number of each entity involved in the relationship is known as its *cardinality*. The relationships can be one-to-one, where one record links to exactly one other record. They can also be one-to-many, such as the employee-to-manager relationship in the example.
>
> A relationship can also be many-to-many. This relationship is best explained by an example. Suppose you introduced a new table of tasks. Each task could have many employees assigned to it. At the same time, each employee could have several tasks. There is, therefore, a many-to-many relationship between employees and tasks.
>
> Much of the work in any database application is focused on maintaining the many-to-many relationships within the database. Several forms of graphical notation (known as *entity-relationship diagrams*) are used to describe database structures. Most of these notations have a strong emphasis on showing the cardinality of each relationship.

You are not restricted to linking data within a single table. You can create another table for `Salary`. A salary can be related to `Grade`, and so you get a second table like Table 3-4.

TABLE 3-4: Salary Data

SALARYID	GRADE	AMOUNT
000010	Foreman	60000
000011	Laborer	35000

To determine employee John Brown's salary, you would first look up John's grade in the main employee data table. You would then consult the `Salary` table to learn what an employee of that grade is paid. Thus you can see that John, a foreman, is paid $60,000.

Relational databases take their name from this ability to link table rows together in *relationships*. Other database types include *network* databases, *hierarchical* databases, and *flat-file* databases (which includes the DBM databases you looked at earlier in the chapter). For large volumes of data, relational databases are by far the most common.

You can do much more sophisticated queries, too, and you look at how to do this in the next few sections. But before you can query anything, you need to create a database and insert some data.

Structured Query Language

The Structured Query Language, or SQL (pronounced either as Sequel or as the letters S-Q-L), is the standard software tool for manipulating relational databases. In SQL an expression is often referred to as a *query*, regardless of whether it actually returns any data.

SQL is comprised of two parts. The first is the *data definition language* (DDL). This is the set of commands used to create and alter the shape of the database itself—its structure. DDL tends to be quite specific to each database, with each vendor's DLL having a slightly different syntax.

The other part of SQL is the *data manipulation language* (DML). DML, used to manipulate database content rather than structure, is much more highly standardized between databases. You spend the majority of your time using DML rather than DDL.

> **NOTE** In this book you use the SQLite database system, which has three big advantages. First, it has an API module provided as part of Python's standard library. Second, it is a simple dialect of SQL to learn. Third, and by no means least, SQLite works from a single data file and code library so you don't need to set up a database server or worry about any of the database administration duties normally associated with maintaining relational databases.

You only look briefly at DDL, just enough to create (with the CREATE command) and destroy (with the DROP command) your database tables so that you can move on to filling them with data, retrieving that data in interesting ways, and even modifying it, using the DML commands (INSERT, SELECT, UPDATE, and DELETE).

> **NOTE** *To use the SQL interactive prompt you need to download the SQLite interpreter because it does not come with Python. You can find it on the SQLite website at* `http://www.sqlite.org/download.html`. *The versions may not match exactly, but the database format is sufficiently stable that the latest interpreter can generally be used with the Python* `sqlite3` *module without difficulty, although the versions might not match exactly. You only need to download the binary for your OS labeled "shell"; the libraries are already installed with Python. (Linux users can usually find SQLite in the package manager, and this is the easiest way to install it, if available.)*
>
> *You can find the official guide to the SQLite interpreter at* `http://sqlite.org/cli.html`.

Creating Tables

To create a table in SQL you use the CREATE command. It is quite easy to use and takes the following form:

```
CREATE TABLE tablename (fieldName, fieldName,....);
```

> **NOTE** *SQL statements in the interpreter must be terminated with a semicolon. This is because SQL statements can span multiple lines, so the interpreter needs to be told when you are done. SQL executed by Python code is passed as a single, complete string, so a closing semicolon is not necessary.*

SQL is not case-sensitive and, unlike Python, does not care about whitespace or indentation levels. An informal style convention is used, but it is not rigidly adhered to, and SQL itself cares not a jot!

Try creating your Employee and Salary tables in SQLite. The first thing to do is start the interpreter, which you do simply by invoking sqlite3 with a single command-line argument, the database filename. If that database file exists, the interpreter will open it, otherwise it will create a new database file by that name. (If you omit the database filename entirely, the interpreter will still process your commands, but your data will exist only in RAM, and will disappear irretrievably when you exit the interpreter.)

Thus, to create an employee database you execute the SQLite interpreter like this:

```
$ sqlite3 employee.db
SQLite version 3.8.2 2013-12-06 14:53:30
Enter ".help" for instructions
Enter SQL statements terminated with a ";"
sqlite>
```

The interpreter creates an empty database called employee.db and leaves you at the sqlite> prompt, ready to type SQL commands. You are now ready to create some tables:

```
sqlite> create table Employee
   ...> (EmpID,Name,HireDate,Grade,ManagerID);
```

```
sqlite> create table Salary
   ...> (SalaryID, Grade,Amount);
sqlite> .tables
Employee    Salary
sqlite>
```

Note that you moved the list of fields into a separate line, making it easier to see them. The fields are listed by name but have no other defining information such as data type. This is a peculiarity of SQLite; most databases require you to specify the type along with the name. It is possible to specify types in SQLite too, but it is not essential (you look at this in more detail later in the chapter).

Also note that you tested that the create statements had worked by using the .tables command to list all the tables in the database. The SQLite interpreter supports several of these dot commands that you use to find out about your database. .help provides a list of the commands along with a brief description of their functions.

You can do lots of other things when you create a table. As well as declaring the types of data in each column, you can also specify constraints on the values. Constraints are rules that the database enforces to help ensure the data remains consistent. For example, NOT NULL means the value is mandatory and must be filled in, and UNIQUE means that no other record can have the same value in that field. Usually you specify the primary key field to be NOT NULL and UNIQUE. You can also specify which field is the PRIMARY KEY. You look more closely at these more advanced creation options later in the chapter.

> **NOTE** *SQLite provides a modest set of constraints that you can apply. Some commercial databases provide very rich and powerful constraint options, and it is tempting to use constraints to implement much of the business logic around the data. This is usually a mistake because it forces you to insert or modify your data in a particular order, which can become increasingly difficult to figure out. It is best to keep constraints for controlling data integrity and build the application logic into the program code.*

For now you leave the basic table definition as it is and move on to the more interesting topic of actually creating some data.

Inserting Data

The first thing to do after creating the tables is to fill them with data. You do this using the SQL INSERT statement. The structure is very simple:

```
INSERT INTO Tablename ( column1, column2... ) VALUES ( value1, value2... );
```

An alternate form of INSERT uses a query to select data from elsewhere in the database, but that's too advanced at this stage. You can read about it in the SQLite manual, which you can find at: http://sqlite.org/lang.html.

To insert some rows into your `Employee` table, do the following:

```
sqlite> insert into Employee (EmpID, Name, HireDate, Grade, ManagerID)
   ...> values ('1020304','John Brown','20030623','Foreman','1020311');
sqlite> insert into Employee (EmpID, Name, HireDate, Grade, ManagerID)
   ...> values ('1020305','Fred Smith','20040302','Laborer','1020304');
sqlite> insert into Employee (EmpID, Name, HireDate, Grade, ManagerID)
   ...> values ('1020307','Anne Jones','19991125','Laborer','1020304');
```

And for the `Salary` table:

```
sqlite> insert into Salary (SalaryID, Grade,Amount)
   ...> values('000010','Foreman',60000);
sqlite> insert into Salary (SalaryID, Grade,Amount)
   ...> values('000011','Laborer',35000);
```

And that's it. You have created two tables and populated them with data corresponding to the values described in the introduction. Notice that you used actual numbers for the salary amount, not just string representations. SQLite tries to determine the correct data type based on the INSERT input values we provide. Because it makes the most sense to have SQLite maintain salary data as a numeric type, it behooves you to inform SQLite of that preference in your INSERT statements by specifying salary data in numeric—not string—format.

Now you are ready to start experimenting with the data. This is where the fun starts!

Reading Data

You read data from a database using SQL's SELECT command. SELECT is the very heart of SQL and has the most complex structure of all the SQL commands. You start with the most basic form and add additional features as you go. The most basic SELECT statement looks like this:

```
SELECT column1, column2... FROM table1,table2...;
```

> **NOTE** You can use the special wildcard character (*) instead of a list of field names to return all of the fields. You should only use this when working at the interactive prompt. If you were to use it in application code and someone later added an extra column to the database, your application would break. By specifying the exact fields to be returned, your code becomes much more resilient to changes in the database.

To select the names of all employees in your database, you use:

```
sqlite> SELECT Name from Employee;
John Brown
Fred Smith
Anne Jones
```

You are rewarded with a list of all of the names in the `Employee` table. In this case that's only three, but if you have a big database that's probably going to be more information than you want. To restrict the output, you need to be able to limit your search somewhat. SQL enables you to do this by adding a WHERE clause to your SELECT statement, like this:

```
SELECT col1,col2... FROM table1,table2... WHERE condition;
```

The condition is an arbitrarily complex boolean expression that can even include nested SELECT statements within it.

Now, add a WHERE clause to refine your search of names. This time you only look for names of employees who are laborers:

```
sqlite> SELECT Name
   ...> FROM Employee
   ...> WHERE Employee.Grade = 'Laborer';
Fred Smith
Anne Jones
```

You only get two names back, not three (because John Brown is not a laborer). You can extend the WHERE condition using boolean operators such as AND, OR, NOT, and so on. Note that = in a WHERE condition performs a case-sensitive test. When using the = test, the case of the string is important; testing for 'laborer' would not have worked!

SQLite has some functions that can be used to manipulate strings, but it also has a comparison operator called LIKE that uses % as a wildcard character for more flexible searching. The example just shown, written using LIKE, looks like this:

```
sqlite> SELECT Name FROM Employee
   ...> WHERE lower(employee.grade) LIKE 'lab%';
Fred Smith
Anne Jones
```

After converting grade to lowercase, you then tested it for an initial substring of 'lab'. When used in conjunction with lower(), upper(), and SQLite's other string-manipulation functions, LIKE can greatly increase the scope of your text-based searches. The SQLite documentation has a full list of the functions available.

> **NOTE** You can test out the SQLite functions in the interpreter using the following technique. In a SELECT statement the return value can be any expression and the table clause can be empty. By combining these two features you can write code like SELECT lower('FREDDY'); and SQLite returns the value 'freddy'. This is very useful when you want to quickly experiment with a function to see what it does.

Notice too that in the WHERE clause you used dot notation (employee.grade) to signify the Grade field. In this case it was not really needed because you were only working with a single table (Employee, as specified in the FROM clause) but, where multiple tables are specified, you need to make clear which table the field belongs to. As an example, change your query to find the names of all employees paid more than $50,000. To do that, you need to consider data in both tables:

```
sqlite> SELECT Name, Amount
   ...> FROM Salary, Employee
   ...> WHERE Employee.Grade = Salary.Grade
   ...> AND Salary.Amount > 50000;
John Brown|60000
```

As expected, you only get one name back—that of the foreman. But notice that you also got back the salary, because you added Amount to the list of columns selected. Also note that you have two parts to your WHERE clause, combined using an AND boolean operator. The first part links the two tables by ensuring that the common fields are equal; this is known as a *join* in SQL. A couple other features of this query are worth noting.

Because the fields that you are selecting exist in two separate tables, you have to specify both of the tables from which the result comes. The order of the field names is the order in which you get the data back, but the order of the tables doesn't matter so long as the specified fields appear in those tables.

You specified two unique field names so SQLite can figure out which table to take them from. If you had also wanted to display the Grade, which appears in both tables, you would have had to use dot notation to specify which table's Grade you wanted, like this:

```
sqlite> SELECT Employee.Grade, Name, Amount
   ...> FROM Employee, Salary
   etc/...
```

Note in particular that SQL would require such qualification even though the choice of table here for the Grade field really does not matter, because the WHERE condition *guarantees* that for any result row displayed the grades of the two tables will have the identical value in any case.

The final feature of SELECT discussed here (although you can read about several more in the SQL documentation for SELECT) is the capability to sort the output. Databases generally hold data either in the order that makes it easiest to find things, or in the order in which they are inserted; in either case that's not usually the order you want things displayed! To deal with that you can use the ORDER BY clause of the SELECT statement. It looks like this:

```
SELECT columns FROM tables WHERE expression ORDER BY columns;
```

Notice that the final ORDER BY clause can take multiple columns; this enables you to have primary, secondary, tertiary, and so on sort orders.

You can use this to get a list of names of employees sorted by HireDate:

```
sqlite> SELECT Name
   ...> FROM Employee
   ...> ORDER BY HireDate;
Anne Jones
John Brown
Fred Smith
```

(It is interesting to note that HireDate was perfectly acceptable as an ORDER BY column, even though HireDate is not a column SELECTed for display.)

And that's really all there is to it; you can't get much easier than that! The only thing worthy of mention is that you didn't use a WHERE clause. If you had used one, it would have had to come before the ORDER BY clause. Thus, although SQL doesn't require that all components of a SELECT statement be present, it does require that those elements that are present will appear in a prescribed order.

That's enough about reading data; you now look at how to modify your data in place.

Modifying Data

You can change the data in your database in two ways. You can alter the contents of one or more records, or, more drastically, you can delete a record or even the contents of a whole table. Changing the content of an existing record is the more common case, and you do that using SQL's UPDATE command.

The basic format is:

```
UPDATE table SET column = value WHERE condition;
```

You can try it out on the Employee database by changing the salary of a foreman to $70,000:

```
sqlite> UPDATE Salary
   ...> SET Amount = 70000
   ...> WHERE Grade = 'Foreman';
```

Be careful to get the WHERE clause right. If you don't specify one, every row in the table is modified, and that's not usually a good idea. Similarly, if the WHERE clause is not specific enough, you end up changing more rows than you want. One way to check you have it right is to do a SELECT using the same WHERE clause and check that only the rows you want to change are found. If all is well, you can repeat the WHERE clause from the SELECT in your UPDATE statement.

A more drastic change you might need to make to your database table, rather than merely modifying certain fields of a given row or rows, is to entirely delete one or more rows from the table. You would do this using SQL's DELETE FROM command, whose basic form looks like this:

```
DELETE FROM Table WHERE condition
```

So, if you want to delete Anne Jones from your Employee table you can do it like this:

```
sqlite> DELETE FROM Employee
   ...> WHERE Name = 'Anne Jones';
```

If more than one row matches your WHERE condition, all of the matching rows are deleted. SQL always operates on all the rows that match the specified WHERE condition. In this respect SQL is quite different from, say, using a regular expression in a Python program to perform substring substitution on a string (where the default behavior is to modify *only the first* occurrence found, unless you specifically request otherwise).

An even more drastic change you might want to make to your database is to delete not only all of a table's rows, but to delete the entire table itself. This is done using SQL's DROP command.

Obviously, destructive commands like DELETE and DROP must be used with extreme caution.

Linking Data Across Tables

The possibility of linking data between tables was mentioned earlier, in the section on SELECT. However, this is such a fundamental part of relational database theory that you consider it in more depth here. The links between tables represent the *relationships* between data *entities* that give a *relational database* such as SQLite its name. The database maintains not only the raw data about the entities, but also information about the relationships.

The information about the relationships is stored in the form of database constraints, applied when you define the database structure using the CREATE statement. Before you see how to use constraints to model relationships, you first need to look deeper into the kinds of constraints available in SQLite.

Digging Deeper into Data Constraints

You normally express the constraints on a field-by-field basis within the CREATE statement. This means you can expand the basic CREATE definition from,

```
CREATE Tablename (Column, Column,...);
```

to:

```
CREATE Tablename (
ColumnName Type Constraints,
ColumnName Type Constraints,
...);
```

The most common constraints are:

➤ NOT NULL

➤ PRIMARY KEY [AUTOINCREMENT]

➤ UNIQUE

➤ DEFAULT value

NOT NULL is fairly self-explanatory; it indicates that the value must exist and not be NULL. A NULL value is simply one that has no specified value, rather like None in Python. If no suitable value is provided for a field governed by a NOT NULL constraint, data insertion will utterly fail—quite possibly not only for that particular field, but also for the entire row. (Or, far worse, violation of the constraint could cause a very large database update transaction—possibly involving hundreds or thousands of rows—to fail in its entirety.)

PRIMARY KEY tells SQLite to use this column as the main key for lookups (in practice this means it is optimized for faster searches). The optional AUTOINCREMENT keyword means that an INTEGER type value is automatically assigned on each INSERT and the value automatically incremented by one. This saves a lot of work for the programmer in maintaining separate counts. Note that the AUTOINCREMENT "keyword" is not normally used; rather, it is implied from a type/constraint combination of INTEGER PRIMARY KEY. This not-so-obvious quirk of the SQLite documentation trips up enough people for it to appear at the top of the SQLite Frequently Asked Questions page, found here: http://sqlite.org/faq.html.

The UNIQUE constraint means that the value of the field must be unique within the specified column. If you try to insert a duplicate value into a column that has a UNIQUE constraint, an error results and the row is not inserted. UNIQUE is often used for non-INTEGER type PRIMARY KEY columns.

DEFAULT is always accompanied by a value. The value is what SQLite inserts into that field if the user does not explicitly provide one.

Here is a short example showing some of these constraints, including the use of DEFAULT:

```
sqlite> CREATE table test
   ...> (Id INTEGER PRIMARY KEY,
   ...> Name NOT NULL,
   ...> Value INTEGER DEFAULT 42);
sqlite> INSERT INTO test (Name, Value) VALUES ('Alan', 24);
sqlite> INSERT INTO test (Name) VALUES ('Heather');
sqlite> INSERT INTO test (Name, Value) VALUES ('Laura', NULL);
sqlite> SELECT * FROM test;
1|Alan|24
2|Heather|42
3|Laura|
```

The first thing to notice is that although none of the INSERT statements had an Id value, there is an Id value in the SELECT output. That's because by specifying Id to be an INTEGER PRIMARY KEY, it is automatically generated by SQLite. Notice too how the entry for Heather has the default Value set. Also, note that the Value for Linda is nonexistent, or NULL. There is an important difference between NOT NULL and DEFAULT. The former does not allow NULL values, either by default or explicitly. The DEFAULT constraint prevents unspecified NULLs, but does not prevent deliberate creation of NULL values.

You can also apply constraints to the table itself, such as how to handle data conflicts like duplicates in a UNIQUE column. For example, a table constraint could specify that where a conflict occurs the entire database query will be cancelled, or it could specify that only the changes to the conflicting row be cancelled. Table constraints are not discussed further in this chapter; you should consult the documentation for details.

Revisiting SQLite Field Types

The other kind of constraint that you can apply, as already mentioned, is to specify the column type. This is very like the concept of data types in a programming language. The valid types in SQLite are as follows:

➤ TEXT

➤ INTEGER

➤ REAL

➤ NUMERIC

➤ BLOB

➤ NULL

These types should be self-evident, with the possible exceptions of NUMERIC, which enables the storage of floating-point numbers as well as integers, and BLOB, which stands for Binary Large Object, typically used for media data such as images. NULL is not really a type, but simply suggests that no explicit type has been specified. Most databases come with a much wider set of types including, crucially, a DATE type. As you are about to see, however, SQLite has a somewhat unconventional approach to types that renders such niceties less relevant.

> **NOTE** *The SQL standard, having been defined by committee, including many database vendors with existing products, is very broad in its list of types. SQLite tries to accommodate this by aliasing several different names to the same underlying type. Thus, the native* TEXT *type can also be expressed as a* STRING *or as a* VARCHAR *because these are terms used by other vendors. The idea is that porting SQL code from another database to SQLite should be as painless as possible.*

Most databases strictly apply the types specified. However, SQLite employs a more dynamic scheme, where the type specified is more like a hint and any type of data can be stored in the table. When data of a different type is loaded into a field, SQLite uses the declared type to try to convert the data, but if it cannot be converted, it is stored in its original form. Thus, if a field is declared as INTEGER, but the TEXT value '123' is passed in, SQLite converts the string '123' to the number 123. However, if the TEXT value 'Freddy' is passed in, the conversion fails, so SQLite simply stores the string 'Freddy' in the field! This can cause some strange behavior if you are not aware of this foible. Most databases treat the type declaration as a strict constraint and fail if an illegal value is passed.

Modeling Relationships with Constraints

Having seen the various kinds of constraints available and how you can use them in your database, it's time to return to the topic of modeling relationships. So how do constraints help you to model data and, in particular, relationships? Look again at your simple two-table database, as summarized in Table 3-5 and Table 3-6.

Looking at the Employee table first you see that the EmpID value should be of INTEGER type and have a PRIMARY KEY constraint; the other columns, with the possible exception of the ManagerID, should be NOT NULL. ManagerID should also be of type INTEGER.

TABLE 3-5: Employee Database Table

EMPID	NAME	HIREDATE	GRADE	MANAGERID
1020304	John Brown	20030623	Foreman	1020311
1020305	Fred Smith	20040302	Laborer	1020304
1020307	Anne Jones	19991125	Laborer	1020304

TABLE 3-6: Salary Database Table

SALARYID	GRADE	AMOUNT
000010	Foreman	60000
000011	Laborer	35000

For the `Salary` table you see that, once more, the `SalaryID` should be an `INTEGER` with `PRIMARY KEY`. The `Amount` column should also be an `INTEGER`, and you should apply a `DEFAULT` value of, say, `20000`. Finally, the `Grade` column should be constrained as `UNIQUE` because you don't want more than one salary per grade! (Actually, this is a bad idea because normally salary varies with things like length of service as well as grade, but you ignore such niceties for now. In fact, in the real world, you should probably call this a `Grade` table and not `Salary`.)

The modified SQL looks like this:

```
sqlite> CREATE TABLE Employee (
   ...> EmpID INTEGER PRIMARY KEY,
   ...> Name NOT NULL,
   ...> HireDate NOT NULL,
   ...> Grade NOT NULL,
   ...> ManagerID INTEGER
   ...> );

sqlite> CREATE TABLE Salary (
   ...> SalaryID INTEGER PRIMARY KEY,
   ...> Grade UNIQUE,
   ...> Amount INTEGER DEFAULT 20000
   ...> );
```

You can try out these constraints by attempting to enter data that breaks them and see what happens. Hopefully you see an error message!

One thing to point out here is that the `INSERT` statements you used previously are no longer adequate. You previously inserted your own values for the ID fields, but these are now auto-generated so you can (and should) omit them from the inserted data. But this gives rise to a new difficulty. How can you populate the `ManagerID` field if you don't know the `EmpID` of the manager? The answer is you can use a *nested select* statement. In this example, you do this in two stages using `NULL` fields initially and then using an `UPDATE` statement after creating all the rows.

To avoid a lot of repeat typing you can put all of the commands in a couple of files, called `employee.sql` for the table creation commands and `load_employee.sql` for the `INSERT` statements. This is the same idea as creating a Python script file ending in .py to save typing everything at the >>> prompt.

The `employee.sql` file looks like this (and is in the SQL folder of the `Chapter3.zip` download):

```
DROP TABLE Employee;
CREATE TABLE Employee (
EmpID INTEGER PRIMARY KEY,
```

```
Name NOT NULL,
HireDate NOT NULL,
Grade NOT NULL,
ManagerID INTEGER
);

DROP TABLE Salary;
CREATE TABLE Salary (
SalaryID INTEGER PRIMARY KEY,
Grade UNIQUE,
Amount INTEGER DEFAULT 10000
);
```

Notice that you drop the tables before creating them. The DROP TABLE command, as mentioned earlier, deletes the table and any data within it. This ensures the database is in a completely clean state before you start creating your new table. (You will get some errors reported the first time you run this script because no tables exist to DROP, but you can ignore them. Subsequent executions should be error free.)

The load _ employee.sql script looks like this (and is also available in the SQL folder of the .zip file):

```
INSERT INTO Employee (Name, HireDate, Grade, ManagerID)
        VALUES ('John Brown','20030623','Foreman', NULL);
INSERT INTO Employee (Name, HireDate, Grade, ManagerID)
        VALUES ('Fred Smith','20040302','Labourer',NULL);
INSERT INTO Employee (Name, HireDate, Grade, ManagerID)
        VALUES ('Anne Jones','19991125','Labourer',NULL);

UPDATE Employee
SET ManagerID = (SELECT EmpID
                    From Employee
                    WHERE Name = 'John Brown')
WHERE Name IN ('Fred Smith','Anne Jones');

INSERT INTO Salary (Grade, Amount)
        VALUES('Foreman','60000');
INSERT INTO Salary (Grade, Amount)
        VALUES('Labourer','35000');
```

Notice the use of the nested SELECT statement inside the UPDATE command, and also the fact that you used a single UPDATE to modify both employee rows at the same time by using The SQL IN operator that works like the Python in keyword for testing membership of a collection. By extending the set of names being tested, you can easily add more employees with the same manager.

This is typical of the problems you can have when populating a database when constraints are being used. You need to plan the order of the statements carefully to ensure that, for every row that contains a reference to another table, you have already provided the data for it to reference! It's a bit like starting at the leaves of a tree and working back to the trunk. Always create, or insert, the data with no references first, then the data that references that data, and so on. If you are adding data after the initial creation, you need to use queries to check that the data you need already exists, and add it if it doesn't. At this point a scripting language like Python becomes invaluable!

Finally, you run these from the SQLite prompt like this:

```
sqlite> .read employee.sql
sqlite> .read load_employee.sql
```

Make sure you have the path issues sorted out, though: Either start sqlite3 from wherever the .sql scripts are stored (as you did earlier) or provide the full path to the script.

Now try a query to check that everything is as it should be:

```
sqlite> SELECT Name
   ...> FROM Employee
   ...> WHERE Grade IN
   ...> (SELECT Grade FROM Salary WHERE amount >50000)
   ...> ;
John Brown
```

That seems to work; John Brown is the only employee earning more than $50,000. Notice that you used an IN condition combined with another embedded SELECT statement. This is a variation on a similar query that you performed previously using a cross table join. Both techniques work, but usually the join approach will be faster.

Although this is an improvement over the original unconstrained definition and it ensures that the ManagerID is an integer, it does not ensure that the integer is a valid EmpID key. You need the embedded SELECT statement for that. However, SQLite offers one more constraint that helps you ensure the data is consistent, and that is the REFERENCES constraint. This tells SQLite that a given field references another specified field somewhere in the database. You can apply the REFERENCES constraint to the ManagerID field by modifying the CREATE statement like this:

```
CREATE TABLE Employee (
...
ManagerID INTEGER REFERENCES Employee(EmpID)
);
```

You see that the REFERENCES constraint specifies the table and the key field within it. At the time of writing, SQLite does not actually enforce this constraint by default (although it is worth including in your code as documentation of your intentions). However, you can turn checking on by using a *pragma* statement. A pragma is a special command that is used to control the way the interpreter works. It looks like this:

```
PRAGMA Foreign_Keys=True;
```

> **NOTE** The term foreign key *signifies that it is a key from a different row in the database. This could be a key from the same table, as in the case of the* ManagerID, *or it could be a reference to another table entirely. In either case the key being referenced comes from a different row and is therefore described as being "foreign."*

If you now modify the `employee.sql` file to add the pragma and modify the create statement, it should look like this:

```
PRAGMA Foreign_Keys=True;

DROP TABLE Employee;
CREATE TABLE Employee (
EmpID INTEGER PRIMARY KEY,
Name NOT NULL,
HireDate NOT NULL,
Grade NOT NULL,
ManagerID INTEGER REFERENCES Employee(EmpID)
);

DROP TABLE Salary;
CREATE TABLE Salary (
SalaryID INTEGER PRIMARY KEY,
Grade UNIQUE,
Amount INTEGER DEFAULT 10000
);
```

After running the script and reloading the data with the `load_employee.sql` script, you can check that it works by trying to insert a new employee with a `ManagerID` not already in the table. Like this:

```
sqlite> .read employee.sql
sqlite> .read load_employee.sql
sqlite> insert into Employee (Name,HireDate,Grade,ManagerID)
   ...> values('Fred', '20140602','Laborer',999);
Error: FOREIGN KEY constraint failed
sqlite>
```

This is a big advantage in keeping your data consistent. It is now impossible for a non-valid worker-to-manager relationship to be created (although you can still use NULL values that indicate that no manager relationship exists).

Many-to-Many Relationships

One scenario you haven't covered is where two tables are linked in a *many-to-many* relationship. That is, a row in one table can be linked to several rows in a second table and a row in the second table can *at the same time* be linked to many rows in the first table.

Consider an example. Imagine creating a database to support a book publishing company. It needs lists of authors and lists of books. Each author may write one or more books. Each book may have one or more authors. How do you represent that in a database? The solution is to represent the relationship between books and authors as a table in its own right. Such a table is often called an *intersection table* or a *mapping table*. Each row of this table represents a book/author relationship. Now each book has potentially many book/author relationships, but each relationship only has one book and one author, so you have converted a many-to-many relationship into two one-to-many relationships. And you already know how to build one-to-many relationships using IDs. It looks like this (you can find the code in the file `books.sql` in the SQL folder of the `.zip` file):

```
PRAGMA Foreign_Keys=True;

drop table author;
```

```
create table author (
ID Integer PRIMARY KEY,
Name Text NOT NULL
);

drop table book;
create table book (
ID Integer PRIMARY KEY,
Title Text NOT NULL
);

drop table book_author;
create table book_author (
bookID Integer NOT NULL REFERENCES book(ID),
authorID Integer NOT NULL REFERENCES author(ID)
);

insert into author (Name) values ('Jane Austin');
insert into author (Name) values ('Grady Booch');
insert into author (Name) values ('Ivar Jacobson');
insert into author (Name) values ('James Rumbaugh');

insert into book (Title) values('Pride & Prejudice');
insert into book (Title) values('Emma');
insert into book (Title) values('Sense &; Sensibility');
insert into book (Title) values ('Object Oriented Design with Applications');
insert into book (Title) values ('The UML User Guide');

insert into book_author (BookID,AuthorID) values (
(select ID from book where title = 'Pride &; Prejudice'),
(select ID from author where Name = 'Jane Austin')
);

insert into book_author (BookID,AuthorID) values (
(select ID from book where title = 'Emma'),
(select ID from author where Name = 'Jane Austin')
);

insert into book_author (BookID,AuthorID) values (
(select ID from book where title = 'Sense & Sensibility'),
(select ID from author where Name = 'Jane Austin')
);

insert into book_author (BookID,AuthorID) values (
(select ID from book where title = 'Object Oriented Design with Applications'),
(select ID from author where Name = 'Grady Booch')
);

insert into book_author (BookID,AuthorID) values (
(select ID from book where title = 'The UML User Guide'),
(select ID from author where Name = 'Grady Booch')
);

insert into book_author (BookID,AuthorID) values (
(select ID from book where title = 'The UML User Guide'),
(select ID from author where Name = 'Ivar Jacobson')
);
```

```
insert into book_author (BookID,AuthorID) values (
(select ID from book where title = 'The UML User Guide'),
(select ID from author where Name = 'James Rumbaugh')
);
```

If you look at the values inserted into the tables, you see that Jane Austin has three books to her credit, while the book *The UML User Guide* has three authors.

If you load that into SQLite in a database called `books.db` (or just use the file `books.db` found in the SQL folder of the `Chapter3.` zip file), you can try some queries to see how it works:

```
$ sqlite3 books.db
SQLite version 3.8.2 2013-12-06 14:53:30
Enter ".help" for instructions
Enter SQL statements terminated with a ";"
sqlite> .read books.sql
Error: near line 3: no such table: author
Error: near line 9: no such table: book
Error: near line 15: no such table: book_author

sqlite> .tables
author        book          book_author
```

Notice the errors resulting from the DROP statements. You always get those the first time you run the script because the tables don't exist yet. Now you can find out which Jane Austin books are published:

```
sqlite> SELECT title FROM book, book_author
   ...> WHERE book_author.bookID = book.ID
   ...> AND book_author.authorID = (
   ...> SELECT ID from Author
   ...> WHERE name='Jane Austin');
Pride & Prejudice
Emma
Sense & Sensibility
```

Things are getting a bit more complex, but if you sit and work through it you'll get the idea soon enough. Notice you need to include both of the referenced tables—book and book _ author—in the table list after the SELECT. (The third table, author, is not listed there because it is listed against its own embedded SELECT statement.) Now try it the other way around—see who wrote *The UML User Guide*:

```
sqlite> SELECT name FROM author, book_author
   ...> WHERE book_author.authorID = author.ID
   ...> AND book_author.bookID = (
   ...> SELECT ID FROM book
   ...> WHERE title='The UML User Guide');
Grady Booch
Ivar Jacobson
James Rumbaugh
```

If you look closely you see that the structure of the two queries is identical—you just swapped around the table and field names a little.

That's enough for that example; you now return to your lending library. You now see how you convert it from file-based storage to a full SQL database. You then go on to build an accompanying Python module that enables application writers to ignore the SQL and just call Python functions.

MIGRATING LENDYDB TO AN SQL DATABASE

In this section you re-create the LendyDB database using a combination of SQL and Python code. Before getting into the nitty-gritty, you need to see how Python and SQL come together.

Accessing SQL from Python

SQLite provides an *application programming interface* or *API* consisting of a number of standard functions that allow programmers to perform all the same operations that you have been doing without using the interactive SQL prompt. The SQLite API is written in C, but wrappers have been provided for other languages, including Python. Python has similar interfaces to many other databases, and they all provide a standard set of functions and provide very similar functionality. This interface is called the Python DBAPI, and its existence makes porting data between databases much easier than if each database had its own interface.

The DBAPI defines a couple of useful conceptual objects that form the core of the interface. These are *connections* and *cursors*.

Using SQL Connections

A connection is the conduit between your application code and the database's SQL engine. The name comes from the client-server architecture used by most SQL databases whereby the client must connect to the server over a network. For SQLite the connection is actually to the data file via the SQLite library. The arguments passed to create the connection are of necessity database-specific. For example, many databases require a user ID and password, and some require IP addresses and ports, whereas SQLite just requires a filename. It looks like this:

```
>>> import sqlite3
>>> db = sqlite3.connect('D:/PythonCode/Chapter3/SQL/lendy.db')
```

Once a connection has been established, you can go on to create cursors, which are the mechanism used to issue SQL commands and receive their output. In principle you can have more than one cursor per connection, but in practice that is rarely needed.

Using a Cursor

When accessing a database from within a program, one important consideration is how to access the many rows of data potentially returned by a SELECT statement without running out of memory. The answer is to use what is known in SQL as a *cursor*. A cursor is a Python iterator so it can be accessed iteratively one row at a time. Thus, by selecting data into a cursor and using the cursor methods to extract the results either as a list (for smaller volumes of data), or row by row, you can process large collections of data. You now try that out.

In this Try It Out, you use the `sqlite3` module to create a table, populate it with data, and perform some queries with SELECT. You then delete the data, drop the tables, and exit. To achieve that complete the following steps:

1. Start the Python interpreter and type the following code:

```
>>> import sqlite3
>>> db = sqlite3.connect(':memory:')
>>> cur = db.cursor()
>>> cur.execute("create table test(id,name)")
<sqlite3.Cursor object at 0x7fd28ca0>
>>> cur.execute(
... "insert into test (id,name) values (1,'Alan')")
<sqlite3.Cursor object at 0x7fd28ca0>
>>> cur.execute(
... "insert into test (id,name) values (2,'Laura')")
<sqlite3.Cursor object at 0x7fd28ca0>
>>> cur.execute(
... "insert into test (id,name) values (3,'Jennifer')")
<sqlite3.Cursor object at 0x7fd28ca0>
>>> cur.execute("Select * FROM test")
<sqlite3.Cursor object at 0x7fd28ca0>
>>> print(cur.fetchall())
[(1, 'Alan'), (2, 'Laura'), (3, 'Jennifer')]
```

2. As you can see, the cursor returns a list of tuples. This is very similar to what you started off with, back in the "Using Comma-Separated Values" section of Chapter 2! And you could simply use this list in your program as if you had read it from a file—using the database merely as a persistence mechanism. However, the real power of the database lies in its ability to perform sophisticated queries using SELECT. Try out a few queries using the following code:

```
>>> def findData(cursor, aString):
...     cursor.execute("select * from test where name like ?",(aString,))
...     return cur.fetchall()
...
>>> findData(cur,'A%')
[(1, 'Alan')]
>>> findData(cur,'%a%')
[(1, 'Alan'), (2, 'Laura')]
```

3. Finally, try a few data manipulation commands:

```
>>> cur.execute("delete from test")
<sqlite3.Cursor object at 0x7fd28ca0>
>>> cur.execute("drop table test")
<sqlite3.Cursor object at 0x7fd28ca0>
>>> cur.close()
>>> db.commit()
>>> db.close()
```

How It Works

You started by importing the `sqlite` module. The next step was to create a connection to the database file, which in this case was `:memory:`, indicating you wanted a temporary database held in the computer's memory. You then created a cursor object that you subsequently used for all the SQL interaction.

You created a test table and inserted three records. You then used the `Select *` idiom to extract all the data from the table. You used the `fetchall()` method of the cursor to view the output as a list of tuples. (Other options include using `fetchone()` within a loop or `fetchmany()` to return batches of results.)

The next step involved defining a Python function that used a string to locate records of interest. This demonstrates how Python functions can be created to hide the details of the SQL from the user. You use this technique later to create an API for the lending library applications.

Having shown that the function works, you deleted the records, dropped the tables, and closed the cursor. You then executed the connection `commit()` method that permanently applies any changes you made, followed by closing the database connection itself.

The use of `commit` is slightly complex, with the DBAPI sometimes calling `commit` for you, and at other times you need to do it explicitly. As a general rule, you should always call `commit` before closing the database connection. In this example it makes no real difference because the database exists only in memory and disappears whenever you close the connection. If you are using a file-based database, you need the `commit()` to ensure your changes are visible next time you open the database.

Creating the LendyDB SQL Database

The database design is not significantly different from its previous incarnations. You just have to translate it into SQL syntax and add in some constraints to improve data integrity.

The initial database setup is usually easiest to do using raw SQL commands as you did in the earlier sections. Although it is possible to do it all from Python, occasionally another tool is better suited to the task at hand.

> **NOTE** If you don't have the SQLite interpreter installed, you can still execute a SQL script using the `executescript()` method of the cursor object. This method takes an SQL script as an argument. The script can be read from a file or a standard Python string, which could be a multiline triple-quoted string. Note that you need to terminate the SQL statements with semicolons just as you did when using the `sqlite3` interpreter.

The code looks like this (and is available in the file `lendydb.sql` in the SQL folder of the `.zip` file):

```
PRAGMA Foreign_Keys=True;

drop table loan;
```

```
drop table item;
drop table member;

create table member (
ID INTEGER PRIMARY KEY,
Name TEXT NOT NULL,
Email TEXT);

create table item (
ID INTEGER PRIMARY KEY,
Name TEXT NOT NULL,
Description TEXT NOT NULL,
OwnerID INTEGER NOT NULL REFERENCES member(ID),
Price NUMERIC,
Condition TEXT,
DateRegistered TEXT);

create table loan (
ID INTEGER PRIMARY KEY,
ItemID INTEGER NOT NULL REFERENCES item(ID),
BorrowerID INTEGER NOT NULL REFERENCES member(ID),
DateBorrowed TEXT NOT NULL,
DateReturned TEXT);
```

You need to drop all the tables at the top of the script, and the order is important because otherwise the referential constraints fail, and an error results. Notice also that you used the NUMERIC type for the item price because this caters for both integer and floating-point values. It also means you don't need to worry about those pesky dollar signs that you had to strip off in the previous incarnations of the data. Apart from the various key fields, the other fields are all declared as TEXT.

Now that the database is ready, you can insert the test data.

Inserting Test Data

The database design now includes some referential constraints so you need to think about the order in which you populate the data. The member data has no references, so it can be loaded first. The item data only references members, so it comes next. Finally, the loan data references both members and items, so it must come last.

For the data insertion, you are essentially repeating the same INSERT operation over and over with different data values. This time Python is the better solution because you can write the SQL once and execute it many times using either the executemany() method of the cursor object or by calling the execute() method from within a Python for loop. It looks like this (and the code is in the file lendydata-sql.py):

```python
import sqlite3

members = [
    ['Fred', 'fred@lendylib.org'],
    ['Mike', 'mike@gmail.com'],
    ['Joe', 'joe@joesmail.com'],
    ['Rob', 'rjb@somcorp.com'],
    ['Anne', 'annie@bigbiz.com'],
```

```
    ]
    member_sql = '''insert into member (Name, Email) values (?, ?)'''

    items = [
        ['Lawnmower','Tool',    0, 150,'Excellent', '2012-01-05'],
        ['Lawnmower','Tool',    0, 370,'Fair',      '2012-04-01'],
        ['Bike',     'Vehicle', 0, 200,'Good',      '2013-03-22'],
        ['Drill',    'Tool',    0, 100,'Good',      '2013-10-28'],
        ['Scarifier','Tool',    0, 200,'Average',   '2013-09-14'],
        ['Sprinkler','Tool',    0,  80,'Good',      '2014-01-06']
    ]
    item_sql = '''
    insert into item
    (Name, Description, ownerID, Price, Condition, DateRegistered)
    values (?, ?, ?, ?, ?, date(?))'''
    set_owner_sql = '''
    update item
    set OwnerID = (SELECT ID from member where name = ?)
    where item.id = ?
    '''

    loans = [
        [1,3,'2012-01-04','2012-04-26'],
        [2,5,'2012-09-05','2013-01-05'],
        [3,4,'2013-07-03','2013-07-22'],
        [4,1,'2013-11-19','2013-11-29'],
        [5,2,'2013-12-05', None]
    ]
    loan_sql = '''
    insert into loan
    (itemID, BorrowerID, DateBorrowed, DateReturned )
    values (?, ?, date(?), date(?))'''

    db = sqlite3.connect('lendy.db')
    cur = db.cursor()

    cur.executemany(member_sql, members)
    cur.executemany(item_sql, items)
    cur.executemany(loan_sql, loans)

    owners = ('Fred','Mike','Joe','Rob','Anne','Fred')
    for item in cur.execute("select id from item").fetchall():
        itemID = item[0]
    cur.execute(set_owner_sql, (owners[itemID-1], itemID))

    cur.close()
    db.commit()
    db.close()
```

Several things are noteworthy in this script. The first point is the format of the dates. Although SQLite does not have a Date data type, it does have a number of functions that can be used to create standardized date strings and values that it then stores as text (or in some cases as floating-point numbers). The date() function used here requires the date string to be in the format shown, and an invalid date string will be stored as NULL. Using date() therefore improves data quality by ensuring only valid and consistently formatted dates get stored.

> **NOTE** *SQLite's use of date functions to handle date fields is very unusual, but it fits well with SQLite's dynamic typing mechanism.*
>
> *The other date functions include a version of the* `strftime()` *function that you met in the "Using the time Module" section of Chapter 2. The SQLite version adds some extra features.*
>
> *One point to note about SQLite's time structure is that it always uses UTC (aka GMT) because this avoids any of the complex issues surrounding time zones and daylight saving time. For display of the data in local time format, you need to use time functions within Python to convert the times returned by SQLite. A page in the SQLite documentation describes how the various date functions can be used in several common scenarios* (`http://www.sqlite.org/lang_datefunc.html`).

The item `OwnerID` field is specified as `NOT NULL`, so you filled it with a dummy value (0) that is then overwritten by the `UPDATE` code later in the script.

You could have used a `for` loop to process the `INSERT` statements, but instead used the `executemany()` method that takes the statement and a sequence (or iterator or generator) and repeatedly applies the statement until the iteration is completed.

The variable values are inserted into the query strings by using a question mark as a placeholder. This is very similar to the string formatting method that uses {} as a place marker.

> **NOTE** *You may wonder why string formatting was not used to insert the values into the SQL statements. This is because string formatting is vulnerable to a security attack known as an injection attack, whereby harmful code can be injected into the SQL statement. Using the SQLite* `execute()` *mechanism as the formatting tool eliminates this risk because it checks for rogue values.*

At this point you have created the database and populated it with some test data. The next stage is to make that data accessible to applications via an application programming interface (API).

Creating a LendyDB API

When defining an API for a database, it's normal to start off by thinking about the basic entities and providing functions to create, read, update, and delete the items. (This is often known as a CRUD interface after the initials of the operations.) The temptation is to provide these functions as a thin wrapper around the corresponding SQL commands. However, to the application programmer it is not particularly useful to just be given an ID of a member—for example, it would be much better in most cases to get the member name instead. Otherwise, the programmer must perform multiple reads of the member database to create a useful display for the user. On the other hand, there may be times when an ID is the best option because the programmer may want to get more specific details about the member. The skill in building a good API comes from being able to resolve these contradictions in a way that makes the application programmer effective while retaining full access to the data.

Although the CRUD operations are a good foundation, it is often more useful to the application programmer if some higher-level operations are also available that span entities. To do this you need to think about how your data is likely to be used in an application. What kinds of questions will the designer want to ask? If you are also the application programmer, this is relatively easy, but if you are providing the database as part of a bigger project, it gets more difficult.

For the lending library example, you focus only on the CRUD interface to items and members. The principles should be obvious, and you have the opportunity to extend the API to cover loans in Exercise 3.3 at the end of the chapter. (The code for items and members is in the lendydata.py file in the SQL folder of the .zip file.)

```
'''
Lending library database API

Provides a CRUD interface to item and member entities
and init and close functions for database control.
'''

import sqlite3 as sql

db=None
cursor = None

##### CRUD functions for items ######

def insert_item(Name, Description, OwnerID, Price, Condition):
    query = '''
    insert into item
    (Name, Description, OwnerID, Price, Condition, DateRegistered)
    values (?,?,?,?,?, date('now'))'''
    cursor.execute(query, (Name,Description,OwnerID,Price,Condition))

def get_items():
    query = '''
    select ID, Name, Description, OwnerID, Price, Condition, DateRegistered
    from item'''
    return cursor.execute(query).fetchall()

def get_item_details(id):
    query = '''
    select name, description, OwnerID, Price, Condition, DateRegistered
    from item
    where id = ?'''
    return cursor.execute(query,(id,)).fetchall()[0]

def get_item_name(id):
    return get_item_details(id)[0]

def update_item(id, Name=None, Description=None,
            OwnerID=None, Price=None, Condition=None):
    query = '''
    update item
```

```
         set Name=?, Description=?, OwnerID=?, Price=?, Condition=?
         where id=?'''
         data = get_item_details(id)
         if not Name: Name = data[0]
         if not Description: Description = data[1]
         if not OwnerID: OwnerID = data[2]
         if not Price: Price = data[3]
         if not Condition: Condition = data[4]

         cursor.execute(query, (Name,Description,OwnerID,Price,Condition,id))

    def delete_item(id):
        query = '''
        delete from item
        where id = ?'''
        cursor.execute(query,(id,))

##### CRUD functions for members ######

    def insert_member(name, email):
        query = '''
        insert into member (name, email)
        values (?, ?)'''
        cursor.execute(query, (name,email))

    def get_members():
        query = '''
        select id, name, email
        from member'''
        return cursor.execute(query).fetchall()

    def get_member_details(id):
        query = '''
        select name, email
        from member
        where id = ?'''
        return cursor.execute(query, (id,)).fetchall()[0]

    def get_member_name(id):
        return get_member_details(id)[0]

    def update_member(id, Name=None, Email=None):
        query = '''
        update member
        set name=?, email=?
        where id = ?'''
        data = get_member_details(id)
        if not Name: Name = data[0]
        if not Email: Email = data[1]
        cursor.execute(query, (Name, Email, id))

    def delete_member(id):
        query = '''
        delete from member
        where id = ?'''
        cursor.execute(query,(id,))

##### Database init and close #######
```

```
def initDB(filename = None):
    global db, cursor
    if not filename:
        filename = 'lendy.db'
    try:
        db = sql.connect(filename)
        cursor = db.cursor()
    except:
        print("Error connecting to", filename)
        cursor = None
        raise

def closeDB():
    try:
        cursor.close()
        db.commit()
        db.close()
    except:
        print("problem closing database...")
        raise

if __name__ == "__main__":
    initDB()   # use default file
    print("Members:\n", get_members())
    print("Items:\n",get_items())
```

In this module you create two global variables for the database connection and the cursor. The initDB() function initializes these variables, and the same cursor is used in each of the query functions within the module. The closeDB() function then closes these objects when you are finished using the module. This approach means that the initDB()/closeDB() functions must be called to initialize and finalize the database, which adds a little bit of complexity for the user, but it means that the individual queries are much simpler because you do not need to manage the database and cursor objects each time a query is called. Notice, too, that you set the Foreign _ Keys pragma in the initDB() function to ensure that all the transactions are checked for referential integrity.

The query functions all follow the same pattern. A SQL query string is created, using triple quotes to allow multiple line layouts, and then that string is passed to the cursor.execute() method. The retrieved values are passed back where appropriate. The cursor.execute() parameter substitution mechanism is used throughout.

The two update methods have an extra twist in that they have defaulted input parameters. This means that the user can provide only those fields that are changing. The other fields are populated based on the existing values that are retrieved by using the appropriate get-details function.

The two get-name functions are provided for the convenience of the user to easily map from the database identifiers returned in the get-details queries to meaningful names. Typically, the application programmer should use these functions before displaying the results to the end user.

The final section of the module, inside the if test, is a very basic test function just to check that the connection and cursor objects are working as expected. It does not comprehensively test all of the API functions; you will do that in the Try It Out that follows.

TRY IT OUT Using the LendyDB API

In this Try It Out, you use the `lendydata.py` module to insert, read, update, and delete entities from the `lendy.db` database created earlier. To do this, complete the following steps:

1. Switch to the folder containing your `lendy.db` database file.

2. Start the Python interpreter and type the following code:

```
>>> import lendydata as ld
>>> ld.initDB()
>>> ld.get_members()
[(1, 'Fred', 'fred@lendylib.org'), (2, 'Mike', 'mike@gmail.com'),
    (3, 'Joe', 'joe@joesmail.com'), (4, 'Rob', 'rjb@somcorp.com'),
    (5, 'Anne', 'annie@bigbiz.com')]
>>> ld.get_items()
[(1, 'Lawnmower', 'Tool', 1, 150, 'Excellent', '2012-01-05'),
    (2, 'Lawnmower', 'Tool', 2, 370, 'Fair', '2012-04-01'),
    (3, 'Bike', 'Vehicle', 3, 200, 'Good', '2013-03-22'),
    (4, 'Drill', 'Tool', 4, 100, 'Good', '2013-10-28'),
    (5, 'Scarifier', 'Tool', 5, 200, 'Average', '2013-09-14'),
    (6, 'Sprinkler', 'Tool', 1, 80, 'Good', '2014-01-06')]
```

3. Having proved you can access the data, you now add an item by typing:

```
>>> ld.insert_item('Python Projects','Book',6,30,'Excellent')
Traceback (most recent call last):
  File "<stdin>", line 1, in <module>
  File "lendydata.py", line 20, in insert_item
  cursor.execute(query,(Name,Description,OwnerID,Price,Condition))
sqlite3.IntegrityError: FOREIGN KEY constraint failed
```

4. The preceding error proves that the referential integrity check works; you first need to add a member and then add the new item. Type this:

```
>>> ld.insert_member('Alan','alan@emailaddress.com')
>>> ld.get_members()
[(1, 'Fred', 'fred@lendylib.org'), (2, 'Mike', 'mike@gmail.com'),
    (3, 'Joe', 'joe@joesmail.com'), (4, 'Rob', 'rjb@somcorp.com'),
    (5, 'Anne', 'annie@bigbiz.com'), (6, 'Alan', 'alan@emailaddress.com')]
>>> ld.insert_item('Python Projects','Book',6,30,'Excellent')
>>> ld.get_items()
[(1, 'Lawnmower', 'Tool', 1, 150, 'Excellent', '2012-01-05'),
    (2, 'Lawnmower', 'Tool', 2, 370, 'Fair', '2012-04-01'),
    (3, 'Bike', 'Vehicle', 3, 200, 'Good', '2013-03-22'),
    (4, 'Drill', 'Tool', 4, 100, 'Good', '2013-10-28'),
    (5, 'Scarifier', 'Tool', 5, 200, 'Average', '2013-09-14'),
    (6, 'Sprinkler', 'Tool', 1, 80, 'Good', '2014-01-06'),
    (7, 'Python Projects', 'Book', 6, 30, 'Excellent', '2014-06-23')]
```

5. You successfully added an item. Now modify the item and member by typing this:

```
>>> ld.update_item(7,Price=25)
>>> ld.get_item_details(7)
('Python Projects', 'Book', 6, 25, 'Excellent', '2014-06-23')
```

```
>>> ld.get_member_name(6)
'Alan'
>>> ld.update_member(6,Name='Alan Gauld')
>>> ld.get_member_details(6)
('Alan Gauld', 'alan@emailaddress.com')
```

6. To delete the data you added, type this:

```
>>> ld.delete_member(6)
Traceback (most recent call last):
  File "<stdin>", line 1, in <module>
  File "lendydata.py", line 97, in delete_member
    cursor.execute(query,(id,))
sqlite3.IntegrityError: FOREIGN KEY constraint failed
>>> ld.delete_item(7)
>>> ld.delete_member(6)
```

7. To see how the API can be used for arbitrary queries, type the following:

```
>>> ld.cursor.execute('''
... select * from item
... where OwnerID in (select id from member where name like '%e%')
... ''').fetchall()
[(1, 'Lawnmower', 'Tool', 1, 150, 'Excellent', '2012-01-05'),
    (2, 'Lawnmower', 'Tool', 2, 370, 'Fair', '2012-04-01'),
    (3, 'Bike', 'Vehicle', 3, 200, 'Good', '2013-03-22'),
    (5, 'Scarifier', 'Tool', 5, 200, 'Average', '2013-09-14'),
    (6, 'Sprinkler', 'Tool', 1, 80, 'Good', '2014-01-06')]
>>> ld.cursor.execute('''
... select * from item
... where OwnerID not in (select id from member where name like '%e%')
... ''').fetchall()
[(4, 'Drill', 'Tool', 4, 100, 'Good', '2013-10-28')]
>>> ld.get_member_name(4)
'Rob'
```

8. Finally, close the database like this:

```
>>> ld.closeDB()
```

How It Works

You started by importing the `lendydata.py` module and assigning a shorter alias, `ld`. You then initialized the module by calling `initDB()`. You proved that the connection was valid by fetching the list of members and items.

You next proceeded to try to add an item, but the `OwnerID` value was for a nonexistent member and the database `Foreign _ Keys` constraint check prevented the operation from completing. You then added the missing member followed by the item, which, this time, was successfully added.

Having added data, you went on to explore the update functions by modifying the price of the new item and the name of the new member. You also used the `get _ member _ name()` helper function to verify that the `OwnerID` of 6 was indeed the member that you had created.

You next tried to delete the new member but, again, referential integrity checks prevented this because the member was being referenced by an item. First you needed to delete the item and then the member.

Having exercised the high-level functions of the API, you proceeded to use the cursor object directly to execute arbitrary SQL statements. In this case you found all items owned by members with an "e" in their name followed by all items owned by members without an "e". You used the get_member_name() helper function to verify that the only such member with an ID of 4 was in fact Rob.

Finally, you closed the database, which ensured that all changes were committed, and that the connection and cursor objects were properly finalized.

You have now built a high-level API for application programmers to use and have seen that by making the underlying cursor object accessible you enable the user to issue arbitrary low-level SQL commands, too. This kind of flexibility is usually appreciated by application programmers, although if they find that they must use SQL extensively, they should request an addition to the functional API.

Of course SQLite is not the only tool available for working with large data volumes, and Python can provide support for these alternatives, too. In the next section, you look at some alternatives to SQLite and how Python works in these environments.

EXPLORING OTHER DATA MANAGEMENT OPTIONS

You have many options for managing large amounts of data. In this section you look at traditional client-server databases, newer databases known as "NoSQL" databases, and how cloud storage is changing approaches to data management. Finally, you consider some powerful data analysis tools that can be accessed from Python using third-party modules.

Client-Server Databases

The traditional SQL database is rather different from SQLite in the way it is constructed. In these databases you have a database server process accessed over a network by multiple clients. The Python DBAPI is designed so that you can work with these databases just as easily as you did with SQLite. Only minor changes in the way you initialize the database connection are usually all that is necessary. Occasionally you'll see minor changes to the SQL syntax, and the parameter substitution symbol is sometimes different, too. But, in general, swapping from one SQL interface to another is a relatively painless experience.

Several reasons exist for wanting to adopt a client-server database or to migrate to one from SQLite. The first is capacity; most client-server databases can scale up to much larger volumes of data than SQLite. In addition, they can be configured to distribute their processing over several servers and disks, which greatly improves performance when multiple users are accessing the data concurrently. The second reason for migrating from SQLite is that larger databases usually come with a much richer set of SQL commands and query types as well as more data types. Many even support object-oriented techniques and have their own built-in programming languages that enable you to write stored procedures, effectively putting the API into the database itself. Usually, a much richer set of database constraints can be used to tighten up data integrity far beyond the simple foreign key checks that SQLite performs.

The biggest downside of selecting a client-server database is the extra complexity of administering the database. Usually a dedicated administrator is needed to set up users, adjust their access privileges, tune the SQL query engine performance, and do backups, data extracts, and loads.

Popular client-server databases include commercial offerings such as SQL Server, Oracle, and DB2, as well as open source projects such as MySQL, PostGres, and Firebird.

NoSQL

As data storage needs have expanded both in size and in variety, several projects have been exploring alternatives to SQL. Many of these projects are associated with what is called "Big Data," which usually relates to the harvesting of large volumes of, often unstructured, data from places such as social media sites or from sensors in factories or hospitals and so on. One of the features of this kind of data is that most of it is of little significance to the database user, but amongst the detritus are gems to be had that can influence sales strategy or alert you to imminent failure of components or processes so that action can be taken in advance. The nature, volumes, and need for rapid access of such data means that traditional SQL databases are not well suited to the task.

The solution has been a variety of technologies that go under the collective term *NoSQL*. NoSQL does not mean that no SQL is used, but rather it stands for Not Only SQL. SQL may still be available for traditional queries on these new databases, but alternative query techniques are also used, especially for searching unstructured data. Some examples of NoSQL approaches (with typical implementations) are Document (MongoDB), Key-Value (Dynamo), Columnar (HBase), and Graphs (Allegro). All of these diverge to some degree or other from the traditional relational model of multiple, two-dimensional tables with cross-references. To get the best from these systems, you need to consider which architecture best suits the nature of your data. Many solutions are open source, but commercial offerings exist, too.

Although NoSQL databases do provide the potential for faster and more flexible access to a wider variety of data, they generally sacrifice qualities like data integrity, transactional control, and usability. The products are all evolving rapidly, although at the time of writing they require lower-level programming skills to utilize the data compared to traditional SQL databases that could change quite quickly. Most of the popular databases offer Python modules that facilitate programming them from Python.

The Cloud

Cloud computing has become popular in recent years with its promise of computing on-demand. This potentially offers lower costs, more flexibility, and lower risks than traditional data center–based solutions. It brings its own set of concerns, of course, especially for sensitive data or where network reliability is an issue. The biggest use of cloud technologies in the database world has been in combination with the NoSQL solutions, discussed in the previous section, and other Big Data solutions such as Hadoop. Many cloud storage providers offer these technologies on a software-as-a-service (SAAS) basis. This offers an attractive option for those just dipping a toe into the Big Data or NoSQL world.

> **NOTE** *Cloud services usually rely on the premise that the data can be physically moved, without notifying the client, so long as the service is not interrupted. New data centers can be brought online and data transferred to these transparently. Unfortunately, many corporate clients insist on knowing where their data is being stored. There may be concerns about data protection regulations—or more likely the lack of such—in some countries. These concerns are frequently written into project contracts in sectors such as, defense, government, and finance. If your cloud provider cannot guarantee adherence to the contract terms, you may need to look elsewhere or may even decide that cloud storage is not appropriate.*

The advantage of cloud computing for the application programmer is that the data is abstracted into a virtual database located at a single consistent network address. The physical location of the data may change over time, or the amount of storage available may grow or shrink, but to the programmer it doesn't matter. (This does not mean that normal error handling can be ignored, but it does mean that the code can be largely decoupled from the physical design of the data storage.)

One of the biggest providers of cloud storage and database technology is the online retailer Amazon. It provides storage and an API (Amazon Web Services, or AWS) as well as a proprietary NoSQL database called SimpleDB, in addition to several other open source offerings. Other cloud suppliers are starting to offer similar products. Many providers offer small amounts of free storage and access as an incentive to try the product before committing to a significant investment.

Amazon AWS has Python support available, including a comprehensive tutorial to both Python and the AWS interface, at `http://boto.readthedocs.org/en/latest/`. Similar interfaces are available, or will likely soon become available, from the other providers.

Data Analysis with RPy

Though client-server SQL, NoSQL, and cloud computing all provide solutions for handling large data volumes or many users, you have other data management issues to consider. Often, the processing of large volumes of data is more important than the storage or retrieval. If that processing involves a high degree of statistical exploration or manipulation, Python offers a basic `statistics` module (introduced to the standard library in version 3.4). If that is not enough, there is the R programming language. R is a specialized language designed for statistical number crunching on a large scale. Like Python it has accumulated a large library of add-in modules, and many statistical researchers use R as their platform of choice, publishing their research using R.

The good news for Python programmers is that there is an interface from Python to R called `rpy2` that opens up this processing power without having to become an expert in R. Knowing the basics of R, especially its data handling concepts, is pretty much essential, but much of your Python knowledge can be applied, too. You can find `rpy2` on the Python Package Index and install it via `pip`.

Data management has many facets, and this chapter has reviewed how Python supports you, from small volumes to large, from simple data persistence through to complex data analysis. Once you have control of your data, you are in a much stronger position to create powerful, user-friendly applications whether on the desktop or on the web. That's the subject of the next two chapters.

SUMMARY

In this chapter you learned how to store and retrieve data so that your application can pick up from where it left off or so that you can work on multiple different projects. You saw how you could do this with flat files using indexed files (DBM), pickles, and shelves. You then looked at SQL and relational databases using SQLite and concluded with a review of some alternative technologies.

Flat files are good for storing small amounts of data or for saving the program's state information when it shuts down. They are less useful where multiple queries have to be made, especially if querying on more than one key value. DBM files act like persistent dictionaries that can only store strings. Pickles turn binary objects into strings. Shelves combine DBM and `pickle` to act like persistent dictionaries, albeit limited to using strings for the keys.

SQL is used to manage data in a relational database management system (RDBMS). Relational databases are conceptually made up of one or more two-dimensional tables, each representing one logical entity. Cross-references between tables act as a model for the relationships between entities. SQL provides commands to build and manage the tables in a database as well as operations to create, delete, query, and update the data within those tables.

Python provides the DBAPI, which is a standard protocol for accessing SQL-based databases. The DBAPI primarily consists of two objects: a connection and a cursor. The cursor is the primary object used for executing SQL commands and retrieving their results. Results are returned as a list of tuples.

The SQLite database interface is provided in Python's standard library, and you can download a standalone interpreter. SQLite, as the name suggests, is a lightweight version of SQL that stores the entire database in a single file and supports a lightweight subset of the SQL language. SQLite can be used on small- to medium-sized projects, and it is then relatively easy to migrate to a larger database if the project expands in scale. DBAPI libraries are available for most major databases and can be downloaded from third parties.

By using the DBAPI it is possible to build a data abstraction layer that hides both the details of the database design and the SQL language from the application programmer, further facilitating the migration process if it becomes necessary.

Several other database technologies exist, and this is an active area of development with several NoSQL projects vying for popular support. These databases tend to have quite specific areas of applicability, and no single solution suits all scenarios. Many are focused on the challenges of managing "Big Data" and are well suited to cloud-based solutions.

EXERCISES

1. To appreciate the work that `pickle` does for you, try building a simple serialization function for numbers, called `ser_num()`. It should accept any valid integer or float number as an argument and convert it into a byte string. You should also write a function to perform the reverse operation to read a byte string produced by your `ser_num()` function and convert it back to a number of the appropriate type. (Hint: You may find the `struct` module useful for this exercise.)

2. Write a version of the employee database example using `shelve` instead of SQLite. Populate the shelf with the sample data and write a function that lists the name of all employees earning more than a specified amount.

3. Extend the `lendydata.py` module to provide CRUD functions for the loan table. Add an extra function, `get_active_loans()`, to list those loans that are still active. (Hint: That means the `DateReturned` field is `NULL`.)

4. Explore the Python `statistics` module to see what it offers (only available in Python 3.4 or later).

▶ WHAT YOU LEARNED IN THIS CHAPTER

KEY CONCEPT	DESCRIPTION
Persistence	The ability to store data between program executions such that when a program is restarted it can restore its data to the state it was in when the program was last stopped.
Flat file	A standard file containing data. The data may be in text form or binary form.
DBM	A form of file storage that uses a combination of a flat file to store the data and index files to store the location of individual data records for rapid retrieval. Both keys and data must be in string format. In Python a dictionary-like interface is provided by the dbm module.
Serialization	The process of converting binary data into a string of bytes for storage or transmission over a network.
Pickle	A Python-specific format for serializing binary data. Most Python objects can be serialized using Pickle. Because it poses some security risks, care must be exercised when reading data from untrusted sources.
Shelve	A combination of DBM and Pickle technologies to provide a persistent dictionary. Arbitrary binary data can be stored against a string-based key.
Relational Database	A database comprising one or more tables. Table rows represent records, and columns represent the fields of the record. Field values can refer to other records within the database, thus representing relationships between entities.
Relationship	Each record in a relational database has a unique "primary key," and other records can store references to the primary key of another record, thus establishing a relationship between the two records and their two tables. Relationships can span tables.
Constraint	Various rules can be defined to ensure data integrity is maintained within the database. These rules are known as constraints and regulate such things as data types, whether a value is required or optional, and whether a cross-reference must contain a valid key from another entity.
Cardinality	Relationships in a database can represent various types of mapping. The numbers of each entity in the mapping are called its cardinality. For example, if one entity refers to exactly one other entity, that is a 1-1 mapping. If several entities refer to one other entity, that is a 1-N mapping. If many entities refer to many other entities, that is a many-to-many mapping.
Structured Query Language (SQL)	A standardized mechanism for working with relational databases. The language contains commands for defining the database structure, known as the data definition language (DDL), and commands for manipulating and retrieving the data within the database, known as data manipulation language (DML).

continues

(continued)

KEY CONCEPT	DESCRIPTION
DBAPI	A standard programming protocol for accessing relational databases from Python. The DBAPI implementations vary slightly in details, but porting code between DBAPI libraries is much easier than porting at the native database library level.
NoSQL	Not Only SQL is a term used to describe several database technologies that do not conform to the traditional relational model. Many of these technologies are focused on managing very large volumes of data with a variety of data types, much of it unstructured, such as documents and social media data. SQL is not well suited to handling such unstructured data, and hence NoSQL technology has become increasingly important.

4

Building Desktop Applications

WHAT YOU LEARN IN THIS CHAPTER:

➤ How to structure and build command-line applications

➤ How to enrich command-line applications

➤ How to structure and build GUI applications with Tkinter

➤ How to enrich Tkinter applications with Tix and ttk

➤ How third-party frameworks extend your GUI options

➤ How to localize and internationalize your applications

WROX.COM DOWNLOADS FOR THIS CHAPTER

For this chapter the wrox.com code downloads are found at www.wrox.com/go/
pythonprojects on the Download Code tab. The code is in the Chapter 4 download, called
Chapter4.zip, and individually named according to the names throughout the chapter.

Python is a general-purpose programming language. That means it can be used for many
different types of programs. You have already seen how it can be used as a scripting language
to glue applications together, as well as its use in managing data persistence and access. You
now look at how it can be used to build complete desktop applications.

Desktop applications are the mainstay of personal computing. They include such standard
facilities as word-processing programs, spreadsheets, and even games. They often function
entirely on the desktop, with no network access required. At other times they may be
inherently network oriented, as is the case with a web browser or a client–server database
application. The distinguishing feature is that the bulk of the functionality is executed on the
local PC.

Desktop applications can have a graphical user interface (GUI) or a command-line interface (CLI). In this chapter you see how an application can be structured in such a way that different user interfaces can be created on top of the same underlying program logic. This means you can start off with a simple text interface and then add a graphical front end on top of the existing code. This idea can be taken even further, and a web user interface can often be added, too, making your desktop application into a network application. You see how to do that in the next chapter.

You start off by looking at the basic structure, or *architecture*, of an application. You then build a simple command-line application that is then extended using some Python modules to provide a much richer user experience. You then move on to build a GUI front end using Python's standard GUI toolkit: Tkinter. This incorporates all the standard GUI features such as controls, menus, and dialogs. You then incorporate extra GUI features and enhance the appearance of the interface using more Python module magic. Next, you take a look at other GUI frameworks that offer even more powerful capabilities. Finally, you look at how to support local configurations and multiple languages.

STRUCTURING APPLICATIONS

The key to building effective, extensible applications is to apply a layered architecture. The most common approach is to split the application into three layers: the user interface, the core logic (also known as the business logic), and the data. There may also be a network layer when the application uses the network extensively.

> **NOTE** There is a more formal version of this multi-layer architecture known as client-server computing. In the client-server model, a strict hierarchy of request–response operation is maintained. Each layer is a client of the layer below and makes requests that receive responses. The lower layers are servers to the layers above. The core logic layer acts as both a server to the user interface layer and a client of the data layer. True client-server design is beyond the scope of this book, but the multilayer approach demonstrated incorporates many of the same concepts.

The user interface should present the application logic to the user, but not implement that logic. Its role is to make navigation of the application's features as simple as possible and to display results or outcomes as clearly as possible. The user interface controls which functions are available at any point in time—for example, it should not be possible to close a document if no document is open. If using an object-oriented program (OOP), the objects will typically represent things like menus, buttons, and windows. The user interface accesses the core logic by calling functions or methods provided by the logic layer.

The core logic layer contains all of the algorithms and state management of the data. This is where you write the code that changes the data values, creates new entities, opens and closes files, and so on. The aim here is to provide a set of functions, or services, that can be accessed from the user interface. For this to be effective, the core logic functions should not print results, but should return them as values (that is, strings, numbers, lists, objects and so on) that the user interface can present in the appropriate place and format. The core logic only presents the information; it does not concern itself with how that information is displayed. It is this separation of concerns between logic and display that enables you to build different user interfaces on top of the same core logic. The core logic operates on data provided by the data layer. If using OOP, the objects will represent the conceptual entities of the problem, such as bank accounts, people, network messages and locations, and so on.

The data layer manages data. It stores the data in a safe place and retrieves it on demand. It should not contain sophisticated algorithms or logic specific to the application; it simply delivers raw data to the core logic layer for processing. The data layer may include some basic data-integrity processing to ensure consistency of the data. It may also incorporate security features such as password control or encryption. It should expose the data via a set of objects, functions, or services. If using OOP, your objects will typically represent queries, tables, data connections, and so on. Ideally, you should be able to build multiple applications using the same basic data services. The data layer was discussed in more detail in Chapter 3, "Managing Data."

> **NOTE** There are many ways to represent a software design, and many books have been written on the subject. Nowadays most of the industry uses a notation called the Unified Modeling Language (UML). Essentially, it is a graphical representation of classes and their structure, as well as the corresponding objects and their interactions. UML is a formally defined design language that in its pure form can result in automated code generation. It consists of many diagrams and associated icons. For small projects such as the ones in this book, UML is an unnecessary overhead, but if you ever work on larger projects and need a way to record and share the structure of your program, then you should research UML.

The interaction between the user interface, logic, and data layers is often designed using a pattern called Model View Controller (MVC). In general, the model represents the core logic and data layers, while the view represents the display elements in the user interface, and the controller represents the interaction and dependencies between those display elements. You use a simplified version of the MVC pattern in this chapter for the GUI design.

> **NOTE** The MVC model was originally developed at Xerox Parc as part of the Smalltalk 80 programming environment. Over the years MVC has been adopted by many different languages and UI frameworks and in the process has diverged significantly from the Smalltalk original. However, the core ideas remain the same: separation of data (model) from the presentation (view) and interaction (controller).

BUILDING COMMAND-LINE INTERFACES

In this section you build a very simple command-line interface application for the well-known game tic-tac-toe. The principles discussed in the earlier sections are applied, but in a very simple form so that you can focus on the program structure rather than the detail of what the code is doing. (The code is included in the `Chapter4.zip` file under the folder OXO.)

Building the Data Layer

You start off creating this game by designing the data layer. For this game you need only a simple text file to hold the state of the game so that it can be saved or resumed. A tic-tac-toe game consists of a board with nine squares. Each square can be empty or have the letter 'X' or 'O' in it. You can represent those three options with a simple list of characters. For storage you convert that list into a simple character string.

The only other piece of data needed is which player is due to move next but, in a computer versus human game, you can assume the human is always next to go. So your data layer interface consists of only two exposed, or published, methods:

```
saveGame()
restoreGame()
```

Because you want to keep your layers separate, you should put these methods into a module. To create this module, type the following code and save it as `oxo_data.py` (or load it from the OXO folder of the `Chapter4.zip` download):

```
''' oxo_data is the data module for a tic-tac-toe (or OXO) game.
    It saves and restores a game board. The functions are:
        saveGame(game) -> None
        restoreGame() -> game
    Note that no limits are placed on the size of the data.
    The game implementation is responsible for validating
    all data in and out.'''

import os.path
game_file = ".oxogame.dat"

def _getPath():
    ''' getPath -> string
    Returns a valid path for data file.
    Tries to use the users home folder, defaults to cwd'''

    try:
        game_path = os.environ['HOMEPATH'] or os.environ['HOME']
        if not os.path.exists(game_path):
            game_path = os.getcwd()
    except (KeyError, TypeError):
        game_path = os.getcwd()
    return game_path

def saveGame(game):
    ''' saveGame(game) -> None
```

```
        saves a game object in the data file in the users home folder.
        No checking is done on the input, which is expected to
        be a list of characters'''

        path = os.path.join(_getPath(), game_file)
        with open(path, 'w') as gf:
            gamestr = ''.join(game)
            gf.write(gamestr)

    def restoreGame():
        ''' restoreGame() -> game

        Restores a game from the data file.
        The game object is a list of characters'''

        path = os.path.join(_getPath(), game_file)
        with open(path) as gf:
            gamestr = gf.read()
            return list(gamestr)

    def test():
        print("Path = ", _getPath())
        saveGame(list("XO  XO OX"))
        print(restoreGame())

    if __name__ == "__main__": test()
```

The first function, _getPath(), is a helper function that uses the os module to try to determine the user's home folder and, if that fails, use the current folder. By convention, functions that are not intended to be called by module users have a leading underscore in front of their name, like _getPath(). The saveGame() function uses _getPath() to create a new file containing the string representation of the game. The final function restoreGame() also uses _getPath() to locate the saved file and open it, reading back the stored game data.

Ideally, you would include a more sophisticated test function (or a set of unit tests, like those described in Chapter 6, "Python on Bigger Projects"). In the interest of brevity, these are not shown here.

> **NOTE** In the data module, you have included documentation strings for the module and functions. You should always do this in your working code, but because full descriptions of the code are provided in the text, and to save space in the book, documentation strings have been omitted in the other modules.

Building the Core Logic layer

You now create the core logic of the game. For that you need to define a number of functions that are used throughout the course of a game. However, to know what those functions are, you first need to think about how the game will be played. So, before diving into logic code, you need to map out the sequence of play and, for that, you can use a sequence diagram.

The game starts by presenting the user with a menu of options. These will include the options to start a new game or restore a saved game. In either case, once the game has been set up, the board will be displayed and the user prompted to select a cell. The computer then analyzes the move and responds with its own. The board is then shown again until a winner is found. The sequence diagram for this is as shown in Figure 4-1.

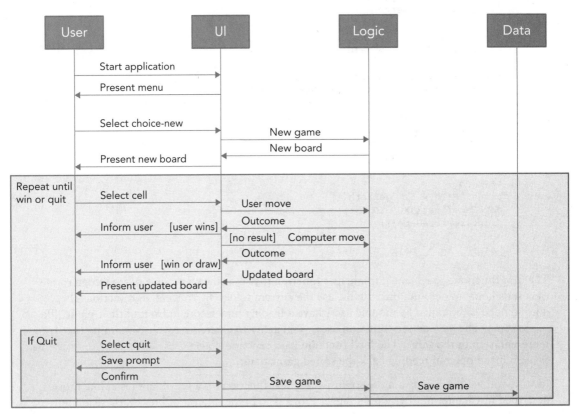

FIGURE 4-1: Module interaction sequence diagram

The sequence diagram is a simplified version of a UML sequence diagram. Each of the "objects" (modules in this case), along with the user, are represented by a vertical line. The arrows indicate messages flowing between the modules (and user). The messages have descriptive titles. Some messages are optional, and the conditions that cause them are indicated in square brackets (called guards). Some sequences of arrows are enclosed in boxes, and these represent loops or conditional blocks with a description given in the upper-left corner. In this case the main game-play sequence is repeated until there is a win, or draw, or until the user selects quit. If the user selects quit, then the sequence in the box at the bottom is executed. Sequence diagrams are a very powerful analysis and design tool.

From the sequence diagram, you can see that you need to provide functions to handle the user's menu choices (only new is shown in the diagram), as well as a function to play the game. The latter would need to return different results depending on the outcome, which is usually a bad idea. However, if you create separate functions for the user's and computer's moves, you can then use the same analysis helper function for both the user and the computer. With that in mind you need to write the following functions:

```
newGame()
saveGame()
restoreGame()
userMove()
computerMove()
```

You need helper functions to generate a random move and analyze whether a given move wins the game. The list of helper functions is therefore:

```
_generateMove()
_isWinningMove()
```

Once again, to keep the separation between the layers, you should put the logic code into a separate module, this time called oxo_logic.py. It looks like this:

```
''' This is the main logic for a tic-tac-toe game.
It is not optimised for a quality game it simply
generates random moves and checks the results of
a move for a winning line. Exposed functions are:
newGame()
saveGame()
restoreGame()
userMove()
computerMove()
'''

import os, random
import oxo_data

def newGame():
    return list(" " * 9)

def saveGame(game):
    oxo_data.saveGame(game)

def restoreGame():
    try:
        game = oxo_data.restoreGame()
         if len(game) == 9:
            return game
        else: return newGame()
    except IOError:
        return newGame()

def _generateMove(game):
    options = [i for i in range(len(game))
                    if  game[i] == " "]
    return random.choice(options)

def _isWinningMove(game):
    pass
```

The newGame() function simply returns a new list of nine spaces.

The saveGame() function calls the oxo_data function of the same name. The restoreGame() function is marginally more complex in that it catches any errors arising because the data file cannot be found and validates the length of the restored game. It could do more data validation on the content of the data, but you can add that later if you wish.

The _generateMove() function looks for the unused cells in the current game and then randomly selects a cell to place the computer's move. This is not optimal, and a more intelligent algorithm would greatly improve the quality of the game.

The _isWinningMove() method has been left unfinished because it is the most complex of the logic functions. This is where the real processing takes place. The approach you take is very simple and relies on the fact that there are only eight possible wining lines. They can be listed in terms of the indices of the game cells involved:

```
wins = ((0,1,2), (3,4,5), (6,7,8),
        (0,3,6), (1,4,7), (2,5,8),
        (0,4,8),(2,4,6))
```

To assess whether a move has resulted in a win, you need to check each winning line. You can extract the character in each cell of the candidate line and construct a three-character string. For a win all three characters need to be either 'X' or 'O'. The function looks like this:

```
def _isWinningMove(game):
    wins = ((0,1,2), (3,4,5), (6,7,8),
            (0,3,6), (1,4,7), (2,5,8),
            (0,4,8), (2,4,6))

    for a,b,c in wins:
        chars = game[a] + game[b] + game[c]
        if chars == 'XXX' or chars == 'OOO':
            return True
    return False
```

Finally, you need a pair of functions that can analyze a user move and a computer move. The former takes a cell value input by the user; the latter needs only the game because it uses _generateMove() internally. They return the outcome of the move as one of four character codes. An empty string means the game is still on, an 'X' or 'O' signifies the victor, and a 'D' means it's a draw. These functions look like this:

```
def userMove(game,cell):
    if game[cell] != ' ':
        raise ValueError('Invalid cell')
    else:
        game[cell] = 'X'
    if _isWinningMove(game):
        return 'X'
    else:
        return ''

def computerMove(game):
    cell = _generateMove(game)
```

```
        if cell == -1:
            return 'D'
        game[cell] = 'O'
        if _isWinningMove(game):
            return 'O'
        else:
            return ''
```

You could have implemented all of these functions as methods of a Game class. That would have removed the need to pass the game data into each function.

Finally, you need a test function:

```
def test():
    result = ''
    game = newGame()
    while not result:
        print(game)
        try:
            result = userMove(game, _generateMove(game))
        except ValueError:
            print("Oops, that shouldn't happen")
        if not result:
            result = computerMove(game)

        if not result: continue
        elif result == 'D':
            print("Its a draw")
        else:
            print("Winner is:", result)
        print(game)

if __name__ == "__main__":
    test()
```

The test function keeps on generating moves until either somebody wins or the board fills up (at which point _generateMove() returns -1). The moves are generated entirely randomly, so there is no intelligence in the selections. You can run the code, and you should see something like this (the actual results you get are random because you use the random module to generate the moves):

```
[' ', ' ', ' ', ' ', ' ', ' ', ' ', ' ', ' ']
[' ', ' ', ' ', ' ', ' ', 'O', ' ', 'X', ' ']
[' ', 'X', ' ', 'O', ' ', 'O', ' ', 'X', ' ']
Winner is: X
[' ', 'X', ' ', 'O', 'X', 'O', 'O', 'X', ' ']
```

It's not very pretty, but then, it's not supposed to be. Presentation is in the user interface, and that's what you build next.

Building the User Interface

In the previous section, you started to think about how the user would perceive the application, that is, the *user experience*. The user experience is the key factor in driving the user interface design. You need to consider the flow of control from entering the application through normal use to exit. In a command-line application, the most common approaches are to offer menus, often nested to several levels, or to accept commands typed at a prompt. In this section you build a set of very simple menus and create a simple prompt-based solution. This process illustrates both techniques while keeping the code size small.

If you walk through the user experience in playing a game of tic-tac-toe, the game starts by offering a menu that allows the user to start a new game, resume a saved game, request help, or quit. (The ability to quit easily is an important, but often overlooked, feature of good user interface design.)

The quit option just exits the program. The help screen displays a page of explanatory text. Both of the other options take the user into a tic-tac-toe game. Once in that game, the user can either select a cell, save the game, or quit. If they choose to quit while the game is still in progress, they should be asked if they want to save the game first. If they choose a cell, then the computer analyzes the move, makes its own move, analyzes that, and presents the result. If either move results in a win or in all cells being used, then a message is displayed to the user and an option to quit or return to the main menu.

The user interface presents the information and manages the flow from screen to screen. It does not perform any of the computational logic; that is provided by the core logic layer. The user interface simply calls the functions that you defined in the oxo_logic module.

You start by defining a function to display a menu and return a valid user selection. The function could be specific to the menu and include the menu definition within it; however, it is not much harder to write a function that takes a menu as input and is therefore reusable for all menus in the system. You could even extract it to a module for reuse across projects.

The menu code, which you can save in oxo_ui.py (or load it from the zip file), looks like this:

```
''' CLI User Interface for Tic-Tac-Toie game.
    Use as the main program, no reusable functions'''

import oxo_logic

menu = ["Start new game",
        "Resume saved game",
        "Display help",
        "Quit"]

def getMenuChoice(aMenu):
    ''' getMenuChoice(aMenu) -> int

        takes a list of strings as input,
        displays as a numbered menu and
        loops until user selects a valid number'''

    if not aMenu: raise ValueError('No menu content')
    while True:
        print("\n\n")
        for index, item in enumerate(aMenu, start=1):
            print(index, "\t", item)
```

```
    try:
        choice = int(input("\nChoose a menu option: "))
        if 1 <= choice <= len(aMenu):
            return choice
        else: print("Choose a number between 1 and", len(aMenu))
    except ValueError:
        print("Choose the number of a menu option")

def main():
    print(getMenuChoice(menu))
    getMenuChoice([])   # raise error

if __name__ == "__main__": main()
```

Notice that the enumerate function is used to generate the menu option numbers and that they start at 1 because most users find 0 a strange option choice. The function keeps repeating until the user selects a valid choice, with prompts to correct invalid choices.

Having presented some choices, you now need to write code to do all of those things. The methods are named after the menu options and are shown as follows:

```
def startGame():
    return oxo_logic.newGame()

def resumeGame():
    return oxo_logic.restoreGame()

def displayHelp():
    print('''
Start new game:  starts a new game of tic-tac-toe
Resume saved game: restores the last saved game and commences play
Display help: shows this page
Quit: quits the application
''')

def quit():
    print("Goodbye...")
    raise SystemExit
```

Your next step is to write a function to process the user's choice. That can be done using an if/elif chain, but that can become difficult to maintain if there are many options. Although the number of possible choices in this project is small, you use a dispatch table because this is a powerful, efficient, and flexible technique. You also need to change the main() function to loop over the menu and game code until the user quits. Make the following modifications to your program:

```
def executeChoice(choice):
    ''' executeChoice(int) -> None

        Execute whichever option the user selected.
    If the choice produces a valid game then
    play the game until it completes.'''
```

```
        dispatch = [startGame, resumeGame, displayHelp, quit]
        game = dispatch[choice-1]()
        if game:
            # play game here
            pass

def main():
    while True:
        choice = getMenuChoice(menu)
        executeChoice(choice)
```

That only leaves the task of actually playing the game. You need to write a function that takes a starting game position and interacts with the user until the game completes, either because there are no more moves or a winner is found. In addition, it helps if you have a function that displays the game in the usual grid layout rather than the flat data format that you are using internally. These are shown here:

```
def printGame(game):
    display = '''
       1 | 2 | 3       {} | {} | {}
       ----------      ------------
       4 | 5 | 6       {} | {} | {}
       ----------      ------------
       7 | 8 | 9       {} | {} | {}'''
    print(display.format(*game))

def playGame(game):
    result = ""
    while not result:
        printGame(game)
        choice = input("Cell[1-9 or q to quit]: ")
        if choice.lower()[0] == 'q':
            save = input("Save game before quitting? [y/n] ")            if
            save.lower()[0] == 'y':
                oxo_logic.saveGame(game)
            quit()
        else:
            try:
                cell = int(choice)-1
                if not (0 <= cell <= 8):  # check range
                    raise ValueError
            except ValueError:
                print("Choose a number between 1 and 9 or 'q' to quit ")
                continue

            try:
                result = oxo_logic.userMove(game,cell)
            except ValueError:
                print("Choose an empty cell ")
                continue
            if not result:
                result = oxo_logic.computerMove(game)
            if not result:
                continue
            elif result == 'D':
                printGame(game)
                print("Its a draw")
```

```
        else:
            printGame(game)
            print("Winner is", result, "\n")
```

The `printGame()` function uses formatting to insert the game values into the display. Note the use of the asterisk (`*game`) that expands the list into its individual elements.

The `playGame()` function displays the user interface prompt for the game screen. You ask for a number representing the cell that the user wishes to place an 'X' into. You also provide the option to quit, and if it is selected, offer the chance to save the game. If the user's choice is valid, you then use the `oxo_logic` functions to determine the outcome of the selection, and if not, a finishing move to get the computer to take a turn. Notice how all of the rules of the game and the data management are in the lower layers. The user interface layer is dealing with presentation and control flow only. One slight quirk of the design is that the board is passed into both the `userMove()` and `computerMove()` functions, but the updated board is not returned by the functions. That is because the board object is a mutable list and, as such, can be changed by the function and the original variable will reflect those changes.

Later in this chapter, you revisit this game and see how easily you can create a new GUI-based user interface layer on top of the existing `oxo_logic` and `oxo_data` modules. Before you do that, there are a couple of interesting options you can use to enhance your command-line applications. You look at them in the next sections.

USING THE CMD MODULE TO BUILD A COMMAND-LINE INTERFACE

Python has a module in its standard library called `cmd` that is specifically designed for building command-line interfaces. In particular it creates the type of interface that you use for Python's help and debugger systems. It presents a command prompt, and you can type in a command. You can request help, and a help screen is presented with the list of available commands. If you type "help <command>", you get a screen explaining how to use the specified command.

In this section you build a cmd-based version of the tic-tac-toe game from the previous section. It has the same four options that you displayed in the opening menu. The game play part is exactly the same as before. (The finished code is in the file `oxo-cmd.py` in the OXO folder of the `Chapter4.zip` download.)

cmd is based on an object-oriented framework whereby you define a new subclass of the `cmd.Cmd` class. This subclass overrides some key methods to provide your application-specific behavior. You then define a set of methods whose names begin with the string `do_`. The class then interprets the part following the underscore as a command word that the user can type.

You can build a skeleton version of your tic-tac-toe game by defining some methods that simply print a message to see how it works. It looks like this:

```
import cmd

class Oxo_cmd(cmd.Cmd):
    intro = "Enter a command: new, resume, quit. Type 'help' or '?' for help"
    prompt = "(oxo) "
```

```
        def do_new(self, arg):
            print("Starting new game")

        def do_restore(self, arg):
            print("Restoring previous game")

        def do_quit(self, arg):
            print("Goodbye...")
            raise SystemExit

    def main():
        game = Oxo_cmd().cmdloop()

    if __name__ == "__main__":
        main()
```

With the preceding code, you created a new class derived from cmd.Cmd. To that you added an intro message and a prompt string. You then defined the command-response methods.

Notice that you don't need a help command because that is built into the class mechanism for free. Also notice that you need to provide a second dummy parameter in the method definitions, even if it is not used in the method.

Finally, in the main function you instantiate the game object and execute its cmdloop() method.

If you run that, you see that it produces a fully functioning command interpreter application.

To turn it into a working tic-tac-toe game, you need to make only a couple of minor tweaks. You import both the oxo_logic and oxo_ui modules. You create a game class variable to hold the game data. Then you call the ui_logic module functions from your command methods. Finally, you call the oxo_ui.playGame() method to initiate the original game play.

The final game looks like this:

```
import cmd, oxo_ui, oxo_logic

class Oxo_cmd(cmd.Cmd):
    intro = "Enter a command: new, resume, quit. Type 'help' or '?' for help"
    prompt = "(oxo) "
    game = ""

    def do_new(self, arg):
        self.game = oxo_logic.newGame()
        oxo_ui.playGame(self.game)

    def do_resume(self, arg):
        self.game = oxo_logic.restoreGame()
        oxo_ui.playGame(self.game)

    def do_quit(self, arg):
        print("Goodbye...")
        raise SystemExit

def main():
    game = Oxo_cmd().cmdloop()
```

```
if __name__ == "__main__":
    main()
```

There are many other options and features for you to explore in the cmd.Cmd class, but hopefully this example has shown you how easy it is to build a command interpreter style application using cmd. It should also have demonstrated how powerful the separation of the presentation from the logic is. For a very small amount of coding, you have created an entirely different version of the tic-tac-toe game, but the logic and data layers are completely identical.

In the next section, you take a look at the command line itself and see how to read those command-line input arguments.

READING COMMAND-LINE ARGUMENTS

When you start a command-line program, the command line itself is stored as a list of strings in sys.argv. The first element is the script name, and the following elements are the arguments to the command. Thus, if you had a file copying script you might call it like this:

```
$ python mycopy.py originalfile copyfile
```

And the sys.argv value would be:

```
["mycopy.py", "originalfile", "copyfile"]
```

However, it's often the case that command-line scripts take optional arguments to control the display or functionality. For example, many programs offer a "-h" or "--help" option that causes the command's help information to be displayed. You can process those options by examining the contents of sys.argv, but it's a nontrivial task so Python includes the argparse module to assist in handling these kinds of command options.

You now modify the original tic-tac-toe code to display the help message if either -h or --help is specified on the command line. It also goes direct to a new game if -n or --new is specified, and it goes straight to a restored game if -r or --res or --restore is given. This enables experienced tic-tac-toe players to bypass the initial menu if they wish.

> **NOTE** *Python argument processing assumes UNIX-style arguments—that is, they start with either one or two hyphens. The traditional option style on DOS or Windows is a forward slash;* argparse *does not process those arguments by default, but you can specify prefix characters as an optional argument when creating the parser if you need to support other styles.*

The first thing you need to do is import the module:

```
import argparse as ap
```

Next, modify the main function as shown:

```
def main():
    p = ap.ArgumentParser(description="Play a game of Tic-Tac-Toe")
    grp = p.add_mutually_exclusive_group()
    grp.add_argument("-n","--new", action='store_true',
                     help="start new game")
    grp.add_argument("-r","--res", "--restore", action='store_true',
                     help="restore old game")
    args = p.parse_args()

    if args.new:
        executeChoice(1)
    elif args.res:
        executeChoice(2)
    else:
        while True:
            choice = getMenuChoice(menu)
            executeChoice(choice)
```

Now, if you try it out, the -h (or --help) option produces a standard help screen format produced by argparse:

```
usage: oxo_args_ui.py [-h] [-n | -r]

Play a game of Tic-Tac-Toe

optional arguments:
  -h, --help              show this help message and exit
  -n, --new               start new game
  -r, --res, --restore  restore old game
```

If you specify -n (or --new), it goes straight into a new game. Specifying -r, --res, or --restore brings back the last saved game.

You should notice a couple of features of the argparse code. First, you created the options as a mutually exclusive group. That was because it makes no sense to specify both new and restore options in the same command. Also you provided a description of the program in the constructor of ArgumentParser and this then appears in the help screen. Finally, by specifying an action of store_true, you made the options into boolean flags that enabled them to be used as truth values in the if/elif tests.

The argparse module has many other tricks up its sleeve. It can interpret arguments as different types, it can count options and it can associate multiple options, and so on. There is a tutorial on its use, and the documentation has several examples.

The last thing to point out here is that you have effectively given your code yet another user interface mechanism without any modification to the game logic or the data layer. Separating presentation from logic and data is a very powerful design technique.

In the next section, you take a look at a different way to make a command-line application more professional looking for your users, by adding a few GUI features while not implementing a full GUI application.

JAZZING UP THE COMMAND-LINE INTERFACE WITH SOME DIALOGS

It is possible to add a few GUI elements to a command-line interface application without the complexity of building a completely graphical user interface. In particular you can pop up information or warning boxes instead of simply printing a message on the terminal. This often makes the messages stand out more to the user—they do not get lost in the mass of text on the screen. You can also use the standard file selection dialogs when choosing filenames. In this section you add some GUI message boxes to the tic-tac-toe user interface to highlight error messages and to notify the user of the final outcome of a game.

> **TIP** It is usually a good idea to allow the code to write to the terminal, too, just in case the user is not running a GUI environment—for example, if they are logging in remotely over ssh or similar. You can do this as a matter of course or have a command-line option, such as --nogui, to control how the prompts are displayed.

Before you start modifying the game itself, you can explore how these message boxes work at the command-line prompt. They are defined in submodules of the tkinter package that you explore more fully later in the chapter. These submodules are:

➤ tkinter.messagebox

➤ tkinter.filedialog

➤ tkinter.simpledialog

➤ tkinter.colorchooser

➤ tkinter.font

You only use the first module in this section, but the principle is the same for all of them. Unfortunately, the official documentation is very sparse, so a bit of experimentation at the Python prompt goes a long way. You can try that now with the tkinter.messagebox module.

TRY IT OUT Exploring Tkinter Message Boxes

In this Try It Out, you play with the various message boxes available in Python's tkinter.messagebox module. You learn how to incorporate these into a non-GUI program and how to deal with a couple of minor niggles that arise. Complete the following steps:

1. Start the Python interpreter and type the following code:

```
>>> import tkinter.messagebox as mb
>>> mb.showinfo("Title", "Your message here")
'ok'
>>>
```

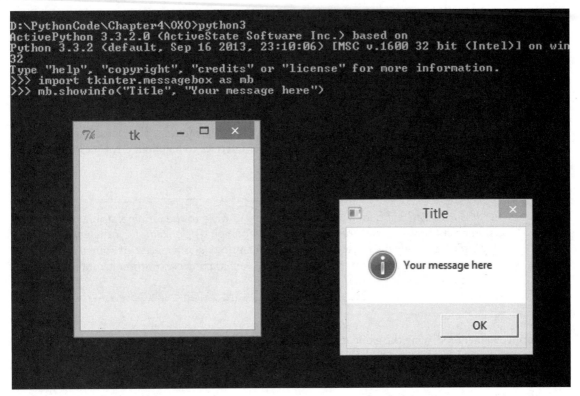

FIGURE 4-2: Initial message box screenshot

The result should look like Figure 4-2. Notice the message box has the title and message specified, plus an icon indicating that it is an informational message. Also notice the strange blank window that appeared. You want to hide that!

2. To remove the blank window, close both of the displayed Tkinter windows and type the following:

    ```
    >>> import tkinter
    >>> tk = tkinter.Tk()
    >>> tk.withdraw()
    ' '
    ```

3. Notice the empty window reappeared on its own this time, then disappeared once you typed the command `withdraw()`.

4. You can now bring up your message box by itself by typing:

    ```
    >>> mb.showinfo("Title", "That's better!")
    'ok'
    >>>
    ```

5. Dismiss the dialog box and try some other message box variants, like this:

```
>>> dir(mb)
['ABORT', 'ABORTRETRYIGNORE', 'CANCEL', 'Dialog', 'ERROR', 'IGNORE',
    'INFO', 'Message', 'NO', 'OK', 'OKCANCEL', 'QUESTION', 'RETRY',
    'RETRYCANCEL', 'WARNING', 'YES', 'YESNO', 'YESNOCANCEL',
    '__builtins__', '__cached__', '__doc__', '__file__',
    '__initializing__', '__loader__', '__name__', '__package__',
    '_show', 'askokcancel', 'askquestion', 'askretrycancel',
    'askyesno', 'askyesnocancel', 'showerror', 'showinfo',
    'showwarning']
>>> mb.showerror("An Error", "Oops!")
'ok'
>>> mb.showwarning("Title","This may not work...")
'ok'
>>> mb.askyesno("Title", "Do you love me?")
True
>>> mb.askokcancel("Title", "Are you well?")
True
>>> mb.askquestion("Title", "How are you?")
'yes'
>>> mb.askretrycancel("Title","Go again?")
True
>>> mb.askyesnocancel("Title", "Are you well?")
>>>
```

How It Works

You started off by importing the messagebox submodule and giving it an alias to reduce typing. You then tried to display an error, but discovered a secondary empty window appeared in addition to the expected information message. This secondary window is, in fact, the main Tkinter application window where you would normally put your controls and menus and so on. To prevent that from appearing, you have to import the main Tkinter module and instantiate the top level Tk object. You then make that invisible by calling withdraw(). Having done that, you can call on the messagebox objects as often as you like, and the top-level window remains invisible.

You then explored the module further. By taking a dir() listing, you could see the other functions available and tried each of them in turn. Notice that some return strings such as 'ok' while others return boolean results. It's best to experiment at the interactive prompt to determine what each one returns. Notice that clicking Cancel, when it appears, returns a None value.

You can experiment in a similar way with some of the other standard dialogs, such as the file dialogs or font and color pickers.

Having seen how the standard dialogs work, you can put them to use in your tic-tac-toe game by presenting the results using showinfo dialogs. You also ask the user if they want to save an incomplete game before quitting with an askyesno dialog. Although you could make all of the prompts use dialogs, this actually leads to a very cumbersome user interface with dialogs popping up and disappearing constantly. It is better to use this technique judiciously to highlight important information only.

The modifications you need to make are in the `playGame()` function. You could modify any of the previous versions of the game, but in this example you use the original `oxo_ui.py` file as the basis and save it as `oxo_dialog_ui.py`. (Or simply load it from the `Chaper4.zip` file.)

The first thing to do is add the `import` statements:

```
import tkinter
import tkinter.messagebox as mb
```

Then you need to modify `main` to get rid of the top level window:

```
def main():
    top = tkinter.Tk()
    top.withdraw()
    while True:
        choice = getMenuChoice(menu)
        executeChoice(choice)
```

Finally, you modify `playGame()` as shown here:

```
def playGame(game):
    result = ""
    while not result:
        printGame(game)
        choice = input("Cell[1-9 or q to quit]: ")
        if choice.lower()[0] == 'q':
            save = mb.askyesno("Save game","Save game before quitting?")
            if save:
                oxo_logic.saveGame(game)
            quit()
        else:
            try:
                cell = int(choice)-1
                if not (0 <= cell <= 8):
                    raise ValueError
            except ValueError:
                print("Choose a number or 'q' to quit")
                continue

            try:
                result = oxo_logic.userMove(game,cell)
            except ValueError:
                mb.showerror("Invalid cell", "Choose an empty cell")
                continue
            if not result:
                result = oxo_logic.computerMove(game)
            if not result:
                continue
            elif result == 'D':
                printGame(game)
                mb.showinfo("Result", "It's a draw")
            else:
                printGame(game)
                mb.showinfo("Result", "Winner is {}".format(result))
```

Although there is quite a lot of code shown here, there are only a few lines of changes. Once again no changes were needed in the logic or data layers.

The next section takes you into the world of GUIs.

PROGRAMMING GUIS WITH TKINTER

In this section you find out how to create GUIs using Python's standard GUI toolkit, Tkinter. All GUIs are built on top of a toolkit of functions or, more commonly, a class library. You look at some of the other toolkits that you can use with Python later in the chapter, but for now the Tkinter toolkit provides a solid foundation for the basic principles.

You start out by examining some of the basic concepts of GUI design, including how GUI toolkits are structured and used.

Introducing Key GUI Principles

Virtually all GUIs are event driven. That means you need to write your code to respond to certain events generated by the GUI toolkit. GUIs come with a whole language of their own in terms of the objects from which a GUI is built. There are windows, frames, controls, and so on. These objects are all connected by something called a *containment tree*. You see what each of these concepts means and how they fit together to form a GUI in the following sections.

Event-Based Programming

You saw how programs can be event driven back in Chapter 2, "Scripting with Python," when you explored the parsing of XML and HTML files. Essentially, the parsers used an internal loop, and whenever they encountered an item of interest, they sent a message to your code. In effect they called a function that you provided.

> **NOTE** This type of function is sometimes called a "callback" because you register it with the framework and then the framework calls it back. GUI programming uses callback functions extensively.

GUI programs function in a similar manner. The toolkit has an infinite loop within it and, as the user clicks buttons, moves the mouse, or presses keys, the toolkit generates events that result in functions being called. You write functions and register them with particular events so that when a user selects, say the `File-> Save` menu item, your function `doFileSave()` gets called.

This means the shape of your program code changes. Instead of you controlling the flow of the program from beginning to end, you instead initialize your data and then hand control over to the toolkit. This can be an unsettling experience for some programmers at first, but once you get used to it, you will find it actually frees you from a lot of mundane control-flow programming and lets you focus on what your program needs to do.

GUI Terminology

One of the first things you notice when dealing with GUIs is the number of new terms you need to learn. You've already met event, and will no doubt be familiar with many more, such as menu, button, scrollbar, and so on. As a programmer you find that, sometimes, the common understanding of terms is not quite what the programming meaning is. In addition, there are a bunch of other terms that are not usually exposed to users. Table 4-1 lists some of the most important GUI terms and their meaning from a programmer's perspective.

TABLE 4-1: Explanations of Key GUI Terms

TERM	DESCRIPTION
Window	An area of the screen controlled by an application. Windows are usually rectangular but some GUI environments permit other shapes. Windows can contain other windows and frequently every single GUI control is treated as a window in its own right.
Control	A control is a GUI object used for controlling the application. Controls have properties and usually generate events. Normally controls correspond to application level objects and the events are coupled to methods of the corresponding object such that when an event occurs the object executes one of its methods.
Widget	A visible control. Some controls (such as timers) can be associated with a given window but are not visible. Widgets are that subset of controls that are visible and can be manipulated by the user or programmer.
Frame	A type of widget used to group other widgets together. Often a frame is used to represent the complete window and further frames are embedded within it. Frames sometimes have visible borders and background colors but at other times are invisible and solely used as a container object.
Label	A widget containing some text or a simple image. It does not generate any events but can be modified in response to an event elsewhere.
Button	A widget with text and/or images that can be pressed by the user and emits an event in response.
Text Entry	A widget that can display and/or receive text. It can be a single line entry on a form or a multiline entry such as a text editor pane. Text widgets can often contain other widgets such as images.
Menu	A widget representing a menu control. The menu contains menu items and/or sub-menus. Menus provide all the mechanisms for the navigation of the menu widget hierarchy. Menu Items, when selected, emit events that can be processed.
Canvas	A widget for containing graphical shapes and images. Canvas objects normally contain methods that permit drawing of geometrical shapes, charts, and so on.

TERM	DESCRIPTION
Geometry	Every window and widget has a geometry, or set of coordinates indicating its location and size. Different toolkits represent this information differently. Tkinter uses the format (width, height). Location information if needed is shown as: (x-coordinate, y-coordinate) and is relative to the containing widget.
Dialog	A special kind of window that is owned by the parent application but can be moved around the screen independently. Dialogs can be modal, that means you must close the dialog before the application responds to any other actions, or modeless where the dialog operates in parallel to the main application window.
Messagebox	A small dialog box that generally presents very simple prompts or requests simple types of user input. You have already used Tkinter's message boxes in an earlier section.
Layout	Controls are laid out within a frame according to a particular set of rules or guidelines. These rules form a layout. The layout may be specified in a number of ways, either using on-screen coordinates specified in pixels, using relative position to other components (left, top etc.) or using a grid or table arrangement. A coordinate system is easy to understand but difficult to manage when, for example, a window is resized. You are advised to use non-resizable windows if working with coordinate-based layouts. Better still use non-coordinate layouts and let the toolkit manage things for you.
Parent-Child	GUI applications tend to consist of a hierarchy of widgets/controls. The top level frame comprising the application window contains sub frames that in turn contain still more frames or controls. These controls can be visualized as a tree structure with each control having a single parent and a number of children. In fact it is normal for this structure to be stored explicitly by the widgets so that the programmer, or more commonly the GUI environment itself, can often perform some common action to a control and all of its children. For example, closing the topmost widget results in all of the child widgets being closed too. The containing widget is called the parent.
Focus	When a window gets focus it becomes the active window in that all keystrokes and mouse clicks will go to that window and its child widgets. For example a word processor may have a modeless dialog box for searches. The user can switch focus between the main window and the dialog by clicking with the mouse on whichever window is to receive input.

The Containment Tree

Every GUI application is constructed in a tree-like manner with a top-level window containing other windows that in turn contain more windows until you eventually reach the lowest level controls and widgets. This hierarchy can be represented as a tree structure and is known as the *containment tree*.

Events arrive at a child widget, which, if it is unable to handle it, passes the event to its parent and so on up to the top level. Similarly, if a command is given to draw a widget, it will send the command on down to its children; thus a draw command to the top-level widget redraws the entire application, whereas one sent to a button likely only redraws the button.

This concept of events percolating up the tree and commands being pushed down is fundamental to understanding how GUIs operate at the programmer level. It is also the reason that you always need to specify a widget's parent when creating it, so that it knows where it sits in the containment tree. An example containment tree is shown in Figure 4-3.

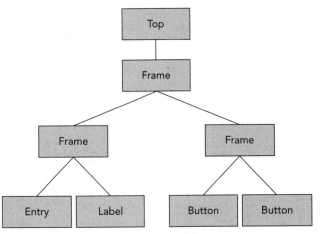

FIGURE 4-3: Example of a GUI containment tree

This illustrates the top-level widget containing a single `Frame` that represents the outermost window border. This in turn contains two more `Frames`; the first contains a text `Entry` widget and a `Label`, and the second contains the two `Buttons` used to control the application. You should refer back to this diagram when you get ready to build a simple GUI in the next section.

Building a Simple GUI

It's time to turn this discussion into real code. You start by building the application illustrated in Figure 4-3 in the previous section. The code looks like this (and can be loaded from the file `demo1.py` in the `Tkinter` folder of the `Chapter4.zip` file):

```
import tkinter as tk

# create the top level window/frame
top = tk.Tk()
F = tk.Frame(top)
F.pack(fill="both")

# Now the frame with text entry
fEntry = tk.Frame(F, border=1)
eHello = tk.Entry(fEntry)
eHello.pack(side="left")
lHistory = tk.Label(fEntry, text="      ", foreground="steelblue")
lHistory.pack(side="bottom", fill="x")
fEntry.pack(side="top")
```

You start by importing `tkinter` and creating a top-level widget. (You already saw this in the earlier section on using message boxes.) Next, you create a `Frame` to hold all of the other widgets. The first parameter of all widget creation methods is the parent widget, so in this case you specify the parent as being `top`. The next step calls `F.pack()`. The `pack()` call invokes a simple layout manager that, by default, simply packs components into the containing object starting at the top and working down. You are packing your `Frame` object into its parent, `top`, that represents the main window. The `fill` option tells the widget to expand to fill the window in `both` vertical and horizontal directions.

You then create a second `Frame` to hold the `Entry` and `Label` widgets. You use named parameters of the constructor to set a `border` around the entry widget and set the `foreground` color of the label font. Notice also that you are using arguments to tell the packer to place the widgets at the sides of the frame rather than its default vertical stacking arrangement. You can see the usage pattern developing—create a widget then pack it. Finally, you pack the new `fEntry` frame itself.

> **NOTE** A naming convention for widget variables is used in the example where the first character indicates the type of widget. This is sometimes useful as a reminder of what each variable is, but can create a maintenance issue if you change the widget type later. The use of such a convention is entirely optional; it makes no difference to Python or Tkinter.

The next step is to create the buttons and associate some behavior with them. For that you need to create an event handler that is activated when the user presses a button:

```
# create the event handler to clear the text
def evClear():
    lHistory['text'] = eHello.get()
    eHello.delete(0,tk.END)
```

The event handler sets the text of the `lHistory` label to the contents of the `eHello` entry field and then deletes the text from the `eHello` field itself. You use a dictionary style access to set the `Label`'s text. This technique works for any of the attributes of the widget. The `delete()` method takes `0` as the first argument. That indicates the start of the text, and the special value `tk.END`, used as the second argument, means the end of the text.

You create the buttons and connect the event handler with the following code:

```
# Finally the frame with the buttons.
# sink this one for emphasis
fButtons = tk.Frame(F, relief="sunken", border=1)
bClear = tk.Button(fButtons, text="Clear Text", command=evClear)
bClear.pack(side="left", padx=5, pady=2)
bQuit = tk.Button(fButtons, text="Quit", command=F.quit)
bQuit.pack(side="left", padx=5, pady=2)
fButtons.pack(side="top", fill="x")

# Now run the eventloop
F.mainloop()
```

Once again, you create a frame to hold the buttons and then pack the buttons using side arguments. You also added some padding to the buttons so that you can create some space around them. The bClear button is connected to your event handler function by specifying the function name, evClear, as the command argument. The bQuit button uses the predefined quit method on the top-level frame, F.

> **WARNING** *It is very important that you specify the name of the function only and do not call it using parentheses after the name. Doing so would assign the return value of the function (in this case None) as the event handler.*

Finally, you start the Tkinter mainloop() running and wait for the user to do something. If you run the code, the resulting window should look like Figure 4-4, which shows before and after versions of the application.

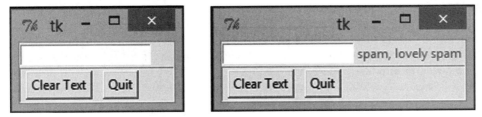

FIGURE 4-4: demo1.py in action

You'll find that you can resize, iconify, and move the window just like any other window in your desktop. Pressing the Quit button closes the application (as does the usual close icon on the title bar) and pressing the Clear button calls your evClear function.

Referring back to the containment tree diagram from the previous section, you see that it describes the layout of this application with three frames, a label and entry box, and two buttons.

Now that you've seen the basics in action, you can move onto a more realistic example using more widgets and linking the controls to more substantial event handling functions. It's time to revisit your tic-tac-toe game.

Building a Tic-Tac-Toe GUI

In this section you build a GUI for your tic-tac-toe game using exactly the same logic and data layers as previously. This GUI is much closer to the kind of GUI you would expect to see on a modern desktop application, complete with menus, buttons, and mouse interaction rather than relying on keyboard input. By using the same tic-tac-toe logic as before, you can focus on the structure of the GUI without thinking too much about how the application itself works.

Sketching a UI Design

When building a substantial GUI application, it often helps to sketch out roughly what you want it to look like before jumping into code. For a tic-tac-toe game, you want a menu bar with File and Help menus. The File menu has New, Resume, Save, and Exit menu items. (You could have called the menu the Game menu, but File is the conventional choice for GUI applications and consistency of style is one of the advantages of using GUIs.) The Help menu has Help and About options.

The board itself will be represented by nine buttons laid out in the usual grid style. When a button is clicked, its label will display the player's mark.

A status bar on the bottom will display messages to the user and the final results will be presented using message boxes. It should look something like Figure 4-5.

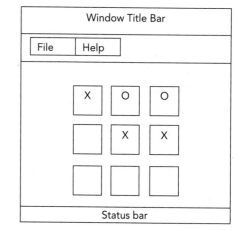

With a clear idea of the layout, you now want to start thinking about the code structure. The GUI essentially consists of three areas: the menu bar, the board, and the status bar. The board needs to be treated as a group and centered in its frame so you could make the board itself another frame inside the central frame. The status bar just displays text so it will consist only of a label widget. That just leaves the menu bar.

FIGURE 4-5: Tic-tac-toe GUI design

Building Menus

Menus in Tkinter are a little more complex than the widgets you've used so far. The initial menu bar is actually quite easy to create because it's the default for a new menu. But, how do you create the drop-down menus? The answer is that the menu class has a method called add_cascade() that applies a submenu to a higher level menu. Tkinter knows about menus so it automatically creates drop-down and pop-out menus as necessary without you having to do anything clever. The final anomaly to menus is that they are not added to the window using the normal layout manager methods, like pack(). Instead the top-level widget's menu attribute is set to the top-level menu object.

Creating menus can become rather tiresome with a lot of repetitive typing so it's often easier to model the menus as data and then use a loop to process the data structure into a menu hierarchy. You can use that approach here even though your menus are actually quite short.

The code to build the menus looks like this (you can load it from the zip file as oxo_menu.py in the OXO folder):

```python
import tkinter as tk
import tkinter.messagebox as mb
import oxo_logic

top = tk.Tk()

def buildMenu(parent):
    menus = (
        ("File", (("New", evNew),
                  ("Resume", evResume),
                  ("Save", evSave),
                  ("Exit", evExit))),
        ("Help", (("Help", evHelp),
                  ("About", evAbout)))
    )
```

```
        menubar = tk.Menu(parent)
        for menu in menus:
            m = tk.Menu(parent)
            for item in menu[1]:
                m.add_command(label=item[0], command=item[1])
            menubar.add_cascade(label=menu[0], menu=m)

        return menubar

    def dummy():
        mb.showinfo("Dummy", "Event to be done")

    evNew = dummy
    evResume = dummy
    evSave = dummy
    evExit = top.quit
    evHelp = dummy
    evAbout = dummy

    mbar = buildMenu(top)

    top["menu"] = mbar

    tk.mainloop()
```

After the initial imports and creation of the top level widget, you define the menu-building function.

The menu structure is defined as a set of nested tuples. The leaf node menu items consist of name-function pairs. You then create the top-level menu bar object and loop over the data structure building the submenus and inserting them into the menu bar. The complete menu bar object is returned.

The next section of code defines the event handler functions—at least, it will do so when you are finished. For now you simply define a dummy function to handle all events (except evExit, which is trivial) and assign it to each of the event handler variables. Soon, you return to these variable assignments and convert them into definitions of the real event handling functions for your game.

Finally, you execute the buildMenu() function and assign the result to the top widget's menu attribute. You then run the mainloop().

When you run this program, you should get a window with a menu bar and when you select any menu item it calls the dummy function.

Building a Tic-Tac-Toe Board

Having created the menu structure, you now want to extend the program to create the board. This sits within a Frame that itself sits centrally inside an outer Frame. The reason for this design is that it separates out the tasks of laying out the board buttons from the layout of the board as a whole.

In the same way that you did for the menus, you create a function that builds the board. The board is the part of the game that is connected to the logic layer and the basic game play so you also need to define code to convert the logical layer's data model of a game into the displayed board within your GUI and vice-versa. You can do that in small helper functions. You also need to add an event handler function to set the button label when a button is clicked; the interplay between the GUI and logic layer is also part of the button click event handler code.

You tackle the GUI building part first. The code is as shown here (and can be loaded from oxo_gui_board.py from the OXO folder of the zip file):

```
def evClick(row,col):
    mb.showinfo("Cell clicked", "row:{}, col:{}".format(row,col))


def buildBoard(parent):
    outer = tk.Frame(parent, border=2, relief="sunken")
    inner = tk.Frame(outer)
    inner.pack()

    for row in range(3):
        for col in range(3):
            cell = tk.Button(inner, text=" ", width="5", height="2",
                             command=lambda r=row, c=col : evClick(r,c) )
            cell.grid(row=row, column=col)
    return outer

mbar = buildMenu(top)
top["menu"] = mbar

board = buildBoard(top)
board.pack()
status = tk.Label(top, text="testing", border=0,
                  background="lightgrey", foreground="red")
status.pack(anchor="s",  fill="x", expand=True)

tk.mainloop()
```

You have started to use some of the more cosmetic features of Tkinter to improve the widget's appearance and more clearly separate them on the screen. In this case you used the border and relief attributes to make the board frame more clearly distinct from the menu and status bar (that you also defined here because it's just two extra lines and gets you close to your final GUI structure). You also set the color options for the status bar and "anchor" it to the bottom of the top-level frame (signified by using a value of s, for south).

The board construction itself is just a couple of for loops creating the grid pattern. (The width and height values were determined by trial and error.) The command argument for the buttons is interesting because it uses the lambda function mechanism. The reason for this is that the command argument must be a function that takes no arguments, but you need to pass in the row and column values. You do that by setting up two, default-valued parameters where the values are the row and col values at the point of button creation. Each button calls the evClick function with its own unique set of values. This is a common trick when programming with Tkinter. You also used the grid layout manager rather than the packer because the board layout is a perfect match to the grid style of layout. You simply specify the row and column locations of each control and the grid does the rest.

Connecting the GUI to the Game

Having gotten the basic GUI structure in place, you can now turn your attention to writing the game play code and hooking up the various menus to the final event handling functions. You can tackle the game code first as it sits mainly in the evClick event handler and is aided by a couple of helper functions that you can call cells2game and game2cells.

The modifications look like this (and can be loaded from the file oxo_gui_game.py in OXO folder of the zip file):

```
gameover = False
def evClick(row,col):
    global gameover
    if gameover:
        mb.showerror("Game over", "Game over!")
        return
    game = cells2game()
    index = (3*row) + col
    result = oxo_logic.userMove(game, index)
    game2cells(game)

    if not result:
        result = oxo_logic.computerMove(game)
        game2cells(game)
    if result == "D":
        mb.showinfo("Result", "It's a Draw!")
        gameover = True
    else:
        if result == "X" or result == "O":
            mb.showinfo("Result",  "The winner is: {}".format(result))
            gameover = True

def game2cells(game):
    table = board.pack_slaves()[0]
    for row in range(3):
        for col in range(3):
            table.grid_slaves(row=row,column=col)[0]['text'] = game[3*row+col]

def cells2game():
    values = []
    table = board.pack_slaves()[0]
    for row in range(3):
        for col in range(3):
            values.append(table.grid_slaves(row=row, column=col)[0]['text'])
    return values
```

If you compare the evClick code to the original playGame() function, you will see that there are many similarities. The game2cells() function is analogous to the original printGame() function. The cells2game() function uses some widget methods to retrieve the child widgets, in this case the buttons. You could have, as an alternative, stored the lists of buttons in a global data structure that would have given more direct access. The game logic of userMove and computerMove is unchanged even though the user interface is vastly different.

The last thing to do is fill in the menu event handlers. These are almost trivial to complete, and the finished program looks like this (it is found as `oxo_gui_complete.py` in the OXO folder of the zip file):

```python
import tkinter as tk
import tkinter.messagebox as mb
import oxo_logic

top = tk.Tk()

def buildMenu(parent):
    menus = (
        ("File",( ("New", evNew),
                  ("Resume", evResume),
                  ("Save", evSave),
                  ("Exit", evExit))),
        ("Help",( ("Help", evHelp),
                  ("About", evAbout)))
        )

    menubar = tk.Menu(parent)
    for menu in menus:
        m = tk.Menu(parent)
        for item in menu[1]:
            m.add_command(label=item[0], command=item[1])
        menubar.add_cascade(label=menu[0], menu=m)

    return menubar

def evNew():
    status['text'] = "Playing game"
    game2cells(oxo_logic.newGame())

def evResume ():
    status['text'] = "Playing game"
    game = oxo_logic.restoreGame()
    game2cells(game)

def evSave():
    game = cells2game()
    oxo_logic.saveGame(game)

def evExit ():
    if status['text'] == "Playing game":
        if mb.askyesno("Quitting","Do you want to save the game before
        quitting?"):
            evSave()
    top.quit()

def evHelp ():
    mb.showinfo("Help",'''
File->New:  starts a new game of tic-tac-toe
File->Resume: restores the last saved game and commences play
```

```
            File->Save: Saves current game.
            File->Exit: quits, prompts to save active game
            Help->Help: shows this page
            Help->About: Shows information about the program and author''')


    def evAbout():
        mb.showinfo("About","Tic-tac-toe game GUI demo by Alan Gauld")


def evClick(row,col):
    if status['text'] == "Game over":
        mb.showerror("Game over", "Game over!")
        return

    game = cells2game()
    index = (3*row) + col
    result = oxo_logic.userMove(game, index)
    game2cells(game)

    if not result:
        result = oxo_logic.computerMove(game)
        game2cells(game)
    if result == "D":
        mb.showinfo("Result", "It's a Draw!")
        status['text'] = "Game over"
    else:
        if result =="X" or result == "O":
            mb.showinfo("Result",  "The winner is: {}".format(result))
            status['text'] = "Game over"

def game2cells(game):
    table = board.pack_slaves()[0]
    for row in range(3):
        for col in range(3):
            table.grid_slaves(row=row,column=col)[0]['text'] = game[3*row+col]

def cells2game():
    values = []
    table = board.pack_slaves()[0]
    for row in range(3):
        for col in range(3):
            values.append(table.grid_slaves(row=row, column=col)[0]['text'])
    return values

def buildBoard(parent):
    outer = tk.Frame(parent, border=2, relief="sunken")
    inner = tk.Frame(outer)
    inner.pack()

    for row in range(3):
        for col in range(3):
            cell = tk.Button(inner, text=" ", width="5", height="2",
                             command=lambda r=row, c=col : evClick(r,c) )
            cell.grid(row=row, column=col)
    return outer
```

```
mbar = buildMenu(top)
top["menu"] = mbar

board = buildBoard(top)
board.pack()
status = tk.Label(top, text="Playing game", border=0,
                  background="lightgrey", foreground="red")
status.pack(anchor="s", fill="x", expand=True)

tk.mainloop()
```

The event functions mirror the original functions in that they mostly just call the oxo_logic functions and then use the game2cells() function to display the board. You now use the status text instead of the global gameover flag. The Help menus simply display text in a showinfo dialog.

The final working game looks like Figure 4-6.

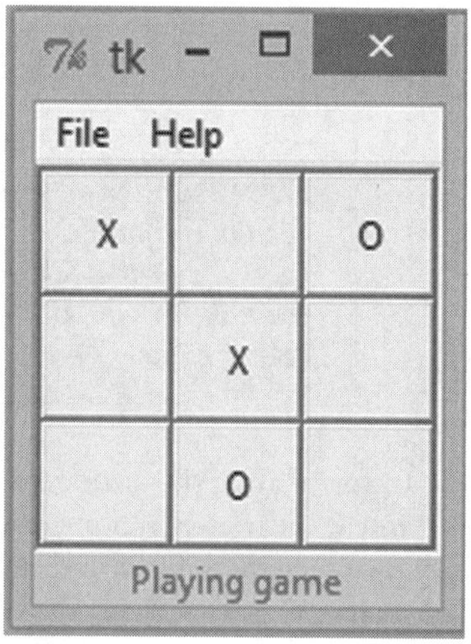

There is a lot more you could do to add polish to this game, but it provides enough to show what can be done using Tkinter as a user interface toolkit and illustrates once again the power of separating the logic and data layers from the presentation layer. You have now written more than 600 lines of code to play the various versions of tic-tac-toe. That's enough for anyone, so it's time to move onto new pastures.

FIGURE 4-6: Final Tkinter GUI

Tkinter has many other widgets and tricks for you to play with. Experiment with the simple GUI application we started with and add or modify the different options that affect layout and appearance. You haven't even looked at how to display formatted text or images or plot graphs or build complex dialogs. All of these things are possible and build on the foundation you saw here. There are many Tkinter tutorials and sample programs around, including IDLE, the default IDE for Python. Reading the code and seeing how these programs control appearance and use widgets is a great way to learn.

> **NOTE** *There is an excellent online tutorial on Tkinter programming, available from New Mexico Tech, which includes some material on the newer features of Tkinter:*
>
> `http://infohost.nmt.edu/tcc/help/pubs/lang.html`
>
> *Unfortunately, it is based on the old Python 2 Tkinter package structure so examples need tweaking for version 3.*
>
> *There is also one book,* Python and Tkinter Programming, *by John Grayson dedicated to Tkinter that is quite out of date now, but does contain useful reference material and some longer, more sophisticated, examples than you find in other tutorials.*
>
> *Mark Lutz also has extensive coverage of Tkinter in his massive reference work* Programming Python *(O'Reilly, 2011). The latest edition of Lutz's book uses Python version 3.*

Tkinter has a couple of extension modules that are included in the standard library (although some Linux distributions omit them for some reason). In the next section, you see what these extension modules can add to your programs.

Extending Tkinter

The two biggest criticisms leveled at Tkinter are that it doesn't have enough widgets and it looks ugly. In comparison to the other GUI toolkits, these are valid issues. However, in recent releases, Tkinter has been fighting back with the introduction of two new modules built on top of Tkinter. These are `tix`, which adds several new widgets, and `ttk`, which enables *theming*, which basically, just means the GUI can look more like the native OS GUI.

> **NOTE** Both `tix` and `ttk` are dependent on the underlying libraries from the Tcl/Tk project being installed. If you have problems getting `tix` or `ttk` to work, check that the Tcl/Tk libraries are all installed. Normally, the Python installers do this for you, but sometimes conflicts can arise, and you need to sort things out manually.

Unfortunately, the documentation for these modules is not as comprehensive as you would want, and at the time of writing, the Python documentation often just contains links to the Tcl/Tk documentation. Once you get used to it, you can usually figure out what options you need from there, but it's not ideal. However, the power of the Python interactive prompt comes to the rescue once again, because you can play with them and experiment to find out what they have to offer. Both modules support most of the same Tkinter widgets that you have used so far; so you should be able to take your Tkinter program and convert it to using ttk or Tix fairly easily. For Tix it is as simple as changing the `tkinter` import line as shown:

```
import tkinter.tix as tk
```

This is one benefit of using the `tk` alias when importing—you don't need to change all your `tkinter` prefixes to `tix`; you simply set the import to use the same alias. You can try that on your tic-tac-toe game if you like. It functions identically to the Tkinter version except that the title bar of the window displays `tix` instead of `Tk`.

For `ttk` it's marginally more complicated because `ttk` uses the `tkinter mainloop` and top-level window so you need to import both. You then refer to `ttk` when creating widgets and `tkinter` when controlling the top window and event loop. You see this in practice later, in the "Using ttk" section.

Using Tix

Because `tix` is so similar to `tkinter`, you can translate all you know about `tkinter` into `tix` and jump straight into learning about the new widgets. There are more than 40 of them, but some are very poorly documented, even in the Tcl/Tk community. If you stick to the subset listed on the Python documentation page, you should be fine. You only dip a toe in the water here, but hopefully it is enough to demonstrate that `tix` is a valuable addition to the Tkinter family.

The widgets that you look at here are the `ComboBox`, the `ScrolledText`, and the `Notebook`.

You can see how a `ComboBox` input control can be used to set a label's text by typing the following code at the Python interactive prompt:

```
>>> import tkinter.tix as tix
>>> top = tix.Tk()
>>> lab = tix.Label(top)
>>> lab.pack()
>>> cb = tix.ComboBox(top,command=lambda s:lab.config(text=s))
>>> for s in ["Fred","Ginger","Gene","Debbie"]:
...     cb.insert("end",s)
...
>>> cb.pick(0)
>>> lab['text'] = "Pick any item"
>>> cb.pack()
>>> top.mainloop()
>>>
```

There are several things to note here. First, you used `config()` to set the text attribute rather than the dictionary style access you used previously. The advantage of `config()` is that you can set multiple attributes at once just by passing them as named arguments. Second, the event handler `lambda` function uses a string argument, s, which is passed in by the widget event. The string holds the currently selected value. Figure 4-7 shows the resulting window in action.

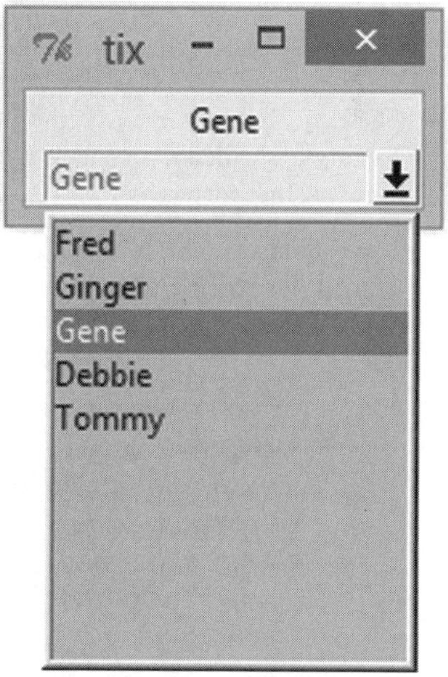

The `ScrolledText` widget is an extension of the standard `Text` widget. As such it can display images as well as formatted text. The Tix version adds scrollbars automatically, which is a useful addition that involves quite a lot of work using the standard toolkit. In use it is very much like the other Tkinter widgets. You can play with it by typing the following code:

FIGURE 4-7: A Tix ComboBox

```
>>> top = tix.Tk()
>>> st = tix.ScrolledText(top, width=300, height=100)
>>> st.pack(side='left')
>>> top.mainloop()
```

Figure 4-8 shows the resulting text box with enough text to activate the vertical scrollbar.

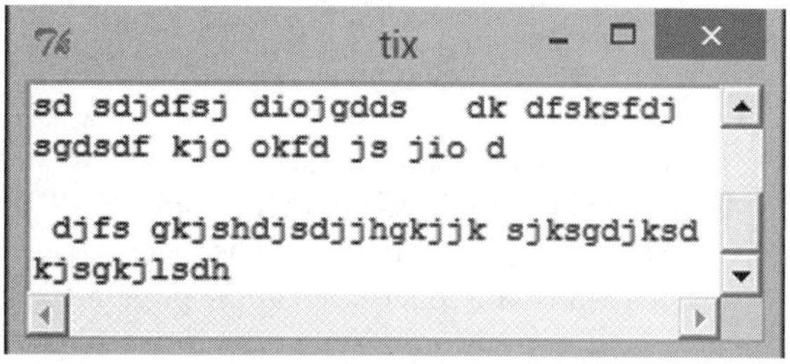

You can simply type into the text box manually or insert text programmatically, like so:

```
>>> t = st.subwidget('text')
>>> t
```

FIGURE 4-8: A Tix ScrolledText Widget in Action

```
<tkinter.tix._dummyText object at 0x019186D0>
>>> t.insert('0.0',"Some inserted text")
>>> t.insert('end',"\n more inserted text")
>>>
```

Notice that you used the `subwidget()` method to get a reference to the underlying text widget and then used its `insert()` method to insert the text. This technique of fetching the underlying standard widget is quite common when working with Tix widgets.

You can also select areas of text in a text widget. Carrying on the previous example, you can change the font and weight of the first line of the previous text like so:

```
>>> t.tag_configure('newfont', font=("Roman", 16, "bold"))
>>> s = t.get('1.0','1.end')
>>> t.delete('1.0','1.end')
>>> t.insert('1.0',s,'newfont')
```

The `tag_configure()` method creates a new *tag*, that is to say a style that you can apply to text. The style is called `newfont` and uses a `Roman` font, of size `16` points and weight `bold`. This triplet font specifier format is standard across Tkinter (and therefore Tix and ttk).

You then used `get()` to fetch the text from the first character through to the `end` of line `1`. You then deleted the existing text from the widget and replaced it with the same text but using the `newfont` tag as a third argument of the `insert()` method.

> **NOTE** Text indexing in Tkinter uses strings that contain numbers formatted like a floating-point number, but actually contains row and column coordinates separated by a period. Rows start from 1, but columns from 0, so 1.0 is the first character in the first row. You can use the string `end` or the predefined constant `tkinter.END` to signify the end of a line, or the end of all text, depending on context.

The result is as shown in Figure 4-9. Note that all of this is being displayed in a Tix `ScrolledText` widget, but you are actually using the underlying standard Tkinter `Text` widget to manipulate the text.

The final widget you look at is an altogether more complex contraption. It is a `NoteBook` widget. It consists of a number of pages, each with an associated tab that the user can select to activate the page. The page is

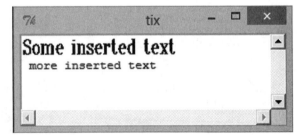

FIGURE 4-9: Modifying Text appearance in a text widget

just a Tkinter container that can be populated with whatever controls you want to use. Often it is a text window or a form. You create a two-page notebook, the first pane containing a `ScrolledText` widget and the other a set of buttons that launch various message box dialogs.

To see the `Notebook` in action, type the following code into a file and execute it from the command line or your IDE (or load it from the file `tix-notebook.py` in the `Tkinter` folder of the zip file, if you prefer):

```python
import tkinter.tix as tix
import tkinter.messagebox as mb

top = tix.Tk()

nb = tix.NoteBook(top, width=300, height=200)
nb.pack(expand=True, fill='both')

nb.add('page1', label="Text")
f1 = tix.Frame(nb.subwidget('page1'))
st = tix.ScrolledText(f1)
st.subwidget('text').insert("1.0", "Here is where the text goes...")
st.pack(expand=True)
f1.pack()

nb.add('page2', label="Message Boxes")
f2 = tix.Frame(nb.subwidget('page2'))
tix.Button(f2, text="error",  bg="lightblue",
                command=lambda t="error", m="This is bad!":
                        mb.showerror(t,m) ).pack(fill='x',expand=True)
tix.Button(f2, text="info",  bg='pink',
                command=lambda t="info", m="Information":
                        mb.showinfo(t,m) ).pack(fill='x',expand=True)
tix.Button(f2, text="warning", bg='yellow',
                command=lambda t="warning", m="Don't do it!":
                        mb.showwarning(t,m) ).pack(fill='x',expand=True)
tix.Button(f2, text="question", bg='green',
                command=lambda t="question", m="Will I?":
                        mb.askquestion(t,m) ).pack(fill='x',expand=True)
tix.Button(f2, text="yes-no", bg='lightgrey',
                command=lambda t="yes-no", m="Are you sure?":
                        mb.askyesno(t,m) ).pack(fill='x',expand=True)
tix.Button(f2, text="yes-no-cancel", bg='black', fg='white',
                command=lambda t="yes-no-cancel", m="Last chance...":
                        mb.askyesnocancel(t,m) ).pack(fill='x',expand=True)

f2.pack(side='top', fill='x')

top.mainloop()
```

In this example you imported the modules and created the top-level widget as usual. You then created a `tix.Notebook` object called nb. To this you added a page and called it `page1`. You then created a frame and made its parent the `page1` page that you just created. You added a text widget and some text, and then packed the widget and frame.

Next, you created a second page, called `page2`, and added a frame to that page as before. You then created a bunch of buttons and linked them to the various message boxes using `lambda` functions as commands. You modified the `pack()` options of both the buttons and the frame to make the buttons occupy the full width of the page, and you gave them different colors to make them stand out.

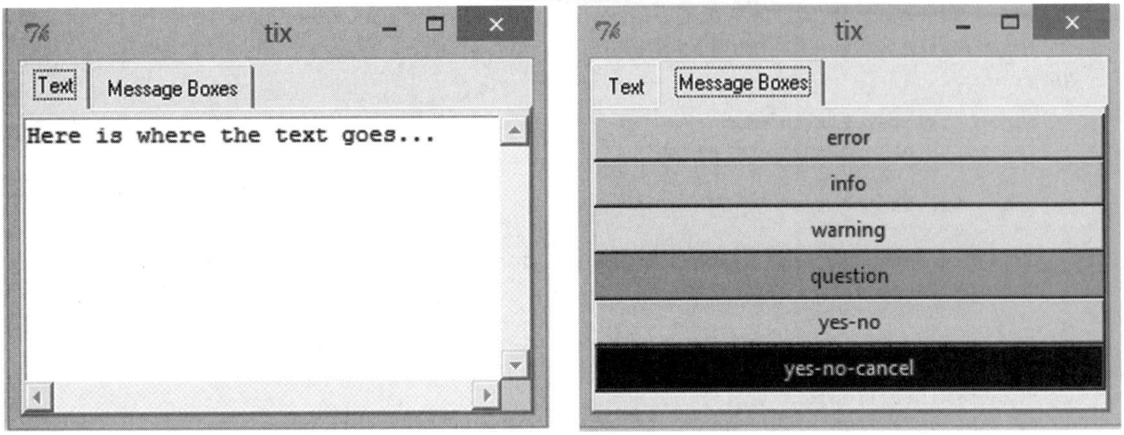

FIGURE 4-10: Tix Notebook showing two pages

Notice that for the notebook, buttons, and ScrolledText widgets, we specified the expand option to the packer. expand tells the layout manager to expand the widget when the window is resized. By using expand in combination with fill and anchor, you can very precisely control how your widgets behave when resizing the window. (It is well worth experimenting with the options to get a feel for them.)

Finally, you started the mainloop() function. When you ran it, the result should have looked like Figure 4-10, which shows both pages of the notebook in action.

Using ttk

As mentioned earlier, the ttk module brings the concept of themes to Tkinter and Python. A theme is a graphical style and enables the same GUI structure to take on the look and feel of the native operating system. There are several themes that ship with ttk, but you can also create bespoke themes of your own.

The predefined themes vary by operating system, and you can find the names for your platform by looking at the output of ttk.Style().theme_names(). On Windows they include Classic (the default), winnative, vista, and xpnative.

ttk comes with its own versions of 11 of the standard Tkinter widgets that are theme aware as well as 6 new widgets of its own, including a ComboBox and NoteBook. You can change the look of applications just by changing the theme. Figure 4-11 shows a very simple Tkinter GUI presented first using classic, then using vista, and then using classic again, but this time on the Ubuntu Linux platform. Notice that the top button doesn't change too much, but the new ttk button is different in each image. The code looks like this:

```
>>> import tkinter as tk
>>> import tkinter.ttk as ttk
>>> top = tk.Tk()
>>> s = ttk.Style()
>>> s.theme_use('classic')
```

```
>>> tk.Button(top,text="old button").pack()
>>> ttk.Button(top,text="new button").pack()
>>>
```

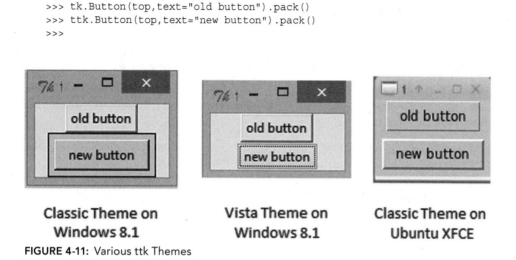

Classic Theme on Windows 8.1   **Vista Theme on Windows 8.1**   **Classic Theme on Ubuntu XFCE**

FIGURE 4-11: Various ttk Themes

Obviously, you need to swap vista for classic in the style object to get the Vista theme. It should be obvious that you need to do a small amount of extra work to define the style object, but otherwise the use of ttk mostly looks like normal Tkinter programming. You should notice when you run the code that the differences are more than simple tweaks to the appearance of the button. The behavior is different too. For example, when you mouse over the button, it changes color differently to the old style button object.

That's all you really need to know about ttk for now. There are lots of options that you can play around with; you can even define your own styles and themes. Mostly, you just use it as shown, and you get small but significant improvements to your Tkinter program's look and feel.

Revisiting the Lending Library

You've now looked at several parts of the Tkinter toolset. It is time to wrap things up by bringing these pieces together in a larger example based on something less frivolous than a tic-tac-toe game. You revisit the lending library database that you created in Chapter 3 and build a GUI front end. This will reinforce much of what you have already done, but also introduces some new elements and techniques:

➤ The ScrolledListBox widget

➤ How to capture low-level events such as mouse double-click and window-level events

➤ How to create and use custom dialog boxes

➤ How to set fonts

➤ How to activate/deactivate widgets using the state attribute

➤ How to build a GUI using object-oriented techniques

You'll build this in the following Try It Out.

Building a Lending Library GUI

In this Try It Out, you add a GUI to the Lending Library database you created in Chapter 3. (There is quite a lot of code, so you may want to load it from the download zip file for Chapter 4. The files are in the Lendy folder and named as described in the text.) To do this, follow these steps:

1. Create a project folder called Lendy and copy your lendydata.py module from Chapter 3, as well as the lendy.db database, into the new folder. (Alternatively, just use the Chapter 2 project folder for this example; it's your choice.)

2. Open your text editor or IDE and create a file called lendy-gui.py (or load it from the zip file). Type the following:

```python
import tkinter.tix as tix
import tkinter.messagebox as mb
import optionsdialog as od
import lendydata as data
import os

class LendingLibrary:
    def __init__(self, root):
        self.isDirty = False
        self.top = root
        root['menu'] = self.buildMenus(root)
        mainWin = self.buildNoteBook(root)
        mainWin.pack(fill='both', expand=True)
        self.top.protocol('WM_DELETE_WINDOW', self.evClose)
        self.top.title('Lending Library')
        data.initDB()    # use default file
        self.items = data.get_items()
        self.members = data.get_members()
        self.populateItemList()
        self.populateMemberList()

    def buildMenus(self, top):
        menus= (
            ("Item", (("New",     self.evNewItem),
                      ("Edit",    self.evEditItem),
                      ("Delete", self.evDeleteItem),
                      )),
            ("Member", (("New",     self.evNewMember),
                        ("Edit",    self.evEditMember),
                        ("Delete",self.evDeleteMember),
                        )),
            ("Help", (("Help",   self.evHelp),
                      ("About", lambda : mb.showinfo(
                            "Help About",
                            "Lender application\nAuthor: Alan Gauld""")
                      ))))

        self.menubar = tix.Menu(top)
        for menu in menus:
            m = tix.Menu(top)
            for item in menu[1]:
                m.add_command(label=item[0], command=item[1])
            self.menubar.add_cascade(label=menu[0], menu=m)
```

```
        return self.menubar

def buildNoteBook(self, top):
    mono_font = self.getMonoFont()
    nb = tix.NoteBook(top)

    nb.add("itemPage",label="Items",
            raisecmd=lambda pg="item": self.evPage(pg))
    fr = tix.Frame(nb.subwidget("itemPage"))
    self.itemFmt = "{:15} {:15} {:10} ${:<8} {:12}"
    tix.Label(fr, font=mono_font,
                text=self.itemFmt.format("Name","Description",
                                        "Owner","Price",
                                        "Condition")).pack(anchor='w')
    slb = tix.ScrolledListBox(fr, width=500, height=200)
    slb.pack(fill='both', expand=True)
    fr.pack(fill='both', expand=True)
    self.itemList = slb.subwidget("listbox")
    self.itemList.configure(font=mono_font, bg='white')
    self.itemList.bind('<Double-1>', self.evEditItem)

    nb.add("memberPage",label="Members",
            raisecmd=lambda pg="member": self.evPage(pg))
    fr = tix.Frame(nb.subwidget("memberPage"))
    self.memberFmt = "{:<15} {:<40}"
    tix.Label(fr, font=mono_font,
                text=self.memberFmt.format("Name","Email Address")).pack
                (anchor='w')
    slb = tix.ScrolledListBox(fr, width=40, height=20)
    slb.pack(fill='both', expand=True)
    fr.pack(fill='both', expand=True)
    self.memberList = slb.subwidget("listbox")
    self.memberList.configure(font=mono_font, bg='white')
    self.memberList.bind('<Double-1>', self.evEditMember)

    return nb

def getMonoFont(self):
    if os.name == 'nt':
        return ('courier','10','')
    else:
        return ('mono','10','')

def populateItemList(self):
    self.itemList.delete('0','end')
    for item in self.items:
        item = list(item[1:])
        item[2] = data.get_member_name(item[2])
        self.itemList.insert('end', self.itemFmt.format(*item))

def populateMemberList(self):
    self.memberList.delete('0','end')
    for mbr in self.members:
        self.memberList.insert('end', self.memberFmt.format(*mbr[1:]))
```

```
    def evClose(self, event=None):
        data.closeDB()
        self.top.quit()
```

3. If you are typing this by hand, you might want to stop there and replace all of the references to event handlers (`self.evXXXXX`) in the widget creation and bind lines, except `evClose`, with `None`. That will allow you to run the GUI and see what it looks like. You will need to add the following starter code at the bottom of the file before you run it:

```
if __name__ == "__main__":
    top = tix.Tk()
    app = LendingLibrary(top)
    top.mainloop()
```

4. Having seen the UI in action, you can now restore the original event handler references in the class code to how it was and continue to add the event handler code below to the class definition:

```
##### notebook event handler #####
def evPage(self, page):
    if page=='item':
        self.menubar.entryconfigure('Item', state='active')
        self.menubar.entryconfigure('Member', state='disabled')
    if page=='member':
        self.menubar.entryconfigure('Item', state='disabled')
        self.menubar.entryconfigure('Member', state='active')


######### Item Event Handlers #######
def evNewItem(self):
    dlg = od.OptionsDialog(top,(
                        ["Name",        "" ],
                        ["Description", "" ],
                        ["Owner",       "" ],
                        ["Price",       "" ],
                        ["Condition",   "" ]))
    if dlg.changed:
        ownerID = self.get_member_id(dlg.options[2][1])
        data.insert_item(dlg.options[0][1],dlg.options[1][1],
                    ownerID,     int(dlg.options[3][1]),
                    dlg.options[4][1])
        self.items = data.get_items()
        self.populateItemList()

def evEditItem(self, event=None):
    # get selected member
    indices = self.itemList.curselection()
    index = int(indices[0]) if indices else 0
    item = self.items[index]
    ownerID = item[3]
    ownerName = data.get_member_name(ownerID)
    dlg = od.OptionsDialog(top,(
                        ["Name",        item[1] ],
                        ["Description", item[2] ],
                        ["Owner",      ownerName ],
                        ["Price",       item[4] ],
                        ["Condition",   item[5] ]))
```

```
            if dlg.changed:
                if dlg.options[2][1] != ownerName:  # its changed
                    ownerID = self.get_member_id(dlg.options[2][1])
                data.update_item(item[0],dlg.options[0][1],dlg.options[1][1],
                                            ownerID,      int(dlg.options[3][1]),
                                            dlg.options[4][1])
                self.items = data.get_items()
                self.populateItemList()

    def evDeleteItem(self):
        indices = self.itemList.curselection()
        index = int(indices[0]) if indices else 0
        item = self.items[index]
        data.delete_item(item[0])
        self.items = data.get_items()
        self.populateItemList()


    # Ideally should use a combo box in options dialog.
    # this gives potential error if more than one member with same name
    def get_member_id(self, name):
        for member in self.members:
            if member[1] == name:
                return member[0]


    ######### Member Event Handlers #######
    def evNewMember(self):
        dlg = od.OptionsDialog(top,(
                            ["Name",""],
                            ["Email",""]))
        if dlg.changed:
            data.update_member(None,dlg.options[0][1],dlg.options[1][1])
            self.members = data.get_members()
            self.populateMemberList()


    def evEditMember(self, event=None):
        indices = self.memberList.curselection()
        index = int(indices[0]) if indices else 0
        mbr = self.members[index]
        dlg = od.OptionsDialog(top,(
                            ["Name",mbr[1]],
                            ["Email",mbr[2]]))
        if dlg.changed:
            data.update_member(mbr[0],dlg.options[0][1],dlg.options[1][1])
            self.members = data.get_members()
            self.populateMemberList()


    def evDeleteMember(self):
        indices = self.memberList.curselection()
        index = int(indices[0]) if indices else 0
        mbr = self.members[index]
        data.delete_member(mbr[0])
        self.members = data.get_members()
        self.populateMemberList()
```

```
     #### Help event handler #
     def evHelp(self):
          mb.showinfo("Help", """
Lending Library Application

Item->New:
     Create a new item in the library
Item->Edit:
     Modify the attributes of the
     selected item (default is first)
Item->Delete:
     Delete selected item (no default)

Member->New:
     Add a member to the library
Member->Edit:
     Modify selected members data
     (default is first)
Member->Delete:
     Delete selected member (no default)

Help->Help:
     Display this screen
Help->About:
     About the program.""")


if __name__ == "__main__":
    top = tix.Tk()
    app = LendingLibrary(top)
    top.mainloop()
```

5. The code uses another class called OptionsDialog, which is defined in another file. Create a new file called optionsdialog.py (or open it from the Chapter4.zip file) containing the following code:

```python
import tkinter.tix as tix
import tkinter.simpledialog

class OptionsDialog(tkinter.simpledialog.Dialog):
    def __init__(self, master, options, *args):
        self.options = options
        self.entries = []
        self.changed = False
        super().__init__(master, *args)

    def body(self, top):
        ''' define GUI elements'''
        f = tix.Frame(top)
        f.pack(expand=True, fill='x')
        for row, opt in enumerate(self.options):
            tix.Label(f,text=opt[0]).grid(row=row, column=0, sticky='w')
            e = tix.Entry(f)
            e.grid(row=row, column=1, sticky='e')
            e.insert('end', str(opt[1]))
            self.entries.append(e)
```

```
        def apply(self):
            ''' store entry values in options '''
            for index, opt in enumerate(self.options):
                opt[1] = self.entries[index].get()
            self.changed = True

    if __name__ == "__main__":
        top = tix.Tk()
        app = OptionsDialog(top,(["First","my value"],["Second","Another value"]))
        top.mainloop()
```

6. Run `lendy-gui.py`.

You should find the items and members listed in their respective tabs, and the menus will activate/deactivate in synchronization with the tabs. You can use the menus to edit a row of either tab, or you can double-click to do the same. The window close icon should shut everything down cleanly.

How It Works

The main GUI follows the basic pattern that you have already seen for GUI applications except that this time you put the code into a class. The class initializer, __init__(), sets up some instance variables and calls various helper functions to build the GUI. The first of these creates the menus from a data structure as you did in the tic-tac-toe GUI, and the second builds the tix.NoteBook, which is the main window of the application. The big difference this time is that you use a tix.ScrolledListbox instead of a tix.ScrolledText widget. The Scrolled ListBox widget has the advantage of making selection of a row easier. To help with the layout, in particular to align the columns with the Label bar at the top of the NoteBook pages, you changed the font to a monospaced variant. To overcome discrepancies in installed fonts on different operating systems, you used the os.name attribute, which you learned about in Chapter 2, to set the font to an appropriate value. You also set the background color to white, which helps identify selected rows.

You also used the bind() method to link a double-click of the left mouse button (<Double-1>) to the appropriate edit event handler .bind() is the mechanism used for any kind of event handling that lies beyond the scope of the default widget command handler. The biggest difference is that the callback function must accept an event argument. The event object will contain information about things like which key has been pressed, the location of the mouse, or whatever is needed to process the event. In this case you simply ignore the event object and give the parameter a default value of None so that it can still be used by the normal command callback mechanism as well as the double-click binding. You use a conversion function from the lendydata module, get_member_name(), to turn the OwnerID value returned by the database into a more user-friendly name on the display. There is no inverse function to return the OwnerID for a given name because there could be several members with the same name. To get around that, you create your own helper method, get_member_id(), which simply returns the first matching ID from self.items. (Ideally, you would create a combo box in the options dialog, but that would complicate the data-driven nature of the dialog significantly. For now you can live with the compromise.)

The event handlers are all fairly self-explanatory. The evPage() handler is fired when a new NoteBook page is selected, and it simply switches the active menu to track the active page. This ensures you can't use member functions when looking at the items and vice versa. It is simply a case of modifying the state attribute of the appropriate Menu widgets.

The new and edit event handlers contain a lot of similar code, and a helper function could be created to simplify them and avoid repetition, but doing so introduces an extra level of complexity in marshalling the correct input values so it was decided to leave them as-is. They both utilize the get_member_id() method to derive an OwnerID value from the supplied owner name value.

Similarly, a helper function could have been used to pick out the selected index, but the function is only two lines so again it was left as-is. Notice that the selection is potentially a list of indices and that these are returned as strings so you explicitly convert to integers to get a numeric index.

Most of the work is done by the data module, which is as you would expect; the GUI, after all, should be about presentation only. You might notice that there is no core logic layer in this application. That is because you are essentially just modifying the data so there is no business logic to speak of and therefore no need of a core logic layer. The GUI just calls the data layer directly. By exposing the data layer as an API, you have allowed the GUI to be written without any reference to SQL. This means you could swap out the underlying SQLite implementation and replace it with, say, Postgres or MySQL, and the API would remain the same; the GUI would not need to change.

The final piece of the puzzle is the OptionsDialog. This is implemented in a separate module because, potentially, you could reuse this in other projects. It takes a list of names and values and displays them as a form. You can then edit the values and save any changes. The dialog is built as a class that inherits from a generic dialog framework included in the standard library. The framework provides several methods that can be overridden to change how the dialog functions. The body() method is called when the dialog is created and is where the GUI layout is defined. The apply() method is called if the user clicks the OK button, and the method processes and stores the data in any way that is needed by the calling program. Other methods exist that allow you to change the button layout and behavior and to validate data entry. In this case you simply store the incoming data in a list and then update that list (in the apply() method) if the user clicks the OK button. After the dialog is closed, the list can be accessed by the call to extract the new values.

You've now covered enough Tkinter to see how it can wrap a GUI around your application logic and data. It's not the most powerful toolkit around, but it is quick and easy to get started, and it comes out of the box with Python. In the next section, you review some of the more powerful third-party GUI toolkits available.

Exploring Other GUI Toolkits for Python

There are many GUI toolkits around, ranging from the very specific native toolkits for Windows, MacOS X, and X windows, to more generic, multiplatform toolkits. Most of them have a wrapper layer of some kind available for Python. They all have the same core ideas and concepts that you saw in Tkinter, although some require an object-based approach while others, like Tkinter, permit a procedural style of programming, too. If Tkinter is not working for you, or if your main area of interest is GUI development, then these other toolkits may hold the answer. In the following sections, you find out about the strengths and weaknesses of each, and for the platform independent toolkits a very short "hello world" style sample program. If you want to run these, you need to install the toolkits because they are all provided by third parties.

That having been said, there are no absolute best or worst toolkits here. Each has its fans, and different programmers prefer different toolkits. It is worth taking some time to try out each toolkit of interest and at least work through their introductory tutorial to see whether it fits your personal style of coding. There are also some useful online videos that introduce their features, too.

wxPython

This is a long-standing toolkit that is a wrapper around the C++ wxWidgets project. wxWidgets is a C++ toolkit designed to work on all the popular operating systems while maintaining a native look and feel. Version 3.0 of wxPython was released late in 2013.

It has a rich set of widgets and powerful features supporting things like cross platform printing. (Printing from a GUI is one of those functions that sounds like it should be easy, but very rarely is!) There are some graphical GUI building tools that can generate code for you, or you can do everything by hand by crafting the code, as you did for Tkinter. While wxPython is powerful, it is still much simpler than some of the other toolkits discussed.

There are active mailing lists and forums for both wxWidgets and wxPython. There are a couple of books available on wxPython, including one written by the lead developers. The wxPython website is: `http://www.wxpython.org`.

A sample wxPython program looks like this:

```
import wx

app = wx.App(False)
frame = wx.Frame(None, wx.ID_ANY, size=(320,240), "Hello World")
frame.Show(True)

app.MainLoop()
```

PyQt

The Qt toolkit came to prominence in the development of the KDE desktop environment for Linux although it had been developed some time before that as a commercial product. Over time the licensing arrangements of Qt have been simplified such that it is now widely used in open source projects and supports most operating systems with a native look and feel. Qt is a C++ toolkit, and PyQt is the Python wrapper around that. Version 5.2 was released in early 2014.

To give some idea of the scale, Qt has more than 400 classes available and several thousand functions and methods. The learning curve is considerable, but so is the power. Some advanced features are available only to commercial users (who pay license fees), and this mixed mode of free and licensed software is probably the biggest drawback of Qt and hence PyQt. There is a full-featured graphical GUI building tool for PyQt.

A true open source (LGPL) alternative has been released in the form of PySide that offers similar functionality to PyQt and was developed by Nokia while they owned the Qt toolkit. Version 1.2.1 of PySide was released mid-2013.

There are at least two books available on PyQt programming. The website is: `http://www.riverbankcomputing.com/software/pyqt/intro`. The PySide web site is: `http://qt-project.org/wiki/PySide`.

A sample PyQt program looks like this:

```
import sys
from PyQt4 import QtGui

app = QtGui.QApplication(sys.argv)
win = QtGui.QWidget()
win.resize(320, 240)
win.setWindowTitle("Hello World!")
win.show()

sys.exit(app.exec_())
```

A sample PySide program looks like this:

```
import sys
from PySide import QtGui

app = QtGui.QApplication(sys.argv)
win = QtGui.QWidget()
win.resize(320, 240)
win.setWindowTitle("Hello World!")
win.show()

sys.exit(app.exec_())
```

As you can see, they are effectively identical, apart from the import statements.

PyGTK

The Gimp ToolKit, or GTK+ as it's now known, was originally developed in C as the GUI toolset for the GNU GIMP graphics editor. It then developed into a generic graphical toolkit and has become the toolkit behind the GNOME desktop environment used on many Linux distributions. PyGTK is the name used for the Python wrapper around the GTK+ toolkit. However, the situation has become more complex, and there are several parts to PyGTK matching the various parts of GTK+ itself. PyGObject is now the official module supporting most of the GNOME software platform including the GUI. As part of the GNU stable, it is an open source project so it has no complex license issues to contend with. New versions are released regularly.

There is a graphical design tool called Glade that can be used to create the GUI. In typical GNU fashion, the documentation is comprehensive, but not tailored to beginners. The system is very powerful and multiplatformed. Once installed it is reasonably simple to use.

There are several books on GTK+ programming, but they are focused on the underlying C API, not on the Python bindings. This leaves the online, but excellent, documentation found here: `https://live.gnome.org/PyGObject`.

A sample GTK program looks like this:

```
from gi.repository import Gtk

win = Gtk.Window(title="Hello World")
win.resize(320,240)
```

```
win.connect("delete-event", Gtk.main_quit)
win.show_all()

Gtk.main()
```

Native GUIs: Cocoa and PyWin32

Cocoa and Win32 are the native GUI toolkits for the Mac OS X and Windows operating systems respectively. Both can be programmed from Python. The PyObjC toolkit for Cocoa is provided by the MacPython project, and the native MacOS X development tools can be used to create and connect the GUI to code. You have already met the Pywin32 package back in Chapter 2, where its ability to expose the Win32 API was discussed. The Win32 API is not only about low-level Windows functions, but also it has all the functions used to build Windows native GUIs. The mechanisms are the same; you just call different functions.

The disadvantages to both these toolkits, especially the Win32 API, is the complexity involved combined with the fact that they are strictly limited to their own operating system. If you know that you will never need to support anything else, that may not be a problem. The Cocoa option does at least provide a useful set of development tools, but the Windows option is not so richly endowed.

A far better option for native Windows development is the use of IronPython. This is a version of Python written in Microsoft .NET and supported on Microsoft's Visual Studio development environment as a standard .NET language. This gives access to all the .NET functionality, but is still limited to Windows. (There is a .NET clone for other platforms known as Mono, but it is not widely used for desktop applications.)

The MacPython website is `http://homepages.cwi.nl/~jack/macpython/`. The IronPython website is `http://ironpython.net/`.

Dabo

Dabo is rather different from the other toolkits described in that it is more than just a GUI toolkit. Dabo is a fully featured application framework and toolset. It specializes in database applications such as those commonly found in businesses. It comes with a set of GUI widgets, currently based on a wxWidgets foundation but modified for Dabo (theoretically, another GUI toolkit could be used but the development team has found more productive ways to spend its time!). On top of the GUI, it provides a set of classes that contains the business logic and bridges the gap between the user interface and data layer. The data layer can be any of half a dozen databases, including SQLite.

It is possible to build complex logic into a Dabo application, although its natural home is in building forms-based tools that provide a view and editing capability to the base data. Version 0.9.12 was released June 2013. The Dabo website is found at `http://www.dabodev.com/`.

You've now covered a fair amount of ground, especially regarding user interface options. You now look at some other issues you will likely meet in building real-world desktop applications in Python: storing configuration data and localization.

STORING LOCAL DATA

In Chapter 3 you saw various strategies for storing data. Earlier in this chapter, you saw how an application can be structured in layers with a data layer at the bottom of the stack. That data layer is concerned with managing the core entities of your application. Those core entities are not the only kinds of data you need to store. You often need to store data about the application itself. That configuration data is specific to a single user or perhaps to the local computer system and hence is called local data. Typically, it is stored in a configuration file or as environment variables. You saw how to read that data in Chapter 2. In this section you consider the various kinds of local data that an application may need to maintain and the options available for storing it.

Applications have several different types of configuration data. Some of it is concerned with getting the application to work in the first place, for example, the network address of a server or the location of the data files. These values are typically specific to a given installation or computer system rather than to an individual user.

Other types of configuration data are things like user preferences. For example, the user may have some control over the layout of the user interface, the colors used, the location and size of the Windows on screen, and so on. Another common category of user-configured data is the selection of helper applications used, for example, the user's preferred text or image editing software. Some of these details could be exposed in a preferences dialog that the user edits and explicitly saves. Indeed it may even be possible to store different preferences for different usage scenarios for the same application.

Other settings may be stored by the application itself so that it can restore itself to the last state when it restarts. These settings might include the last opened file, the currently open windows and dialogs, and the screen coordinates of each.

The final data type you might want to store is information about how the application is functioning. In particular, error conditions or unexpected inputs can be recorded. This is generically known as logging and involves storing information in a log file that can be examined later either as part of a debug process or to improve effectiveness of the design.

Storing Application-Specific Data

Application specific data could be stored on the local computer, or it could be stored in a local network location that all instances of the application can reach. This raises the question of how the computer knows where to look. The usual solution to this problem is to set an environment variable or use a local configuration file stored in the startup folder of the application. This can then be set as part of the installation procedure. It can even be provided as a startup parameter.

The advantage of storing this kind of information on the network is that it is shared so that any changes made, for example if the database is moved, can be detected immediately by all of the installed instances on the network without having to manually reconfigure each machine or user configuration. It also allows for a backup configuration to be available in the event of a system failure and by changing one environment variable or configuration setting on the local computers the new central configuration can be accessed with minimal downtime.

The physical storage medium is relatively unimportant because the data are relatively static and normally only read once when the application starts up. A simple configuration file using plaintext, XML, or even Windows INI format will likely suffice. Python provides tools for creating and reading all of these; refer to Chapter 2 for details.

Storing User-Selected Preferences

User preferences are nearly always stored in the local computer, and often in a configuration file stored in the user's home directory. Occasionally, applications store user preferences in the main database, especially if the database contains a significant amount of user data anyway. The disadvantage of using the database is that the application can access the preferences only if the database is accessible, which may not be the case if the user is mobile. It is disconcerting for a user to find that the application appears or functions differently depending on whether they are connected to their network or not. Local storage is definitely the preferred option for this kind of data.

Locating the data should be straightforward if a standard filename is used and the location is the home directory, because the home directory is nearly always obtainable either as an environment setting or as a user database value. (See Chapter 2 for guidance on how to determine user details such as the home directory.)

The format is normally a text file using either Windows INI or XML format. If the number of settings is very large, a small local database using SQLite might be appropriate, but this would be separate from the main application data store.

One other factor to consider when dealing with user preferences is how these are set and modified. If the settings are few and simple in nature (for example boolean or integer values), then it might be acceptable to generate a default preferences file and ask the user to manually edit the file. This does carry a risk if the user is not familiar with text editors and uses a rich format word processor to edit the file. This can render the configuration file unreadable by the application. However, if the users are likely to be experienced in editing text, such as developers or system administrators, then this approach can work well. If the configuration data is not simple or is stored in a structured file using XML or similar, then user editing is much less suitable and error prone, and a preferences dialog needs to be included in the application itself.

STORING AND NAMING CONFIGURATION DATA

Some operating systems or environments have preferred ways to store configuration data. Microsoft recommends that Windows applications use the Windows Registry (for which Python provides the winreg module). The registry can store data for individual users or for the computer as a whole. The disadvantage of the registry is that it is Windows specific, and if your code is intended to run on multiple operating systems, you need to have two storage mechanisms, so many developers prefer to standardize on configuration files even for Windows.

The X Windows system has its own configuration database (managed via the xrdb program) and expects its configurable data in a specific format. The local settings for all X applications are stored in the file .Xresources in the user's home directory. Fortunately, if you are creating X-based programs in Python, you are likely to be using one of the GUI toolkits discussed earlier, and they hide these details from you. However, if your application uses X-based programs as helper applications, you may need to read or modify these X configuration files. This should be treated as a scripting challenge, and the principles found in Chapter 2 apply.

Finally, most operating systems have recommended naming conventions for configuration files. On UNIX systems they often start with a period (that makes them invisible to normal file listing tools), end with the letters rc, and are typically stored in the user's home directory (for user settings) and the application directory (for systemwide settings and defaults). For example, the vim text editor uses the file .vimrc to store user preferences. It is also becoming common for configuration data files to be stored under the hidden directory .config in the user's home directory, and this is the location recommended by the freedesktop.org standards. On Windows the configuration files are usually in Windows INI format and have an extension of .ini.

Storing Application State

Storing application state is the least standardized form of local data storage. The location and format of the storage is down to the developer. Some applications make the choice of whether to save-state a user preference; others do it automatically, while most do not save state (except perhaps for a list of recently accessed files). You need to decide how much state information you want to store, where to store it, and what format to use.

To keep application behavior consistent, you should choose a local storage option so that the application behaves as expected even when disconnected from the network. However, you need to be careful with error handling because, if the application was closed while online but then opened offline, many of the resources previously used may not be accessible. You need to have a working fallback configuration that can be used when things go wrong.

The format of the state data is likely to be quite complex because it may involve multiple windows and even tabs and control settings within windows. This almost inevitably requires a rich storage format such as XML. On the other hand, if you are only saving the open file history, a simple text file may suffice, or you could even append it to the user's preference data in their configuration file.

Logging Error Information

You often want to keep a record of unexpected events or inputs so that you can analyze them later. This could be during testing, following a system failure, or even as a continuous improvement activity. The usual way to do this is to record messages in a log file. The log file might be a single file that just grows continuously or, more commonly, a file whose name is based on the date. Housekeeping (archiving or deleting of old files) of old files might be done manually, automatically, or via a shell script.

Python provides the `logging` package to assist in this process. It can generate standard information in a standard file with different levels of logging (that is it can flag a message with different category markers: debug, info, warning, error, and critical). The package is very flexible and allows for many different configuration options to control how it works. The basic usage is straightforward and you can extend its functions as you need them.

At the most basic level you import the module and then call one of several logging methods corresponding to the categories mentioned. For example:

```
>>> import logging
>>> logging.basicConfig(level=logging.DEBUG)
>>> logging.info('Heres some info')
INFO:root:Heres some info
>>> logging.error('Oops, thats bad')
ERROR:root:Oops, thats bad
>>> logging.critical('AAARGH, Its all gone wrong!')
CRITICAL:root:AAARGH, Its all gone wrong!
```

It's important that you call `basicConfig()` before using any of the logging methods; otherwise, it has no effect, and you use the default values. The level setting indicates the minimum level of message that is displayed; DEBUG is the lowest level, so everything gets printed. In addition to setting the level, you can also specify an output filename.

You can also specify the format of the log message including things like the date of the message, the file and function where it was generated, and so on. (The options are all documented in the `LogRecord` section of the logging documentation.) Because the default format doesn't include any date or time information, you usually want to set something like this:

```
>>> import logging
>>> logging.basicConfig(format="%(asctime)s %(levelname)s : %(message)s")
>>> logging.error('Its going wrong')
2014-04-24 16:12:44,832 ERROR : Its going wrong
>>> logging.error('Its going wrong')
2014-04-24 16:12:54,415 ERROR : Its going wrong
>>>
>>> logging.critical('Told you...')
2014-04-24 16:13:08,431 CRITICAL : Told you...
```

You can also use a `datefmt` argument to `basicConfig()` to change the date format using the same options as you used in `time.strftime()`. Here is a short example:

```
>>> import logging
>>> logging.basicConfig(format="%(levelname)s:%(asctime)s %(message)s",
                        datefmt="%Y/%m/%d-%I:%M")
>>> logging.error("It's happened again")
ERROR:2014/04/24-04:21 It's happened again
>>>
```

There are many other things you can do, but the basic usage described here should be enough for all but the largest projects.

UNDERSTANDING LOCALIZATION

Localization is the name given to the various actions required to make a computer application usable in different localities. That includes such features as time zone differences, date and time formatting, currency symbols, numeric formatting and, of course, language differences. In extreme cases it might require a new UI layout to take account of reading direction, such as right to left. Your computer operating system likely has many of these features controlled by a configuration setting, usually created when the operating system is first installed. Most users never change this setting and therefore take it for granted and never think about it. As a programmer your code may have to run on different computers each with potentially different localization options.

In this section you learn about how Python provides support for localization through the use of *locales* and the *Unicode* character set. A *locale* is simply a code value that indicates a standardized group of localized settings (time zone, date format, currency, and so on). Unicode is an international standard for representing characters in different alphabets, for example, Latin, Arabic, Chinese, and so on, as well as different symbols such as punctuation marks and math.

Unicode is all very well in that it enables you to use different alphabets, but how do you translate the strings used in your applications into different languages? That process is known as *internationalization*. There is a standard industry process for this using a mechanism called *gettext* that generates language-specific files containing mappings from your embedded strings to the different language versions. Python supports this mechanism via the `gettext` module. Localization includes the ability to select the correct string translation using `gettext`.

Using Locales

Python supports different locales via the locale module. The way the module works is quite complex and uses a layered approach; however, mostly you don't need to know about that. You can use a very small subset and generally you pick up the correct locale for your user.

When your program starts, it is usually set to the "C" locale by default (although that may not always be the case, and local configuration settings may have changed it). However, you usually want to set the locale that your user has chosen. The way to do that is to call the `locale .setlocale()` function with an empty locale argument. This causes the system locale to be selected. Most of the time, that's all you need to do. You are strongly recommended to do this only once in your program and to do so near the start of your code.

You can then use `locale.getlocale()` to fetch the local details if you need to find out what has been set up (you see that in action in the next section where you look at how to translate your program's strings into the local language).

Unfortunately, setting the locale is not the end of the story. If you want that change to take effect, there are some changes you need to make to your code. Specifically, there are some type conversion and comparison operations that are not locale-aware in the standard library and built-in functions. To get around that, the locale module provides alternatives. In other cases the standard functions do understand locales if you give them the right hints. For example, the `time.strftime()` function can format times to the local style if you use the appropriate formatting specifications such as `%x` for the localized date and `%X` for the localized time. Similarly, to `print()` numbers in the locale specific format, you need to specify the n style instead of d or f or g in the string `format()` method.

The following interpreter session demonstrates some of these features:

```
>>> import locale as loc
>>> import time
>>> loc.setlocale(loc.LC_ALL,'')
'English_United States.1252'
>>> loc.currency(350)
'$350.00'
>>> time.strftime("%x %X", time.localtime())
'4/22/2014 7:44:57 PM'
>>>
```

Repeating those in a cygwin session set to the en _ GB locale, you can see some differences:

```
>>> import locale as loc
>>> import time
>>> loc.setlocale(loc.LC_ALL, '')
'en_GB.UTF-8'
>>> loc.currency(350)
'£350.00'
>>> time.strftime("%x %X", time.localtime())
'22/04/2014 19:32:23'
```

The locale itself is clearly very differently specified. The currency uses the appropriate symbols, and the dates and times are quite different with the UK version using a 24-hour clock format and with the day and month of the date transposed.

You can now try some of the conversion and comparison functions. These work the same in both UK and U.S. English, so there is no point in doing a comparison this time.

```
>>> print("{:n}".format(3.14159))
3.14159
>>> print("{:n}".format(42))
42
>>> loc.strcoll("Spanish", "Inquisition")
1
>>> loc.strcoll("Inquisition", "Spanish")
-1
>>> loc.strcoll("Spanish","Spanish")
0
```

These examples show how the string formatting n specifier works for both integers and floating-point numbers. The `locale.strcoll()` string comparison examples are useful because they take account of locale specific ideas on character ordering. The return values are 1 if the first string is "higher" valued, -1 if it is "lower" valued, and 0 if the two arguments are the same.

Locale provides the following conversion functions that are useful in particular situations: `atoi()`, `atof()`, `str()`, `format()`, and `format _ string()`.

Using Unicode in Python

Computers store data as binary numbers. Characters are mapped onto these numbers so that when the computer prints a string of characters it maps the numeric data in memory to a set of character representations on screen. Back in the dawn of computing, characters were represented by as few as 5 bits and more commonly using 7 or 8 bits. All of these encodings could fit into a single 8-bit byte of storage, so it was very compact. Unfortunately, a single byte can only cater to 256 different combinations, which is fine for the Latin alphabets, used in the Western nations where modern computing originated, but nowhere near enough for all the alphabets in the world as a whole. Over time each country and corporation invented its own encoding system, and software engineers had to write lots of code to cater to these if their software was to be used in different localities. The solution was the Unicode standard.

Unicode is a 32-bit character catalog that can store a huge number of possible characters. Unicode characters are represented by entities called *code points* that are the numeric values that map onto characters. Code points are described using the format U+xxxx. The U+ indicates that it is a Unicode code point and the xxxx is the hexadecimal number representing the location of the code point in Unicode (there can be up to 8 hex digits not just 4). Code points are then mapped to characters that also have descriptive names. Thus the character "A" is listed as "U+0041 LATIN CAPITAL LETTER A". The Python representation of the Unicode encoding is \uxxxx for 4 digits or \Uxxxxxxxx for 8 digits, which is a fairly obvious translation of the Unicode format, simply replacing U+ with \u or \U. The codes and names can all be found on the Unicode website at http://www.unicode.org/Public/UNIDATA/NamesList.txt. It is important to realize that Unicode defines the character only, not its appearance. What you see as a character on your computer screen, or printed out on paper, is known as a *glyph,* which is a graphical representation of that character in some font or other. Unicode does not specify the font family, weight, size, or any other details about appearance, only the actual character.

The Unicode data has to be stored on the computer as a set of bytes that, as you recall, can only store values from 0–255. The simplest translation, or *encoding*, of Unicode is known as UTF-32 and is a one-to-one mapping from the Unicode code point value to a 32-bit number. This is simple to understand, but requires 4 bytes for every character, making it very memory and bandwidth hungry. To conserve space two other encodings are used. UTF-16 uses 16-bit blocks to represent most characters, but with an option to extend that to two 16-bit blocks for some rarely used characters. Microsoft Windows uses UTF-16 by default.

> **NOTE** *The extension in UTF-16 is known as a surrogate and is indicated by a block containing a value in the range 0xD800-0xDFFF. UTF-8 uses a different scheme whereby if a byte has a value greater than 128 it indicates that it is part of a multibyte sequence.*

UTF-8 stores the most commonly used characters in a single 8-bit block, but can be extended to use 2, 3, or 4 blocks for less commonly used characters. This makes UTF-8 the most compact format if you are using the right set of characters—specifically the Latin alphabet. UTF-8 also has the convenient feature of having the original ASCII character set as its lowest set of bytes, making interworking with older non-Unicode applications much easier. UTF-8 is the default encoding for Python version 3.

That is all pretty complicated, so how does Python help you handle all of this? Python version 3 uses Unicode strings with UTF-8 as its default encoding, although you can change that if you need to. The way to change the encoding is to put a special comment as the very first line of your code, like this,

```
# -*- coding: <encoding name> -*-
```

where the encoding name is whatever encoding you choose to use, typically utf-16 or ascii.

You can also use the Unicode characters in literal strings. You can even use their long names, for example:

```
>>> print('A')
A
>>> print('\u0041')
A
>>> print("\N{LATIN CAPITAL LETTER A}")
A
```

They all print the same character, A.

You can use the encode() method of a string to get the raw bytes used to store the data:

```
>>> print("\u00A1Help!")
¡Help!
>>> print("\u00A1Help!".encode('utf-8'))
b'\xc2\xa1Help!'
>>> b'\xc2\xa1Help!'.decode('utf-8')
'¡Help!'
>>>
```

Notice that the second version printed the UTF-8 two-byte representation of the inverted exclamation point represented by \u00A1. The third line converted the encoding back into a string using encode()'s complementary method decode().

So far you've seen how to represent single Unicode characters, how to change the default encoding used by Python, and how to convert a string into its byte representation using encode() and how to turn bytes into a Unicode string using decode(). Mostly that is all you need to know about Unicode and Python. The interpreter does most of the work for you. You can go on to define your own encodings, too, but that requires some more detailed knowledge and a study of the codecs module. You really shouldn't need to do that in most situations.

To conclude this section, you should be aware of the unicodedata module that is particularly useful at the interactive prompt as a way of finding out about Unicode characters. Combined with the data published on the Unicode website you should be able to answer most questions that arise during regular coding.

You can tell the Unicode name and category of a given character using the unicodedata module and that can then be used to look up the website for more details. Assume you have just stored some data that you believe to contain a Unicode string and you want to know about the characters it contains. You might try this:

```
>>> data = b'\xd9\x85\xd8\xb1\xd8\xad\xd8\xa8\xd8\xa7 \xd8\xa3\xd9\x84\xd8\xa7\
    xd9\x86'
>>> print(data.decode('utf-8'))
ألان مرحبا
>>> for ch in data.decode('utf-8'):
...     print(ord(ch), ud.name(ch))
...
1605 ARABIC LETTER MEEM
1585 ARABIC LETTER REH
1581 ARABIC LETTER HAH
1576 ARABIC LETTER BEH
1575 ARABIC LETTER ALEF
32 SPACE
1571 ARABIC LETTER ALEF WITH HAMZA ABOVE
1604 ARABIC LETTER LAM
1575 ARABIC LETTER ALEF
1606 ARABIC LETTER NOON
>>>
```

Here you have a byte string that you suspect is UTF-8 characters and you want to find out what kind of data it is. You can try decoding it, to check that it is valid UTF-8, and that works, but you don't recognize the printed character set. You then import the unicodedata module and run a for loop over the data printing out the long Unicode name of each character. From this it is obvious that the data is in Arabic.

Using gettext

To translate your program strings using the gettext mechanism, there is a standard set of steps you need to take. First, you have to use gettext functions to identify the strings in your code that you want translated. Second, you run a utility to extract those strings into a template file, typically called messages.po. After that you have to produce translation files based on messages.po, ideally by hiring a set of translators or perhaps by trusting Google translate or similar tools! Third, use another tool to convert the translation files to the language specific .mo format used by getttext, for example, messages_en.mo for the English version. Finally, you need to ship the folder with the .mo files in it along with your translation. There are various different tools available depending on the operating system. For Windows users there are a couple of scripts in the Tools/i18n folder of your Python distribution. For UNIX-like systems there are operating system utilities available that are Python aware.

You now walk through a simple example—the ubiquitous "Hello world" script. The first step is to use the gettext module and its functions to mark your program strings that require translation. You start by creating a new Python code file called gettext_demo.py (or load it from the gettext folder of the zip file):

```
import gettext
import locale as loc


# Set up the locale and translation mechanism
##############################
```

```
loc.setlocale(loc.LC_ALL,'')
filename = "res/messages_{}.mo".format(loc.getlocale()[0][0:2])

trans = gettext.GNUTranslations(open(filename,'rb'))
trans.install()

# Now the main program with gettext markers
############################
print(_("Hello World"))
```

This sets the locale as discussed in the previous section and uses it to dynamically create the name of the translation file to be used. You are only creating an English translation so you could have hard-coded the name, but using `getlocale()` demonstrates how it would be done if you had more than one language available.

Next, you instantiate a `gettext.GNUTranslations` object and `install()` it. This activates the magic function `_()` that you then use to surround all the strings you need translated. In this case that's the single string `"Hello World"`.

Your next step is to generate the `messages.po` template file. If you are on a UNIX-like operating system, you can run the tool `xgettext` like this:

```
$ xgettext gettext_demo.py
```

> **NOTE** The Windows equivalents of the UNIX tools are `pygettext.py` and `msgfmy.py`. Both are found in the `Tools/i18n` folder of a standard Python install.

You should now find a `messages.po` file in the same folder as your Python file. Open this in your text editor and replace the string CHARSET with UTF-8 and insert a translation of `"Hello world"` in the empty string at the bottom. Just to prove that the translation is being picked up, you should use something like `"Hello beautiful world"` but normally, for English, you would just repeat the same string. (There are a bunch of other metadata fields that you could fill in, but they are not needed for this demonstration so you can just ignore them.) Now save the file as `messages_en.po`. It should look like this:

```
# SOME DESCRIPTIVE TITLE.
# Copyright (C) YEAR THE PACKAGE'S COPYRIGHT HOLDER
# This file is distributed under the same license as the PACKAGE package.
# FIRST AUTHOR <EMAIL@ADDRESS>, YEAR.
#
#, fuzzy
msgid ""
msgstr ""
"Project-Id-Version: PACKAGE VERSION\n"
"Report-Msgid-Bugs-To: \n"
"POT-Creation-Date: 2014-04-22 18:05+0100\n"
"PO-Revision-Date: YEAR-MO-DA HO:MI+ZONE\n"
```

```
"Last-Translator: FULL NAME <EMAIL@ADDRESS>\n"
"Language-Team: LANGUAGE <LL@li.org>\n"
"Language: \n"
"MIME-Version: 1.0\n"
"Content-Type: text/plain; charset=UTF-8\n"
"Content-Transfer-Encoding: 8bit\n"

#: gettext-demo.py:14
msgid "Hello World"
msgstr "Hello beautiful world"
```

Next, you want to create the res (for resource) folder that you specified in the filename in the Python script. The name is not critical, but res is a reasonable convention. You now run another utility called msgfmt like this:

```
$ msgfmt -o res/messages_en.mo messages_en.po
```

Note the different file endings! This creates the translation file that you told gettext to read when running your script. You are now ready to run the demo:

```
$ python3 gettext_demo.py
```

You should find that the translated string "Hello beautiful world" is printed instead of the original "Hello World" that you had in your code. This proves that the translation worked. You can go on to make more translation files by repeating the steps after running xgettext for each new language. To test them you need to change the local language settings.

Localization is a complex and growing area of study. However, if you plan on distributing your applications to multiple language users or in different countries, it is something you cannot afford to ignore.

SUMMARY

In this chapter you saw the power of structuring applications in layers to separate out the data processing from the core, or business, logic and the presentation. In particular you saw how you could build multiple user interfaces on top of the same core logic and data layers. In the process you explored several variations of command-line interfaces including different styles of user interaction and powerful command-line options.

You also saw how to build GUI applications using Tkinter, the standard GUI toolkit in Python, along with its ancillary modules that offer more widgets and improved appearance. You concluded this exploration by building a significant user interface on top of an existing data layer using many of the features already explored but using an object-oriented style rather than a procedural approach. Finally, you reviewed some alternative third-party GUI frameworks that offer even more power than Tkinter should you wish to get more serious about GUI applications.

The chapter looked at some wider issues in building applications for other people to use. It covered the various types of non-core data (such as configuration values) that you can store and the options available for each type. You also covered the use of the Python logging module to record significant events and how you can manage the levels of logging and how it is stored.

You concluded the chapter with a look at the issues around localizing applications for the user. This includes using localized settings for currency and time formats as well as different alphabets. Python supports Unicode character sets, and you used encode() and decode() methods to convert strings to and from their raw bytes. Finally, you experimented with the gettext mechanism for displaying different languages within your application.

EXERCISES

1. Convert the oxo-logic.py module to reflect OOP design by creating a Game class.

2. Explore the Tkinter.filedialog module to get the name of a text file from a user and then display that file on screen.

3. Replace the label in the first GUI example program with a Tix ScrolledText widget so that it displays the history of all the entries from the Entry widget.

4. Rewrite the first GUI example to be compatible with gettext and generate a new English version with different text on the controls.

▶ WHAT YOU LEARNED IN THIS CHAPTER

KEY CONCEPT	DESCRIPTION
Desktop application	A program that runs primarily on the user's local computer. Generally an interactive program that, for example, modifies data or plays a game.
Data layer	The part of an application that stores, modifies, and retrieves data. It has little or no knowledge of the application logic or business rules and no knowledge of how the data will be presented.
Core logic	The part of the application that processes the data. This is where the complex algorithms and business rules will be located. The data will be fetched or written via the data layer. The logic is not concerned with how the results are presented merely that the correct data are created.
Presentation layer (aka User Interface)	The part of the application with which the user interacts. This is all about presenting the data in a clear manner and enabling the user to access the functions of the application in a logical and obvious manner. The presentation layer should not depend on the correctness of the underlying data to function, it is only concerned with presenting the data it is given. (Some basic data validation could legitimately occur, such as ensuring that a given field contains an integer within a given range.)
Localization	The process and mechanisms whereby different users can use the same application regardless of their location and still see the output in terms that they recognize. That is the application should comply with local layouts of structured data such as dates or currency.
Unicode	An internationally agreed set of standards for presenting character sets. Unicode is not concerned with the shape of the characters it represents (their glyphs) but only with the content, or meaning, of the individual characters.
Internationalization	The process of translating the strings on a display such that they are legible by users of different languages.

5

Python on the Web

WHAT YOU WILL LEARN IN THIS CHAPTER:

- ➤ Understanding how Python works on the web
- ➤ Creating a web app with Python
- ➤ Connecting a web app to a database
- ➤ Creating an API
- ➤ Parsing and manipulating data in a web app

WROX.COM DOWNLOADS FOR THIS CHAPTER

For this chapter the wrox.com code downloads are found at www.wrox.com/go/
pythonprojects on the Download Code tab. The code is in the Chapter 5 download, called
Chapter5.zip, and individually named according to the names throughout the chapter.

Up to this point you've been using Python locally to investigate and parse data on your local
machine. But what about when you want to use Python for remote data manipulation, or
across "the wire"?

Python is a very powerful language, and it's not just for doing system administration tasks or
file system tasks locally. You can use Python across networks to handle tasks using REST and
XMLRPC. This chapter looks into both of these, but the focus is on the most popular method
of using Python remotely: HTTP using REST.

In this chapter you use some of the more popular web technologies with Python, including
HTTP and REST, to create a web app that links to a database. You use technologies such as
Flask and SQLite to complete the web app, and finally, you create an application programming
interface (API) and learn to parse and manipulate data in the web app.

REST stands for *Representational State Transfer.* It's a fancy name for the technology and architecture style of a certain web service. This service doesn't rely on the implementation of components or protocol syntax; instead, it worries about how to interact with data (sending it back and forth within the constraints placed upon it). We explain RESTful architecture in the section on building an API with Flask. For now, just know that REST is a thing that makes up the architecture of web services.

> **NOTE** *Because it is beyond the scope of this book to teach the fundamentals of front-end web development, we've provided you with the files you need to have a nice interface. We will be focusing on the middle layer of Python and how to hook up the front end to the database and web server. We can only lightly touch on the JavaScript that is provided. It is recommended that you familiarize yourself with modern front-end technologies should you be focusing your Python development on the web.*

PYTHON ON THE WEB

As you may know, the web is made up of a few technologies, not just one. Figure 5-1 shows a high-level overview of the structure of a modern web app.

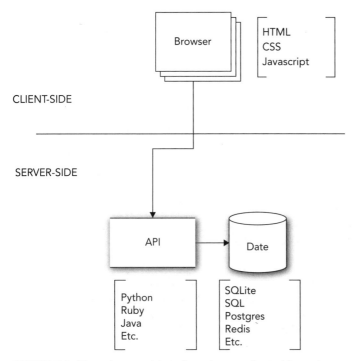

FIGURE 5-1: Note the two sides of a web app: client-side and server-side. Server-side data is served via a web server such as Apache or Nginx.

As you can see, the front end of a web app consists of a browser that handles the HTML, CSS, and JavaScript. The middle layer, in this case, is Python, but in general this is usually some scripting language such as Ruby, Perl, or PHP, or JavaScript. The back end will house your database (SQLite) and web server, or HTTP Daemon (commonly, Nginx or Apache). Although it is beyond the scope of this book to explain the fundamentals of the back end and front end, you will learn how to set up a very simple server.

> **NOTE** *Should you need to make this server public, it is highly recommended that you fully understand the fundamentals of any technology with which you are unfamiliar. So, read the docs and know what you're getting into, and learn how to securely set up a public-facing web server before doing so.*

Let's move on and start explaining how each of these pieces work together.

Parts of a Web Application

You can serve data across networks in a few ways. Python is a language that can handle almost all of those ways. We briefly touch on the most common uses of Python as a server-side language, and then we use the most modern and most common way of using Python on the web: building a web application.

The basic structure of any network request is shown in Figure 5-2. What happens between "Server Receives Request" and "Server Returns Data to Requestor"? That is where Python lives.

Request Is Made

↓

Server Receives Request

↓

Server Returns Data to Requestor

FIGURE 5-2: Structure of a network request

Because browsers can't ship with every interpreter ever created—and we certainly don't want them to come with compilers—we needed to find a way to bridge static pages and dynamic data so that we could have interactive, dynamic web pages. We know that we have a web server that is serving up files that make up our web app, but how does the server know what files we're using? How can the server tell that the app is written in Python and not, say, Ruby?

Welcome WSGI! WSGI, or *Web Server Gateway Interface*, is how your web server (like Apache) knows about and can run Python files. It is beyond the scope of this book to delve into the intricacies of WSGI; just know that most modern web servers support it, and if you want to run Python on a server, that server needs to have WSGI available. If you're interested in a deeper understanding of server operations and what is known as "DevOps," it is recommended that you research the more lower-level technologies, such as WSGI. For our purposes, however, we'll be using a framework that has already taken care of that piece of server architecture for us and uses WSGI. You will see this term referenced throughout when discussing Python on the web, so hopefully you'll remember it and understand what part it plays in the grand scheme of things.

The Client-Server Relationship

What is a client? In web development, a *client* usually refers to a web browser, which sends out requests to your web server for files. However, you will see other uses of the term "client" to mean another server that is requesting data from a second server. For the purposes of this chapter, a client is basically a browser—in other words, the part of the web app that wants to display the data that the app is returning. This is also the part of the web app that the user will be interacting with. If you've ever heard the term "client-side JavaScript" and never really understood it, this should clear up that confusion: Client-side JavaScript is JavaScript that is only on the client side and performs actions directly in the client (a web browser), and not on the server. This includes, for example, changing colors or styles on a webpage when certain events are fired (i.e., a button-click changes the color of a background). These functions never actually talk to a server and can be used locally, if needed (without an Internet connection).

So, what is server-side JavaScript, then? As you probably guessed, it's JavaScript that is executed on the server, usually by an event from the client side, such as a GET request or client-side JavaScript. We won't be dealing with any server-side JavaScript in this book because we're using Python, which is our server-side language of choice. This is where our logic will live. This is the part of the app that takes the actions from the client and makes magic happen.

Middleware and MVC

Middleware is a fairly new term in web development. It refers to the part of the technology stack that will take in data from the front end (the client), manipulate it, pass it into or out of the database (or other service that may be running), and then send it back to the front end. Basically, the logic of your system/app should live in your middle layer, your data should live in your data layer, and your styles should live in the front end. It is never ideal to have your front end (JavaScript) doing much data logic, which can be better handled in your middle layer.

All of these pieces actually have a nice name—it is called *model-view-controller* (MVC). Most modern frameworks use some sort of MVC architecture. The benefit of MVC is that your client doesn't have to deal with the logic of your app, and your logic doesn't have to deal with your data models. You can set your data models and forget 'em! (sorta).

Say you're working on a large project and you have web designers writing your HTML and CSS and some of the JavaScript that makes your web app look slick and shiny. Then you have very smart mathematicians working on your data layer, because you need precise numbers to be calculated from data inputted from your slick, shiny client. What happens if you have your logic code in your client-side files? Let's say you put your calculations in the templates that the web designers were working on. Furthermore, let's say that your web designers wanted to manipulate something and they thought your calculation was the problem. This isn't ideal, is it? MVC somewhat solves this problem by separating out your data layer (the data *model* that is storing your precise calculations), from the *controllers* you're writing to do your precise calculations, with the *view* that your web designers are working on to make a shiny, slick web app.

So, what does all this mean in the Python world? Well, you're going to come across the term "MVC" and you should understand the overview of the architecture. We use a framework in this chapter that utilizes a sort of MVC architecture, so you should now have a better understanding of why we've made most of the decisions we've made, moving forward.

HTTP Methods and Headers

HTTP stands for *HyperText Transfer Protocol*. This is the protocol that is used to pass data around on the web, usually via a web browser. When a client makes a request, it uses this HTTP protocol. This might look familiar to anyone who's done any web programming with HyperText Markup Language (HTML). HTTP is made to pass HTML.

HTTP methods are the verbs of the web. The two most basic methods are GET and POST. These do what you might expect. When you send the web server a GET request, you are requesting to *get* data *from* the server. This request, or GET, is used every time you load a web page into your browser. So, when you go to twitter.com, your browser is sending a GET request to the Twitter servers and asking for information.

What about when you type out a tweet and hit the Tweet button? When you are sending data *to* the server, you are using a POST method call. This indicates to the server that you are going to attempt to *post* data *to* the server. (We lightly touch on some other method calls as you go through the process of building your app.)

> **NOTE** If you plan to use Python for web development, it is highly recommended that you familiarize yourself with all the HTTP methods available.

So, how does the web server know what method is being sent? It does this via the HTTP headers (see Figure 5-3).

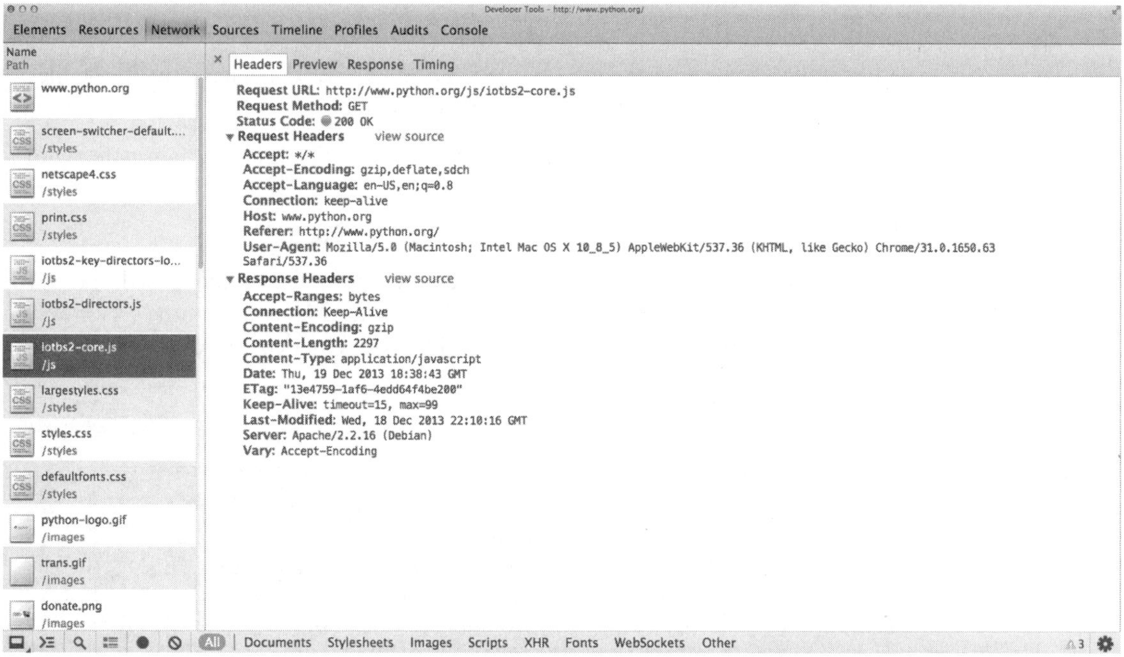

FIGURE 5-3: The Chrome Developer Tools, illustrating the headers of a server request for a file

As you can see in Figure 5-3, we have gone to `http://www.python.org` and in doing so, have sent a GET request to the server for a JavaScript file that is named `iotbs2-core.js`. The server responded with a status code of "200 OK," which simply means that the file was available to be served and was served. Other HTTP Status Codes exist: the code 404 is the most widely known—it means "Not Found," meaning the file was not found on the server, so it could not be served.

Headers contain information for the server, to know what you are requesting from the server. This helps the HTTP, or web, server to respond properly to requests that are made from the Internet. Headers also contain metadata, such as what browser was being used to make the request. As you can see in Figure 5-3, the request was made using Chrome on a Macintosh running OS X 10.8.5.

If you're going to be developing for the web and you don't have a dedicated front-end team to check your API's implementation, you're going to have to do your own debugging. It's also helpful to know how your API will be accessed and to be able to replicate that for testing and debugging purposes. To do this, you will be using the Chrome Developer Tools (or DevTools, for short).

TRY IT OUT   Using the Chrome Developer Tools

In this Try It Out, you practice using the Chrome Developer Tools, which you will be using later in this chapter.

1. Open your Chrome browser. From the menu, click View and then select Developer. Finally, click Developer Tools.

2. In the DevTools window, click the Network tab (see Figure 5-4).

3. Go to `http://www.python.org`.

    You should see a list of files, some ending with `.js`, such as `jquery.min.js`. These are all the files that have been requested when we told the browser to get us python.org.

4. Click one of the files ending with .js. You should see a new window appear in the right pane, with the Preview tab highlighted (see Figure 5-5).

5. Click the Headers tab, to the left of the highlighted Preview tab (see Figure 5-6).

You should now see the HTTP header that was sent to the server, requesting the file along with the response headers that the server returned. Feel free to click the Response tab to see what the server actually returned. You work more with the Response tab later on, when you start debugging your own API.

NOTE *DevTools will be one of the most used tools you'll work with if you are doing web development. Another tool that may come in handy while testing your API, if you don't want to test using a live page, is SimpleRestClient. This is a free Chrome plug-in that you can find in the Chrome App store and install directly into Chrome. Of course, other REST clients are available, so feel free to find one that suits you.*

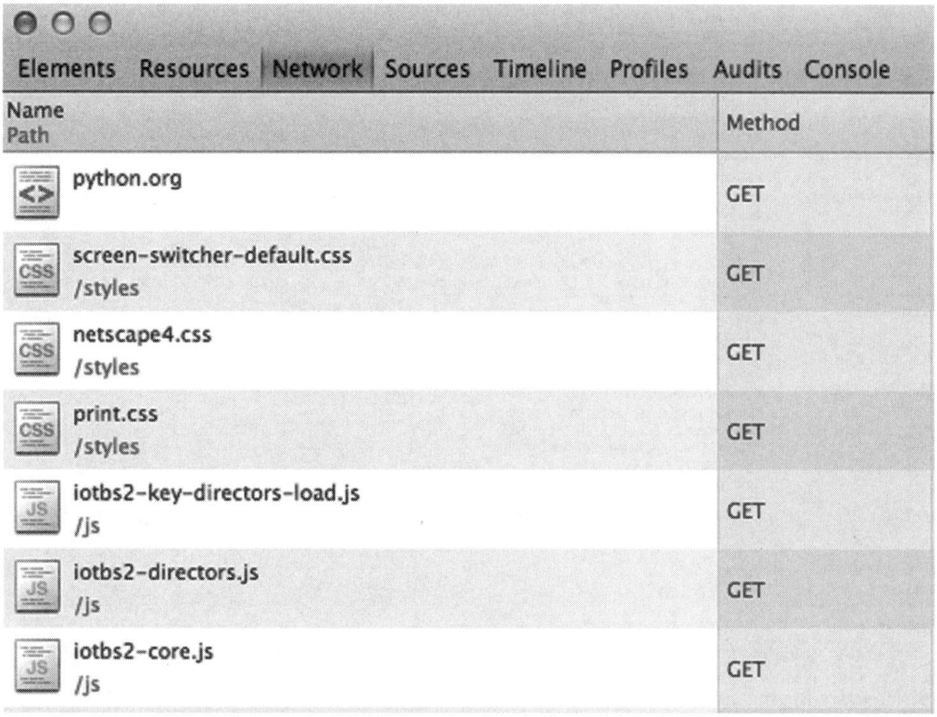

FIGURE 5-4: The DevTools Network tab

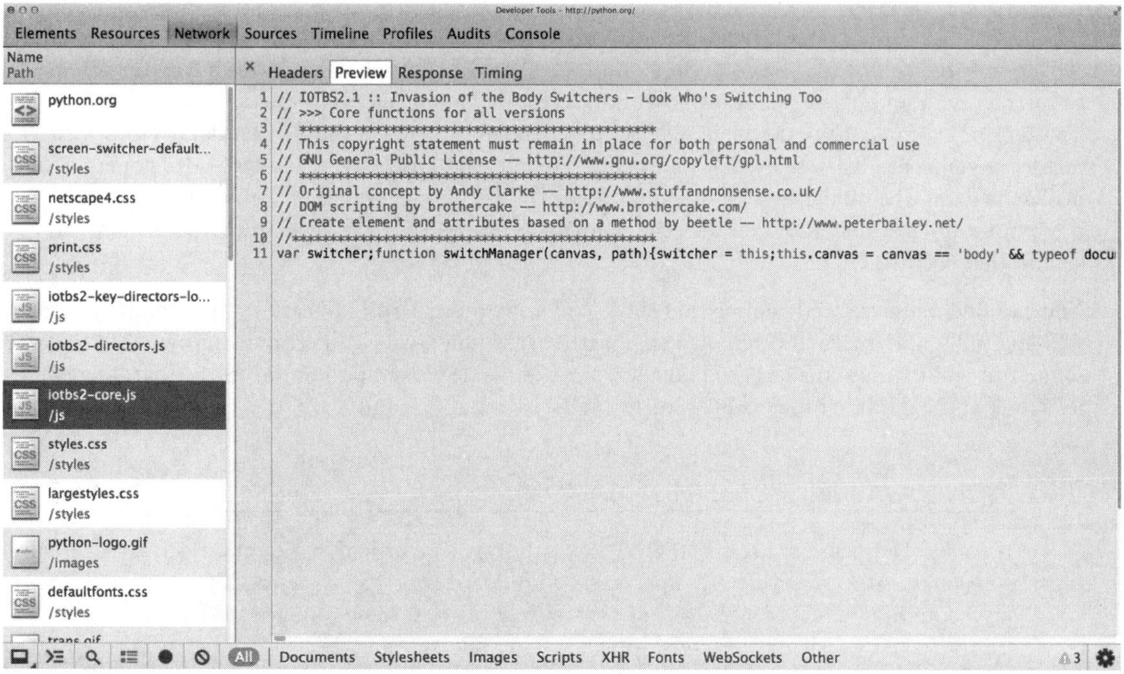

FIGURE 5-5: Preview of the selected file

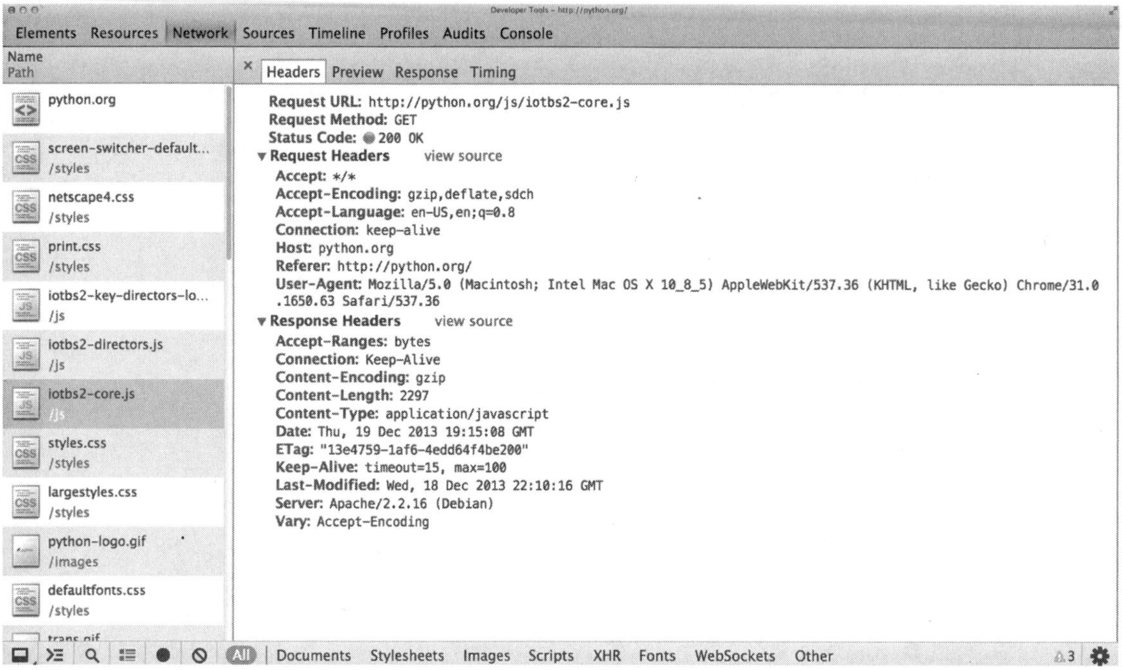

FIGURE 5-6: Headers for the selected file

What Is an API?

API stands for *application programming interface*. An API is simply the approved way for others to interact with an outside application, without actually having access to the database itself. Take Twitter, for example. How do the many Twitter clients out there get the Twitter data? Does Twitter just let anyone onto its systems? No, not really. Twitter uses an API to allow other developers to utilize its data. The modern use of an API is a RESTful API, meaning that you use URLs to talk to the remote application's API, and the remote application returns data depending on the data you've sent to the specified URL.

You can find many tutorials online that show you how to use certain libraries in Python to access an API and pull data. You will be going a step farther than that—you will create your own API to serve data. You will then use that API to code up your client-side files to pull in the correct data. But first, let's look at the data that most APIs return: JSON.

> ### JSON (JAVASCRIPT OBJECT NOTATION)
>
> If you've ever heard the term "JSON" (jay-sahn), you've probably thought it was some magical secret that only supersmart computer scientists understood. Or you just thought it was some weird thing that web developers kept going on about. Either way, it's very easy—almost too easy—to understand.

JSON is simply key:value pairs that are formatted to resemble a JavaScript object. Like dicts in Python, JavaScript has a data structure that is very similar. They are called *objects* in JavaScript, and they look like this:

```
{ name: "Henry",
  email: "henry@henry.com",
  job: "Accountant"
}
```

This is simply an object with three keys: `name`, `email`, and `job`. Each key has a corresponding value.

When we talk to most modern APIs, the format of the data that is sent and received is usually JSON. This means that we simply have to structure our data as key:value pairs and wrap it in curly braces ({}). Some APIs can have JSON sent to them along with them sending JSON back out. And some APIs simply provide JSON data. We'll look at a third-party API that sends data as JSON. We'll also look at how to parse that data, how to read it, and how Python handles it.

In the following Try It Out, you learn how to access a third-party API to get data. For this example, you use the USDA's API for Farmer's Markets in a given area. You can find plenty of other governmental APIs at `www.data.gov`. You can find the documentation for this example at `http://search.ams.usda.gov/farmersmarkets/v1/svcdesc.html`.

TRY IT OUT Using a Third-Party API

In this Try It Out, you'll find lists of farmers markets for a given U.S. ZIP code.

1. Install the requests library:

```
pip install requests
OR
easy_install requests
```

2. Open a new Terminal window and start your Python interpreter:

```
~$ python

Python 3.3.3 (default, Feb 14 2014, 12:35:03)
[GCC 4.2.1 Compatible Apple LLVM 5.0 (clang-500.2.79)] on darwin
Type "help", "copyright", "credits" or "license" for more information.
```

3. Import the requests library. If you have requests properly installed, you should simply see your prompt returned once you press Return/Enter. If you don't, you haven't installed requests properly. Check out the documentation on the requests website to see how to remedy this.

```
>>>import requests
>>>
```

4. Make a request to the USDA's API. Save the object returned from the request into a variable and then print that result:

```
>>>url = requests.get("http://search.ams.usda.gov/farmersmarkets/v1/data.svc/
zipSearch?zip=46201")
```

```
// Feel free to replace the zip code '46201' with your own zip code to see local
farmer's markets in your area
```

```
>>>print(url)
<Response [200]>
```

Here you are calling `requests.get()`. Earlier we talked about HTTP request methods—this request is sending a GET request to the server, to get back some data (a JSON object in this case). What do we know about an HTTP response status code of 200? This simply means that the request was received and returned `'OK'`, meaning everything is OK.

5. Call the `.json()` method on the object so that it is in a form that Python can understand. Save the result of calling the `.json()` method on the object that was returned, and print the variable:

```
>>>results = url.json()
```

```
>>>print(results)
{'results': [{'id': '1003905', 'marketname': '1.7 Irvington Farmers Market & Art
    Fair'}, {'id': '1005421', 'marketname': "2.4 Original Farmers' Market at
    Indianapolis City Market"}, {'id': '1006165', 'marketname': '2.4 Indy Winter
    Farmers Market'}, {'id': '1002600', 'marketname': '2.9 Statehouse Market'},
    {'id': '20312', 'marketname': '2.9 Stadium Village Farmers Market '}, {'id':
    '1002467', 'marketname': '3.8 Farmers Market at the Barn'}, {'id': '1004011',
    'marketname': "4.2 Hurlock Farmers' and Watermen's Market"}, {'id': '1003161',
    'marketname': '4.4 38th & Meridian Farmers Market'}, {'id': '1006494',
    'marketname': '6.1 52 & Shadeland Avenue Farmers Market'}, {'id': '1005505',
    'marketname': '6.6 Broad Ripple Farmers Market'}, {'id': '1006523',
    'marketname': '6.7 Binford Farmers Market'}, {'id': '1003901', 'marketname':
    '7.9 Cumberland Farmers Market'}, {'id': '1004663', 'marketname': '12.1 Geist
    Farmers Market'}, {'id': '1009026', 'marketname': '12.1 Farm to Fork Farmers
    Market at Normandy Farms'}, {'id': '1007367', 'marketname': '13.5 Carmel
    Farmers Market'}, {'id': '1000748', 'marketname': '13.6 Fishers Farmers
    Market'}, {'id': '1004686', 'marketname': '14.5 Zionsville Farmers Market'},
    {'id': '1008028', 'marketname': '16.0 Brownsburg Farmers Market'}, {'id':
    '1000129', 'marketname': "16.2 Plainfield Chamber Farmers' Market"}]}
```

What you're seeing here is a list of all the markets that is returned when you query for that ZIP code. The data for this query lives on the USDA's servers; however, because the USDA has provided an API, you can access this data without actually accessing the database itself.

What data type is being *returned*? It's a one-item dict with the key "results" containing a list of dicts as its value. How do you know? { = dict indicator..... [= list indicator..... { = dict indicator. The first dict item is titled "results," and its data is a list. Remember dicts are key:value pairs. Remember lists are simply number indices (0th indexed). So, how do you get the list out of the first dict? You have to reference the dict with its key—in this case the key is the word "results" after the { and u.

6. To get the value of that key, call it like so:

```
>>>for result in results['results']:
```

```
...    print(result)
{'id': '1003905', 'marketname': '1.7 Irvington Farmers Market & Art Fair'}
{'id': '1005421', 'marketname': "2.4 Original Farmers' Market at Indianapolis City
Market"}
{'id': '1006165', 'marketname': '2.4 Indy Winter Farmers Market'}
{'id': '1002600', 'marketname': '2.9 Statehouse Market'}
{'id': '20312', 'marketname': '2.9 Stadium Village Farmers Market '}
{'id': '1002467', 'marketname': '3.8 Farmers Market at the Barn'}
{'id': '1004011', 'marketname': "4.2 Hurlock Farmers' and Watermen's Market"}
{'id': '1003161', 'marketname': '4.4 38th & Meridian Farmers Market'}
{'id': '1006494', 'marketname': '6.1 52 & Shadeland Avenue Farmers Market'}
{'id': '1005505', 'marketname': '6.6 Broad Ripple Farmers Market'}
{'id': '1006523', 'marketname': '6.7 Binford Farmers Market'}
{'id': '1003901', 'marketname': '7.9 Cumberland Farmers Market'}
{'id': '1004663', 'marketname': '12.1 Geist Farmers Market'}
{'id': '1009026', 'marketname': '12.1 Farm to Fork Farmers Market at Normandy
Farms'}
{'id': '1007367', 'marketname': '13.5 Carmel Farmers Market'}
{'id': '1000748', 'marketname': '13.6 Fishers Farmers Market'}
{'id': '1004686', 'marketname': '14.5 Zionsville Farmers Market'}
{'id': '1008028', 'marketname': '16.0 Brownsburg Farmers Market'}
{'id': '1000129', 'marketname': "16.2 Plainfield Chamber Farmers' Market"}
```

When you run this code, you should see a Unicode-encoded list of farmers markets for the area of Indianapolis within the ZIP code 46201 (or your ZIP code if you changed that data point).

How It Works

You just used an API from the USDA to search for farmers markets within a certain ZIP code, based on the data housed in the USDA's databases. You got the result back from the server and using the requests library's .json() method, you got that information out of the data the server sent back to you in the JSON format, so that you could read it. You then noted the structure of the data, so that you could get each individual listing and list them out via a for loop.

What if you wanted to get the name of the farmers market and search for it via Google?

Luckily, the USDA has done the heavy lifting of finding each market via Google Maps, by providing a link to the corresponding Google map for each market. This search, according to the USDA API docs (http://search.ams.usda.gov/farmersmarkets/v1/svcdesc.html), will return some market details, provided you pass in a market ID, which you can get from the earlier inquiry. Included in the results is a link to the Google map. Let's watch it in action:

```
>>>market = "http://search.ams.usda.gov/farmersmarkets/v1/data.svc/mktDetail?id="

>>>for result in results['results']:
...     id = result['id']
...     details = requests.get(market + id).json()
...     print(details['marketdetails']['GoogleLink'])
http://maps.google.com/?q=39.7776%2C%20-86.0782%20(%22Irvington+Farmers+Market+%26+
Art+Fair%22)
This is the example of one of the links that may be returned.
```

What does this code do? Can you decipher it? Try to write it out in human-readable format using pen and paper, or type it out as if you were explaining it to someone else. If you are unsure what is going on exactly, insert print statements after each line to see what the code looks like as it is going through each line, like this:

```
>>>for result in results['results']:
...     id = result['id']
...     print(id) [RS - all these need parenthesss[
...     print result['id']
...     details = requests.get(market + id).json()
...     print details
...     print details['marketdetails']
...     print details['marketdetails']['GoogleLink']
```

As a fun exercise, open Chrome and go to the URL: http://search.ams.usda.gov/farmersmarkets/v1/data.svc/zipSearch?zip=46201. Notice the results you get back. Open the DevTools and take a look at the response headers (see Figure 5-7). Notice the response is identical to the response you got back when you queried the URL in the Python interpreter (200 OK). Next, click the Preview tab, and you should see each result returned as a JSON object. Feel free to click around and inspect the data the browser can see with the data you've been inspecting.

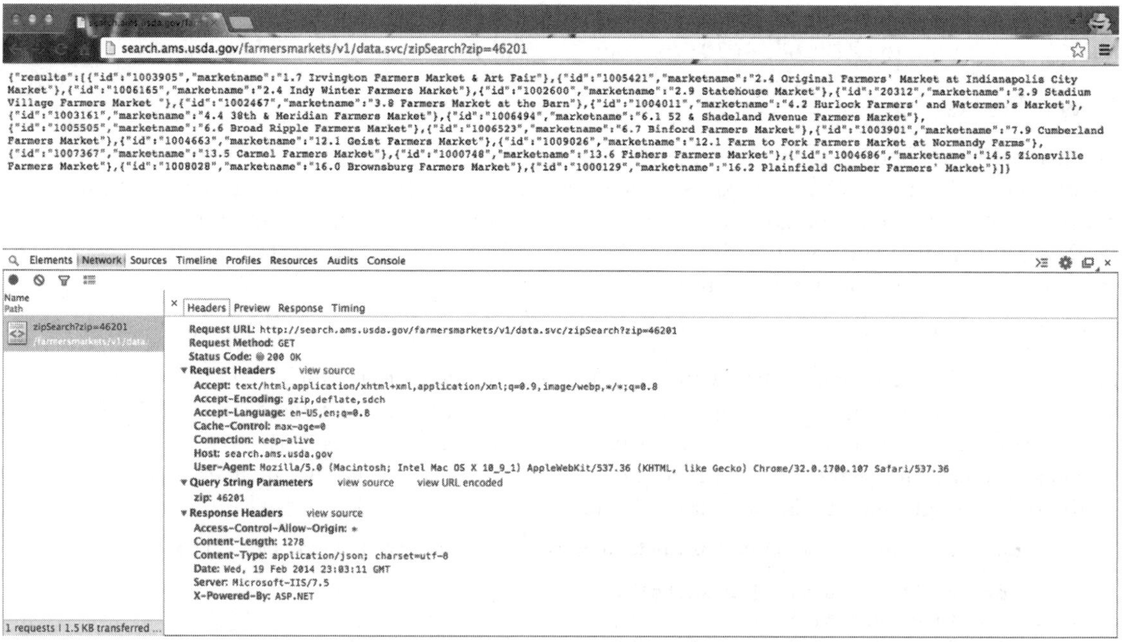

FIGURE 5-7: The Headers tab in Chrome's DevTools, illustrating the HTTP response from the USDA website

So, now the question is: How does that work? How does the Requests library do that? That's for our next section, "Web Programming with Python." Though we won't be making our own requests-like library, we will look at the underlying logic and functionality that Python provides in order to make such a library.

WEB PROGRAMMING WITH PYTHON

In the preceding section, you took a look at the Requests library. In this section you're going to see a little bit of the technologies Requests employs under the hood. Then, using the Flask web framework (http://flask.pocoo.org), you'll take the lending library, give it a web interface, and make it interactive via a browser. But first, you should understand just how things are working before you put big bows on them.

Using the Python HTTP Modules

Python is incredibly powerful, versatile, and easy to use. Part of the reason for this is all the built-in functionality that comes with the base Python install. When you install Python, you also get a plethora of modules that you can use. Included in these modules are the http modules—http .server, http.client—and a few others. In this section you work with the http.server module to see just how easy it is to spin up a quick HTTP server so that you can quickly begin serving web pages for debugging/testing purposes. This section also illustrates just how some of the more popular third-party libraries use Python's built-in modules to create incredibly powerful tools for the Python developer.

Let's take a look at the http.server module and see just how quickly you can get an HTTP server up and running locally.

Creating an HTTP Server

In this Try It Out, you set up, in just a few lines of code, an HTTP server that will run locally and serve up pages that you'll create and serve out of your local directory. After this exercise, you should have a good idea of just how some of the more popular frameworks and third-party libraries implement Python's built-in modules to harness incredible power to create easy-to-use tools.

TRY IT OUT Serving Local Files via http.server

This Try It Out demonstrates how you can serve files in your local directory, via a web browser, to test or debug any code that may need a web server running. This also illustrates just how powerful Python's built-in modules can be.

1. In your project directory, create a directory for Chapter 5 and, using your editor of choice, create an index.html file with the following code and save it:

```
<!doctype html>
<html>
  <head>
    <title>HELLO WORLD!</title>
  </head>
<body>
  <p>Hello World! I am serving this page via Python! WOWZERS!</p>
</body>

</html>
```

2. Open a new Terminal window and start up your Python interpreter. Import the two built-in modules you'll need:

```
    Python'
Python 3.3.3 (default, Feb 14 2014, 12:35:03)
[GCC 4.2.1 Compatible Apple LLVM 5.0 (clang-500.2.79)] on darwin
Type "help", "copyright", "credits" or "license" for more information.
>>>import socketserver
>>>import http.server
```

3. Decide which port you want to use to serve the data—you're free to use any port you want, but this example uses 8080:

```
>>> PORT = 8080
```

Note that the variable PORT is in all caps because it is a constant, which means it will not be changed within your program.

4. Set up a handler called Handsy to handle the requests you'll be sending:

```
>>>Handsy = http.server.SimpleHTTPRequestHandler
```

5. Now that you have a request handler, you can set up your simple HTTP Daemon (or httpd, because that's how most UNIX conventions name these things):

```
>>>httpd = socketserver.TCPServer(("", PORT), Handsy)
```

What are you doing here? You're passing in an empty string, the PORT constant, and then the variable Handsy, which is a request handler object. Can you explain, in plain words, what may be happening? It may help to write this down on paper in paragraph form.

6. Finally, you need to serve the directory to the correct port so that you can access it via your browser:

```
>>> httpd.serve_forever()
```

7. Leaving the Terminal window open and running, open a browser and point it to http://localhost:8000/. You should see something like the web page shown in Figure 5-8.

FIGURE 5-8: Note how this displays the HTML file we created earlier.

8. Go back to your Terminal window, where your server is running. You should see the following:

```
>>> httpd.serve_forever()
127.0.0.1 - - [14/Feb/2014 14:17:02] "GET / HTTP/1.1" 200 -
127.0.0.1 - - [14/Feb/2014 14:17:04] "GET / HTTP/1.1" 200 -
```

Remember what a status code of 200 means? "OK," meaning the server found index.html and was able to serve it to the client. Easy, huh?

How It Works

Python's built-in HTTP modules enable you to quickly "spin up" a small HTTP server to serve simple pages. The http.server module will search in the directory provided for an index.html file (you provided "", which means the directory you were in when you started the server), and if there is an index.html file, it will serve that file. If that file is not present, http.server uses the list _ directory() method to list the contents of the present directory. This is helpful for debugging and testing code, but it shouldn't be used for production systems. However, if you want to make a larger library, such as the Flask library you'll be using, or the Requests library that you used earlier, you can write code around these built-ins that will create helpful tools to use later on.

> **NOTE** Python 3 makes creating an HTTP server even easier. You can go to the directory that you want to serve through the HTTP server and simply run this command:
>
> python -m http.server 8000.
>
> That command will serve the directory, on localhost, at the port you provided. So, if you go to your Chapter 5 directory, where your index.html file is stored, and run this command in a Terminal, you'll be able to point your browser to http://localhost:8000 and see your index.html! Try it on a directory that doesn't have an index.html file and see what the results are.

Exploring the Flask Framework

Now, you take a closer look at the Flask framework. It is a third-party library written in Python that will help you to do everything from creating your own APIs to creating a full web-based application. Flask supports templating, using the Jinja template system, and therefore you can use it as an all-in-one web framework. You use this functionality for the next part of this chapter.

Before you begin, you'll need to install Flask (pip install flask). You'll be using SQLite3 for your database. Luckily, SQLite3 comes with Python 3. SQLite is a smaller database that is perfect for this simple example app. If you're doing a larger app, we recommend you take the time to research larger databases such as PostgreSQL, SQLAlchemy, or many of the others available, including the NoSQL databases such as Redis. For the purposes of this chapter, however, you'll use SQLite, which is a very easy, small, and lightweight database.

Once you have Flask installed, you'll set up a very simple app, which you will build on to complete the larger app.

> **NOTE** *Flask has Python 3 support, but only in 3.3 and newer; older versions of Python 3 (3.2 and older) will not work. Also, most plug-ins are developed under 2.7, so porting them to Python 3, though possible, is an undertaking left to the reader. Should you encounter any abnormalities and cannot find help via an Internet search, going back to Python 2.7 and using Flask in that environment is recommended.*

To start, you want to set up the directory structure where each part of your project will live. You can set up projects in many different ways, and each tutorial shows you a different way, but the basic idea is the same. Because you'll be working in an MVC-like environment, you're going to want to separate out each piece of the project. In the following Try It Out, once you unzip the `lendy.zip` file, you should have a directory structure similar to this:

lendy (the silly name of your lending app)

    static

    templates

This structure is similar to how most projects start out. You want to separate each piece of the project. The `static` directory will hold static files, such as images and scripts. The `templates` directory is where the templates will live.

Let's look at each piece of a typical MVC architecture:

➤ **Model:** This is where the data models live, or the tables in the database. This is going to be the table for your users (not secure) and the items that you'll be lending.

➤ **View:** This is what the users will see—what you show to them in a browser; or how they interact with the data, and where the data will go, once the next step does its job.

➤ **Controller:** This is the part of the app that "controls" the data flow. Users interact with this part. So, a user may send form data to the back end, which is picked up via the controller part of the project. This part interacts with the model and can initiate either an update, creation, or even deletion. This is also the "heaviest" part of the app, in that this part receives data from the model layer and returns it to the view. This is, basically, the brain of your web app.

Let's see how all of these pieces fit together by creating the basics for your web app.

Creating Data Models in Flask

In this example you will be use the lendydb database that you created in Chapter 3, in the section "Creating the LendyDB SQL Database." You will use two of the data entities: a member and an item. Members will be able to log in and view the inventory of items and add items to the inventory. You will be using a text editor and saving files in this exercise. You will not be using any security measures, for the sake of time. However, you should be very familiar with the most common security practices before setting up public web interfaces.

The data model for this application consists of the two files from Chapter 3: `lendydata.py`, which is the API, and `lendy.db`, which is the actual database. You need to copy both of these into your `lendy` folder.

Creating Core Flask Files

Now it's time to really get to the meat of the app—everything that will give us functionality and allow us to have a working web app. Let's create the Python files for the app.

TRY IT OUT Setting Up a Simple Flask App (lendy.zip)

This Try It Out demonstrates how to get a Flask project started.

1. In your project directory (`lendy`), open the filenamed `lendy.py`, which contains the following:

```
import sqlite3, os, lendydata
from flask import Flask, request, session, g, redirect, url_for, abort, \
    render_template, flash
```

These first two lines import the libraries and modules you'll be using. The first line is importing the sqlite3 and os modules, which come with Python, as well as the lendydata API module you created in Chapter 3. The second line is importing only the modules from the Flask library that you will be using. This is good practice when it comes to imports. Only import those modules and libraries that you'll actually be using. Remember, when you import you are running all the code in that file that you've designated in the import. So, if a module has 40 methods, you're importing all those method definitions. So, import only that which you'll be using.

2. Set up the config for your app:

```
app = Flask(__name__)

# Load default config and override config from an environment variable
app.config.update(dict(
    DATABASE=os.path.join(app.root_path, 'lendy.db'),
    DEBUG=True,
    SECRET_KEY='nickknackpaddywhack',
    USERNAME='admin',
    PASSWORD='thisisterrible'
))
app.config.from_envvar('LENDY_SETTINGS', silent=True)
```

Here you are creating your Flask object and assigning it the name of app. You are then setting up your Flask config properties. Because everything in Python is a first-class object, you can modify this object as needed.

Note the __name__ variable being passed around in the first two lines. Remember, when a Python script runs, depending on how it was run—directly, as the __main__ module, by running it with the command `python app.py`, or indirectly, by importing it from another (main) Python file. The Python interpreter sets the __name__ variable to either __main__ or the name of the file that was being imported. Here you are passing the __name__ variable to Flask and to the `config.from_object` methods. This will be determined by how you're running your script, as __main__ or as the name of your script (in our case the __name__ variable here will be set to `lendy`).

Next, you are updating the dict that goes along with your Flask object. Python objects are basically dicts all the way down, which is the reason you can modify them at any time. The all caps indicate that you are setting constant variables (variables that will never change). These variables are going to be passed around in the app and help you to run your program.

First, you have the DATABASE variable, which is declaring where the database file will reside. SQLite creates a simple file that is the database, which is why it's "lite." This os.path.join() call is simply setting up the path to the SQLite file that you'll be making in a moment.

Second, you have DEBUG=True. This is because you are in development mode. When you're ready to send your Flask project to production, you want to set this variable to FALSE.

Next, you have the SECRET_KEY. This variable should be something random, long, and hard to guess. Here it is set to be none of those things, for illustrative purposes. This key will help to keep your client-side session secure.

Finally, you have USERNAME and PASSWORD. These are the credentials for your app. Because you're making a very simple app, you're going to store these in the config, and not in a database. These of course, should be set up to be more difficult than shown here and put into a database and encrypted, but again for our purposes, security isn't the first concern. Also, it is assumed that your app will remain private and locally hosted for now.

The last line is important for later. This sets up an environment variable called LENDY_SETTINGS, which contains the config variables. However, you've set those here, so this config file doesn't exist (yet!), which is why the silent= True flag is set. This will ignore errors if the config file isn't found. Should you want to add a config file, you'd need the LENDY_SETTINGS variable to point to said config file.

3. Now, dissect the database connections, because this is where the heart of the app lies:

```
def get_db():
    """Opens a new database connection if one does not exist for our current request
    context (the g object helps with this task)"""

    if not hasattr(g, 'sqlite_db'):
        lendydata.initDB()
        g.sqlite_db = lendydata.db
    return g.sqlite_db


@app.teardown_appcontext
def close_db(error):
    """Closes the database again at the end of the request. Note the 'g'
object which makes sure we only operate on the current request."""
    if hasattr(g, 'sqlite_db'):
        lendydata.closeDB()
```

This code, in a nutshell, opens a database connection so that you have a handle on the SQLite database and can perform functions on it. There is an init_db function in there, which you will use in a moment. There is also a bit of Flask magic with the get_db() method call. This is opening a new connection if one doesn't exist yet, and the g variable is a special object in Flask that is valid for the active request only. This keeps data integrity through various request objects. Finally, the code opens the database; then, once the app is done using the connection, it closes the connection with the lendydata.close() function.

Note in the @app.teardown_appcontext decorated method, you are once again using the g object. This object is really flask.g, but because you imported it directly, you can use it as simply g. This object keeps each request separate so that if you close a database connection you aren't closing all the database connections, or other connections. This is part of the ease and simplicity of using libraries. Many times libraries will include things like this g object, which makes your job much easier so that you can simply do the tasks that you need to do (in this case, open and close database connections per connection) without having to fuss with the minute details/intricacies of each part.

4. Add the magic:

```
if __name__ == '__main__':
    app.run()
```

Here is where the magic of all Python scripts is invoked and made. Remember earlier we spoke about __name__ and __main__? What do they mean, exactly? When Python runs a script, a hidden variable called __name__ is set. When the script is run as the first Python script, this __name__ property is set to __main__ to let the interpreter know that this is the first script. Any subsequent scripts that are called after __main__ (through import statements) have their __name__ variables set to their filenames, so if you import os, then the os script (which is just a .py file) will have its __name__ variable set to os. This is a lot like namespacing in other languages and is basically Python's version of the practice.

5. Open Terminal, and in the directory where you saved your lendy.py file, run this command:

```
python lendy.py
```

You should see this:

```
* Running on http://127.0.0.1:5000/
* Restarting with reloader
```

6. Now, go to localhost:5000 in your web browser. You should get a 404 error in your browser and see this in your Terminal window:

```
127.0.0.1 - - [18/Feb/2014 12:10:44] "GET / HTTP/1.1" 404 -
```

7. The server returned a 404 because you don't have any views (or templates) yet. Let's add those. In the lendy.py file add the following lines:

```
@app.route('/')
@app.route('/login', methods=['GET', 'POST'])
def login():
    error = None
    if request.method == 'POST':
        if request.form['username'] != app.config['USERNAME']:
            error = 'Invalid username'
        elif request.form['password'] != app.config['PASSWORD']:
            error = 'Invalid password'
        else:
            session['logged_in'] = True
            flash('You were logged in')
            return redirect(url_for('show_inventory'))
    return render_template('login.html', error=error)
```

This is the real magic and power of Flask in action. Note that Flask uses decorator methods to create your HTTP routes. This saves you a ton of time and makes the code easier to maintain. With these specific routes, you're telling Flask that if anyone hits the endpoint of /login or the root directory (/), the login() function will be called, and you'll evaluate the value of the request method (we discussed this earlier in the chapter; here we allow POST and GET methods, and handle each specifically). Then you check the username and password values that are passed in, and if they are true, you alert the user that he's been logged in and you take him to the login.html template via the render_template() method. Basically, you want the user to hit the login page when visiting the site.

8. Set up the other views for your other pages. In your lendy.py file, add the following:

```python
@app.route('/inventory')
def show_inventory():
    get_db()
    allItems = lendydata.get_items()
    inventory = [dict(zip(['name','description'],[item[1],item[2]]))
                    for item in allItems]
    return render_template('items.html', items=inventory)
```

This code is similar to the preceding code. When a user hits the endpoint /inventory, the show_inventory function will be invoked and run. This function is calling the get_db() function shown earlier and then is executing the get_items() API function, making a query for all the items in the table. You then construct a dictionary of the field names and values used in the Web page. You are then passing this dictionary to your template for population. Note this endpoint doesn't have a methods= argument being passed to the route() method. That is because the default method is GET, so there is no need to pass that argument to the function.

9. What if you want to add items to your inventory? Let's add that endpoint to your lendy.py file:

```python
@app.route('/add', methods=['POST'])
def add_item():
    if not session.get('logged_in'):
        abort(401)
    get_db()
    ownerID = [row[0] for row in lendydata.get_members()
                if row[1] == request.form['owner']]
    try: ownerID = ownerID[0]
    except IndexError:
        # implies no owners match name
        # should raise error/create new member
        ownerID = 1      # use default member for now.

    lendydata.insert_item(request.form['name'],
                        request.form['description'],
                        ownerID,
                        request.form['price'],
                        request.form['condition'])

    flash('New entry was successfully posted')
    return redirect(url_for('show_inventory'))
```

This method uses the `get_members()` API function to find the owner's ID from the name captured in the form. It then calls the `add_item()` API function to add the item to the database.

You still can't see anything because you haven't actually created the templates. The templates are what the browser will actually show to the user. This is where the HTML magic lives. However, the real magic lies in the power of having those templates be able to pass data to your Python middleware. Let's see just how this happens.

Next you'll take a look at the templates.

They are already provided for you in the `lendy.zip` file in the lendy/templates folder. We'll just briefly discuss each one to give you a sense of how everything is interacting.

10. Open the `base.html` file in the `templates` directory and review its contents:

```
<!doctype html>
<title>Inventory Of Things</title>
<link rel=stylesheet type=text/css href="{{ url_for('static',
filename='style.css') }}">
<div class=page>
  <h1>Lendy</h1>
  <div class=metanav>
  {% if not session.logged_in %}
    <a href="{{ url_for('login') }}">log in</a>

  {% endif %}
  </div>
  {% for message in get_flashed_messages() %}
    <div class=flash>{{ message }}</div>
  {% endfor %}
  {% block body %}{% endblock %}
</div>
```

When dealing with templates, there is usually a base HTML file that will hold the base scaffolding for your site. This usually includes navigation and other pieces of the page setup that will not be changing throughout the app. This is how many of your favorite one-page web apps work: templates.

Once you have your base template in order, you can start making your other screens. You will need a login screen, an inventory list screen, and an inventory add screen. Let's look at the important parts of each so that you have a better understanding of just how each piece is working with the others.

11. In your `templates` folder for your lendy app, create the login screen by creating a `login.html` file and adding the following code:

```
{% extends "base.html" %}
{% block body %}
  <h2>Login</h2>
  {% if error %}<p class=error><strong>Error:</strong> {{ error }}{% endif %}
  <form action="{{ url_for('login') }}" method=post>
    <dl>
      <dt>Username:
      <dd><input type=text name=username>
      <dt>Password:
      <dd><input type=password name=password>
      <dd><input type=submit value=Login>
    </dl>
  </form>
{% endblock %}
```

Note how the first line indicates that this template is extended from the `base.html`. You declare that first so that your templating engine understands that you want to include all the pieces of `base.html` on your page. Each page will have this line included so as to indicate which HTML file you'll be extending from.

Secondly, note the `{% block body %}` line. This indicates that you have a body block, which will include the HTML that you want to display. All of the HTML is wrapped in the `{% block body %}` ... `{% endblock %}` notation. These tags indicate the dynamic parts of the template. For instance, let's look at the following line:

```
{% if error %}<p class=error><strong>Error:</strong> {{ error }}{% endif %}
```

Notice the difference between the `{% if error %}` tag and the `{{ error }}` tag. The double curly braces (`{{...}}`) indicate that you will be populating that space with data from your app; the value inside those braces is a variable that you will be passing to the template via your functions in the Flask code. The curly brace with a percent sign (`{%...%}`) indicates an action for the template engine to act upon. So the `{% blockbody %}` indicates to the template engine that you are starting the block body, and the `{% if error %}` tag indicates that you will be performing some logic in the template. This notation is very common in many templating engines, so you'll probably see it often.

12. Reload the app in your browser. You should see a login page when you hit either `http://localhost:5000` or `http://localhost:5000/login`. If you get an error, double-check your typing and your indentation. Also, recall the first Try It Out section in this chapter and use the Chrome DevTools to inspect your requests for any clues about your error.

Now you want to add the screens you'll use to list your items and add an item to your inventory. Again, we've provided these screens, but feel free to type them all out for your own muscle memory. We'll just be looking at the important parts of the templates.

13. Open `items.html` and note the use of `{%` and `{{`. Can you explain what is going on based on what you learned from the `login.html` template?

```
{% extends "base.html" %}
{% block body %}
  {% if session.logged_in %}
    <form action="{{ url_for('add_item') }}" method=post class=add-item>
      <dl>
        <dt>Item Name:
        <dd><input type=text size=30 name=name>
        <dt>Item Description:
        <dd><textarea name=description rows=5 cols=40></textarea>
        <dt>Item Condition:
        <dd><input type=text size=30 name=condition>
        <dt>Item Price:
        <dd><input type=text size=30 name=price>
        <dt>Owner Name:
        <dd><input type=text size=30 name=owner>          <dd><input type=submit
  value=Submit>
      </dl>
    </form>
  {% endif %}
  <ul class=entries>
  {% for item in items %}
    <li class="item_list">
      <h2>{{ item.name }}</h2>{{ item.description|safe }}

  {% else %}
    <li><em>There doesn't seem to be anything here. Add some items, maybe?</em>
  {% endfor %}
  </ul>
{% endblock %}
```

Here you are passing a form action and method. If you're logged in, you're setting up the form to take the new item and create a POST method that will then be passed to the `'add_item'` URL, which is a mapping to the `add_item` function in the `lendy.py` file.

Another interesting part in this template is that it contains two functionalities in this one template. One is the adding of items, and the other is the listing. If you are logged in, you can add items and see the item listing. If you are not logged in, you can only see the list of items. You have many ways to display this information. You could make separate screens for listing items and adding items. You can hide divs using CSS and display the adding of items only if the user clicks a button. Feel free to try a few options for this functionality to find one you like best. We'll stick with a quick and dirty way for now.

The next step is adding in the CSS. This step is very simple. The CSS has been provided for you in the `static` folder, named `style.css`. It is very common for `style.css` to be the base CSS file in a project. Our CSS is very simple; however, the power of CSS is great, and its functionality can be amazing. Feel free to experiment with other ways to implement your app using different CSS values.

14. Open the `style.css` file from the `static` folder and take a look:

```
body{
        font-family: sans-serif;
        background: #eee;
}
```

```css
a, h1, h2{
    color: #377ba8;
}

h1, h2{
    font-family: 'Georgia', serif;
    margin: 0;
}

h1{
border-bottom: 2px solid #eee;
}

h2{
font-size: 1.2em;
}

.page{
    margin: 2em auto;
    width: 35em;
    border: 5px solid #ccc;
    padding: 0.8em;
}

.inventory{
    list-style: none;
    margin: 0;
    padding: 0;
}

.inventory li{
    margin: 0.8em 1.2em;
}

.inventory li h2{
    margin-left: -1em;
}

.add-item{
    font-size: 0.9em;
    border-bottom: 1px solid #ccc;
}

.add-item dl{
    font-weight: bold;
}

.metanav{
    text-align: right;
    font-size: 0.8em;
    padding: 0.3em;
    margin-bottom: 1em;
    background: #fafafa;
}
```

```
.flash{
    background: #cee5F5;
    padding: 0.5em;
    border: 1px solid #aacbe2;
}

.error{
    background: #f0d6d6;
    padding: 0.5em;
}
```

Note that you are defining some base styles for your basic elements (body, h1, h2, and so on); then you define some classes (those lines beginning with a period; the period denotes a class name in CSS, and ID names are denoted with the pound, or sharp sign, #).

The most important part to note is the .flash class. This is a Flask feature. Flask has 'flash', which will flash error messages or other system feedback to the user by displaying the text on the screen. You can go back and look at the previous code and see where the flash function was called and how you're using it.

That's it! You're done! You've created a small Flask app to help you keep track of your inventory of things!

15. Start your Flask app like you did before (when you got the 404 error) and see if you now have a working web app.

You may encounter some errors, so check over your code for spelling and syntax mistakes (most especially, in Python, indention errors). If you still can't figure out what may be causing your error, fire up your Chrome DevTools and start inspecting the requests that you're sending and what the server is returning upon the request. This may help you. Remember to check out the Network tab. You may need to refresh the page to populate the Network tab with the requests that have been made.

How It Works

You've just set up a small web app using the Flask framework to do the heavy HTTP lifting. You set up an app that creates a database and allows you to connect to the database. You created tables in said database to store your data. You then set up your views, which tell the app how and when to return data, and what data to return. You set up endpoints (the /<foo> part of your URL) and mapped those to functions to help you pass data back and forth from the templates to the database. You then created templates to display all the information, and using Jinja as your templating engine, you set things up so that the templates can pass data back and forth with the lendy.py file. You then styled things to make them pretty and easier on your user (us!).

MORE ON PYTHON AND THE WEB

Creating web apps with Python is incredibly easy. You can do all the heavy lifting yourself, or you can try one of the many open source frameworks out there to help you with it, or help with just a few parts. You can build websites in two main ways with Python: static site generators and full-on web frameworks. This section briefly describes both methods and includes a list of some of the more popular generators and frameworks.

Static Site Generators

Static site generators are usually used for things like blogs and other documentation—where you may make a new page at a time and want to serve out that page but the content on the page won't be changing once it's published. Some of the more popular static site generators include, but are not limited to:

➤ **Pelican:** Probably the most popular and well-known static site generator in Python. There is also lots of community support, including plug-ins and themes for Pelican.

➤ **Hyde:** A little larger than Pelican, with a bit more of a learning curve, but quite robust.

➤ **Nikola:** Fully featured, lots of community involvement and support. Also supports customization, including themes and plug-ins.

➤ **Mynt:** Used by `www.pyladies.com` and a few other sites. Mynt lauds itself as having the features of a content management system (CMS) without the rigid implementation.

Web Frameworks

Web frameworks are all-in-one systems that give you the power to create APIs, web apps, and even a comprehensive CMS. Here are a few we recommend:

➤ **Flask:** Flask is quite versatile, from creating simple APIs that others will access to creating full web apps.

➤ **Django:** Django is quite popular and very robust. It even includes an admin interface that allows users to put entries in the database with an easy-to-navigate user interface that is highly customizable.

➤ **Bottle:** Bottle is smaller than Flask and simply gives you just what you need to create a website, with very little overhead and limited functionality. It's perfect for smaller websites and pages.

➤ **Pyramid:** Pyramid is similar to Flask in that it can be used for small projects, but you can also use it for larger projects, and it can be scaled up as needed.

Of course, many more web frameworks are available. We recommend finding one that suits you and your project, or just play around with a few to find one you feel more comfortable with.

USING PYTHON ACROSS THE WIRE

You can do many different tasks across a network connection. Whether that connection is the public Internet, a local area network, or a private network, you can process data, serve web pages, and even run Python scripts remotely. This section introduces a few of the simple, different ways you can run Python across a wire. None of the examples are production-ready code, but this should be a good way to get you familiar with the different powers Python can provide.

XML-RPC

XML-Remote Procedure Call (XML-RPC) is an older technology that is still used in a few legacy systems. This is how data was once processed across the Internet, using XML. We now use JSON to pass data back and forth; however, some systems still use XML and require remote procedural calls. Because of this Python has a built-in XML-RPC module. Let's make one and watch it in action.

In this Try It Out, you set up, in just a few lines of code, an XML-RPC server that will run locally in one Terminal and serve up a simple Python script, which you create. You then open another Terminal window and run the code remotely.

TRY IT OUT Running Python Code Remotely

This Try It Out demonstrates how you can serve files in your local directory, via an XMLRPC server.

1. Open your Python interpreter and import the `xmlrpc.server` object from the SimpleXMLRPCServer module:

```
Python 3.3.3 (default, Feb 14 2014, 12:35:03)
[GCC 4.2.1 Compatible Apple LLVM 5.0 (clang-500.2.79)] on darwin
Type "help", "copyright", "credits" or "license" for more information.
>>>from xmlrpc.server import SimpleXMLRPCServer
```

2. Similar to the HTTP code earlier in the chapter, you have to create a server object. You also want to create some sort of system feedback that will tell you that your code is working:

```
>>>server = SimpleXMLRPCServer(("localhost", 8080))
```

3. Set up your server with the code you will be running, in this case a simple function that will square a number that is passed in:

```
>>>def square(n):
...     return n * n
...     print("We've got a connection and are listening on port 8080...huzzah!")
```

4. Next you're going to register your function, so that it can be used by the client code you'll be creating in just a moment:

```
>>>server.register_function(square, "square")
```

5. Finally, you want to start the server:

```
>>>server.serve_forever()
```

You should now see your print statement print out to let you know that you're serving on port 8080.

Do not close this Terminal or stop the process; you need it to continue running to complete the next part of the example.

6. Open a new Terminal window, start a Python interpreter, and import the `xmlrpc.client` library:

```
Python 3.3.3 (default, Feb 14 2014, 12:35:03)
[GCC 4.2.1 Compatible Apple LLVM 5.0 (clang-500.2.79)] on darwin
Type "help", "copyright", "credits" or "license" for more information.
>>>import xmlrpc.client
```

If you happened to read any of the documentation on the `http.server` library you probably discovered that there is an `http.client` library as well, which will allow you to access URLs via a client. The `xmlrpc` library is set up in much the same way.

7.   Now you want to set up a server proxy object like so:

```
>>>proxy = xmlrpc.client.ServerProxy("http://localhost:8080")
```

8.   Finally, you want to call your remote procedure (or the Python function that is sitting on the server in the other Terminal window):

```
>>>print("the square root of 3 is %s" % proxy.square(3))
```

You should see the string print out "the square root of 3 is 9." Now, go look in your server Terminal window, and you should see that the server received a request and returned with a status of 200, like so:

```
127.0.0.1 - - [19/Feb/2014 23:14:41] "POST /RPC2 HTTP/1.1" 200 -
```

9.   To stop the server, simply go into the Terminal window where the server is running and hit Ctrl+C to stop the server.

This should stop the server and open that port back up for use.

How It Works

We just showed you how to set up an `xmlrpc` server and an `xmlrpc` client and have them talk to one another. This is the power of Python in action. Both of these modules are built into Python and are available for use out of the box.

Many people ask just what you could use such functionality for in the real world. XML processing was once the way we processed data across the wire. Some organizations still use this method. However, the power that we wanted to illustrate was that you can even set up Python to run remotely. So, if you had a large data file and wanted to process it remotely, you could set up code on a remote server and then call that code from another machine. Next, you'll look at some other examples that can also accomplish these tasks.

Socket Servers

If you've ever heard anyone talk about "Websockets" or "streaming data," they're usually talking about TCP and socket servers. These servers utilize TCP, or *Transmission Control Protocol*. You may have heard of TCP/IP, which this is the same thing. Python, of course, has some built-in libraries that can enable you to create TCP sockets to send and receive data between two points using the Internet Protocol.

In this Try It Out you get a bit more involved with some Python, and do some things in a more "pythonic" way. You're going to again set up a server and a client, so you'll need two Terminal windows running to complete this task. However, you're also going to create a class to handle your TCP requests to illustrate the use of classes in Python.

TRY IT OUT Running Python Code Remotely via TCP

This Try It Out demonstrates how to set up a socket server via Python for using TCP to send/receive data directly from one machine to another over the Internet.

1. Create a new file, `server.py`, and import the SocketServer module:

```
#server.py

import socketserver
```

2. Set up your class for the request handler. This class is going to be instantiated once per connection, and each time you will want the `handle()` method to be overridden so that you can communicate with the client:

```
class TCPHandler(socketserver.BaseRequestHandler):
    def handle(self):
    self.data = self.request.recv(1024).strip()
    print("{} wrote:".format(self.client_address[0]))
    print(self.data)
    # just send back the same data, but upper-cased
    self.request.sendall(self.data.upper())
```

`self` is the instance of the `TCPHandler` class. This is the TCP socket that is connected to the client (this will make more sense when you get to the client code). Here you are taking the request that is being sent over from the client, stripping it, and saving it to the data property on the instance (`self.data`). You then are calling some illustrative print statements, so that you can see things as they happen. Finally, you are sending the data back to the client, but transforming the string into all uppercase characters, so that you can see a change has happened.

3. Now you do something familiar—you check to see if you're running as main, and if so, you want to set the HOST and PORT variables to let the code know what host and port you want to listen to for connections:

```
if __name__ == "__main__":
    HOST, PORT = "localhost", 8080
```

4. Finally, you do something that you've done each time you've set up a new server—create a server object that will allow your client to connect—and then you serve it forever:

```
server = SocketServer.TCPServer((HOST, PORT), TCPHandler)
server.serve_forever()
```

Now you need to create the client code.

5. Create a new file, `client.py`, and import the proper libraries:

```
#client.py

import socket
import sys
```

6. Now you need to define the host and port you'll be connecting to—remember, the `server.py` code is *listening* on this host and port for incoming connections:

```
HOST, PORT = "localhost", 8080
```

7. Next, create some data that you can send over to the server. You'll use `sys.argv` to parse the arguments you'll be passing in; this will be your data:

```
data = " ".join(sys.argv[1:])
```

8. Now you need to set up your socket. The `socket.SOCK_STREAM` is simply the type of socket (TCP) that you'll be connecting through:

```
sock = socket.socket(socket.AF_INET, socket.SOCK_STREAM)
```

9. Now use a `try:finally` to try and connect:

```
try:
    sock.connect((HOST, PORT))
     sock.sendall(bytes(data + "\n", "utf-8"))

    received = str(sock.recv(1024), "utf-8")

finally:
    sock.close()
```

What is happening here is that you are trying to connect to the server and send your data. You are then storing the received data into the "received" variable. Finally, no matter what happens (success or failure of gaining a connection and sending/receiving data), you are closing your socket.

10. Finally, you want to print out the results of your connection:

```
print("Sent:     {}".format(data))
print("Received: {}".format(received))
```

11. Run the code and see what happens. You will, again, need two Terminal windows. In the first Terminal window, you want to run your Python code:

```
$ python server.py
```

12. In the other Terminal window, run the client code and pass in a string as an argument:

```
$ python client.py Hello from Python Projects' TCP server!
```

13. Verify that the following displays in the server window:

```
$ python server.py
127.0.0.1 wrote:
b'Hello from Python Projects TCP Server!'
```

14. Verify that the following displays in the client window:

```
$ python3 client.py Hello from Python Projects TCP Server!
Sent:     Hello from Python Projects TCP Server!
Received: HELLO FROM PYTHON PROJECTS TCP SERVER!
```

The server is *very* excited that you were able to connect!

How It Works

You successfully created a TCP socket and connected to it via a client script, and then had each script send and receive data back and forth. By setting up a server and telling it what host and port to listen to, you were able to create a client that would send data to that host at that port, and the two pieces were able to rendezvous and send/receive data successfully.

We've only shown you the very basics of what Python sockets can do. Our job here is to familiarize you with all the tools that are available in the Python ecosphere. There may be times when a direct data connection is needed, for updating data feeds in real time—this is where the power of sockets and streaming data comes in very handy. Luckily for you, Python makes this fairly easy. We, of course, recommend that if you're going to be creating network connections on a lower level, you understand the security risks and cautions that you will need to be aware of before undertaking such a task.

MORE NETWORKING FUN IN PYTHON

You may be interested in delving a bit deeper into networking with Python. If so, here is a short list of some of the more popular networking libraries available for download:

➤ **Twisted** (`http://twistedmatrix.com`): Twisted is very large, very powerful, and full of networking goodness. However, as of this writing it is not fully functional with Python 3. If you're interested in doing some event-driven networking, Twisted is for you. Support for SMTP, POP3, IMAP, SSHv2, and DNS is included. So if you've always wanted to make your own e-mail server, you and Twisted may be a match made in heaven. If you're interested in setting up your own SSL server—get Twisted!

➤ **Tornado** (`http://www.tornadoweb.org`): Tornado is lauded as a web framework and asynchronous networking library. Mainly made for larger applications that may need long-lived connections, Tornado uses non-blocking I/O and is perfect for Websockets and long polling. We put Tornado in the "networking" section rather than the "web frameworks" section because it's more focused on the networking side of web frameworks than on creating templates and making things pretty.

➤ **gevent** (`http://www.gevent.org`): According to gevent's own website, gevent is "a coroutine-based Python networking library....that provides a high-level synchronous API..." When you need to do some crazy coroutines across your network, you may want to take a gander at gevent. Currently, gevent is only for Python 2.

You should now have a good idea of the power and ease with which Python can be used to send and receive data across the wire. If you're interested in any sort of data passing using Python, this chapter should have given you a nice jumping-off point to go explore more and hopefully create interesting things with your discoveries.

Python's community is full of helpful people, so if you happen to find a framework or library that you particularly like, join the mailing lists, the IRC channels, and any other conversations you can find. Contribute to those projects, and help the communities grow larger and stronger. Participation in technologies that you find interesting and/or helpful not only helps the projects and organization that is offering the technology, but it helps all developers who may need to use or want to learn that technology.

SUMMARY

You started off this chapter by learning about how Python works on the web. The front end of a web app consists of a browser that handles the HTML, CSS, and JavaScript. The middle layer, in this case, is Python. The back end houses your database (SQLite) and web server. You also learned about APIs (application programming interfaces), which is the approved way for others to interact with an outside application, without actually having access to the database itself. Next, you practiced using a third-party API and the Requests library. Along with that, you explored the technologies Requests employs under the hood. Then, using the Flask web framework, you took the lending library, gave it a web interface, and made it interactive via a browser. Finally, you learned a few of the various easy ways you can run Python across a wire.

EXERCISES

1. Consider our code from earlier in this chapter:

```
>>>for result in results['results']:
...     id = result['id']
...     print(id)
...     print(result['id'])
...     details = requests.get(market + id).json()
...     print(details)
...     print(details['marketdetails'])
...   print(details['marketdetails']['GoogleLink'])
```

Using what you know about Python, can you figure out a way to create a list comprehension that will do the same thing as the preceding code? Remember that list comprehensions are constructed like this:

```
[expression for item in list if conditional]
```

2. Using what you know so far about how to use files in Python, can you save the output of your call to the USDA's API to a file on your machine, to parse later? (Is saving it as a .txt file fine?)

3. Can you find the docs for Flask that would help us to break our app into smaller, modularized files with our endpoints/views in a separate file, rather than having one big Python file with everything in it? (Hint: It is one concept/feature that Flask offers.)

4. What other HTTP methods can you find? Can you find ways to use them in a Flask app?

5. By reading the Requests docs, can you find the method call needed to output the HTML of a website by passing the URL to a requests method?

► WHAT YOU LEARNED IN THIS CHAPTER

TOPIC	KEY CONCEPTS
Where Python fits on the web	Python is the language that the server uses to manipulate the actual data that is being passed back and forth between machines on the web.
HTTP and HTTP methods	The basic "language" of how machines communicate over the web. GET and POST methods and their purposes.
APIs	Application programming interface, or how to interface with other servers in order to retrieve or manipulate data. You can produce or consume APIs.
How to create a Flask app	The Flask framework is very powerful for creating web apps using Python as the server-side code. This also illustrated how to produce an API.
Templates in Flask	Templates are very common in web apps. They are ways to introduce logic and create dynamic content on web pages.
XMLRPC	Python has built-in functionality to create XMLRPC servers to pass data over the wire. This is really helpful only to people who will be supporting older/legacy systems, which still use this method of data passing.
Socket servers	Python has a very handy built-in library named "socketserver," which will allow you to create sockets to connect to via other scripts. This is incredibly powerful for processing data over the wire.
SimpleHTTPServer	This is a way to make a simple HTTP server to test files locally or to integrate into making a larger framework to use as a debug mode.

6

Python in Bigger Projects

WHAT YOU WILL LEARN IN THIS CHAPTER:

- ➤ Testing your Python code
- ➤ Debugging your Python code
- ➤ Handling errors in your Python code
- ➤ Structuring and releasing your Python code
- ➤ Tuning the performance of your Python code

WROX.COM DOWNLOADS FOR THIS CHAPTER

You can find the wrox.com downloads for this chapter at www.wrox.com/go/pythonprojects on the Download Code tab. The code is in the Chapter 6 download, called Chapter 6.zip, and individually named according to the names throughout the chapter.

So far you've looked at many ways to use Python. You've made local scripts to handle small tasks, you've handled medium-sized tasks locally, and you've even made a small web app using Flask. But what if you find yourself in the midst of a larger project? Python, as you have seen by now, is a very powerful language. It's also very open, meaning you, the developer, have access to all aspects of the language. This openness, however, makes testing your Python code more important than ever. Every object in Python is a first-class object, so you can change and manipulate any object available to you. Because you can change and manipulate objects, you must make sure to test and verify the logic of our code.

Python is not a "typed" language in the same way that C and Java are explicitly typed. You can pass objects around in Python and the interpreter will try to manipulate them to the best of its ability. If it cannot perform an operation on an object or data that is available, however, it raises an exception, which causes your program to crash. So, how can you prevent this? How can you write code, share that code, and guarantee that others can use it and that the code will function as expected? Testing.

TESTING WITH THE DOCTEST MODULE

The simplest form of testing in Python is the doctest module. This module is made for testing the simpler parts of your code, to verify that it will function as expected, as written in your document strings (triple quotes '''...''' or """...""", single or double quotes will both work). Doctest tests are written like this:

```
'''
this function should take in a number and return its squared value
>>> sq(3)
9
'''

def sq(n):
    return n*n
```

> **WARNING** *With doctest, your code indentation matters. The indentation of your first line dictates further indentations, so you are committed to that pattern. Your doctest strings will be fed into the interpreter exactly as you have written them—if the interpreter is expecting a certain indentation, you need to make sure your doctest strings have that indentation pattern.*
>
> *Also, keep in mind that as Python changes and evolves, indentation patterns may change, so your doctest strings may fail in the future. This is one reason why many people do not rely heavily on doctest for significant testing.*

The usual way of writing doctest tests is to use the interpreter, write the code, and then run it in the interpreter. Then you copy and paste the interpreter text into the doctest string, as follows:

```
Python 3.3.3 (default, Feb 14 2014, 12:35:03)
[GCC 4.2.1 Compatible Apple LLVM 5.0 (clang-500.2.79)] on darwin
Type "help", "copyright", "credits" or "license" for more information.
>>> def sq(n):
...     return n*n
...
>>> sq(3)
9
>>>
```

So you would simply copy the following lines, and put them in your doctest strings:

```
>>> sq(3)
9
```

Doctest is not suitable for testing of large, complicated methods or functions. But it is really good at "contract programming." By using doctest strings and saying "this function, when passed a 3 as an argument, will return a 9" and then calling the function, you are setting up a contract: if you pass a certain piece of data, the function will behave as you expect it to. However, you cannot test every possible outcome, so doctest will hit its limitations fairly quickly with larger projects.

In the following example you create and then run a small Python script with some doctest strings to test your code.

TRY IT OUT Creating and Executing Simple Doctest Tests

This Try It Out demonstrates how you can test a simple file that has a few functions using doctest, which houses testing strings in documentation strings, using triple quotes (''' ... ''').

1. Create a directory for Chapter 6 in your project directory, and then using your editor of choice, create a Python filenamed `simple_doctest.py`. Include the following function and test:

```python
def simple_math(x, y):
    '''
    >>> simple_math(1, 2)
    3

    >>> simple_math('k', 'v')
    'kv'
    '''

    return x + y
```

You *must* have a space after the interpreter prompt (>>>) for the tests to run. Your first line with the interpreter prompt (>>> simple_math(1,2)') would not run properly if it were formatted as >>>simple_math(1,2). The space is mandatory.

2. Open a new Terminal window and from your Chapter 6 directory and run the following command:

```
python -m doctest -v simple_doctest.py
```

Here you are calling Python, but by passing it the -m flag, you are telling Python you want to execute the file using a module—in this case the doctest module. The -v flag means that you want "verbose" output. If you take off the -v flag and rerun the code, you will see that it simply finishes silently, meaning the code runs, but then you are given another Terminal prompt and nothing further from the Python interpreter. Finally, the last argument is, of course, the file you are testing. With the -v flag, you should see the following output:

```
~chapter6$ python -m doctest -v simple_doctest.py
Trying:
    simple_math(1, 2)
Expecting:
    3
ok
Trying:
    simple_math('k', 'v')
Expecting:
    'kv'
ok
1 items had no tests:
    simple_doctest
1 items passed all tests:
    2 tests in simple_doctest.simple_math
2 tests in 2 items.
2 passed and 0 failed.
Test passed.
```

Note that you must have a space after the interpreter prompt (>>>) for the tests to run.

3. Next, write these tests as if you wanted fully documented contract programming. In your editor, open your `simple_doctest.py` file and add these lines:

```
def simple_math(x, y):
    '''
    This function will return x + y
    we can use it on numbers. Passing 1 and 2:

    >>> simple_math(1, 2)
    3

    We should get 3 as a return value

    It will also work on strings. Passing the strings 'k' and 'v':

    >>> simple_math('k', 'v')
    'kv'

    We should get 'kv'
    '''
    return x + y
```

Note that you must have a newline between your expected result and any documentation string that you are putting into the doctest string. So, when you have your expected 3 after your `simple_math(1,2)` call, you must have that newline in place before you specify the behavior you want. Otherwise, the interpreter will try to evaluate that line as expected output, therefore rendering that test a failure.

4. There are times where you will need to evaluate a value that cannot be consistently predicted (like an address in memory). Add the following to your `simple_doctest.py` file (after your first test is fine):

```
class SimpleClass():
    pass

def class_testing_method_ahoy(obj):
    ''' Should return a list containing the object

    >>> SimpleClass(class_testing_method_ahoy())
    [<doctest_class_testing_method_ahoy.SimpleClass object at /
    0x10382a390]
    '''

    return [obj]
```

Now run the tests and observe the output. You should see that your tests fail because the code is evaluating a location in memory that we cannot reliably predict each time. Note the memory addresses in your output.

```
chapter6 $ python -m doctest -v simple_doctest.py
Trying:
    class_testing_method_ahoy(SimpleClass())
Expecting:
    [<doctest_class_testing_method_ahoy.SimpleClass object at /
    0x10382a390>]
***************************************************************
```

```
File "./simple_doctest.py", line 27, in /
simple_doctest.class_testing_method_ahoy
Failed example:
    class_testing_method_ahoy(SimpleClass())
Expected:
    [<simple_doctest.SimpleClass object at 0x10382a390>]
Got:
    [<simple_doctest.SimpleClass object at 0x10af0fe50>]
Trying:
    simple_math(1, 2)
Expecting:
    3
ok
Trying:
    simple_math('k', 'v')
Expecting:
    'kv'
ok
2 items had no tests:
    simple_doctest
    simple_doctest.SimpleClass
1 items passed all tests:
    2 tests in simple_doctest.simple_math
********************************************************************
1 items had failures:
    1 of   1 in simple_doctest.class_testing_method_ahoy
3 tests in 4 items.
2 passed and 1 failed.
***Test Failed*** 1 failures.
```

Doctest requires the actual output to match the expected output exactly. When we specify a memory address to Doctest as the expected output, the actual memory address received from the test must precisely match the declared expected value. When we:

```
[<simple_doctest.SimpleClass object at 0x10382a390>]
```

Doctest wants an object at the memory location `0x10382a90`, but you're going to be creating a new object in a new memory location. You don't really care about the memory location, only that the object is created. Doctest provides a way to work around this:

```
>>> class_testing_method_ahoy(SimpleClass()) /
    # doctest: +ELLIPSIS
[<simple_doctest.SimpleClass object at 0x...>]
```

The ELLIPSIS option lets doctest know that what follows can be any value. This will return a successful test:

```
Trying:
    class_testing_method_ahoy(SimpleClass()) # doctest: +ELLIPSIS
Expecting:
    [<simple_doctest.SimpleClass object at 0x...>]
ok
```

```
Trying:
    simple_math(1, 2)
Expecting:
    3
ok
Trying:
    simple_math('k', 'v')
Expecting:
    'kv'
ok
2 items had no tests:
    simple_doctest
    simple_doctest.SimpleClass
2 items passed all tests:
    1 tests in simple_doctest.class_testing_method_ahoy
    2 tests in simple_doctest.simple_math
3 tests in 4 items.
3 passed and 0 failed.
Test passed.
```

The ELLIPSIS constant is also useful if you are checking that a list is returned, such as when using the range() method. Say you want to make sure you get back the numbers 1–4,590 when you call range(4589). Rather than print the entire list of 4,590 numbers, you can use the ELLIPSIS constant and simply have your result be [0, 1, ... , 4588, 4589]. Doctest has many of these constants for different situations. Refer to the full doctest documentation for a list of all of them.

How It Works

The doctest module is built into the Python language. It takes in strings that are usually copied directly from the interpreter and then evaluates those strings when the file is called. It does this by using the module (calling Python on the command line with the -m flag, followed by the module 'doctest' and then the filename).

Although doctest is good for evaluating whether your documentation strings are true and the code behaves as expected, it is not meant for thorough, robust testing of more complicated codebases. There are many other facets to the doctest API. You should check out the documentation to familiarize yourself with the full functionality of the module.

TESTING WITH THE UNITTEST MODULE

What if you need significant testing and you want to verify that your codebase is operating as expected? This is a job for the unittest module. This module is more robust than the doctest module, and will test your code thoroughly. Unittest is like the baseline testing module on which most testing libraries are based. It is also an excellent introduction to test-driven development (TDD) in Python.

The term *unit test* is not unique to Python. If you're familiar with other languages and programming, you have no doubt heard of unit testing. Unit testing is simply testing your code in units. So, if you have five functions in your code, you want to have a minimum of five units in your testing harness for each unit of functionality in your codebase. Unit tests also consist of a test file, which contains all of your tests, written in the same structure or format as any other Python file. The only difference is that each test begins with *test*, and each test harness is a class from the Unittest.Test object. For example, if you have a function named `login`, and you want to test that function, create a test named `test _ login`, which would then call your `login` function and run your tests against the output of that function.

Don't forget that when you are writing unittest classes, you need to import the code module you'll be testing into your test code. If you were testing `users.py`, you would need to `import users` into your `test.py` file, so that you can test the functions in the users module with your unittests.

You create unittest tests by creating classes that are subclasses to the `TestCase` class, as follows:

```
import unittest

class PythonProjectsTest(unittest.TestCase):
      eturn
```

You want to put statements within your class that will be evaluated when the test is run and return an assertion value of `True` or `False`:

```
import unittest

class PythonProjectsTest(unittest.TestCase):
        def test_to_fail(self):
              self.failIf(False)

if __name__ == '__main__':
      unittest.main()
```

In the preceding example, you use the assertion method `failIf()` to evaluate the value in the parentheses. If the value is true, you will receive a failure message when you run the test. In this case, you're passing in `False`, which will, of course, evaluate to false. Therefore, this test will return a failure.

If you run this test you should see the following output:

```
======================================================================
FAIL: test_to_fail (__main__.PythonProjectsTest)
----------------------------------------------------------------------
Traceback (most recent call last):
  File "<stdin>", line 3, in test_to_fail
AssertionError: True is not false


----------------------------------------------------------------------
Ran 1 test in 0.000s

FAILED (failures=1)
```

If you change `self.failIf(True)` to `self.failIf(False)`, you should see your output change to:

```
----------------------------------------------------------------------
Ran 1 test in 0.000s
OK
```

Note that unittest doesn't evaluate whether a test is actually passing; it is simply evaluates whether an exception is thrown. Therefore, if an exception is not thrown, the test is considered OK. This could mean that your precise calculation, while returning a not-so precise number, shows as passing, or OK, not because the result is correct—which it isn't—but simply because the test is not raising an exception.

Following are the three possible outcomes of unittest if it doesn't actually have passing tests:

➤ OK: The test is OK; no exception raised.

➤ Fail: An `AssertionError` was raised (the test has failed).

➤ Error: An exception was raised that is not an `AssertionError`.

The best way to understand unit testing and the unittest module is to just do some testing.

TRY IT OUT Building and Running Unit Tests Using the unittest Module

In this Try It Out, you will write functions and test them using the unittest module, to understand the architecture of the unittest module.

1. In your Chapter 6 directory, create the file `ch6_example.py`. This file contains some fairly useless functions, but they are easy to test:

```
#ch6_example.py

def first(chars):
    chars.sort()
    return chars[0]

def last(chars):
    chars.sort()
    return chars[-1]
```

2. Create the test file and call it `unittest_example.py`. Import unittest and then, from your `ch6_example.py` file, import your two functions. Importing these functions directly means you won't have to call `ch6_example.first()` or `ch6_example.last()` when testing them, and you can simply call `first()` and `last()`. Remember, this is called *aliasing* our functions into our code through importing.

```
#unittest_example.py

import unittest
from ch6_example import first, last
```

3. Create two lists, one with numbers and one with strings. You'll be using these lists to test your two different sort functions. Then, set up the testing class, inheriting from the `unittest.TestCase` class:

```
#unittest_example.py

import unittest
from ch6_example import first, last

list_nums = [7,9,5]
list_chars = ['m', 'd', 'Z', 'l']import unittest

class TestPPMath(unittest.TestCase):
```

4. Next, test a few assertions to see how they behave. Start with the most common: `assertEqual`. This test should pass, because when you sort your list of numbers, the first element in the list is 5, so this should return true:

```
import unittest
from ch6_example import first, last

list_nums = [7,9,5]
list_chars = ['m', 'd', 'Z', 'l']

class TestPPMath(unittest.TestCase):

    def test_first(self):
        self.assertEqual(first(list_nums), 5)
```

Remember: All testing functions that you want to run must begin with `test`.

5. Similar to `AssertEqual`, which checks equality, there is also `assertTrue`, which checks that the first value is the second value, and therefore true:

```
import unittest
from ch6_example import first, last

list_nums = [7,9,5]
list_chars = ['m', 'd', 'Z', 'l']

class TestPPMath(unittest.TestCase):

    def test_first(self):
        self.assertEqual(first(list_nums), 5)

    def test_last(self):
        self.assertTrue(last(list_chars), 'm')
```

6. Unittest is only looking for exceptions, like the `assertionError` exception. You can use the `failUnless()` function to tell it to fail that test unless it is returning true:

```
import unittest
from ch6_example import first, last

list_nums = [7,9,5]
list_chars = ['m', 'd', 'Z', 'l']

class TestPPMath(unittest.TestCase):

    def test_first(self):
        self.assertEqual(first(list_nums), 5)

    def test_last(self):
        self.assertTrue(last(list_chars), 'm')

    def testFirstAgain(self):
        self.failUnless(first(list_chars), 'Z')
```

7. If you want the test to fail if it's true, you use the `failIf()` function, which fails if the inputs evaluate to true. So, this test should fail when you run it:

```python
import unittest
from ch6_example import first, last

list_nums = [7,9,5]
list_chars = ['m', 'd', 'Z', 'l']

class TestPPMath(unittest.TestCase):

    def test_first(self):
        self.assertEqual(first(list_nums), 5)

    def test_last(self):
        self.assertTrue(last(list_chars), 'm')

    def testFirstAgain(self):
        self.failUnless(first(list_chars), 'Z')

    def testLastAgain(self):
        self.failIf(last(list_nums), 9)
```

8. Finally, insert your `__main__` check and run the `unittest.main()` method to actually test your new testing class:

```python
import unittest
from ch6_example import first, last

list_nums = [7,9,5]
list_chars = ['m', 'd', 'Z', 'l']

class TestPPMath(unittest.TestCase):

    def test_first(self):
        self.assertEqual(first(list_nums), 5)

    def test_last(self):
        self.assertTrue(last(list_chars), 'm')

    def testFirstAgain(self):
        self.failUnless(first(list_chars), 'Z')

    def testLastAgain(self):
        self.failIf(last(list_nums), 9)


if __name__ == '__main__':
    unittest.main()
```

How It Works

When you write tests, you're simply creating static data to pass into functions you've already defined. You want to pass a known value to the function and then express, in your tests, the value you expect to be returned. If that value isn't returned, the test should fail. If the value is returned, the test passes and the code moves on to the next testing function.

Some readers may quickly realize that testing with static data isn't foolproof. What if the data that is passed in isn't a type that you've tested? This is why writing good tests is important. One function in your program may have multiple tests, or one test could verify multiple situations.

TEST-DRIVEN DEVELOPMENT IN PYTHON

A term that is becoming more and more popular in the Python community is *test-driven development* (TDD). What exactly does that mean? Although TDD is a very important topic when it comes to Python development, it is also a very robust topic. Therefore, this section gives only a very brief introduction of TDD so that you can familiarize yourself with the term and its basic definition.

TDD simply means writing your tests first. Most developers groan when they hear the word "testing." They think it means longer development time and more effort on their part, and less of the fun stuff like writing the actual code that will make their project run. However, testing can be just as fun as the other stuff. And although it does require the developer to write more lines of code, it leads to better quality code and more maintainability later on in the project. Your future self and co-collaborators will thank you for taking the time to write tests first and develop against those tests.

So, how exactly does TDD work? Write tests! It's really that simple. There is, of course, an art form to writing good tests, and it's important that you take the time to study up and become familiar with proper TDD practices. Here are the basics:

1. Write tests first.
2. All tests should fail at first.
3. Write code.
4. Test code against tests.
5. Rewrite code.
6. Retest code against tests.
7. Repeat until all tests are passing.

This is the gist of TDD. You can probably see why doctest may not be the best answer for all testing situations. Once you have to test and retest, and you begin testing more complex ideas, doctest will hit its limitations. As stated, there is an art to writing *effective* tests, however, and that is where the beauty of TDD comes in.

DEBUGGING YOUR PYTHON CODE

Most developers will likely tell you that they hate debugging. It's tedious, persnickety, and can become rather boring or infuriating fairly quickly. It doesn't have to be this way. Taking a new look at debugging and testing can make even the most cynical developer a little less irritated.

When you run into a bug with your code, rather than think about how annoying it is (don't worry, it's the natural reaction), think about how this is actually an opportunity to learn. Something is broken somewhere, some stone has gone unturned. This is your chance to find that stone, turn it over, and see what there is to see! You're well on your way to becoming a seasoned programmer with every bug you squash.

Python makes debugging a little less of a hassle with the Python debugger module, or the pdb. If you read Chapter 5 and explored the Chrome Developer Tools, you may notice some similarities. If you're a web developer by trade who is trying Python on for size, you'll probably find that you like the pdb and it reminds you a little of your favorite web debugging software.

The pdb is fairly powerful in that it enables you to insert breakpoints in your code that will stop your code running, and drop you into a pdb prompt or terminal. This is very handy because you can then begin examining the data you have in scope at that moment. If you find an exception is being raised when a certain function is called, you can put a `pdb()` call in that function and then you can start to examine the data in an interactive interpreter in your terminal. Let's try it out.

The following example illustrates using the pdb module for debugging your Python code.

TRY IT OUT Using the Python Debugger, or pdb module (pdb_example.py)

This Try It Out demonstrates how you can utilize the power of the pdb module to debug or examine your Python code.

1. Open the `pdb_example.py` file. You should see the following:

```
#pdb_example.py

class ExampleClass(object):

    def __init__(self, name, number):
        self.name = name
        self.number = number

    def example_entry(self):
        return "The example name is {0} with the number {1}".format(self.name,
        self.number)


if __name__ == '__main__':
    example = ExampleClass("Carla", 456)

    return example.example_entry()
```

2. Import the pdb module:

```
#pdb_example.py

import pdb

class ExampleClass(object):

    def __init__(self, name, number):
        self.name = name
        self.number = number

    def example_entry(self):
        return "The example name is {0} with the number {1}".format(self.name,
        self.number)
```

```
if __name__ == '__main__':
    example = ExampleClass("Carla", 456)

    return example.example_entry()
```

3.   The pdb module has many powerful features. The first one you look at is the `.set_trace()` method, so add a `set_trace()` to your code:

```
#pdb_example.py

import pdb

class ExampleClass(object):

    def __init__(self, name, number):
        self.name = name
        self.number = number

    def example_entry(self):
        pdb.set_trace()
    return "The example name is {0} with the number {1}".format(self.name,
self.number)


if __name__ == '__main__':
    example = ExampleClass("Carla", 456)

    return example.example_entry()
```

4.   Save the file. Now run your `pdb_example.py` file. You should be dropped into a pdb interpreter, which is noted with the `(Pdb)` prompt:

```
chapter6$ python pdb_example.py
> /Users/lcassell/Documents/Python_Companion/chapter6/pdb_example.py(13)
example_entry()
-> return "The example name is {0} with the number {1}".format( self.name,
self.number)
(Pdb)
```

5.   Type **n** and press Enter/Return:

```
(Pdb) n
--Return--
> /Users/lcassell/Documents/Python_Companion/chapter6/pdb_example.py(13)
example_entry()->'The example ...he number 456'
-> return "The example name is {0} with the number {1}".format( self.name,
self.number)
(Pdb)
```

What you've done is stepped down to the next (n) line in the file. Look at the `pdb_example.py` file and you'll see that the `set_trace()` is placed before your return string:

```
#pdb_example.py

import pdb

class ExampleClass(object):
```

```
def __init__(self, name, number):
    self.name = name
    self.number = number

def example_entry(self):
    pdb.set_trace()
    return "The example name is %s with the number %d" % name, number


if __name__ == '__main__':
    example = ExampleClass("Carla", 456)

    example.example_entry()
```

This means that the program will break at that line and open a pdb interpreter so that you can examine your code. When you type n and then press Enter/Return, you're moving to the next line in the code, which is your return statement. That line will execute and you'll see the printout of the string (with some ellipses to indicate text that was left out for readability (/):

```
> /Users/lcassell/Documents/Python_Companion/chapter6/pdb_example.py(13)
example_entry()->'The example ...he number 456'
-> return "The example name is {0} with the number {1}".format( self.name,
self.number)
(Pdb)
```

6. While still in the debugger, simply press Enter/Return again. You should see that the next line in the code is executed. It's as if you've type n and Enter/Return again. The debugger retains your last command and will simply execute it with the Enter/Return key:

```
(Pdb)
--Return--
> /Users/lcassell/Documents/Python_Companion/chapter6/pdb_example.py(19)<module>()
->None
-> example.example_entry()
(Pdb)
```

If you keep pressing Enter/Return, you'll see that you simply step through the rest of the program until it completes and you're back to your command prompt and out of the pdb environment:

```
(Pdb)
--Return--
> /Users/lcassell/Documents/Python_Companion/chapter6/pdb_example.py(19)<module>()
->None
-> example.example_entry()
(Pdb)
chapter6$
```

7. Start up the debugger again and run through some more handy commands:

```
chapter6$ python pdb_example.py
> /Users/lcassell/Documents/Python_Companion/chapter6/pdb_example.py(13)
example_entry()
-> return "The example name is {0} with the number {1}".format( self.name,
self.number)
(Pdb)
```

8. This time, print the value of some variables. At the debugger prompt, type **p self.name** and press Enter/Return:

```
> /Users/lcassell/Documents/Python_Companion/chapter6/pdb_example.py(13)
example_entry()
-> return "The example name is {0} with the number {1}".format( self.name,
self.number)
(Pdb) p self.name
'Carla'
(Pdb)
```

You can use the print functionality by simply typing **p** followed by the variable name.

9. At your prompt, type **locals()** and press Enter/Return. You should see all objects that are in the local scope at that moment:

```
(Pdb) p self.name
'Carla'
(Pdb) locals()
{'self': <__main__.ExampleClass object at 0x106c66450>}
(Pdb)
```

In this case your current local scope contains just your class, which is what it should be.

10. Type **globals()** and see what you have available in your global scope:

```
(Pdb) locals()
{'self': <__main__.ExampleClass object at 0x106c66450>}
(Pdb) globals()
{'example': <__main__.ExampleClass object at 0x106c66450>, '__builtins__': <module
'builtins' (built-in)>, '__name__': '__main__', '__file__': 'pdb_example.py',
'ExampleClass': <class '__main__.ExampleClass'>, 'pdb': <module 'pdb' from
'/usr/local/Cellar/python3/3.3.3/Frameworks/Python.framework/Versions/3.3/
lib/python3.3/pdb.py'>, '__package__': None, '__loader__': <_frozen_importlib.
SourceFileLoader object at 0x106b9a410>, '__cached__': None, '__doc__': None}
(Pdb)
```

Note that you have many things available to you, including your `ExampleClass` object, your pdb module (that you imported), and your local Python source. There may be times where you are debugging that you need to inspect what is in your local scope, to see if you have that data available to you. The `locals()` and `globals()` functions will be very useful during these times.

11. Type **c** and press Enter/Return. You should be taken out of the pdb, your code should complete, and you should see your normal command prompt. With the pdb, c simply continues running the program.

12. To quit the debugger without running the rest of your program, type **q** at the (Pdb) prompt and press Enter/Return prompt.

How It Works

The pdb is a built-in module in Python's standard library. You simply import the pdb into your file, then either call the stack_trace() method to enter the debugger environment or call other methods to perform certain functions within the file at run time, which will then take you into the debugger interface. The pdb is incredibly useful for debugging code at run time and for examining the data in your code at certain points in a "live" environment. The pdb module contains many commands; consult a reference for a more robust list.

Handling Exceptions in Python

Python is an interpreted language, which means that there is no compiler to compile your code and find any logic or syntax errors before you run it. So how does Python handle this? Python uses exceptions to handle errors. This type of handling can mean that making one small mistake in your code can cause your entire program to fail. Because of this you want to test thoroughly, but on top of that, you also want to set up some fail-safes in case you encounter exceptions with your code during run time.

For example, if you try the following code in your interpreter,

```
>>> def sum(a, b):
...         return a + b
...
>>> sum("no", 4)
```

you'll get the following error:

```
Traceback (most recent call last):
    File "<stdin>", line 1, in <module>
    File "<stdin>", line 2, in sum
TypeError: Can't convert 'int' object to str implicitly
```

As you can see, when you try to pass a string to a mathematic function, which can only operate on integers and floats, it throws a TypeError. This tells you that the data you sent to the function is not of the correct type. Because Python is not a strongly typed language, nor is it compiled, the only errors that you will get are exceptions, which will crop up at run time. When an exception is thrown at run time, your entire program will quit if there is no exception handling in place. It is imperative that you check for these sorts of "gotchas." Not checking for them can render your code unusable, and that's not a very good codebase to have!

A number of exceptions are built into the Python language. Here is a list of those exceptions:

```
BaseException
+-- SystemExit
+-- KeyboardInterrupt
+-- GeneratorExit
+-- Exception
     +-- StopIteration
     +-- StandardError
     |    +-- BufferError
     |    +-- ArithmeticError
     |    |    +-- FloatingPointError
     |    |    +-- OverflowError
     |    |    +-- ZeroDivisionError
     |    +-- AssertionError
     |    +-- AttributeError
```

```
|        +-- EnvironmentError
|        |     +-- IOError
|        |     +-- OSError
|        |           +-- WindowsError (Windows)
|        |           +-- VMSError (VMS)
|        +-- EOFError
|        +-- ImportError
|        +-- LookupError
|        |     +-- IndexError
|        |     +-- KeyError
|        +-- MemoryError
|        +-- NameError
|        |     +-- UnboundLocalError
|        +-- ReferenceError
|        +-- RuntimeError
|        |     +-- NotImplementedError
|        +-- SyntaxError
|        |     +-- IndentationError
|        |           +-- TabError
|        +-- SystemError
|        +-- TypeError
|        +-- ValueError
|              +-- UnicodeError
|                    +-- UnicodeDecodeError
|                    +-- UnicodeEncodeError
|                    +-- UnicodeTranslateError
+-- Warning
      +-- DeprecationWarning
      +-- PendingDeprecationWarning
      +-- RuntimeWarning
      +-- SyntaxWarning
      +-- UserWarning
      +-- FutureWarning
      +-- ImportWarning
      +-- UnicodeWarning
      +-- BytesWarning
```

With so much that can go wrong, how do you gracefully handle exceptions in Python? With a try-except block. The try-except block will try a piece of code and if the code throws one of the preceding exceptions, it will catch that exception and print out an error message, as defined in the base exception class, or you can even print your own error messages for each exception:

```
>>> try:
...     sum("yes", 9)
... except TypeError:
...     print("Both inputs must be integers")
...
Both inputs must be integers
```

You can also have try-except blocks handle exceptions so that your program doesn't fail and you can continue moving down the stack:

```
>>> try:
...     some_function()
```

```
... except:
...     graceful_function()
... else:
...   next_function()
```

Sometimes you will want to run a function no matter if your try-catch catches an exception or runs. In that case you want to use the finally statement.

```
>>> try:
...     some_function()
... except:
...     graceful_function()
... finally:
    cleanup_function()
```

But what if you want your code to throw its own exceptions? What if you want to check for some certain type of data, and if that is not present, you want to alert the user? You can make custom exception classes to use on top of built-ins.

In the following example, you create and use customs exceptions.

TRY IT OUT Creating and Using Custom Exceptions in Python (exceptClass.py)

This Try It Out demonstrates how you can create and then use custom exceptions in your Python code.

1. Open exceptClass.py to familiarize yourself with the class you'll be using:

```
# exceptClass.py

class TestClass(object):

    def __init__(self, name, number):

        name = self.name
        number = self.number


    def return_values(self):

        print ("The values are: ", self.name, self.number)
```

2. Write the exception that you'll throw if self.number isn't a number. The first step to writing an exception is that it must be a class that inherits from the Exception class. Add the following lines to your exceptClass.py file:

```
# exceptClass.py

class TestClass(object):

    def __init__(self, name, number):

        self.name = name
        self.number = number


    def return_values(self):

        print ("The values are: ", self.name, self.number)
```

```
class notANumber(Exception):
    def __init__(self, value):
        self.value = value

    def __str__(self):
        return repr(self.value)
```

Here you've created your own customized exception that will be thrown if the number attribute is not, in fact, a number. You've also overridden the __init__ function for the Exception class, and rather than using args you're going to use value to catch the value that raised the exception. You are also overriding the __str__() method to output the self.value property using the repr() method call, which will give you the correct representation of the value that raised the exception (this is what will be printed out with your exception error message).

3. Next, change your return_values() method into something that can check whether self .number is an int. If the type of self.number isn't an int, you want to raise your exception. Implement a very simple if/else statement to check in your try/catch:

```
# exceptClass.py

class TestClass(object):

    def __init__(self, name, number):

        self.name = name
        self.number = number

    def return_values(self):
        try:
            if (type(self.name) is int):
                return "The values are: ", type(self.name), type(self.number)
            else:
                raise notANumber(self.number)
        except notANumber as e:
            print("The value for number must be an int you passed: ", e.value)

class notANumber(Exception):
    def __init__(self, value):
        self.value = value

    def __str__(self):
        return repr(self.value)
```

What you are doing here is a simple check on the type of self.name. If it is not an int, you are raising the exception you defined earlier. Should the self.number property actually be an int, you're simply returning a string that tells you the types of each property of your instance. If the type is not an int, notANumber will be raised and you'll pass in self.number to be evaluated and output in your error message.

4. Now, run your script in interactive mode. Start up a Python interpreter, but do it using the -i flag and calling your exceptClass.py file, like so:

```
$ python -i exceptClass.py
>>>
```

When you use the `-i` flag when starting a Python interpreter, you can pass in a Python file and this imports the file you've passed in without having to explicitly import in the interpreter. This means you have both classes you've defined in your `exampleClass.py` file, and you don't have to namespace them with `exampleClass.<foo>`; you can simply call things.

5. Next, create a new instance of your `TestClass`, and pass in two strings (rather than a string and an integer):

```
(ch3Ex2)$ python -i exceptClass.py
>>> exampl = TestClass('string1', 'string2')
```

6. Call `return_values()` on your newly created instance and note the output:

```
(ch3Ex2)$ python -i exceptClass.py
>>> exampl = TestClass('string1', 'string2')
>>> exampl.return_values()
The value for number must be an int you passed:  string
```

The `try-except` worked and caught that you were passing in a string rather than an integer

7. Create another instance and pass in a string and an integer; then call `return_values()` on that instance and note the output:

```
>>> exm = TestClass('string1', 42)
>>> exm.return_values()
('The values are: ', <class 'str'>, <class 'int'>)
```

How It Works

When you create an exception class, you're really creating a subclass from the base `Exception` class that is built into Python. With this, you have control over how your own customized exceptions will behave when they are raised. You created a very simple class, and saw that when the exception was raised, your class will give feedback to the user as to what type of data was passed into your class.

As you can see, this feature can be incredibly powerful when writing larger projects. Hopefully this has given you enough of a glimpse into the formulation of exceptions that you can write your own, should the need arise.

WORKING ON LARGER PYTHON PROJECTS

When developing with Python you may find that different projects have different versions of different packages. What do you do when your local environment is Python 2.7, but that project you want to work on (or inherited) is 2.6? Or 3.4? This is a problem that many Python developers have encountered, so of course they created a solution. Enter virtualenv.

Virtualenv is a virtual environment for your Python projects. It enables you to create numerous Python instances and develop against all the libraries you need for certain projects. Say you want to work on a project that uses Python 2.7, which you have installed locally, but the project needs a different version of a library than what you have installed locally. The Python versions match up but the library's versions do not. This is a job for virtualenv!

In this example, you create and then activate a virtualenv to create sandboxes for your individual Python projects.

TRY IT OUT Creating and Activating Virtualenvs

This Try It Out demonstrates how to install, activate, deactivate, and remove virtualenvs from your system.

1. Install virtualenv by using the commands appropriate for your system:

    ```
    OSX:
    brew install virtualenv

    Linux:
    apt-get install python-virtualenv
    pacman -s install python-virtualenv

    Windows (powershell users):
    pip install virtualenv
    ```

2. Move into the directory where you'll be working. Some power users create a `temp_env` directory on their systems and create virtualenvs in that. This is a great workflow if you have many virutalenvs to manage. For your purposes, however, you'll just keep things simple. Once you are in your directory, create your virtualenv:

    ```
    $ cd chapter6
    $ virtualenv ch6Ex3
    $
    ```

3. If you do a directory listing of the contents in the directory where you created your virtualenv, you should see a directory for the name of your environment (in this case `ch6Ex3`). You'll be using that directory to activate your environment. This is also the directory that will house all of your installs and your Python code for this environment. To activate the new virtualenv, simply add the following command:

    ```
    $ source ch6Ex3/bin/activate
    (ch6Ex3)$
    ```

    When you are in an active virtualenv, your command prompt will show the name of the virtualenv within parentheses before your command prompt. In this case you have `(ch6Ex3)$`.

4. Now let's do an experiment. If you did the exercises in Chapter 5, you should have installed requests via `pip install requests`. Start a Python interpreter and see if you can use requests:

    ```
    (ch6Ex3)$ python
    Python 2.7.5 (default, Aug 25 2013, 00:04:04)
    [GCC 4.2.1 Compatible Apple LLVM 5.0 (clang-500.0.68)] on darwin
    Type "help", "copyright", "credits" or "license" for more information.
    >>> import requests
    ```

    What version of the Python shell do you have? Is it 3.4? Or 2.7? How can you change that?

Once you press Enter/Return after importing requests, you should see an `ImportError` exception, declaring there are no module requests. This is because although you imported requests to your system-wide Python, you are not using that Python environment now, and you must reinstall requests if you want to use it in this virutalenv.

5. `exit()` out of the interpreter and pip install requests, while still in your virtualenv:

```
(ch6Ex3)$ python
Python 2.7.5 (default, Aug 25 2013, 00:04:04)
[GCC 4.2.1 Compatible Apple LLVM 5.0 (clang-500.0.68)] on darwin
Type "help", "copyright", "credits" or "license" for more information.
>>> import requests
Traceback (most recent call last):
  File "<stdin>", line 1, in <module>
ImportError: No module named requests
>>>exit()
(ch6Ex3)$ pip install requests
Downloading/unpacking requests
  Downloading requests-2.2.1-py2.py3-none-any.whl (625kB): 625kB downloaded
Installing collected packages: requests
Successfully installed requests
Cleaning up...
(ch6Ex3)$
```

After you install a package you're still in your virtualenv, and you'll remain in your virtualenv until you deactivate that environment.

6. Note that even after installing a package, you are still in your virtualenv and will remain there until you deactivate that environment. Deactivate your environment like so:

```
 (ch6Ex3)$ pip install requests
Downloading/unpacking requests
  Downloading requests-2.2.1-py2.py3-none-any.whl (625kB): 625kB downloaded
Installing collected packages: requests
Successfully installed requests
Cleaning up...
(ch6Ex3)$ deactivate
$
```

You've successfully installed virtualenv, created a new virtualenv to use, installed a package for that environment, and even deactivated the virtualenv. What if you want to remove that environment altogether? Say you're done with that project and you want to remove all those files you installed.

7. To remove a virtualenv, systematically remove the directory it created:

```
 (ch6Ex3)$ pip install requests
Downloading/unpacking requests
  Downloading requests-2.2.1-py2.py3-none-any.whl (625kB): 625kB downloaded
Installing collected packages: requests
Successfully installed requests
Cleaning up...
(ch6Ex3)$ deactivate
$rm -rf ch6Ex3/
$
```

How It Works

Virtualenv provides a way for Python developers to create environments that may have various version requirements. This helps to keep environments separate from others and allows the system to have sandboxes for development of multiple Python projects.

Oftentimes you have projects where more than one person is working in the environment. What happens when you have a long list of requirements that your project needs and you have four people working on the project, on different machines? Do you want to have your teammates simply type `pip install <module _ name>` over and over? No, you do not.

Virtualenv has a very nice feature that enables you to make a `requirements.txt` file and put the packages needed for your program into the file. Anyone using your package can simply type `pip install requirements.txt` and get all the dependencies that your package requires! It really is that easy!

TRY IT OUT Creating a requirements.txt file to Simplify Adding Modules

This Try It Out demonstrates how to create a fake `requirements.txt` file and populate it with some popular packages.

1. Create a new virtualenv:

    ```
    $virtualenv ch6Ex3
    $source ch6Ex3/bin/activate
    (ch6Ex3)$
    ```

2. Write the `requirements.txt` file. In your Chapter 6 directory, create `requirements.txt` and add the following lines:

    ```
    BeautifulSoup==3.2.0
    requests
    https://github.com/django/django/tarball/master
    ```

    These lines are all different. Usually, `requirements.txt` will have uniformity, but for illustrative purposes, these lines show the three most common ways to get a package installed via pip.

    The first line (`BeautifulSoup==3.2.0`) shows that you want to install BeautifulSoup (a web scraping tool), but you want version 3.2.0, hence the double equal signs.

    The second line (`Requests`) installs the current version.

    The final line (`https://github.com/django/django/tarball/master`) indicates that you want to download and install the package at the URL provided. In this case you'll be downloading and installing the entire Django project that is available on the master branch of the Django repository (this is a pretty big file, so be prepared for a short download wait).

3. Save this file and then activate your virtualenv and install those requirements:

    ```
    $ source ch6Ex3/bin/activate
    (ch6Ex3)$ pip install -r requirements.txt
    ```

You should see messages about downloading and installing the three packages we've provided. Once the packages are successfully downloaded and installed, you should see a "Cleaning up..." message, followed by your virtualenv prompt:

```
Successfully installed Django
Cleaning up...
(ch6Ex3)$
```

4. Start up Python and see if you really do have those packages installed:

```
Python 2.7.5 (default, Aug 25 2013, 00:04:04)
[GCC 4.2.1 Compatible Apple LLVM 5.0 (clang-500.0.68)] on darwin
Type "help", "copyright", "credits" or "license" for more information.
>>> import requests
>>> import BeautifulSoup
>>> import django
>>>
```

If you can import without an error being raised, you've successfully installed all of the requirements for your phantom project. Feel free to rm -rf ch6Ex3 virtualenv now. This will remove the virtualenv and all the packages you've installed, including the very large Django project.

How It Works

Requirements.txt is a feature of virtualenv that allows developers to include all the necessary libraries needed for their module to work with their Python package. This allows quick setup of environments so that developers can begin work quickly.

RELEASING PYTHON PACKAGES

The __init__.py ('dunder, init, dunder') file is fairly important when releasing code out into the wild. For Python projects, __init__.py needs to be at each level of the codebase's directory structure. For example, say you have a rather large codebase that has multiple .py files. You start by putting a __init__.py in the first layer of the directory structure:

```
my_package
     |----__init__.py
     |---- my_package.py
            |---- my_subpackage
                     |---- __init__.py
                     |---- my_subpackage.py
```

This tells the Python interpreter that you want to treat the directory as a Python package. The cool part is that you can leave the __init__.py file empty, or you can put configuration variables in it. Commonly, folks will import modules/libraries, or other configurations in their __init__.py file— basic setup work to help the package function.

So what happens when you create an __init__.py file and import something? How does Python's namespacing work now? Suppose you have the following import statement in my_package/__init__.py:

```
from file import File
```

When you want to call that import in the my _ package.py file you would simply say:

```
from my_package import File
```

Another use of the __init __.py file is to import all the modules that you'd like to import into the namespace of your package. You do this by assigning the __all__ variable to your subpackage in your package level __init __.py (the first one):

```
__all__ = ['my_subpackage']
```

Doing this makes it so that when your users declare from my _ package import * it will import all of the modules from my _ subpackage.

> **NOTE** *Can you think of a way you could have used a __init __.py file in the Flask application? That would have made the code more Pythonic. (We did not do this because we wanted to show you the "raw" way of doing things, so that you can understand the inner workings of things before adding more steps and layers).*

Now that you have your code written, and your __init __.py files in place, what if you want to release this code out into the wild? What if you want to be able to install this module on other machines by simply typing pip install <package _ name>?

PIP AND PYPI

You've been using pip to install third-party libraries and modules throughout this book. But just what is pip, and how does it work?

Pip is the Python package installer. It installs packages that are in the PyPI (pronounced pie-P-I, not pie-pie). The PyPI is the Python Package Index, also known as "The Cheese Shop" (another Monty Python reference), to more seasoned Python developers. This is where you can upload your own Python packages so that they will be available via pip install <package _ name>. Sometimes, people will simply upload their own packages to PyPI because it's easier for them to install those packages on multiple machines. Oftentimes people upload their packages because they hope it will be helpful to others.

To find out more about the Package Index, or to search the index, you can go to http://pypi.python.org/pypi. This is the main page for PyPI and has all the information you need to get started.

If you want to upload your own packages to the PyPI you'll need to register with PyPI and then follow the tutorial, which is linked on the homepage. It really is that simple. You register, you upload your package, and then it will be available to you, shortly, via `pip install <package_name>`.

Keep in mind that when you upload a package to PyPI, it is readily available for anyone to download and use. This is why it is so important to practice good, Pythonic programming at all times. You never know when someone will download and use your module, and you want them to be able to use your creation with as little headache as possible.

SUMMARY

We've looked over some of the basics of testing and packaging for your Python projects. You should now have a clear idea of just how most Python packages and modules/libraries are architected and created. A good exercise for the reader is to go back through the beginning of the book and work through the exercises using the concepts you've learned in this chapter. Can you rewrite the code in Chapter 3 to be test-driven? Can you package your Flask app from Chapter 5 and send it to another computer to be run and developed? You should try these things out so that you have a clear idea of just how all parts and pieces of Python packages are working together.

EXERCISES

1. In the zip file for this chapter, open the file `markets.py` and write a doctest string to test the value being returned by the function in the file. Can you think of a reason why a simple doctest string in this code could be incredibly useful for maintaining the code in the future?

2. Write a unittest for a function that will take a string and return that string reversed. Make sure the test fails, because you haven't written the function to test, yet.

3. Write a function for your unittest that takes a string and returns the reverse of that string. Now, run your unittest against that function and modify the function until it passes.

▶ WHAT YOU LEARNED IN THIS CHAPTER

TOPIC	DESCRIPTION
Unit test	Usually a function that is written in a separate testing script, that imports the code to be tested, and that tests each function in the imported code.
Virtualenv	Third-party software that allows developers to create system sandboxes for Python development, using customized versions of Python and Python libraries/modules.
TDD (Test-Driven Development	A development style where one writes tests first, which will fail, then writes the actual functioning code to make the tests past, therefore driving the development cycle based on testing first.
Pdb	Python Debugger, an interactive debugging module for Python.

7

Exploring Python's Frontiers

WHAT YOU WILL LEARN IN THIS CHAPTER:

➤ Specialist application areas using Python

➤ Third-party packages for specialist applications

➤ How to contribute to Python's development

WROX.COM CODE DOWNLOADS FOR THIS CHAPTER

There are no Wrox code downloads for this chapter, but the various solutions discussed all have packages that are available for download. Many of these are available via the Python Package Index (PyPI) or have binary installers that you can download from the package's home site. Each section provides information about download locations for the associated packages.

In the earlier chapters of this book, you looked at how Python can be used to interact with your operating system and other programs, how it can manage data using flat files and databases, and how you can build both desktop and web-based applications. You have also seen some of the techniques and tools that can help you build larger scale programs efficiently and reliably.

In this concluding chapter, you see how Python can support you in many wider areas of programming. You consider the various frameworks, packages, libraries, and even distinct Python distributions that have been developed to support specialist areas of interest such as science and language processing. You also see how some niche application types have acquired specialist tools and packages to support their specific needs. Finally, you look at how you can contribute to the Python community itself to help make Python even better.

DRAWING PICTURES WITH PYTHON

Many tools are available for drawing and processing graphics in Python. These range from simple drawing libraries like `turtle` to highly specialized modules and frameworks like `matplotlib` and `Pillow`. The following sections describe the capabilities and areas of application of each option.

Using Turtle Graphics

The easiest way to draw pictures from code is probably to use *turtle graphics*. Turtle graphics was invented as a way of drawing pictures using the programming language Logo. The idea was to issue directional commands to a robotic device—the turtle—with a pen attached that, in turn, produced a drawing. The concept proved popular, and now most languages provide some kind of turtle graphics support. In Python, it comes in the form of the `turtle` module. By default, the module presents the graphics in a small pop-up window built using Tkinter. You can specify a Tk canvas object (see the next section for more details about canvas objects) when you initialize the turtle system from within an application, or you can use the module at the interactive prompt to experiment with the system. The official documentation gives a comprehensive description of the functions and methods available, and you can get a good feel for what is possible by running the demonstration. Type the following at the OS command prompt:

```
python -m turtledemo
```

This brings up a window with a menu of examples that you can start and stop, and also displays the code of the running example so that you can see how to achieve the same effects in your programs.

Using GUI Canvas Objects

Most GUI frameworks include a *canvas* object. A canvas is an area on-screen in which you can draw lines and shapes, add images, and even insert text. The Tkinter `Canvas` object is fairly typical and supports drawing arcs, ovals (including circles), lines, rectangles, polygons, text, images, and even windows (so you can embed a widget inside a canvas). A minimal canvas program showing a red circle looks like this:

```
>>> import Tkinter as tk
>>> top = tk.Tk()
>>> c = tk.Canvas(top, width=50, height=50)
>>> c.pack()
>>> c.create_oval(10,10,40,40,outline='red',fill='red')
1
>>> top.mainloop()
```

The `Canvas` class contains many, many methods that enable you to build sophisticated graphics programs.

This is all at a very low level of abstraction. For a higher level you can turn to other libraries such as the `turtle` module discussed earlier, or some more exotic, third-party options such as those discussed next.

Plotting Data

The most popular data-plotting tool for Python is `matplotlib`, which you can find at `http://matplotlib.org/` and downloaded from PyPI or included as part of the `scipy` package discussed later in this chapter. The website includes links to many examples and tutorials.

`matplotlib` is closely tied into the other `scipy` packages and, as such, can be rather intimidating if you only want a simple graph. Several other lightweight packages are available on PyPI that attempt to address this and provide an easier-to-use plotting library, but for serious plotting `matplotlib` is the best solution.

Using imghdr

If your graphics interests are more focused on images than data, the `imghdr` module offers some useful help in determining what kind of image file you are dealing with. The module is part of the standard library and is quite simple to use. Rather than relying on the filename extension, it tests the data content of the file to determine the image type.

The module consists of a single function, `what()`, which takes either a filename or filestream as an argument and returns the image type. The module supports most common file types, but you can extend its range by adding your own custom test functions to handle other image types.

Introducing Pillow

For many years the standard solution for manipulating images in Python was the Python Imaging Library (PIL). PIL has not been ported to Python version 3; instead, a replacement library, called Pillow, has been created that builds on PIL but adds some new features.

Pillow's homepage is at `http://pillow.readthedocs.org`. You can install it via PyPI.

Pillow is based on an `Image` class that can be opened and saved. By specifying the appropriate parameters, converting a JPEG file to a PNG file, for example, can be as simple as this:

```
>>> from PIL import Image
>>> Image.open('foo.jpg').save('foo.png')
```

You can also use the `Image` object to retrieve information about the image, such as its size. Many more powerful options are available, too. For example, you can transpose images by flipping them or rotating them, as well as resizing and applying filters. Pillow is like an image editing program that you drive programmatically.

Trying Out ImageMagick

ImageMagick is a similar tool to Pillow, but it's based on the command-line suite of tools of the same name. The command-line website is at `http://www.imagemagick.org/`.

The Python package, `wand`, is on PyPI and uses `ctypes` to harness much of ImageMagick's power. You can find the website here: `http://docs.wand-py.org`. The site has documentation, including a user guide and references.

An image conversion program, similar to the Pillow example in the previous section, looks like this:

```
>>> from wand.image import Image
>>> with Image(filename='foo.jpg') as img:
...     img.format = 'png'
...     img.save(filename='foo.png')
>>>
```

You can find many other modules and packages for graphics work in Python. The PyPI search tool and web search engines will reveal many examples. The tools that have been highlighted in this chapter should cover most eventualities, but don't be afraid to try alternatives.

DOING SCIENCE WITH PYTHON

Python has a long tradition of use within the scientific and mathematical communities. As a result, many modules and packages have been created to meet the specialized needs of the communities. Before looking at the third-party options available, you should first consider the built-in support that Python offers.

Python's native types offer much for scientific computing. In particular, the Python integer type with its effectively unlimited size makes it well suited for working with large volumes and long series calculations. Python's floating-point type is comparable to that of other languages, but in addition you have the options of using decimal and fraction types that reduce errors due to rounding. Finally, Python is one of the few languages that natively supports the complex, or "imaginary," number type used so extensively in science and engineering applications.

Of course, having a variety of data types is only half the story; along with the data you need operations to support them. Once again, Python's built-in operations are supplemented by the standard library with modules like `math`, `cmath`, and `statistics` providing a wide range of options. Modules, such as the `collections` module, also provide support for more exotic data types like named tuples, ordered dictionaries, and chain maps—used as an efficient way to link multiple mappings.

Although these are all powerful tools, they still do not provide the specific support needed for performing detailed scientific analysis, and this is where the special third-party libraries come into play. Chief among these is the SciPy package, discussed next.

Introducing SciPy

SciPy has a long history, evolving out of several independent development streams. These have gradually come together to form a powerful integrated whole. The SciPy project incorporates six separate bundles that form an integrated "stack" of tools. You can find the SciPy website at `http://www.scipy.org/`.

The six bundles are:

➤ **NumPy:** One of the oldest mathematical packages for Python and the foundation of many others. NumPy includes a set of types and operations suitable for numerical analysis and simulations. These include an N dimensional array object, linear algebra, Fourier transforms, and various random number generators. In addition, NumPy offers hooks to access the wealth of scientific and mathematic tools written in Fortran and C.

➤ **SciPy:** The package for which the project is named. It includes functions for integration, signal processing, sparse data structures, and numerous special-purpose functions.

➤ **Matplotlib:** This package was discussed under the "Plotting Data" heading earlier in this chapter. It produces high-quality graphs, suitable for publication, offering a great deal of control over layout, labeling, and so on. It aims to compete with commercial packages such as Mathematica and MATLAB in this regard. It also supports several GUI toolkits for building graphics-rich desktop applications.

➤ **SymPy:** This is designed to perform symbolic math. Rather than display numerical results, it uses concepts like `sqrt(2)` as a symbol within its answers. This would look strange to users without a math background, but to mathematicians it is a standard tool and has the advantage of not being subject to the rounding errors associated with traditional floating-point representations. You can think of it as a tool for doing pure math rather than doing arithmetic. In the former, the result is symbolic; in the latter it is a number. You can use it to solve integral and differential calculus problems, Bessel functions, Eigenvalues, and much more. SymPy includes an interactive shell prompt at which you can enter your expressions, as well as a package you can import into your own applications.

➤ **Pandas:** This is a data analysis toolkit. In Chapter 3 you heard about `rpy` for interfacing with the R statistics analysis language. Pandas is a pure Python alternative to the R environment. At the time of writing, Pandas is less powerful than R in this regard, but it is a project that is growing with each release. In addition, it integrates with the other SciPy packages better than the `rpy` solution. If you are purely interested in statistics, stick with `rpy`, but if you want a more integrated analysis workflow and are using the other SciPy elements, take a close look at Pandas.

➤ **IPython:** This is not specifically aimed at scientific users. It is a powerful replacement for the standard Python interactive interpreter. It replaces the traditional `>>>` prompt with `In[n]:`, where n is the number of the command. Output lines are preceded by `Out[n]:` where n matches the value in the corresponding `In[]:` prompt. As well as understanding all of the usual Python language, IPython adds several new features. For example, there is a shortcut to the `help()` function. It also enables you to run OS commands by prefixing them with an exclamation point (`!`). But IPython is much more than just an interactive prompt. It includes a notebook concept where whole sessions can be stored and retrieved. You can thus work on multiple projects and save the state of each when you are done, then restore that state and continue with all history and so on intact. IPython also works with the other SciPy bundles, including matplotlib and SymPy, and can display graphs or symbolic expressions. You can find examples of what the notebook can do along with full documentation on the IPython website at `http://ipython.org/`. The combination of matplotlib, SymPy, and IPython offers a powerful alternative to commercial packages such as MATLAB or Mathematica.

Finally, several add-ons for SciPy are included under the SciKit banner. These cover areas such as aeronautical engineering; audio, image, and video processing, environmental science, and others.

Doing Bioscience with Python

One area of science that has come to the fore in recent years is bioscience, and particularly the analysis of DNA. The bioPython package has been developed to meet this need (`http://biopython.org/`). The package includes support for reading and writing most of the standard files used in bioinformatics as well as a `Sequence` class for analyzing DNA sequences.

In addition to bioPython, some other modules are available, and you can find them using your preferred search engine. Before trying to reinvent the wheel, it is always wise to check whether somebody else has already done the work for you!

Using GIS

With the explosion of satellite navigation and mobile electronic mapping software, the field of Geographic Information Systems (GIS) has seen an upsurge of interest. ArcGIS (`https://www.arcgis.com`) is a standardized set of tools for geo-processing. Python support for ArcGIS comes in the form of ArcPy, a package that has the goal of providing "access to geo-processing tools as well as additional functions, classes, and modules that enable you to create simple or complex workflows quickly and easily."

There is one big problem. At the time of writing, ArcPy is only available for Python v2.7, not for Python v3. However, for GIS processing ArcPy really is the best option currently available.

Watching Your Language

The study of human language and processing natural languages into data has been an area of study for many years. There have been rapid advances in recent years, and with increased computing power natural language processing is starting to appear in mainstream projects.

Python has the Natural Language ToolKit to support this area, and its homepage is located at `http://www.nltk.org/`. The toolkit provides access to several specialized tools and enables programmers to parse and tokenize text, analyze its structure, and categorize it. You can find and install NLTK from PyPI.

Getting It All

Although all of the previously discussed packages are powerful tools, getting them installed into a standard Python distribution can be a complex process using the normal installation tools. Fortunately, you have alternatives in the shape of Anaconda and Enthought Canopy. These are distributions of Python packaged up with all of the science tools you are likely to need. In addition to the SciPy and NLTK frameworks already discussed, Anaconda has more than 100 other specialist packages built in. The distribution is made available by Continuum Analytics, which also offers other packages on a commercial basis. Canopy is a very similar concept with a free basic version available as well as enhanced, commercial offerings.

Anaconda can be installed on Windows, Mac OS, or Linux and does not interfere with existing installations of Python. Anaconda supports Python versions 2.6 through 3.4 at the time of writing. The Anaconda homepage is located at `https://store.continuum.io/cshop/anaconda/`.

Canopy is likewise available on all the major platforms, and its web page is at `https://www` `.enthought.com/products/canopy/`.

PLAYING GAMES WITH PYTHON

You have already seen how Python can be used to build basic games in Chapter 4, "Building Desktop Applications," where you built several variations on the classic tic-tac-toe game. However, most game players today expect something a tad more exciting and dynamic. Python can support many types of games and has comprehensive support for generating random numbers, an essential part of any game, built right into the `random` module of the standard library. The module has functions that can simulate dice rolls, pick random choices from a selection, or just generate a random number in a variety of formats.

Enriching the Experience with PyGame

If you want a rich game experience using multimedia, the PyGame third-party package is a good place to start. It provides a set of modules that encapsulate the Simple DirectMedia Layer (SDL) that enables programs to access audio, keyboard, joystick, and graphics hardware. It is also cross-platform, so PyGame works with most popular OSes. It is modular so you only need to use the bits that are useful to you, keeping your code small.

Its website at `http://www.pygame.org` includes many example programs, as well as several tutorials. PyGame has an active community of users for help and support. Several books on building games using Python and PyGame are also available.

Exploring Other Options

PyGame is not the only gaming-focused library. You can use several other options. One example is Pyganim, which is a sprite animation module built on top of the PyGame infrastructure, but easier to use. Albow is a GUI toolkit specifically targeted at building games with PyGame. Many other packages are written on top of PyGame, bearing witness to its popularity as a foundation games framework.

Of course, you don't have to use PyGame. Other packages access the low-level hardware and libraries. PyOpenGL, as the name implies, provides access to the OpenGL libraries.

One feature of gaming that is also supported is the back-end physics engines needed to model the real-world behavior of physical objects. Python also has tools to support this in the shape of packages like `pymunk` for 2-D modeling. Panda3d and the Python Computer Graphics Kit (`cgkit`) provide support for 3-D.

In addition to graphics, most games also need sound. For that you can use built-in modules in the standard library including `aifc`, `wave`, and `sunau`. The `winsound` module provides low-level access to Windows sound facilities. On top of these low-level libraries, the gaming community has built several packages to assist in generating suitably exciting sounds to accompany your action.

Many other libraries are available, too. In fact, the number of options available for the games programmer can be bewildering. You can find a useful summary at `https://wiki.python.org/` `moin/PythonGameLibraries`.

GOING TO THE MOVIES

Python has a long history in the movie business, with several computer-generated imagery (CGI) studios adopting Python as a scripting engine. Several well-known movies had Python doing some of the production work behind the scenes. To support this, various packages have been developed and made available to a wider audience. Examples include Nuke, Maya, and Blender. Many of these are built on a foundation provided by the `cgkit` package mentioned in the "Playing Games with Python" section earlier in this chapter. This means that you have lots of scope for using Python while creating and editing your next video masterpiece.

The Computer Graphics Kit

The `cgkit` package provides a set of low-level types and operations needed to create 3-D scenes. It also provides a rendering engine, although the results can be displayed in other rendering engines if required. `cgkit` includes bindings to the Pixar RenderMan API. `cgkit` also includes the Maya plug-ins that enable Maya (see the next section) to interact with Python and vice versa.

Tutorials and reference documentation are available, although they do expect a basic knowledge of 3-D computer graphics principles such as would be acquired by using 3-D modeling applications.

Version 2 of the `cgkit` was released in early 2013. `cgkit` is available for Python versions 2 and 3. The package is stable with very little new development underway.

The homepage for the `cgkit` is at `http://cgkit.sourceforge.net/introduction.html`.

Modeling and Animation

Many tools are available for digital compositing of video images. Those discussed here are a representative selection, and all include some degree of Python integration.

The NUKE family of products is aimed squarely at the professional end of the video graphics market. It is a commercial compositing tool that integrates with Python but has a price to match its target audience, although a free trial is available as is a limited-functionality Personal Learning Edition for non-commercial use. You can find the NUKE homepage at `http://www.thefoundry.co.uk/products/nuke-product-family/`. NUKE uses Python 2.7.

Maya is another 3-D animation and compositing tool. It, too, is a commercial product, competing with NUKE, and also offers a free trial. It can be scripted using Python, and you can incorporate Maya animations into your Python programs. The Maya/Python integration is part of the `cgkit` bundle described in the previous section. You can find the Maya homepage at `http://www.autodesk.co.uk/products/autodesk-maya/overview`.

Blender is yet another animation and compositing package, but it is open source and therefore free, making it much more accessible to the consumer market. It, too, uses Python for its scripting engine. The homepage is at `http://www.blender.org/features/`. Blender uses Python 3.

Photo Processing

For processing photographic images, many of the solutions discussed in the "Drawing Pictures with Python" section at the start of the chapter apply. Pillow and ImageMagick are both effective tools for manipulating photographic images, capable of cropping, changing exposure, and so on. In addition, the SciPy bundle of packages includes features for processing images with features such as Gaussian blur.

You can also find many special-purpose modules in PyPI to perform specific tasks such as resizing or cropping images. There is a module, `psd-tools`, for reading Adobe Photoshop .psd files. For processing the EXIF metadata there is, for example, the `pyexif` module that uses the `exiftool` command-line application under the covers.

The final category of photo tools is that of online media managers. Modules enable you to transfer photos to and from various sites such as Picasa, Flickr, Facebook, and Twitter. An example of this category is `picasa-downloader`. Unfortunately, many of these are still only available for Python v2, and most use the Pillow or ImageMagick tools under the covers anyway.

Working with Audio

You've already heard about the built-in modules in the standard library: `aifc`, `wave`, `sunau`, and the `winsound`. These are just as applicable for non-gaming sound applications.

SciPy and its various packages can also be used to process sound files, especially in conjunction with some of the SciKit add-ons. This is especially useful for analyzing sound content or plotting signal waveforms.

There is a useful Python wiki-page listing many sound- and music-oriented projects at `https://wiki.python.org/moin/PythonInMusic`.

INTEGRATING WITH OTHER LANGUAGES

The normal Python distribution that you have been using until now is written and built using the C language and is often referred to as CPython. There are other implementations of the Python language in other languages. These non-C based interpreters facilitate integration of the other language with Python. Two of the best known of these alternate Python versions are Jython, written in Java, and IronPython, an implementation for Microsoft's .NET environment. A third alternative is Cython, which is not strictly an implementation of Python but a very closely related subset that can be compiled into C to provide very fast performance while still providing the speed of development of a Python-like language. Finally, it is possible to access Tcl/Tk code from within the Tkinter package.

Jython

The Java implementation of Python offers many advantages to Java programmers looking for an interactive environment in which to test their Java classes or to build prototype solutions that can, if necessary, be converted to full Java later.

The distribution includes both an interpreter and a compiler. The interpreter comes with the familiar interactive prompt, as well as the ability to run scripts directly. In addition to importing Python modules (including many of the regular Python standard library modules), Jython can import Java libraries, making the classes available to the Python interpreter as if they were regular

Python classes. This makes it possible to exercise and test new Java classes interactively at the Jython prompt. Jython also enables dynamic prototyping of solutions by mixing Java and Python code together. The interpreter can also be used to run script files with all of these same features for bigger projects or prototypes.

The compiler takes Jython code (either pure Python or a mixture of Java classes and Python code) and compiles it into a .java file. This is a powerful tool for prototyping new classes because they can be developed and written in Python, compiled, and included in Java code. Once proven, the Python version can be seamlessly replaced with a pure Java version.

The downside of Jython is that it tends to produce slower code than pure Java and is also more memory hungry. This is largely due to the fact that the compiler effectively embeds a Python interpreter in the output files.

At the time of writing, Jython is at version 2.7, although work is underway to migrate to version 3.

IronPython

IronPython is a version of Python written for the Microsoft .NET framework. .NET is not a single language system; rather, it depends on a common bytecode to which several languages can be compiled. The modules so produced can then be shared between languages. Thus, code written in IronPython can import modules written in C#, C++, Visual Basic, and several other .NET-compatible languages. Similarly, IronPython modules can be imported by any of those other .NET languages. IronPython is an extremely appealing prospect for developers working on the .NET platform.

Better still is the fact that an open source variant of .NET called Mono has been produced that can run under Linux and Mac OS X and many others, including mainframe computers and games consoles. This is achieved while maintaining binary-level compatibility with the Microsoft .NET implementation. (At the other end of the spectrum, a slightly limited version, called Mono Touch, runs on iOS and Android for building smartphone apps.) As .NET becomes the de facto standard for building applications on Microsoft Windows, the availability of Python within that framework is a major boon for Python programmers.

The IronPython implementation supports most of the standard Python library as well as the .NET module system. Modules in .NET are called assemblies, but they are imported into IronPython in exactly the same way that ordinary Python modules are imported. Some issues exist due to the dynamic typing used by Python and the .NET type system, which is more static in nature. However, once understood these can be worked around using some helper features built into IronPython. Full documentation is provided on the IronPython documentation site at `http://ironpython.net/documentation/`.

At the time of writing, IronPython was compatible with Python version 2.7, and a project was underway to develop a Python 3 version. A set of tools is available to enable IronPython development within the Microsoft VisualStudio IDE, which is the default IDE for .NET development.

Cython

Cython is significantly different from the other language integration options discussed here. It is, in effect, a separate language from Python but is highly compatible with it, describing itself as a super-set of Python. This means Python programmers can easily learn Cython and take advantage of its special features.

So what are these features that would make you want to use Cython? In short, speed. Cython is a compiler that produces C code that, in turn, can be compiled to native machine code and thereby has the potential to run much faster than its Python equivalent. This compiled code can then be imported back into regular Python just like any other module to provide the best of both worlds— easy Python development combined with C-level speed of execution.

The Cython extensions are mainly geared around interacting with native C code, and in this regard are similar to the helper features of the `ctypes` module discussed in the section "Accessing Native APIs with ctypes and pywin32," back in Chapter 2.

> **NOTE** *If your Python code consists of importing a module that is already written in C and executing its functions, converting your program to Cython will have little performance impact. But, if your code contains a lot of pure Python processing, the difference can be significant.*

Cython is not the only Python-to-C translator, but it is probably the easiest to use for the average Python programmer. You can find the Cython website at `http://cython.org/`.

Tcl/Tk

The `tkinter` and `tix` GUI modules are built on top of the Tcl/Tk and Tix toolkits. As such, they have the ability to execute Tcl code from within Python by using a method of the embedded `tk` object: `self.tk.call()`.

This method is the key to how the `tix` module is built. If you look at the code in `tix.py`, you find many method definitions that look like this example from the `Notebook` class:

```
def raised(self):
    return self.tk.call(self._w, 'raised')
```

As you can see, the method is simply a wrapper for a call to the underlying Tix widget (`self._w`). If you are familiar with Tcl/Tk and Tix, you can fairly easily extend the existing Python widgets to utilize some Tcl features that are not otherwise available. An alternative method to `call()` is `eval()`, which evaluates an input string as a Tcl expression.

But the integration does not need to stop with GUI widget access. You can pass arbitrary Tcl code to the `eval()` method and have it executed by the embedded Tcl interpreter. This could include importing Tcl modules that provide features that Python does not. Of course, you need to know Tcl to use this effectively! Here is the basic "Hello World" script that can be run in any command-line console using the standard output stream:

```
>>> import tkinter
>>> tcl = tkinter.Tcl()
>>> tcl.eval('''
```

```
... puts "Hello world"
... ''')
Hello world
''
>>>
```

The section inside triple quotes can be any Tcl script you wish.

GETTING PHYSICAL

There has been an upsurge of hobbyists interested in programming physical devices in recent years. Low-cost, highly flexible products such as the Arduino microcontroller card and the RaspberryPi single board computer (SBC) have become available at very low cost. Python is well suited to programming such devices, and several libraries exist to assist in the process. Indeed, Python is one of the recommended languages for the RaspberryPi.

It is not necessary to spend money on hardware to connect Python to the outside world. Most computers still have a serial port running the RS232 protocol, and it is possible to connect that to various peripheral devices and access them using Python. Similarly, the MIDI interface can be used to access musical instruments, and even the ubiquitous USB interface can be manipulated with the right modules in place.

As is the case in any kind of integration, you need to understand both ends of the connection. If you are not familiar with the physical devices to which you want to connect, you will struggle. The first step in integrating Python with anything is to first find out how the target device interacts with the world. Only then will the libraries discussed in the following sections become useful to you.

Introducing Serial Options

You can access the RS232 communications port on a computer (or indeed any other serial port, including old-style PS-2 mice or pens) using the `serial` module made available by the PySerial project, which has its homepage at `http://pyserial.sourceforge.net/`. Comprehensive documentation and examples are included.

The module provides support for several OSes including Windows and Linux, as well as Jython and IronPython. It can be installed from PyPI, or as a Linux package in most distributions, or, for Windows, as a binary installer. It works with Python versions 2 and 3.

The PyUSB library is available for USB access. It is written in Python using `ctypes` under the covers to access the low-level code. You can find PyUSB at `https://github.com/walac/pyusb`. The website is a tad sparse, but it includes a tutorial with several examples. It is assumed that you already understand how USB interfaces function.

PyUSB is available from the GitHub repository, but is easier to install via the PyPI.

Programming the RaspberryPi

The RaspberryPi is a single board computer, about the size of a credit card, and sold at very low cost. It was originally intended to encourage interest in computing technology and programming.

It has been hugely successful not only in its original objective, but also as a hobbyist tool. Many owners have capitalized on its small size and built the computer into small physical enclosures for applications such as weather monitoring, security systems, robotics experiments, and vehicle control.

The RaspberryPi runs various distributions of Linux, the default being Raspbian Linux. It includes a full Python distribution, and Python is the recommended language for user programming. Used in its basic configuration, it can be treated like any other computer, and indeed, if mounted in a suitable case with monitor, mouse, and keyboard connected, it functions just like any other Linux-powered PC, albeit with modest computing resources. If used as a control system for a custom project, the programming environment may well involve using some of the peripheral access techniques, especially PyUSB for access to the built-in USB ports.

You can find the RaspberryPi homepage at `http://www.raspberrypi.org/`.

There is a free community online magazine called "The MagPi," where enthusiasts can share experiences, tips, and projects. In addition, several books on the subject have been published, as well as regular conferences and local user groups.

Talking to the Arduino

The Arduino products are, in many ways, complementary to the RaspberryPi. Where the RaspberryPi aims to teach about computing and programming, Arduino is more directly aimed at the electronics enthusiast. It enables experimentation with interfaces, both analog and digital. The various microcontroller circuit boards in the Arduino range come in various configurations of inputs and outputs. Typically they include a USB interface, several analog input pins, as well as some digital I/O pins, thus enabling the user to attach various external devices.

Accessories are also available to extend the types of devices that can be connected. Also included is a code library, called Wiring, written in C, that provides access to the various ports. There is an IDE that helps users write their code and provides a single-click mechanism to upload it to the board. The Arduino homepage is at `http://www.arduino.cc/`.

Although the Arduino processor normally has to have a binary application downloaded, it can also be controlled by connecting the Arduino to a controlling computer, such as a RasberryPi. This enables Python to be used to send instructions to the Arduino via the USB or serial ports. There is a library to facilitate this called `pyfirmata`, which is available from PyPI. There is a web page that discusses this further, with several examples of what is possible, at `http://playground.arduino.cc/interfacing/python`.

Exploring Other Options

The popularity of the RaspberryPi and Arduino projects has spawned several competing products. Many of these are simply low-cost clones of the other projects, especially the Arduino, but others are genuine alternatives with a slightly different set of objectives or presentation of the ideas; for example, creating the smallest board possible. In most cases Python can be used to access the boards over a serial link or even by a network connection using standard Python modules.

Your favorite search engine should find many candidates. You should check the nature of the interfaces provided and how the programming is done. Some Arduino clones require you to program the chip on a genuine Arduino and then transfer it to the clone board for installation in the final device.

BUILDING PYTHON

One area of special interest for Python programmers is Python itself. Python is a very open architecture with many features that enable the programmer to inspect the internal workings of the interpreter, as well as the data structures within the program. Being an open source project means that the development of the language is a community affair and everyone who uses Python can share in its development. If there is a feature of Python that you think is broken or can be improved, there is a process for fixing it. If there is a feature you'd like to add, there is a process for adding it.

If you want to get involved in Python development, whether because you have a personal itch to scratch or just as a way of giving back to the community that gave you Python, you have several ways to get started. You can find a good introduction to all of the options at `https://docs .python.org/devguide/index.html`.

Fixing Bugs

Perhaps the most obvious place to start getting involved with Python is in fixing bugs. The very act of reporting bugs is a useful contribution, but supplying fixes is even better. There is an official bug tracker application, and before submitting a bug you should check whether it has already been reported, and what, if anything, is being done to fix it. If it's a new bug, you can fill in a report (and optionally supply a fix).

Once a bug has been reported, the tracker supports a conversational model whereby users can suggest fixes, comment on patches, and so on. The bug tracker homepage is at `https://docs .python.org/3/bugs.html`.

Documenting

In most open source projects, it is easier to get someone to write code than to get someone to write documentation. Python is no exception. Although the official documentation is quite good for an open source project, it still has many areas that are sketchy at best and in some cases completely lacking. (You saw an example of that with the `tix` module used in Chapter 4. Several `tix` widgets are available that are not described in the official documentation.)

Volunteering to document some of these darker corners of Python is a worthwhile endeavor, and one that provides a relatively gentle introduction to open source community. Documentation issues are reported on the standard Python bug tracker that you can use to submit bug reports and suggested fixes. If you want to get more fully involved, you can subscribe to the docs@python.org mailing list. You can find more specific details on the process on this website: `https://docs .python.org/devguide/docquality.html`.

The documentation is actually generated using a purpose-built document processor called Sphinx. The Sphinx content is created in reStructuredText (reST), a lightweight markup system similar to that used on many wiki-pages. (The Python Docutils project supplies the underlying toolset for processing reST files.) The Sphinx website is at `http://sphinx-doc.org/index.html`.

Testing

Unless you plan on getting involved in core Python development, the best way to contribute to testing is to download and use the early beta releases. You can then report bugs found using the bug tracker as usual.

Adding Features

If your itch is not due to a bug but due to a missing or incomplete feature, either in the Python language itself or in a module, you should consider submitting the idea to the `python-ideas` mailing list. You can sign up to the list at `https://mail.python.org/mailman/listinfo/python-ideas`. The list enables your idea to be discussed by the wider community. If yours is considered a good idea, you may be invited to submit a Python Enhancement Proposal, or PEP.

It must be said you have far more chance of getting a module change approved than a core language feature, but language changes do happen, and if it's a good idea it is worth trying.

Attending Conferences

Another, altogether easier, way of getting involved in the Python community is to attend the various local user groups and conferences held every year. These afford opportunities to learn about Python and its infrastructure, hear about successful projects based on Python, and, of course, to present your own experiences with Python.

Several major international Python conferences are held annually, as well as some smaller events either focused on a local area or a special interest group. Details of these are often announced online, in the various Python mailing lists, and a list is maintained here: `https://wiki.python.org/moin/PythonEvents`.

SUMMARY

In this chapter you looked at the wider world of Python. In particular, you considered the specialist areas that are not covered by the standard library but have extensive support from Python in the wider community.

You've seen how graphics can be produced and manipulated using core Python modules as well as various third-party libraries, especially Pillow and ImageMagick.

Many third-party libraries are available in the field of science, and the foundation for many of these is the SciPy bundle of packages and tools. Distributions like Anaconda make installation of these packages much easier.

For games programming you discovered that the PyGame package provides low-level graphics and multimedia access. Third-party computational engines also help you to develop realistic game play.

The video processing and movie world is well served with commercial products using Python. Blender provides an open source option for you to create your own video masterpiece.

Python integration with other languages is available in various forms. Jython provides two-way integration with Java, and IronPython integrates with Microsoft's .NET infrastructure as well as the open source Mono implementation.

You can get Python talking to the physical world via the serial and USB ports either directly or via low-cost microcontroller boards like the Arduino. When combined with small single board computers like the RasberryPi, you can build compact but powerful projects.

Finally, you saw how you can get involved in the Python development activities. Whether it be by fixing documentation or code or simply by getting involved in the discussions on the community mailing lists and forums, you can have a share in improving Python.

EXERCISES

1. In the section on SciPy you discovered that there were many more areas of science with Python libraries available. Pick some areas of science and see what support you can find in the Python community. (Hint: The Anaconda and Enthought Canopy distributions contain much more than the basic SciPy bundle of packages.)

2. In the "Going to the Movies" section you saw that commercial (and open source) applications can be scripted using Python as a macro language. This is not the only area where this is possible. Research the use of Python as a macro language and produce a list of some popular applications that can be scripted using Python.

3. Python is used in many other niche areas. Try to identify an area that you have an interest in and find out what support might be available. (Hint: PyPI has a search facility.)

▶ WHAT YOU LEARNED IN THIS CHAPTER

KEY CONCEPT	DESCRIPTION
Turtle graphics	A graphics technique whereby drawings are produced by moving a virtual turtle around the drawing surface. The turtle has a pen attached that can be raised/lowered, its color changed, and its thickness varied. The turtle can move in a specified direction for a specified distance.
Canvas widget	A low-level drawing widget that supports basic operations such as drawing lines, polygons, and circles. It can also handle text and image files.
Pillow	An extension of the older Python Imaging Library (PIL). Pillow is used to convert and manipulate image files.
ImageMagick	A command-line toolset for manipulating and converting image files. Many libraries and modules encapsulate ImageMagick's capabilities.
SciPy	A set of tools for doing scientific and numerical analysis in Python. There is an eponymous SciPy package that provides general-purpose scientific tools, but the term encompasses a group of other related packages as well.
SciKit	A collection of scientific and numerical processing modules that generally relies upon SciPy but is not part of the formal SciPy bundle of packages. SciKit includes packages covering many fields of scientific investigation.
NumPy	A package within SciPy that provides advanced numerical processing tools.
SymPy	A package within SciPy for doing symbolic math.
Pandas	A package within SciPy that provides a statistical data analysis toolset.
IPython	Interactive Python. A sophisticated replacement for the standard Python command prompt. It includes a powerful notebook mechanism whereby individual sessions can be saved and restored.
bioPython	A suite of tools used for doing bioscience.
ArcGIS	A standard set of tools for doing geographical information processing. ArcPy provides a Python wrapper around the ArcGIS toolset.
NLTK	A set of tools for analyzing natural language text.
PyGame	A toolset for creating games in Python. It includes powerful support for multimedia programming, including graphics and audio as well as interaction with keyboard, mice, joysticks, and other peripherals.
CGI	Computer-generated imagery (CGI) has become a widely used tool in the motion picture industry. Python is used in many of the tools used to create and manage CGI images.
CPython	The standard implementation of the Python language interpreter, written in C.

continues

(continued)

KEY CONCEPT	DESCRIPTION
Jython	An alternative implementation of the Python interpreter written in Java. This enables Jython to import Java classes in addition to Python modules. Jython also features a compiler for turning Python code into Java bytecode that can in turn be imported by Java programs.
Cython	A superset of the Python language that can be compiled into C and from there into Python modules with enhanced performance.
IronPython	An implementation of Python for Microsoft's .NET platform. This makes it compatible with any other modules written for .NET (or the open source clone, Mono).
PySerial	A project that provides tools whereby a Python programmer can access the serial ports of a computer.
PyUSB	A project that provides tools whereby a Python programmer can access the USB devices on a computer.
Sphinx	A purpose-built documentation tool used to create the Python documentation. The content format is reStructuredText, which is a kind of markup language supported by the Python Docutils project and toolset.
PEP	A Python Enhancement Proposal. This is the formal mechanism for getting changes into a Python release.

A

Answers to Exercises

Chapter 1 Solutions

1. **How do you convert between the different Python data types? What data quality issues arise when converting data types?**

   You convert between types using the type functions. Thus, to convert a float or string to an integer, you use the `int()` type function. To convert an object to a string, you use the `str()` type function. And so on.

   When making the conversion, it is possible that you might lose some data in the process. For example, converting a floating-point number to an integer loses the decimal part of the number (for example, `int(2.3)` results in 2). If it's important to retain the detail, you must retain a copy of the original as well.

2. **Which of the Python collection types can be used as the key in a dictionary? Which of the Python data types can be used as a value in a dictionary?**

   Dictionary keys must be immutable. That means that of the basic Python types, integers, booleans, floats, strings, and tuples can all be used as keys (although floats are not recommended due to their imprecision, especially if you will be computing the key value rather than just storing it). Other custom types, such as `frozenset`, can also be used as keys provided they are immutable.

   Dictionary values can be of any type regardless of mutability.

3. **Write an example program using an `if/elif` chain involving at least four different selection expressions.**

   You could use any number of choices here. This example uses colors. Your `if/elif/else` code should look something like the following:

```
(red, orange, yellow, green, blue, violet) = range(6)
color = int(input('Type a number between 1 and 6'))-1
if color == red:
   print ('You picked red')
```

```
elif color == orange:
    print ('You picked orange')
elif color == yellow:
    print ('You picked yellow')
elif color == green:
    print ('You picked green')
else:
    print('I don't like your color choice')
```

4. Write a Python **for** loop to repeat a message seven times.

```
for n in range(7):
    print('Here is a message')
```

5. How can an infinite loop be created using a Python **while** loop? What potential problem might this cause? How could that issue be resolved?

An infinite loop is written using the `while True:` idiom.

The problem is that this is an infinite loop so it never ends. Sometimes that's what you want, but often you need to exit if certain conditions occur. In those cases you can use an `if` check with a `break` statement. Here is a short loop that echoes the user input until the user enters an empty string:

```
while True:
    message = input('Enter a message: ')
    if not message: break
    print(message)
```

6. Write a function that calculates the area of a triangle given the base and height measurements.

```
def area_of_triangle(base, height):
    return 0.5 * base * height
```

7. Write a class that implements a rotating counter from 0 to 9. That is, the counter starts at 0, increments to 9, resets to 0 again, and repeats that cycle indefinitely. It should have **increment()** and **reset()** methods, the latter of which returns the current count then sets the count back to 0.

```
class RotatingCounter:
    def __init__(self, start = 0)
        self.counter = 0

    def increment(self):
        self.counter += 1
        if self.counter > 9:
            self.counter = 0
        return self.counter

    def reset(self, value=0):
        current_value = self.counter
        if 0 < value < 9:
            self.counter = value
        else:
            raise ValueError('Value must be between 0 and 9')
        return current_value
```

Chapter 2 Solutions

1.   Explore the `os` module to see what else you can discover about your computer. Be sure to read the relevant parts of the Python documentation for the `os` and `stat` modules.

Start the Python interpreter and type the following:

```
>>> import os
>>> os.nice(0)          # get relative process priority
0
>>> os.nice(1)          # change relative priority
1
>>> os.times()          # process times: system, user etc...
posix.times_result(user=0.02, system=0.01,
children_user=0.0, children_system=0.0, elapsed=1398831612.5)
>>> os.isatty(0)        # is the file descriptor arg a tty?(0 = stdin)
True
>>> os.isatty(4)        # 4 is just an arbitrary test value
False
>>> os.getloadavg()     # UNIX only - number of processes in queue
(0.56, 0.49, 0.44)
>>> os.cpu_count()      # New in Python 3.4
4
```

There are many other functions you could try. For example: `os.getpriority()`, `os.get_exec_path()`, `os.strerror()`, and so on.

2.   Try adding a new function to the `file_tree` module called `find_dirs()` that searches for directories matching a given regular expression. Combine both to create a third function, `find_all()`, that searches both files and directories.

See Chapter2.zip `solutions/findfiles.py`. The `findfiles.py` module included in the solutions download provides solutions to all three of the functions in the exercise as well as a couple of alternatives that you might find useful. The specific code for the examples is reproduced here:

```
def find_dirs(pattern, base='.'):
    """Finds directories under base based on pattern

    Walks the filesystem starting at base and
    returns a list of directory names matching pattern"""

    regex = re.compile(pattern)
    matches = []
    for root, dirs, files in os.walk(base):
        for d in dirs:
            if regex.match(d):
                matches.append( path.join(root,d) )
    return matches

def find_all(pattern, base='.'):
    """Finds files and folders under base based on pattern

    Returns the combined results of find_files and find_dirs"""
```

```
matches = find_dirs(pattern,base)
matches += find_files(pattern,base)
return matches
```

3. Create another function, `apply_to_files()`, that applies a function parameter to all files matching the input pattern. You could, for example, use this function to remove all files matching a pattern, such as `*.tmp` , like this:

```
findfiles.apply_to_files('.*\.tmp', os.remove, 'TreeRoot')
```

See Chapter2.zip `solutions/findfiles.py` as described previously for Exercise 2.

```
def apply_to_files(pattern, function, base='.'):
    ''' Apply function to any files matching pattern

    function should take a full file path as an argument
    the return value, if any, will be ignored '''

    regex = re.compile(pattern)
    errors = []
    for root, dirs, files in os.walk(base):
        for f in files:
            if regex.match(f):
                try: function( path.join(root,f) )
                except: errors.append(path.join(root,f))
    return errors
```

4. Write a program that loops over the first 128 characters and displays a message indicating whether or not the value is a control character (characters with ordinal values between 0x00 and 0x1F, plus 0x7F). Use `ctypes` to access the standard C library and call the `iscntrl()` function to determine if a given character is a control character. Note this is not one of the built-in test methods of the string type in Python.

See Chapter2.zip `solutions/Ex2-4.py`. The code for the `iscntrl()` function is provided here:

```
import ctypes as ct
# libc = ct.CDLL('libc.so.6')     # in Linux
libc = ct.cdll.msvcrt     # in Windows

for c in range(128):
    print(c, ' is a ctrl char' if libc.iscntrl(c) else 'is not a ctrl char')
```

Chapter 3 Solutions

1. To appreciate the work that `pickle` does for you, try building a simple serialization function for numbers, called `ser_num()`. It should accept any valid integer or float number as an argument and convert it into a byte string. You should also write a function to perform the reverse operation to read a byte string produced by your `ser_num()` function and convert it back to a number of the appropriate type. (Hint: You may find the `struct` module useful for this exercise.)

Create a file containing the following code (located in `Exercise3_1.py` in the `Solutions` folder of the `.zip` file):

```python
import struct

def ser_num(n):
    '''
    ser_num(int|float) -> byte string

    convert n to a byte string if it is a float or int.
    ints are stored using their string representation,
    encoded as UTF-8, since they are arbitrarily long.
    floats are stored as C doubles

    Raise Type error for any other type.'''

    if isinstance(n, int):
        # convert to bytes using str()
        data = bytes('i','utf-8') + bytes(str(n),'utf-8')
    elif isinstance(n, float):
        # convert to bytes with struct.pack
        data = bytes('f','utf-8') + struct.pack('d', n)
    else: raise TypeError('Expecting int or float')
    return data

def get_num(b):
    '''
    get_num(bytes) -> int|float

    convert bytestring b to an int of float'''

    flag = str(b[:1],'utf-8')
    data = b[1:]
    # convert to binary
    if flag == 'i':
        s = str(data, 'utf-8')
        return int(s)
    elif flag == 'f':
        return struct.unpack("d", data)[0]
    else: raise ValueError('Unrecognised byte string format')

if __name__ == '__main__':
    e = 0.000000000000000001
    i = 1234567
    f = 3.1415926
    bi = ser_num(i)
    bf = ser_num(f)
    i == get_num(bi)
    f-e <= get_num(bf) <= f+e
    try: be = ser_num('a string')
    except TypeError: print('Type error on string')
    try: d = get_num(b'1234')
    except ValueError: print('Value Error on invalid bytes')
```

2.   Write a version of the employee database example using `shelve` instead of SQLite. Populate the shelf with the sample data and write a function that lists the name of all employees earning more than a specified amount.

Create a file containing the following code (located in `Exercise3_2.py` in the `Solutions` folder of the `.zip` file):

```python
import shelve

#'ID', 'Name', 'HireDate', 'Grade', 'ManagerID'
employees = [
['1','John Brown', '2006-02-23', 'Foreman', ''],
['2','Fred Smith', '2014-04-03', 'Laborer', '1'],
['3','Anne Jones', '2009-06-17', 'Laborer', '1'],
]

#'Grade','Amount'
salaries = [
['Foreman', 60000],
['Laborer', 30000]
]

def createDB(data, shelfname):
    try:
        shelf = shelve.open(shelfname,'c')
        for datum in data:
            shelf[datum[0]] = datum
    finally:
        shelf.close()

def readDB(shelfname):
    try:
        shelf = shelve.open(shelfname,'r')
        return [shelf[key] for key in shelf]
    finally:
        shelf.close()

def with_salary(n):
    grades = [salary[0] for salary in readDB('salaryshelf') if salary[1] >= n]
    for staff in readDB('employeeshelf'):
        if staff[3] in grades:
            yield staff

def main():
    print('Creating data files...')
    createDB(employees, 'employeeshelf')
    createDB(salaries, 'salaryshelf')

    print('Staff paid more than 30000:')
    for staff in with_salary(30000):
        print(staff[1])
    print('Staff paid more than 50000:')
    for staff in with_salary(50000):
        print(staff[1])

if __name__ == "__main__": main()
```

3.   Extend the `lendydata.py` module to provide CRUD functions for the loan table. Add an extra function, `get_active_loans()`, to list those loans that are still active (Hint: That means the `DateReturned` field is `NULL`.)

Add the following code (located in `Exercise3_3.py` in the `Solutions` folder of the `.zip` file) to the `lendydata.py` module:

```
##### CRUD functions for loans ######

def insert_loan(item,borrower):
    query = '''
    insert into loan
    (itemID, BorrowerID, DateBorrowed, DateReturned )
    values (?, ?, date(?), date(?))'''

    cursor.execute(query, (item,borrower,'now',''))

def get_loans():
    query = '''
    select id, itemID, BorrowerID, DateBorrowed, DateReturned
    from loan'''
    return cursor.execute(query).fetchall()

def get_active_loans():
    query = '''
    select id, itemID, BorrowerID, DateBorrowed
    from loan
    where DateReturned is NULL'''
    return cursor.execute(query).fetchall()

def get_loan_details(id):
    query = '''
    select itemID, BorrowerID, DateBorrowed, DateReturned
    from loan
    where id = ?'''
    return cursor.execute(query, (id,)).fetchall()[0]

def update_loan(id, itemID=None, BorrowerID=None,
                    DateBorrowed=None, DateReturned=None):
    query = '''
    update loan
    set itemID=?,BorrowerID=?,DateBorrowed=date(?),DateReturned=date(?)
    where id = ?'''
    data = get_loan_details(id)
    if not itemID: itemID = data[0]
    if not BorrowerID: BorrowerID = data[1]
    if not DateBorrowed: DateBorrowed = data[2]
    if not DateReturned: DateReturned = data[3]
    cursor.execute(query, (itemID,BorrowerID,DateBorrowed,DateReturned, id))

def delete_loan(id):
    query = '''
    delete from loan
    where id = ?'''
    cursor.execute(query,(id,))
```

You can test it using the following lines in the `if __name__ == '__main__'` stanza (or you can import it and use it interactively):

```
initDB()
print('Testing loans\n\n')
insert_loan(1,3)
print("Loans: ", get_loans())
print("Active Loans: ", get_active_loans())
print('Details of 4:',get_loan_details(4))
update_loan(6,DateReturned='2014-06-23')
print('Details of 6:',get_loan_details(6))
delete_loan(6)
print('All:',get_loans())
closeDB()
```

4. Explore the Python `statistics` module to see what it offers (only available in Python 3.4 or later).

Open a Python 3.4 or later interpreter and type:

```
>>> import statistics as stats
>>> stats.mean(range(6))
2.5
>>> stats.median(range(6))
2.5
>>> stats.median_low(range(6))
2
>>> stats.median_high(range(6))
3
>>> stats.median_grouped(range(6))
2.5
>>> stats.mode(range(6))
Traceback (most recent call last):
  File "<pyshell#13>", line 1, in <module>
    stats.mode(range(6))
  File "C:\Python34\lib\statistics.py", line 434, in mode
    'no unique mode; found %d equally common values' % len(table)
statistics.StatisticsError: no unique mode; found 6 equally common values
>>> stats.mode(list(range(6))+[3])
3
>>> stats.pstdev(list(range(6))+[3])
1.5907898179514348
>>> stats.stdev(list(range(6))+[3])
1.7182493859684491
>>> stats.pvariance(list(range(6))+[3])
2.5306122448979593
>>> stats.variance(list(range(6))+[3])
2.9523809523809526
```

Chapter 4 Solutions

1. Convert the `oxo-logic.py` module to reflect OOP design by creating a `Game` class.

    See the following code (available in the `Chapter4.zip` file, in the `Solutions` folder as `ex4-1.py`):

```
import os, random
import oxo_data

class Game():
    def __init__(self):
        self.board = list(" " * 9)

    def save(self, game):
        ' save game to disk '
        oxo_data.saveGame(self.board)

    def restore(self):
        ''' restore previously saved game.
            If game not restored successfully return new game'''
        try:
            self.board = oxo_data.restoreGame()
            if len(self.board) != 9:
                self.board =  list(" " * 9)
            return self.board
        except IOError:
            self.board = list(" " * 9)
            return self.board

    def _generateMove(self):
        ''' generate a random cell from those available.
            If all cells are used return -1'''
        options = [i for i in range(len(self.board)) if  self.board[i] == " "]
        if options:
            return random.choice(options)
        else: return -1

    def _isWinningMove(self):
        wins = ((0,1,2), (3,4,5), (6,7,8),
                (0,3,6), (1,4,7), (2,5,8),
                (0,4,8), (2,4,6))
        game = self.board
        for a,b,c in wins:
            chars = game[a] + game[b] + game[c]
            if chars == 'XXX' or chars == 'OOO':
                return True
        return False

    def userMove(self,cell):
        if self.board[cell] != ' ':
            raise ValueError('Invalid cell')
        else:
            self.board[cell] = 'X'
        if self._isWinningMove():
```

```
                return 'X'
            else:
                return ""

    def computerMove(self):
        cell = self._generateMove()
        if cell == -1:
            return 'D'
        self.board[cell] = 'O'
        if self._isWinningMove():
            return 'O'
        else:
            return ""

def test():
    result = ""
    game = Game()
    while not result:
        print(game.board)
        try:
            result = game.userMove( game._generateMove())
        except ValueError:
            print("Oops, that shouldn't happen")
        if not result:
            result = game.computerMove()

        if not result: continue
        elif result == 'D':
            print("Its a draw")
        else:
            print("Winner is:", result)
        print(game.board)

if __name__ == "__main__":
    test()
```

2. Explore the **Tkinter.filedialog** module to get the name of a text file from a user and then display that file on screen.

    Create or copy a text file into a folder. Change into that folder and start the Python interpreter. Type the following at the Python interpreter:

    ```
    >>> import tkinter.filedialog as fd
    >>> target = fd.askopenfilename()
    >>> for line in open(target):
    ...     print(line, end='')
    ...
    <Your chosen file contents should appear here>
    ```

3. Replace the label in the first GUI example program with a Tix **ScrolledText** widget so that it displays the history of all the entries from the **Entry** widget.

The solution can be found in the download zip file in the Solutions folder as ex4-3.py. The code is shown here:

```
import tkinter.tix as tk

# create the event handler to clear the text
def evClear():
  txt = stHistory.subwidget('text')
  txt.insert('end',eHello.get()+'\n')
  eHello.delete(0, 'end')

# create the top level window/frame
top = tk.Tk()
F = tk.Frame(top)
F.pack(fill="both")

# Now the frame with text entry
fEntry = tk.Frame(F, border=1)
eHello = tk.Entry(fEntry)
eHello.pack(side="left")
stHistory = tk.ScrolledText(fEntry, width=150, height=55)
stHistory.pack(side="bottom", fill="x")
fEntry.pack(side="top")

# Finally the frame with the buttons.
# We'll sink this one for emphasis
fButtons = tk.Frame(F, relief="sunken", border=1)
bClear = tk.Button(fButtons, text="Clear Text", command=evClear)
bClear.pack(side="left", padx=5, pady=2)
bQuit = tk.Button(fButtons, text="Quit", command=F.quit)
bQuit.pack(side="left", padx=5, pady=2)
fButtons.pack(side="top", fill="x")

# Now run the eventloop
F.mainloop()
```

4. **Rewrite the first GUI example to be compatible with** gettext **and generate a new English version with different text on the controls.**

The solution, based on Ex4-3.py, is found in the zip file under Solutions as ex4-4.py and messages_en.po.

The code, with changes in bold, is as shown:

```
import tkinter.tix as tk

#### gettext mods #####
import gettext
import locale
locale.setlocale(locale.LC_ALL,'')
filename="res/messages_{}.mo".format(locale.getlocale()[0][0:2])
trans=gettext.GNUTranslations(open(filename,'rb'))
trans.install()
#######################
```

```python
# create the event handler to clear the text
def evClear():
  txt = stHistory.subwidget('text')
  txt.insert('end',eHello.get()+'\n')
  eHello.delete(0, 'end')

# create the top level window/frame
top = tk.Tk()
F = tk.Frame(top)
F.pack(fill="both")

# Now the frame with text entry
fEntry = tk.Frame(F, border=1)
eHello = tk.Entry(fEntry)
eHello.pack(side="left")
stHistory = tk.ScrolledText(fEntry, width=150, height=55)
stHistory.pack(side="bottom", fill="x")
fEntry.pack(side="top")

# Finally the frame with the buttons.
# We'll sink this one for emphasis
fButtons = tk.Frame(F, relief="sunken", border=1)
bClear = tk.Button(fButtons, text=_("Clear Text"), command=evClear)
bClear.pack(side="left", padx=5, pady=2)
bQuit = tk.Button(fButtons, text=_("Quit"), command=F.quit)
bQuit.pack(side="left", padx=5, pady=2)
fButtons.pack(side="top", fill="x")

# Now run the eventloop
F.mainloop()
```

The edited messages_en.po file looks like this:

```
# SOME DESCRIPTIVE TITLE.
# Copyright (C) YEAR THE PACKAGE'S COPYRIGHT HOLDER
# This file is distributed under the same license as the PACKAGE package.
# FIRST AUTHOR <EMAIL@ADDRESS>, YEAR.
#
#, fuzzy
msgid ""
msgstr ""
"Project-Id-Version: PACKAGE VERSION\n"
"Report-Msgid-Bugs-To: \n"
"POT-Creation-Date: 2014-05-16 19:40+0100\n"
"PO-Revision-Date: YEAR-MO-DA HO:MI+ZONE\n"
"Last-Translator: FULL NAME <EMAIL@ADDRESS>\n"
"Language-Team: LANGUAGE <LL@li.org>\n"
"Language: \n"
"MIME-Version: 1.0\n"
"Content-Type: text/plain; charset=UTF-8\n"
"Content-Transfer-Encoding: 8bit\n"

#: ex4-4.py:34
msgid "Clear Text"
msgstr "Move to History"
```

```
#: ex4-4.py:36
msgid "Quit"
msgstr "Exit"
```

Chapter 5 Solutions

1. Consider our code from earlier in this chapter:

    ```
    >>>for result in results['results']:
    ...     id = result['id']
    ...     print(id)
    ...     print (result['id'])
    ...     details = requests.get(market + id).json()
    ...     print (details)
    ...     print (details['marketdetails'])
    ...   print (details['marketdetails']['GoogleLink'])
    ```

    Using what you know about Python, can you figure out a way to create a list comprehension that will do the same thing as the preceding code? Remember that list comprehensions are constructed like this:

    ```
    [expression for item in list if conditional]
    ```

    Here is the solution:

    ```
    print([requests.get(market + result['id'].json()['marketdetails']['GoogleLink'])
    for result in results['results']])
    ```

2. Using what you know so far about how to use files in Python, can you save the output of your call to the USDA's API to a file on your machine, to parse later? (Saving it as a .txt file is fine.)

    You can use the list comprehension above to simply write to a file as such:

    ```
    file = open("markets.txt", "w")
    file.write([requests.get(market +
    result['id'].json()['marketdetails']['GoogleLink'])
    for result in results['results']\n])
    file.close
    ```

3. Can you find the docs for Flask that would help us to break our app into smaller, modularized files with our endpoints/views in a separate file, rather than having one big Python file with everything in it? (Hint: It is one concept/feature that Flask offers.)

    Flask docs can be found at (http://flask.pocoo.org/docs/blueprints/#blueprints).

    Blueprints are how we can separate our app into separate files so that we don't have one large python file with every piece of functionality in it.

4. What other HTTP methods can you find? Can you find ways to use them in a Flask app?

    Depending on how the reader researches the question, they will find there are a few other HTTP methods; GET, PUT, DELETE, OPTIONS. The second part of this exercise will vary, but the point is to get the reader reading docs and learning how to find answers, and explore what is available to them.

5. By reading the Requests docs, can you find the method call needed to output the HTML of a website by passing the URL to a requests method?

It's not pretty, but it's easy!

```
>>> import requests
>>> r = requests.get("http://www.python.org")
>>> r.text
```

Chapter 6 Solutions

1. In the zip file for this chapter, open the file **markets.py** and write a doctest string to test the value being returned by the function in the file. Can you think of a reason why a simple doctest string in this code could be incredibly useful for maintaining the code in the future?

Depending on the static data you've decided to use, answers will vary, however here is one example using the ZIP code in the code (you may have changed this):

```
import requests
results = requests.get("http://search.ams.usda.gov/farmersmarkets/v1/data.svc/
zipSearch?zip=46201").json()
def get_details(results):
    '''
    >>> print(get_details(results))
    http://maps.google.com/?q=39.7776%2C%20-86.0782%20(%22Irvington+Farmers+
    Market+%22Error! Hyperlink reference not valid.
    '''
    market = "http://search.ams.usda.gov/farmersmarkets/v1/data.svc/mktDetail?id="
    for result in results['results']:
        id = result['id']
        details = requests.get(market+id).json()
        return details['marketdetails']['GoogleLink']
```

2. Write a unittest for a function that will take a string and return that string reversed. Make sure the test fails, because you haven't written the function to test... yet.

```
import unittest
from reverse import rev
class TestRev(unittest.TestCase):
    def test_rev(self):
        self.assertEqual(rev('robot'), 'tobor')



    '''
```

3. Write a function for your unittest that takes a string and returns the reverse of that string. Now, run your unittest against that function and modify the function until it passes.

```
#reverse.py
def rev(chars):
        chars.sort(reverse=True)
         return chars
```

Chapter 7 Solutions

1.   **In the section on SciPy you discovered that there were many more areas of science with Python libraries available. Pick some areas of science and see what support you can find in the Python community. (Hint: The Anaconda and Enthought Canopy distributions contain much more than the basic SciPy bundle of packages.)**

The Anaconda and Canopy websites list the modules included in their respective distributions. Here is just a sample of the obviously scientific options:

   ➤   astroid

   ➤   astropy

   ➤   biopython

   ➤   bokeh

   ➤   geos

   ➤   libffi

   ➤   libnetcdf

   ➤   libsodium

   ➤   mccab

2.   **In the "Going to the Movies" section you saw that commercial (and open source) applications can be scripted using Python as a macro language. This is not the only area where this is possible. Research the use of Python as a macro language and produce a list of some popular applications that can be scripted using Python.**

The Python wiki has a page dedicated to this topic. Here is the address: `https://wiki` `.python.org/moin/AppsWithPythonScripting`.

As you can see, the list encompasses everything from the GIMP image toolkit, to the vim and emacs editors, to the OpenOffice productivity suite. Doubtless there are others not listed on the wiki-page, but there should be plenty here for you to get going with.

3.   **Python is used in many other niche areas. Try to identify an area that you have an interest in and find out what support might be available. (Hint: PyPI has a search facility.)**

One area many people are passionate about is music. Python supports this in various ways including several audio players, MIDI tools, audio servers, file format convertors, and so on.

However, Python also supports the creation of original music via a piano tutor (The Turcanator), musical notation editors (Frescobaldi), analysis of sounds (pcsets), and generation of sounds (Cabel).

There are many others ranging from easy-to-use applications to highly technical APIs for audio professionals.

Python Standard Modules

The Python standard library contains well over 200 modules, although the exact number varies between distributions. Not all of these modules are recommended for use by the typical Python programmer; many have specialized uses associated with the Python internal modules and are intended mainly for use by developers working on Python itself. And certain other modules, remnants of older Python versions now superseded by more modern alternatives, are retained mainly for compatibility with old code.

This appendix lists all of the standard packages and modules that are recommended for "normal use" and highlights, in bold, those used or discussed in this book. Modules marked in the official documentation as deprecated, or intended for use by core developers, as well as some designed to be development tools, have been omitted from the list. A few minor clarifications to the descriptions have been added. Not all packages have been expanded to show the individual modules, and in these cases a package-level description is provided.

a

aifc	Read and write audio files in AIFF or AIFC format.
argparse	**Command-line option and argument-parsing library.**
array	Space-efficient arrays of uniformly typed numeric values.
asynchat	Support for asynchronous command/response protocols.
asyncio	Asynchronous I/O, event loop, coroutines, and tasks.
asyncore	A base class for developing asynchronous socket-handling services.
atexit	Register and execute cleanup functions.
audioop	Manipulate raw audio data.

Copyright © 2001-2014 Python Software Foundation; All Rights Reserved.

b

base64	RFC 3548: Base16, Base32, Base64 Data Encodings; Base85, and ASCII85.
binascii	Tools for converting data to and from various ASCII-encoded binary representations.
binhex	Encode and decode files in binhex4 format.
bisect	Array bisection algorithms for binary searching.
bz2	Interfaces for bzip2 compression and decompression.

c

calendar	**Functions for working with calendars, including some emulation of the UNIX cal(1) program.**
cgi	Helpers for running Python scripts via the common gateway interface (CGI).
cgitb	Configurable traceback handler for CGI scripts.
chunk	Module to read Interchange File Format (IFF) chunks.
cmath	**Mathematical functions for complex numbers.**
cmd	**Build line-oriented command interpreters.**
code	Facilities to implement read-eval-print loops.
codecs	Encode and decode data and streams.
collections	**Container data types.**
collections.abc	Abstract base classes for containers.
colorsys	Conversion functions between RGB and other color systems.
compileall	Tools for byte-compiling all Python source files in a directory tree or some subset thereof.
concurrent	Execute computations concurrently using threads or processes.
configparser	**Configuration file parser.**
contextlib	**Utilities for with-statement contexts.**
copy	Shallow and deep copy operations.
copyreg	Register pickle support functions.
crypt (UNIX)	The `crypt()` function used to check UNIX passwords.
csv	**Write and read tabular data to and from comma-delimited data files. (Other delimiters can also be used.)**
ctypes	**A foreign function library for Python.**
curses (UNIX)	An interface to the curses library, providing portable terminal handling.

d

datetime	**Basic date and time types.**
dbm	**Interfaces to various key-value database formats.**
decimal	**Implementation of the General Decimal Arithmetic Specification.**
difflib	Helper classes and functions for computing differences between objects.
distutils	Support for building and installing Python modules into an existing Python installation.
doctest	**Test snippets of code appearing within docstrings.**

e

e-mail	Package supporting the parsing, manipulating, and generating of e-mail messages, including MIME documents.
encodings	Package supporting various character encodings.
enum	Implementation of an enumeration class.
errno	Standard errno system symbols.

f

fcntl (UNIX)	The `fcntl()` and `ioctl()` system calls.
filecmp	Compare files efficiently.
fileinput	Loop over standard input or a list of files.
fnmatch	UNIX shell–style filename pattern matching.
fractions	**Rational numbers.**
ftplib	FTP protocol client (requires sockets).
functools	**Higher-order functions and operations on callable objects.**

g

getpass	Portable reading of passwords and retrieval of the user ID.
gettext	**Multilingual internationalization services.**
glob	**UNIX shell–style pathname pattern expansion.**
grp (UNIX)	The group database (`getgrnam()` and friends).
gzip	Interfaces for gzip compression and decompression using file objects.

h

hashlib	Secure hash and message digest algorithms.
heapq	Heap queue algorithm (aka, priority queue).
hmac	Keyed-Hashing for Message Authentication (HMAC) implementation for Python.
html.entities	**Data structures useful for processing HTML.**
html.parser	**A simple parser that can handle HTML and XHTML.**
http	Package supporting use of HTTP including client, server, and cookie management.
http.server	HTTP server and request handlers.

i

imaplib	IMAP4 protocol client (requires sockets).
imghdr	Determine the type of image contained in a file or byte stream.
io	Core tools for working with streams.
ipaddress	IPv4/IPv6 manipulation library.
itertools	**Functions creating iterators for efficient looping.**

j

json	Encode and decode the JSON data format.

k

keyword	Test whether a given string is a Python keyword.

l

linecache	Provides random access to individual lines from text files using a cache.
locale	**Internationalization services.**
logging	**Flexible event logging for applications.**
lzma	A Python wrapper for the liblzma compression library.

m

macpath	Mac OS 9 path manipulation functions.
mailbox	Manipulate mailboxes in various formats.
mailcap	Mailcap file handling.
math	**Mathematical functions [`sin()`, and so on].**
mimetypes	Mapping of filename extensions to MIME types.
mmap	Interface to memory-mapped files for UNIX and Windows.
msvcrt (Windows)	**Miscellaneous useful routines from the MS VC++ run time.**
multiprocessing	Package for process-based parallelism.

n

netrc	Loading of `.netrc` files.
nis (UNIX)	Interface to Sun's NIS (Yellow Pages) library.
nntplib	NNTP protocol client (requires sockets).
numbers	Abstract base classes for numeric types (Complex, Real, Integral, and so on).

o

operator	Functions corresponding to the standard operators (add, subtract, and so on).
os	**Miscellaneous operating system interfaces.**
	As Chapter 2 makes clear, the `os` module is one of several modules used to interact with the OS on Python, and the selection of functions provided is somewhat arbitrary and inconsistent.
os.path	Provides helper functions for manipulating and testing file paths.
ossaudiodev (Linux, FreeBSD)	Access to OSS-compatible audio devices.

p

pathlib	Provides an object-oriented model of file system paths.
pdb	**A debugger for interactive Python interpreters.**
pickle	**Convert Python objects to streams of bytes and back.**
pipes (UNIX)	A Python interface to UNIX shell pipelines.
platform	Retrieves as much platform identifying data as possible.
plistlib	Generate and parse Mac OS X plist files.

poplib	POP3 protocol client (requires sockets).
pprint	Pretty prints Python data structures.
profile	Python source code profiler.
pstats	Statistics object for use with the profiler.
pty (Linux)	Handling of pseudo-terminals for Linux.
pwd (UNIX)	**The password database** [`getpwnam()` **and friends].**

q

| queue | A queue class suitable for communicating between threads. |
| quopri | Encode and decode files using the MIME quoted-printable encoding. |

r

random	Generate pseudorandom numbers with various common distributions.
re	**Regular-expression operations.**
readline (UNIX)	GNU readline support for Python.
reprlib	An alternate `repr()` implementation with size limits.
resource (UNIX)	An interface to provide resource usage information about the current process.

s

sched	General-purpose event scheduler.
select	Wait for I/O completion on multiple streams.
selectors	High-level I/O multiplexing.
shelve	**Python object persistence.**
shlex	**Simple lexical analysis for UNIX shell–like languages.**
shutil	**High-level file operations, including copying.**
signal	Set handlers for asynchronous events.
smtpd	An SMTP server implementation in Python.
smtplib	SMTP protocol client (requires sockets).
sndhdr	Determine the type of sound file.
socket	**Low-level networking interface.**
socketserver	**A framework for network servers.**
spwd (UNIX)	The shadow password database [`getspnam()` and friends].
sqlite3	**A DB-API 2.0 implementation using SQLite 3.x.**
ssl	TLS/SSL wrapper for socket objects.

stat	Utilities for interpreting the results of `os.stat()`, `os.lstat()`, and `os.fstat()`.
statistics	**Mathematical statistics functions.**
string	Common string operations.
stringprep	String preparation, as per RFC 3453.
struct	**Read and write binary data in a byte array.**
subprocess	**Subprocess management.**
sunau	Provide an interface to the Sun AU sound format.
sys	**Access system-specific parameters and functions.**
sysconfig	Python's configuration information.
syslog (UNIX)	An interface to the UNIX syslog library routines.

t

tarfile	Read and write tar-format archive files.
telnetlib	Telnet client class.
tempfile	Generate temporary files and directories.
termios (UNIX)	POSIX style TTY control.
textwrap	Text wrapping and filling.
threading	Parallel processing based on threads.
time	**Time access and conversions.**
timeit	Measure the execution time of code snippets.
tkinter	**Interface to Tcl/Tk for graphical user interfaces.**
tkinter.messagebox	**Standard message dialogs.**
tkinter.tix	**Tk Extension Widgets for Tkinter.**
tkinter.ttk	**Tk themed widget set.**
tkinter.filedialog	**Variations on standard File dialogs.**
tkinter.simpledialog	**A base class for building custom dialogs.**
tty (UNIX)	Utility functions that perform common terminal control operations.
turtle	**An educational framework for developing simple graphics applications.**
types	Names for Python's built-in types.

u

unicodedata	**Access the Unicode database.**
unittest	**Unit testing framework for Python.**
urllib	**Package for processing URLs including requests, responses, errors, and so on.**
uu	Encode and decode file-like objects to and from uuencode format.
uuid	UUID objects (universally unique identifiers) according to RFC 4122.

W

warnings	Issue warning messages and control their disposition.
wave	Provide an interface to the WAV sound format.
weakref	Support for weak references and weak dictionaries.
webbrowser	Easy-to-use controller for web browsers.
win32com.client	**Third-party module providing access to the native Win32 API.**
winreg (Windows)	**Provides helper functions and a Key class for manipulating the Windows registry.**
winsound (Windows)	Access to the sound-playing machinery for Windows.
wsgiref	Package providing a reference implementation of WSGI along with various WSGI utility functions and classes.

X

xdrlib	Encoders and decoders for the External Data Representation (XDR).
xml	**Package containing XML processing modules.**
xml.dom	Document object model (DOM) API for Python.
xml.minidom	Minimal document object model (DOM) implementation.
xml.etree	Implementation of the ElementTree API.
Xml.parsers.expat	An interface to the Expat non-validating XML parser.
xml.sax	Package containing SAX2 base classes and convenience functions.
xml.sax.handler	Base classes for SAX event handlers.
xmlrpc	Package providing support for XMLRPC.
Xmlrpc.client	Provides helper functions and classes for XML-RPC client access.
Xmlrpc.server	Basic XML-RPC server implementations.

Z

zipfile	Read and write zip-format archive files.
zlib	Low-level interface to compression and decompression routines compatible with gzip.

C

Useful Python Resources

This appendix lists some useful resources for the intermediate-level Python programmer. The list does include a few tutorials, but these are either more in-depth than most beginner's tutorials or they cover specific topic areas. Many of the links point to user support forums and mailing lists. Several of the resources were recommended by the Python "Tutor" mailing list community following a request for suggestions.

ASKING QUESTIONS: MAILING LISTS AND MORE

Many Python mailing lists are available, covering a wide variety of topics and interest areas. The Python "Tutor" mailing list is specifically targeted at those learning Python and its standard library along with the fundamentals of programming. The main Python mailing list is a source of information about all aspects of Python, but is populated by a particularly Python-savvy team who may be less tolerant of poorly researched questions. You can find the official Python mailing lists at `https://mail.python.org/mailman/listinfo`.

At the time of writing, almost 200 lists are available; however, many relate to special events such as conferences or local user groups. Nonetheless, many technical lists are available on the official site.

Many third-party packages also have their own mailing lists or web forums for support and maintenance. Examples include the wxPython GUI library and the Django web framework.

The `gmane.org` website and news server offers access to all the official mailing lists as well as many other lists. At the time of writing it hosts more than 230 top-level Python mailing lists, and many of these have several sublists. All of these are available in web, usenet, and e-mail formats. Other related technologies such as SQLite, Tcl/Tk, and the various OSes all have extensive lists available, too.

Newsgroups are a legacy from the early pre-web days of the Internet, but are still heavily used by professional programmers. They often provide more direct access to a true expert than some of the more casual web forums. The general Python mailing list is also available on usenet as `news://comp.lang.python`.

Some people prefer IRC channels because of the immediate response. The problem with that is that you are limited to whoever is logged on at the same time you are. Using a mailing list, web forum, or newsgroup, although slightly slower, is more likely to get you a definitive solution or answer to your question.

Stackoverflow (`www.stackoverflow.com`) is a popular site for asking questions and getting answers. It contains an archive of previous questions and their answers. Some people complain that the answers are not always optimal, but that is the nature of the Internet; if you get an answer that works, it's better than no answer at all. As always with archives, it's best to search the archive before posting a new, duplicate question.

READING BLOGS

If you don't have specific questions and just want to find out what other Python programmers are doing or thinking, a blog may be your best bet. Here are a few blog sites with useful material:

➤ Doug Hellman has a long established website at `http://pymotw.com/2/contents.html` that features different Python modules on a weekly basis. In addition, he maintains a more informal but useful blog at `http://doughellmann.com/`.

➤ The effbot site is not strictly a blog in the traditional sense, but it contains a miscellany of useful articles and information from Python stalwart Frederick Lundh and is well worth a browse. You can find it at `http://effbot.org/`.

➤ The final suggestion is not Python specific, but a general programming blog. The author has strong opinions, sometimes controversial, but that just adds to the interest. It is written by Joel Spolsky and is located at `http://www.joelonsoftware.com/index.html`.

STUDYING TUTORIALS AND REFERENCES

Many universities now use Python in their programming courses. This has led to a number of online courses and tutorials being produced by the universities or their students. Some are basic and aimed at beginners, but others feature specific packages or libraries or teach more advanced techniques.

The University of Cambridge has several short courses available as PDF files. You can find them linked from this site: `http://www.ucs.cam.ac.uk/docs/course-notes/unix-courses/PythonProgIntro`.

You can find other similar courses with the aid of your favorite search engine.

In addition, several computer companies use Python or encourage programmers to learn about it. Two well-known examples are Apple and Google, both of which provide Python courses featuring multimedia instruction. You can find their courses at the following URLs.

This one is for iTunes users: `https://itunes.apple.com/gb/itunes-u/hands-on-python-tutorial-chapter/id448754574?mt=10`. This is for the Google fans: `https://developers.google.com/edu/python/`.

Wikipedia (`http://en.wikipedia.org/wiki/Main_Page`) is a fantastic resource for technical information. If you come across computer science terms that you want to understand, Wikipedia is a great place to try first. It can sometimes be a tad overly technical for beginners, but it usually has links to gentler tutorials at the bottom of the page.

Several online books about Python are available, including the following two titles, each of which focuses on a specific area of interest:

➤ *Dive Into Python* is a beginner's book, but with a slightly deeper than usual treatment. You can find it at `http://www.diveintopython3.net/`. It is also included in the ActiveState Windows distribution of Python.

➤ *Text Processing in Python* is slightly outdated nowadays, but it still contains a lot of useful material on searching and manipulating textual data in all its many forms. The online version of the book is available at `http://gnosis.cx/TPiP/`.

WATCHING VIDEOS

YouTube has several videos on Python. The quality ranges from excellent to poor, as is usually the case on community-based sites like YouTube. However, if you learn well from video it's worth a browse; you can always hit the stop button if you don't like what you find. YouTube is, of course, located at `https://www.youtube.com/`.

ShowMeDo is a web-based video training site. It offers a mix of free and paid-for training materials. The quality is more consistent than YouTube and well worth a browse. Check it out at `http://showmedo.com/`.

AND NOW FOR SOMETHING COMPLETELY DIFFERENT...

As a final treat, you can try the Python Challenge. This is a bit like an adventure game for Python programmers. You start with easy examples, which then become more progressively difficult. The location of the next challenge is revealed by solving the current one. If you find that you are writing a lot of code for any individual challenge, you are probably going the wrong way about solving it. The fun starts here: `http://www.pythonchallenge.com/`.

REFERENCES

A. Church. (1985). *The Calculi of Lambda-Conversion*. Princeton University Press: Princeton, NJ.

M. Hammond & A. Robson. (2000). *Python Programming On Win32: Help for Windows Programmers*. O'Reilly Media: Sebastopol, CA.

J. Grayson. (2000). *Python and Tkinter Programming*. Manning Publications: Shelter Island, NY.

M. Lutz. (2011). *Programming Python*. O'Reilly Media: Sebastopol, CA.

N. Rappin & R. Dunn. (2006). *WxPython in Action*. Manning Publications: Shelter Island, NY.

INDEX

M

Try Safari Books Online FREE
for 15 days and take 15% off
for up to 6 Months*

Gain unlimited subscription access to thousands of books and videos.

With Safari Books Online, learn without limits from thousands of technology, digital media and professional development books and videos from hundreds of leading publishers. With a monthly or annual unlimited access subscription, you get:

- Anytime, anywhere mobile access with Safari To Go apps for iPad, iPhone and Android

- Hundreds of expert-led instructional videos on today's hottest topics

- Sample code to help accelerate a wide variety of software projects

- Robust organizing features including favorites, highlights, tags, notes, mash-ups and more

- Rough Cuts pre-published manuscripts

START YOUR FREE TRIAL TODAY!
Visit: www.safaribooksonline.com/wrox

*Discount applies to new Safari Library subscribers only and is valid for the first 6 consecutive monthly billing cycles. Safari Library is not available in all countries.

Safari
Books Online

An Imprint of ⊛WILEY
Now you know.